THE RISE AND DECLINE
OF THE AMERICAN
CENTURY

THE RISE AND DECLINE OF THE AMERICAN CENTURY

William O. Walker III

CORNELL UNIVERSITY PRESS   ITHACA AND LONDON

First published 2018 by Cornell University Press

Printed in the United States of America

Library of Congress Cataloging-in-Publication Data

Names: Walker, William O., III, 1946- author.
Title: The rise and decline of the American century / William O. Walker III.
Description: Ithaca : Cornell University Press, 2018. | Includes bibliographical
    references and index.
Identifiers: LCCN 2017060538 (print) | LCCN 2017061793 (ebook) |
    ISBN 9781501726149 (pdf) | ISBN 9781501726156 (ret) |
    ISBN 9781501726132 | ISBN 9781501726132 (cloth ; alk. paper)
Subjects: LCSH: United States—Foreign relations—1945–1989. |
    National Security—United States—History—20th century. |
    Hegemony—United States—History—20th century. | Luce, Henry Robinson,
    1898–1967. American century.
Classification: LCC E744 (ebook) | LCC E744 .W24 2018 (print) |
    DDC 327.73009/04—dc23
LC record available at https://lccn.loc.gov/2017060538

In memory of Alexander DeConde,
mentor, scholar, gentleman.
For Sue,
mi querida esposa, tqm.

Above all, the thrall in which an ideology holds a people is best measured by their collective inability to imagine alternatives.

Tony Judt
New York Review of Books, September 30, 2010

Contents

Preface

Imagine that a very large oil painting, a triptych, has recently been discovered. Each of the panels is badly soiled; still, the painting seems recognizable. It is oddly evocative of John Gast's 1872 composition, the allegorical *American Progress*. Among the discernible images in the first panel are Harry Truman and Joseph Stalin at Potsdam and John Foster Dulles refusing to shake Zhou Enlai's hand at Geneva in 1954; in the second one, John Kennedy gives his inaugural address and Lyndon Johnson agonizes over Vietnam; a discarded placard proclaiming the "Year of Europe" and Richard Nixon boarding a helicopter on the White House lawn adorn the third panel. The painting has to be a rendition of the history of the Cold War through August 1974.

Cleaning and restoration of the triptych reveal a much different story. In the lower left of the first panel sits Henry Luce penning his essay "The American Century." Visible along the lower border of each panel are crowds of young people from various locales, some carrying signs of protest. Across the top reside symbols of America's vast material and cultural prowess: a television set, an automobile, an airplane, a movie camera, a trumpet, and more. Present now in the first panel are more people of color than were previously visible; in the second one, gold bars with wings fly out from Fort Knox; the third panel also shows Japan's copious export trade and Chile's presidential palace, La Moneda, in flames.

What to make of this transformed canvas? It could simply be a more complete depiction of the highly familiar tale of the Cold War. Or is something else influencing the brushstrokes of our nameless artist? If context matters, then Luce's presence holds the key. The refurbished images on the triptych should be seen as coming under its sway, their story still to be told.

The germ of an idea for a book akin to this one originated, inchoately to be sure, in 1969 when I was an MA student at Ohio State University. Also at OSU then was the now-superb historian Melvyn P. Leffler. Mel and I and a small number of others spent hours talking about American history, especially the origins of the Cold War, and we speculated endlessly about what the Cold War meant for understanding America's place in the modern world. These latter discussions came to mind when I decided to write this book.

The Rise and Decline of the American Century describes and analyzes what I consider the active lifespan of the American Century as the noted publisher Henry R. Luce conceived it in 1941. Luce very much wanted the United States to seize the reins of global leadership, to exert supremacy over international political and economic affairs. U.S. officials, commencing in 1945, endeavored to spread Luce's vision as widely as possible. I contend that the American Century developed alongside the Cold War yet was a far grander project—one designed to establish the United States as the world's hegemon in strategic, political, and economic realms. To succeed in that effort entailed fostering thoroughgoing change in what became known as the Free World. Hegemony was inconceivable without widespread acceptance of Washington's leadership; in turn, leadership depended both on consultation with allies and client states and on the credibility of U.S. actions throughout what I call the free-world society.

Waging cold war became an integral aspect of the Lucian project. Policymakers from the Truman through the Johnson administrations internalized Luce's vision and were determined to give it practical effect. That effort collapsed by the end of 1968 largely because of the Vietnam War, burgeoning economic troubles that a weakened dollar exemplified, and a general lack of receptivity to U.S. hegemony beyond Western Europe and Japan, most notably in the Americas. Officials rightly worried that if the American Century were not embraced by people and nations close to home, then a positive reception elsewhere was far less likely. Thereafter, Richard Nixon and Henry Kissinger turned to détente in an attempt to chart a path to primacy—a way to exert power and influence—in world affairs; they came up short. More than four decades later, it is worth considering whether the very idea of the American Century has over time become little more than a useful shibboleth. I think not, if only because those who wanted to give it life did bring the American Century into being and then undertook to nurture it for two decades.

My goal in writing this book is in its way nearly as ambitious as that of those who forged the American Century. I want readers to know at the outset that this is not another book about the Cold War. Instead, I seek to revise how we think about U.S. foreign relations from the final months of Franklin Roosevelt's presidency through Nixon's resignation in August 1974. To do so, I scrutinize in greater depth some of the ideas that I developed in the cold-war sections of my book *National Security and Core Values in American History* (2009). Two prominent histories of that era—John Lewis Gaddis, *The Cold War: A New History* (2005), and Campbell Craig and Fredrik Logevall, *America's Cold War: The Politics of Insecurity* (2009)—do not mention the American Century; Craig and Logevall accord Luce only a cameo role. These books confine themselves to narratives placing superpower relations and American politics, respectively, at the heart of their stories.

A secondary, yet essential part of my undertaking is recognition of the role of emotions, most especially fear and anxiety, in the making of U.S. foreign policy. Fear, which I explored at some length in my 2009 book, had a profound impact on threat perception and decision-making and influenced how the United States engaged the world through 1968 as authorities strove to implant abroad the American Century. Fear in dealing with adversaries, whether well founded or self-induced, often seemed near at hand because of the assumption that foes like the Soviet Union and China were inherently ill disposed toward Washington's objectives. Policymakers also worried—sometimes unduly, sometimes not—that the interests of friends and allies, notably in Western Europe and East Asia, might not align with those of the United States in a given situation, which would challenge America's claims to leadership.

Without making a study of emotion central to the core of my story, as Frank Costigliola, for example, has done in his several influential writings about George F. Kennan, I nevertheless purposefully chose to use the verbs "feared" and "worried" on numerous occasions in the first six chapters. U.S. officials were obsessively concerned that what Luce called "the opportunity for leadership" was eluding them—hence my choice of words. Less emotionally laden alternatives, like "thought" or "believed," among others, I employ as appropriate.

The present study is at once original and synthetic. The narrative and thematic structure springs from my years of teaching about the United States in the world. Research relies on the State Department's published documentary volumes, *Foreign Relations of the United States*, and the myriad of online primary documents. Online sources include records on the economy and finance from the Public Record Office in Great Britain, documentary compilations of the Cold War International History Project of the Wilson Center and the National Security Archive, declassified documents released by the Central Intelligence Agency and the State Department (some readily accessible through presidential libraries), and oral histories from presidential libraries and other collections.

This wealth of online material afforded me insights into matters of race, youth and politics, and the growth of revolutionary sentiment, all of which had a discernible impact on efforts to propagate the American Century. These issues are woven into individual chapters as appropriate. (All of the cited websites were active as of January 15, 2018, except that of the Project for the New American Century.) I also draw on research conducted at various repositories, notably the John Fitzgerald Kennedy Presidential Library for materials on Latin America and the Lyndon Baines Johnson Presidential Library for documentation on economic issues and on Latin America in the mid to late 1960s. The book is synthetic in that some of its narrative derives from and reflects what I consider to be the best scholarship of the last several decades in the history of U.S. foreign relations.

I also want my work to convey more than my scholarly interests. This foray into research and writing about America's engagement with the world is meant to appeal to an informed reading public, suggest to students a way of learning that may be novel to them, and aid teachers and scholars in their classrooms and their research. All, I trust, will find it instructive to draw on familiar, lesser known, and unfamiliar episodes in the cold-war era to consider more encompassing developments—the origins, expansion, and travails of the ultimately Sisyphean enterprise that was the making of an American Century.

Some words are in order about the initial three paragraphs. They were conceived in the days following the death at the age of ninety on January 2, 2017, of John Berger, noted British art critic, novelist, and Marxist intellectual. In 1972, when the American Century was in full decline, he published one of his best-known books, *Ways of Seeing*. Berger asserted that how we look at paintings in Western art often constitutes a political act: "When we 'see' a landscape, we situate ourselves in it. If we 'saw' the art of the past, we would situate ourselves in history. When we are prevented from seeing it, we are being deprived of the history which belongs to us" (p. 11). To "see" our fictional landscape not as "The Cold War" but as "The American Century" enables us to recognize and accept its history as part of our own. That is, to alter our way of seeing is to transform our way of learning. That idea, really a lodestar, emerged in the writing of this book.

Four scholars remain an inspiration to me whenever I write: Walter F. LaFeber, Fredrick B. Pike, the late Marilyn B. Young, and the late Tony Judt. I could not have written the first two chapters without the work on George F. Kennan of Frank Costigliola and John Lewis Gaddis. I thank John, and the History Department at Ohio University, for choosing me as his replacement for a year when my career was at risk. The work of George Herring and William J. Duiker on Indochina was essential for the completion of this book, as was that of Michael E. Latham and David Ekbladh on modernization. Alan Brinkley's superb study of Henry R. Luce gave my work context. Richard Immerman, Mark Stoler, Robert Bothwell, Natalia Milanesio, and Cesar Seveso provided encouragement when I needed it.

I owe an intellectual debt to everyone whose work I relied on as I wrote and rewrote. Deserving special mention are Andrew J. Bacevich, Thomas Borstlemann, Elizabeth Cobbs, John W. Dower, Aleksandr Fursenko, Walter L. Hixson, Michael J. Hogan, Michael H. Hunt, Douglas Little, Robert J. McMahon, Timothy Naftali, Frank Ninkovich, Thomas F. O'Brien, Stephen G. Rabe, Emily Rosenberg, Thomas Alan Schwartz, Jeffrey F. Taffet, the late Nancy Bernkopf Tucker, Odd Arne Westad, Randall B. Woods, Thomas W. Zeiler, and Vladislav M. Zubok. I also thank Thomas Tunstall Allcock, Perry Anderson, Fred L. Block, Greg Brazinsky, Alessandro Brogi, Curt Caldwell, Nick Cullather, Thomas C. Field Jr., Luke Fletcher, Jeffrey Glen Giauque, Patrick Iber, John B. Judis, Barbara Keys, Jeremy Kuzmarov, Klaus Larres, Fredrik Logevall, Alfred W. McCoy, David Milne,

Jason Parker, Uta G. Poiger, Geoffrey Roberts, Bevan Sewall, Bradley R. Simpson, Jeremi Suri, Tim Weiner, and Salim Yacub.

I am grateful to three of my former students at Ohio Wesleyan University: Robert Buzzanco, Peter L. Hahn, and Glenn J. Dorn. Without Bob's help, the sections on political economy would be much the poorer; for years, Peter's work on the Middle East has greatly informed me; and Glenn's knowledge of the Southern Cone aided me immensely in this and other projects.

Anyone who writes about post–World War II international history must depend on the Wilson Center's Cold War International History Project and on the National Security Archive. Crucial, too, in my research were the John F. Kennedy Presidential Library and the Lyndon B. Johnson Presidential Library. I thank their staffs, especially the incredible people in Austin. Also, the Electronic Reading Room of the CIA is a must for all serious scholars, as is the trove of online documents at the Dwight D. Eisenhower Presidential Library.

I cannot adequately thank Michael J. McGandy of Cornell University Press for his initial interest in my book and for his good work and enthusiasm throughout the publication process. And I greatly appreciate the copyediting of Westchester Publishing Services, especially the work of Kristen Bettcher and Liz Schueler. I also owe many, many thanks to the anonymous readers for the press. In the penultimate draft of my work, I often engage in conversations with myself. My two readers helped me keep those to a minimum and made invaluable suggestions for improvement. I treated their thoughtful comments as seriously as they did my scholarship.

On a personal level, I am most fortunate to have lived in Santa Fe, New Mexico, since mid-2015, where the Sangre de Cristo mountains welcome the day. Three restaurants literally provided food for thought as I wrote: Tune-Up Café, where the owner Jesús, Brian, Heather, Adán, Josh, and Bree made Sunday evenings such a pleasure; Palacio Café, where Damián and Maria treated me like a close relative. Muchisimas gracias. And then comes The Pantry with its remarkable cast of characters on Wednesday nights starting with Tupper, Flaco, Anabel, Oscar, Tyler, Juan Carlos, and Fernando. Bring into the mix Rick and Susan, Linda, and Melissa. Add BB, who outshines us all in her tenth decade, and her loving son Water, who, I have reason to believe, once found Ken Kesey a tad staid. Finally, singing for our supper is Gary Vigil, whose voice and guitar are sublime, most of all when performing his own wonderful compositions.

But for three people, I would not have written this book. Mel Leffler, as mentioned, was present at the creation. The arcs of our careers soon separated, yet my admiration for his work, even when criticizing him in print, remained undiminished. What I value most about Mel is the honesty, integrity, and humanity he puts into every word he writes. These are precious qualities we all should try to emulate in our work, in our lives.

Words fail in trying to thank Alex DeConde. From his first greeting through every handwritten note to his last email, I felt his encouragement. How very nervous I was when we met in August 1970 in his office at the University of California, Santa Barbara. He quickly put me at ease, asking what I wanted to study. I replied, "U.S.-Latin American relations." Alex, whose focus was on the Federalist era, had on his desk Arnold H. Taylor's book on international drug control. We discussed Operation Intercept, and he asked, "Do you think there's a book in it?" Not a dissertation, a book! I said, "Let's find out." So I became a historian of drugs and U.S. foreign policy. After Alex's death in May 2016, I exchanged emails with Fred Logevall, who replaced him at Santa Barbara. Fred called him a giant in his field, an exemplary colleague, and a better person. Alex was indeed that, as those he guided into the historical profession can attest.

And now, Susan Kellogg. I cannot imagine anyone being more loving and supportive through the emotional and intellectual journey we take when writing a book. Sue was by my side every step of the way since research began. She knows more about the American Century and the cold-war era than I will ever learn about pre-Columbian and early colonial Mexico. Far more, though I promise to be with you, Sue, on all your intellectual journeys, with a few side trips to Ghost Ranch, Chama, Chaco Canyon, and beyond along the way.

List of Abbreviations

ABM	Anti-Ballistic Missile
AEM	American Education Mission
AID	Agency for International Development
AIOC	Anglo-Iranian Oil Company
ARAMCO	Arabian American Oil Company
ARVN	Army of the Republic of Vietnam
BEA	Bureau of Economic Affairs
CENTO	Central Treaty Organization
CFM	Council of Foreign Ministers
CI	Counterinsurgency
CIA	Central Intelligence Agency
CIA, ERR	Central Intelligence Agency, Electronic Reading Room
CIF	Chinese Irregular Forces
CO	Country
COMIBOL	Corporación Minera de Bolivia
CORDS	Civil Operations and Revolutionary Development Support
CPT	Communist Party of Thailand
CRU	Collective Reserve Unit
CWIHP	Cold War International History Project
DDEL	Dwight D. Eisenhower Presidential Library
DDFY	Declassified Documents - Fiscal Year
DDRS	Declassified Documents Reference System
DLF	Development Loan Fund
EC	European Community
ECA	Economic Cooperation Administration
ECSC	European Coal and Steel Community
EDC	European Defense Community
EEC	European Economic Community
ELN	Ejército de Liberación Nacional
EPU	European Payments Union
ERP	European Recovery Program
FAOHC	Foreign Affairs Oral History Collection
FARC	Fuerzas Armadas Revolucionarias de Colombia

FAS, IRP	Federation of American Scientists, Intelligence Resource Program
F & E, BWC	Finance and the Economy, Bretton Woods Conference
F & E, BWS	Finance and the Economy, Bretton Woods System in Practice
FNLA	National Front for the Liberation of Angola
FOA	Foreign Operations Administration
FPCC	Fair Play for Cuba Committee
FRELIMO	Mozambique Liberation Front
FRUS	*Foreign Relations of the United States*
FY	fiscal year
GATT	General Agreement on Tariffs and Trade
GDR	German Democratic Republic
GMD	Guomindang
GNP	gross national product
GPO	Government Printing Office
HSTL	Harry S. Truman Presidential Library
ICA	International Cooperation Administration
IDA	International Development Association
IDB	Inter-American Development Bank
IFC	International Finance Corporation
IIAA	Institute for Inter-American Affairs
IMF	International Monetary Fund
IPC	International Petroleum Company
ITO	International Trade Organization
ITT	International Telephone and Telegraph
IYC	Interagency Youth Committee
LBJL	Lyndon B. Johnson Presidential Library
LDP	Liberal-Democratic Party
JCS	Joint Chiefs of Staff
JFKL	John F. Kennedy Presidential Library
KPR	Korean People's Republic
MAAG	Military Assistance Advisory Group
MACV	Military Assistance Command, Vietnam
M & M	Meetings and Memoranda
MAP	Military Assistance Program
MFN	most favored nation
MIR	Movimiento de Izquierda Revolucionario
MIRV	multiple independently targeted reentry vehicle
MLF	Multi-Lateral Force
MNC	multinational corporation

MNR	Movimiento Nacionalista Revolucionario
MPLA	Popular Movement for the Liberation of Angola
MSA	Mutual Security Administration
NATO	North Atlantic Treaty Organization
NCFE	National Committee for a Free Europe
NGOs	nongovernmental organizations
NIE	National Intelligence Estimate
NLF	National Liberation Front
NSA, EBB	National Security Archive, Electronic Briefing Book
NSAM	National Security Action Memorandum
NSC	National Security Council
NSF	National Security File
NSL	National Security Law
NSSM	National Security Study Memorandum
OAS	Organization of American States
OEEC	Organization for European Economic Cooperation
OPEC	Organization of Petroleum Exporting Countries
OPIC	Overseas Private Investment Corporation
OPS	Office of Public Safety
P.L. 480	Public Law 480
PKI	Indonesian Communist Party
PKP	Philippine Communist Party
PLO	Palestine Liberation Organization
PNAC	Project for the New American Century
PPP	*Public Papers of the Presidents of the United States*
PPS	Policy Planning Staff
PRC	People's Republic of China
PRO, Cab	Public Record Office, Cabinet Papers
RLA	Royal Laotian Army
RMNL	Richard M. Nixon Presidential Library and Museum
ROK	Republic of Korea
RTG	Royal Thai Government
RVNAF	Republic of Vietnam Armed Forces
SALT	Strategic Arms Limitation Treaty
SDRs	Special Drawing Rights
SEATO	Southeast Asia Treaty Organization
SNIE	Special National Intelligence Estimate
TCA	Technical Cooperation Administration
TVA	Tennessee Valley Authority
UAR	United Arab Republic

UN	United Nations
UNITA	National Union for the Total Liberation of Angola
UP	Unidad Popular
USIA	United States Information Agency
USSR	Union of Soviet Socialist Republics

THE RISE AND DECLINE OF THE AMERICAN CENTURY

HENRY R. LUCE AND THE SECURITY ETHOS

Henry R. Luce's plan for his country's future role in the world, "The American Century," appeared in *Life* magazine on February 17, 1941. The war then raging in Europe gave the United States, the magazine's influential publisher observed, "the complete opportunity of leadership." If "the most powerful and the most vital nation in the world" made a clear decision to lead, then civilized peoples everywhere would follow. So entrusted, the United States could dominate the postwar world "for such purposes as we see fit and by such means as we see fit."[1]

Luce's audacious words were a tonic for those Americans desirous of deepening their nation's engagement with the world during the war, and beyond. The quest for leadership was felt both inside and outside Washington, DC, and remained a strong motivational force in U.S. foreign relations in the first three decades after World War II. Not everyone, of course, has shared this view. Many experts have interpreted the early Cold War exclusively in terms of U.S.-Soviet relations. Both superpowers presumed the intentions of the other were grand in scope, limited only by their mutual, yet vague determination to avoid catastrophic strategic conflict. Comprehensive containment held the spotlight as Washington's fundamental goal. In this telling, scholars, whatever their interpretive mien, have depicted containment as a vital means to prevent the aggrandizement of Soviet power and influence, especially in places important to the United States and its friends and allies. My emphasis is different, however. It places efforts to build an American Century in the forefront of analysis. Containment therefore serves as merely one of several means to a larger end.

The intensity of scholarly debates over who held the greater responsibility for the origins and growth of the Cold War has long since subsided. Newer generations of scholars focus more on the conceptual meanings of the Cold War and the cultural and temporal contexts in which it arose than on the hoary issue of human agency.[2] Before we consign agency and the use of power to the margins of history, we should reconsider the period between 1945 and 1974 using the idea of an American Century to examine both U.S. engagement with the world and the responses of allies, friends, adversaries, and nonstate actors. A fresh look supersedes a vantage point giving priority to the Cold War and focuses instead on the American Century, for which growth was the truest mark of success.

Luce's ideas about the active role the country should play in world affairs were not really new. Americans deemed their land—whether as an English colony or an independent nation after 1776—exceptional, worthy of emulation. That other people and nations had not replicated the American experience was all the more reason for the United States to don the mantle of leadership, Luce and like-minded others believed. Given the tradition of political isolationism, the question was how best to lead.

The quest had begun in the 1890s when the United States boldly stepped onto the world stage.[3] In so doing, internationally attuned leaders and citizens developed a "security ethos."[4] They looked at the world as a dangerous place, one in which the nation's vital interests and its fundamental values might be in peril. Rarely did these proto-internationalists pause to consider the extent to which perceived dangers were of their own making. They believed theirs was a God-given mission to make the world a better place. American ends and means were therefore naturally congruent. This faith produced a sense of entitlement that history was theirs to shape. Moreover, American commerce would be the indispensable engine of progress. As then captain Alfred Thayer Mahan advised, building a modern navy was essential if peace, prosperity, and stability were to be had. To the new internationalists of the 1890s, a navy guaranteed security.

Americans who desired to engage the world—if their nation was to fulfill its destiny—were quite willing to lead. To do less, Theodore Roosevelt feared, would consign the fate of civilization to the whims of other powers with less benign intentions. Preventing civilization's decay meant restoring the "iron quality" that valiant men had exhibited since the nation's birth. It would take, he asserted, "the warlike power of a civilized people."[5] Consequently, military might should always be at the ready.

In time, Luce came to epitomize the Republican Roosevelt's thinking. Born in China of missionary parents in 1898 as the security ethos was taking shape, Luce grew up, Alan Brinkley writes, trusting in "the moral superiority of Christianity and the cultural superiority of Western culture."[6] Ever ambitious, Luce merged in his public life the missionary's belief in a providential calling with Roosevelt's literal and metaphorical call to arms in defense of civilization. A strong market-based economy provided another essential component of Luce's worldview.

How had he developed such a perspective?[7] His father Henry's abiding faith in the Social Gospel of the late nineteenth century opens the door to understanding. The senior Luce, known as Harry, having trained at Union Theological Seminary and Princeton Theological Seminary, believed that spiritual and material change would enable China to find its way into the modern world. Luce's mother, Elizabeth, less at ease in China because of her inability to learn Mandarin, focused her energy on fostering social betterment among the members of her household. Were the Luces successful, widespread conversion to Christianity would doubtless follow. The Boxer Uprising, which began in 1899 and forced Harry and Elizabeth to flee to Korea, greatly tested their core beliefs. That they persevered in its wake illumines the evangelical, progressive impulse that defined their ministry.

The young Harry embraced the beliefs and work of his Presbyterian parents as a model even as his daily experiences kept him at a remove from Chinese culture. Well before the age of ten, he became quite the American patriot and admirer of Theodore Roosevelt. These convictions were strengthened during his first trip to the United States in 1906. Luce may then have begun to form a sense of what he would later see as the need for a prominent American presence abroad as he watched his father undertake the hard work of fundraising for the China mission. Success, in short, whether in the religious or secular world, required leadership, creating a union of mission and money. After returning to China in 1908, Luce attended a boarding school at Chefoo, which he hated. While there, he devoted himself to besting the British boys who made up the majority of the student body. Brinkley finds in Luce's exertions "an extraordinary drive for achievement and success that would characterize the whole of his life." The road to self-improvement, which Luce coveted for himself, involved improving the lives of others. The question he long struggled with was how to marry the two objectives.

This task informed Luce's 1941 essay. "We Americans are unhappy," he began. "We are not happy about America. . . . As we look out to the rest of the world we are confused; we don't know what to do. 'Aid to Britain short of war' is typical of halfway hopes and halfway measures. As we look toward the future . . . we are filled with foreboding." He railed against "the virus of isolationist sterility," declaring that global engagement was "needed for the shaping of the future of America and of the world."[8]

In taking this position, one that mirrored the security ethos and reflected extant realist, evangelical, and universal impulses in U.S. foreign policy, Luce did not differ much from either Woodrow Wilson or Franklin D. Roosevelt.[9] Wilson, raised as was Luce in a Presbyterian home, saw it as his duty and the responsibility of the United States to instruct others in the virtues of self-government. Only then could humanity live in a stable, prosperous world.[10] He believed that an exceptional America was obligated to fulfill a noble charge: the responsibility to lead. His legacy, Wilsonian internationalism, served as a general blueprint for how the nation should act as an indispensable world power. The misgivings of isolationists aside, Wilson's profound influence on foreign policy remained in evidence throughout the twentieth century.

FDR, who incurred Luce's ire as a presumed stalking horse for radicalism during the 1940 presidential campaign, even as their views about America's global role converged, gave practical effect to Wilson's worldview.[11] If imperialism could not be vanquished, then empire had to be tempered with the prospect of self-determination; if authoritarian tyranny was to wane as a force in human affairs, then an international organization under the sway of Washington had to be created; and if the global economy was never again going to relegate untold numbers of people to squalid misery as in the Great Depression, then an American-led economic system was imperative.

These tenets formed the basis of what one scholar fittingly terms Roosevelt's "humanistic globalism."[12] Despite the claims of some others to the contrary, there was little that was naive or idealistic in the president's actions.[13] Politically, the American form of government had survived the ravages of World War I and the Great Depression. Strategically, the potential of the United States was unmatched when Luce was penning his essay.[14] In fact, the New Deal had acted systematically to restructure the American economy so as to foster the growth of finance and commerce that would dominate the world economy once World War II ended. Humanism and realism were wholly compatible traits that Roosevelt drew on in making foreign policy.

Luce worried, though, that Roosevelt, like Wilson, would squander an opportunity "to assume the leadership of the world." The current crisis, he insisted, provided perhaps the final opportunity to lead—both in war and in its aftermath. The upshot would be the invigoration of "an American Century" devoted to "a sharing with all peoples of our Bill of Rights, our Declaration of Independence, our Constitution, our magnificent industrial products, our technical skills." Something more was at stake for Luce than markets or the stability of political institutions. It was the nation's image, as reflected "throughout the world [by] faith in the good intentions as well as in the ultimate intelligence and ultimate strength of the whole American people."[15]

This lofty status—the fruit of exceptionalism—was at risk in 1941. The president, Luce asserted, could protect it if he took certain steps. First, the free-enterprise system must become global in scope. Second, the United States must help others develop their technical, scientific, and artistic skills. Third, the nation, through a unique vehicle, food aid, "must undertake now to be the Good Samaritan of the entire world." The frightening alternative was disorder, which nothing short of military preparedness could avert. Luce contended that for "every dollar we spend on armaments, we should spend at least a dime in a gigantic effort to feed the world." Policymakers would subsequently transform his determination to provide the hungry with food into a belief in the efficacy of foreign aid. Finally, the United States had to inculcate in others its basic ideals, namely, freedom, equality of opportunity, self-reliance and independence, and a spirit of cooperation. If it failed to lead, Luce ominously warned, "this nation cannot truly endure."[16] In hyperbole typical of those imbued with the security ethos, Luce intoned: "Most men living [believe] that the 20th Century must be to a significant degree an American Century. This knowledge calls us to action."[17]

Given Luce's conservatism and subsequent distrust of the government, his call to enhance state power merits elaboration. An avid supporter of Wendell Wilkie until disenchantment set in when Wilkie edged closer to Roosevelt's positions in the 1940 presidential campaign, Luce had anticipated Wilkie's "One World" concept.[18] Wilkie's 1943 proposal called for international peacekeeping after the war. Luce shared that sentiment with the proviso that any such activity be U.S.-led, which meant greater power and influence for the state. Luce, in sum, was very much a typical devotee of the security ethos.

To what end would power be put? "We are in a war," Luce wrote, "to defend and even to promote, encourage, and incite so-called democratic principles throughout the world." His essay advocated an American-led international order through the construction of a global society, what became commonly known as the "Free World."[19] To make that society as strong as possible, before the end of the war U.S. authorities helped devise an international economic community. Then, in the early years of the Cold War, they fashioned an Atlantic Community composed of the nations of Western Europe, Canada, and the United States and sought to revitalize the Pan American Community in the Western Hemisphere. In response to cold-war exigencies, they then imagined constructing Pan Asian and Pan African communities—partly in response to the needs and concerns of nonwhite, postcolonial people. (Arabists in the State Department thought that something comparable was possible in the Middle East, trusting their government to act more effectively there than had Great Britain.)

By using power wisely, Luce counseled, the United States could safeguard the Free World. Civilization itself would be strengthened. The state as an agent of civilization in the 1940s was significant given the history of imperial and authoritarian states in the twentieth century and because of America's flight from leadership after World War I.

"The American Century" appeared at a propitious time—between the signing of the Destroyers-For-Bases Agreement in September 1940 and passage of the Lend-Lease Act in March 1941—and briefly transcended partisan politics. The fate of Luce's project lay in the Democrat Roosevelt's hands, indicating just how deeply ingrained was the security ethos among elites of diverse political leanings. To forge an American Century, in which the United States served both as a model for other nations and as the leading actor on the world stage, was to build on the aspirations of prominent men such as Mahan, Theodore Roosevelt, Henry Cabot Lodge, Josiah Strong, Herbert Croly, and Walter Lippmann—each of whom had advocated a greater international presence for the United States before Wilson took a divided country into war in April 1917. However defined at a given moment, globalism meant security and served as the modern guarantor of exceptionalism, or so they believed.[20]

Beneath such convictions lay a large measure of fear. This disquieting emotion had been the handmaiden of expansion and often its vehicle throughout American history. This was true whether it was fear of Indians in the colonies along the Atlantic seaboard, in the territories of the Old Northwest, or on the Great Plains; fear of social disorder brought on by immigrants eager for a share of the nation's bounty; or fear of foreign powers and their interests even as the United States first eyed the world beyond its shores.[21] Fear should not be mistaken for due vigilance against potential threats. By the turn of the twentieth century, historic fears had metamorphosed into a kind of political paranoia. That is, if Boxer-like uprisings were ignited beyond China's borders, if Filipinos and Cubans were not subdued, if Japanese ambitions were not contained, and if Germans did not alter their imperial dreams, then America would somehow be less secure, exceptionalism endangered, and civilization imperiled.

Luce evinced this reasoning in writing about the urgency of American leadership and the dire consequences of its absence. He surely struck a chord among varied observers. Unstinting in her praise, the noted columnist Dorothy Thompson called his essay "an American document . . . that projects a daring future." Like others before her and in her time who found in the security ethos a sense of mission, she exclaimed, "To Americanize enough of the world so that we shall have a climate and environment favorable to our growth is indeed a call to destiny. . . . This will either be an American Century or it will be the beginning of the decline and fall of the American dream." The British weekly *The Economist* conceded in less fulsome language that the "center of gravity [in Anglo-American relations], and the ultimate decision must increasingly lie in America. We cannot resent this historical development."[22] Norman Thomas, America's leading socialist, denounced Luce's ideas as "plain imperialism," whereas Assistant Secretary of State Adolf A. Berle Jr. affirmed, much like Luce, that there would be an American Century only if "the word 'American' is taken in its broadest, finest sense."[23]

Additional consideration of emotion and the American Century seems worthwhile. The security ethos and the foreign policies arising from it after 1900 contained an inviolable pledge by persons in positions of power and influence: to safeguard the United States and civilization as they understood it. No individual in public or private life undertook so crucial a task devoid of emotion. And those emotions, whether expressed as anxiety, fear, hubris, or even a cooperative spirit, profoundly color the story of Luce's American Century.

Roosevelt's death on April 12, 1945, had the potential to cast a pall over Luce's plans. That did not happen, though. By then, the essence of Luce's American Century had become part and parcel of the security ethos, which helped to ensconce his progeny in the making of foreign policy. There came in Roosevelt's stead the insecure and combative Harry S. Truman, who was unschooled in foreign affairs.[24] The seeming contradictions in Truman's behavior early in his presidency have a simple explanation, as his famously contentious meeting with Soviet foreign minister Vyacheslav Molotov on April 23 illustrates. He wanted to honor Roosevelt's postwar plans, set forth at the Yalta Conference in February, while showing his own policymaking bona fides to Soviet leaders.[25] Building an American Century would enable him to reach his goals.

Truman's inner circle was replete with advisers, a coterie of urbane men with similar educational backgrounds and professional lives, for whom the security ethos was gospel. Their ostensibly broad worldview concealed a decidedly parochial, transatlantic caste. Drawing on their vast common experiences, they responded to America's most likely competitor, the war-weakened Soviet Union, with outsized fear. Indeed, anger at the decay of Soviet-American relations among Washington's Soviet experts affected postwar decision-making, born of their belief that U.S. efforts as a wartime partner were underappreciated in Moscow.[26] The sense of alarm officials possessed in the early Cold War complicated the crucial task of threat perception, that is, of distinguishing between the USSR's strategic capability and its political intentions.[27] One result was that by early 1950 the United States became overextended abroad. Seeing mortal danger nearly everywhere, officials relied on a new strategy—global containment—that in time helped undermine Luce's project as a viable international system.

Luce described the structure of his American Century in general terms to avoid partisan bickering while officials and the public warmed to the idea. The specifics would be established in due course, presumably in consultation with friends and allies. And so they were. The United Nations (UN), founded at Dumbarton Oaks in Washington, DC, in October 1944, established principles for the conduct of human affairs echoing basic American values. The United States stood first among a cast of not-quite-equals on the world stage. Economically, with the U.S. dollar as the base currency, the International Bank for Reconstruction and Development (World Bank) and the International Monetary Fund (IMF), created several months earlier in July at Bretton Woods, New Hampshire, offered the prospect of stability in the global economy. To lessen rising pressure on the pound as a source of loans, British authorities supported the creation of the World Bank, admitting that "it is important for the world that a Bank should be set up which will enable *American* money to be adequately and wisely invested in capital development schemes in those countries where capital development is most needed."[28]

Help for the world's needy got started with the Marshall Plan in Europe and then the Point Four program Truman announced in 1949; it became institutionalized in 1961 with the creation of the U.S. Agency for International Development (AID).[29] The promise of widespread aid, which Luce deemed vital for the United States to act as the world's Good Samaritan, found expression in modernization theory as popularized in the 1950s by Walt Whitman Rostow and others. Military aid, not explicitly mentioned by Luce yet an important aspect of the American Century, formally found a home in the Mutual Security Act of October 1951.

Whether Luce's vision was imperial or hegemonic in intent can be debated, though the latter characterization seems more apt because it entails a quest for unassailable and widely accepted predominance.[30] Sounding much like Woodrow Wilson, Luce wrote that "only America can effectively state the war aims of this war." Thus, "it is our duty . . . to exert upon the world the full impact of our influence."[31] These highly charged sentiments understandably conveyed to some an imperial intent. Yet it must be recalled that, for Roosevelt in 1941, the war against Nazi Germany—a war in which the United States was not a formal combatant—was a conflict being waged to demolish the evils of totalitarian empire. The Atlantic Charter of August 1941, which Roosevelt and British prime minister Winston S. Churchill put forth as a declaration of common war aims, envisioned the end of colonialism.

After victory, the United States maneuvered to act as the dominant architect and arbiter of the postwar world. That is what a hegemon does.[32] Hence, it would be on the landscape of hegemony where an American Century was imagined, forged, and challenged by friend and foe alike. Scholars differ over how to assess American power and influence in the cold-war era.[33] Melvyn P. Leffler, in his award-winning book on Truman's grand strategy, *A Preponderance of Power: National Security, the Truman Administration, and the Cold War* (1992), concludes, "Preponderance did not mean domination." Leffler, however, also observes that officials "were ready to assume Britain's former role as financial hegemon. They recognized the connections between the economic and political spheres."[34]

Nearly two decades later, Leffler wrote that Truman and his advisers endeavored "to use American power to forge an international environment conducive to the American way of life."[35] I contend that U.S. leaders actively aspired to hegemony in forging an American Century. They predicated hegemony on the success of grand strategy, close political ties, and economic might. Their goals became less lofty by the late 1960s when officials sought to attain a position of global primacy, which I construe as the possession of substantial power and influence, wielded selectively and flexibly, if not decisively, in a given situation because of external constraints.[36]

Reinforcing the case for hegemony as a goal is the matter of race in America's relations with the world between 1945 and 1974. Drawing on his Christian faith and experiences in China, Luce never lost hope that Asians would become more like Americans. Not the dominant factor, race influenced the making of foreign policy in various ways, including tolerance for a gradual end to European colonialism as policymakers became convinced that colonial peoples from the Middle East to Southeast Asia were not ready for self-determination; the search for Asians—from Japan and South Korea to the Philippines, Vietnam, and Pakistan—to serve as cold-war partners; the disdain shown by the State Department to Latin Americans; and the hard task of bringing black Africans into the American Century. Jason Parker has urged scholars to uncover "connections between the Cold War, the global postwar 'race revolution,' and the course of Third World decolonization."[37] He could have added: "within the context of an 'American Century.'"

Luce's call to arms imagined an international order evocative of the efforts of Great Britain and major continental European powers at the Congress of Vienna in 1815 to bring stability to world affairs. After World War II, it would chiefly be the United States adjudicating what constituted acceptable state behavior. Washington could not summarily impose order on others; there would, however, have to be a large measure of deference to American leadership. Commonality of purpose would hold the system together. *"But the United States must run the show,"* declared Dean Acheson.[38] He was referring to the Marshall Plan, but his words conveyed Washington's belief in the need for American dominance of the postwar international system.

States within this free-world society ought to share an antipathy to communism and a devotion to free-market trading principles. The importance of representative government in the society's structure remained uncertain. Since the late 1890s, citizens and American officialdom had extolled self-determination in principle, while frequently being chary of it in practice.[39] In theory, if the Free World prospered, then the virtues of democracy would become ingrained over time. There was the rub because anticommunism and freer trade were not necessarily precursors of self-determination. In fact, the cause of liberal democracy in any given situation might impede the pursuit of security. Assessing this paradox, Walter LaFeber concludes, "[Those] who held sway over policymaking in the early Cold War considered the advancing of democracy to be of distinctly secondary interest as they built up political, military, and economic systems to contain and roll back communism."[40] And racially based assumptions played a role in such thinking.

To become a reality in the aftermath of war, American hegemony had to exert a presence in the daily lives of others, particularly the Germans and Japanese. Therefore, the Marshall Plan for European reconstruction and the "Reverse Course" in Occupied Japan should be considered more than aspects of cold-war security policy. They were emblematic of the highest aspirations of those who were forging an American Century. In addition, they were intended to facilitate the transformation of Germany and Japan into pro-American outposts where respect for electoral politics and the rule of law would strengthen, where business and industry would be revitalized, where educational reforms would signify progress and order, and where novel cultural norms would engender an ethos of material consumption. Americanization through cultural change, though resisted at times and in places, was essential to the building of an American Century.

To trace the history of the American Century from 1945 through Richard M. Nixon's resignation in August 1974, my book examines five major themes. The first four—the making of grand strategy, relations with allies and client states, political economy (also referred to as containment capitalism), and nation-building—are covered in each chapter as appropriate; the fifth theme, credibility, also mentioned throughout, brings each chapter to a close. The relative paucity of studies about the origins and evolution of the American Century indicates the need for a broad overview to explicate Luce's project. To wit, if U.S. officials could build and expand a free-world society, an American Century replete with the attributes set forth in Luce's essay would thrive. Luce would then have given a name to his hopes and ambitions and a historical era that paralleled and transcended the Cold War.

In order to flourish, the American Century needed a solid foundation, one as strong as the anticommunism U.S. leaders professed in the early Cold War. Underpinning the enterprise was containment on a grand scale. Alliances and patron-client relationships, a market-based economy dependent on a strong dollar and bolstered by the politics of productivity, and foreign aid that enabled people and nations to modernize while striving to replicate the best of America were the building blocks of an organic free-world society.[41] The mortar of credibility would bind them together.

As the founder of a publishing empire, Henry Luce knew that an American Century could not exist, let alone prosper, without credibility, which he equated with the acceptance by others of American leadership and tutelage. The United States had to be a magnet for the hopes and dreams of other peoples and had to create a real affinity for America, its values, culture, and institutions. Laura A. Belmonte has called this undertaking "selling the American way."[42]

"Most important of all," Luce wrote in his essay, "we have that indefinable, unmistakable sign of leadership: prestige."[43] Without credibility, the idea of an American Century made no sense. Although credibility, prestige, and image—emotion-laden concepts that depend not on self-validation but on the perceptions of others—are not exact synonyms, officials used them interchangeably. At stake throughout the cold-war era, concludes Robert J. McMahon, was U.S. "resolve, reliability, believability, and decisiveness," that is, its credibility. The impetus for credibility was thus intimately linked to "the need to maintain America's global supremacy."[44]

The act of creating and sustaining the American Century was not as straightforward an endeavor as the foregoing discussion suggests. At a meta-level, campaigns to transform world affairs constituted a global culture war against both friends and foes. To achieve hegemony, policymakers had to alter how heads of state, high-level government officials, average citizens, and young people understood and lived in what Washington saw as a dangerous world. This "culture war," an apt if anachronistic term, was nothing less than an ideological struggle. From Harry Truman and Dean Acheson through Dwight Eisenhower and John Foster Dulles, John Kennedy and Dean Rusk, and Lyndon Johnson and Walt Rostow, to Richard Nixon and Henry Kissinger, the self-anointed exemplars of realpolitik, U.S. leaders resolutely and passionately encountered and maneuvered to change the world.

The American Century initially had a positive impact in places crucial to emerging U.S. interests—for example, in Japan, where the occupation provided a laboratory for testing the sway of American influence, especially in the wake of protests following the peace settlement and the signing of a bilateral security accord in 1951.[45] And in Europe, cold war never became hot war despite the acrimonious West-East divide over Germany from 1945 until the building of the Berlin Wall in 1961. Yet if the success of the American Century was most evident in Western Europe and Japan, in Latin America and less familiar reaches of the world its reception depended both on local conditions and on how the United States tried to mold the free-world society. The Eurocentrism of U.S. authorities, which generated great unease in the Western Hemisphere, had dismaying consequences.[46] Empathy with the world's poor and racially diverse peoples was not the forte of powerful men in Washington who feared the instability that often accompanied rising expectations in the Third World. Their conviction that American intentions were innately benign was not universally shared.[47]

After contending with the USSR for nearly two decades while simultaneously striving to expand the free-world society, the United States possessed unmatched strategic dominance in late 1963, a year after the Cuban missile crisis. Then there occurred the horrific assassination of President John F. Kennedy. A modern-day nirvana had not been at hand, though, as incipient cracks in the edifice of American supremacy soon broadened into visible fissures. Events over the next eighteen months, notably intervention in the Dominican Republic and the dispatch of troops to Indochina, weakened American leadership. Things worsened in 1968. Beginning with the Tet Offensive at the end of January, Lyndon Baines Johnson witnessed the collapse of his Vietnam policy, the near eclipse of the dollar as the regnant international currency, exasperating assertions of autonomy by America's closest allies, and dispiriting societal problems at home. At the end of March, days before the assassination of Rev. Dr. Martin Luther King Jr., a greatly beleaguered Johnson told a national television audience that he would not run for reelection.

These developments shook America's international credibility to its core and placed on display the decline of the American Century. They also helped elevate Richard Nixon to the presidency. While in office, he and his top foreign policy adviser, Henry A. Kissinger, set out to restore American credibility and keep the United States from becoming "a pitiful, helpless giant," as Nixon famously put it on April 30, 1970, in a televised speech defending the incursion of U.S. troops into Cambodia.[48] In trying to transform the grand strategy of global containment into what I call strategic globalism, they were no more than partly successful.[49] By August 9, 1974, when Nixon resigned in disgrace, Luce's dream was essentially dormant and had lost its relevance to American policymaking even though the security ethos endured.

Assessing how the American Century ultimately fared is a timely endeavor because few systematic studies exist of its origins and evolution.[50] Bruce Cumings dismisses as "nonsense" assertions that the American Century met its demise in the mid-1960s: "The American Century began in 1941 . . . and continues apace." Others disagree in their evaluation of its longevity or value as a metaphor for America's ambitions.[51] Mary Nolan, who tracks European and American engagement since 1890, contends, "From the seventies onward, American influence began to erode."[52] David F. Schmitz places the blame for the end of the American Century squarely on Richard Nixon.[53] In fact, Walter LaFeber, coauthor of a multi-edition textbook, *The American Century*, doubts its existence: "It had never begun. . . . The American Century was stillborn." Indicative of these differing views, one of his students, Sayuri Guthrie-Shimizu, observes that the "postwar world [was] where visions of the 'American century' now reigned supreme."

I argue that the forging of an American Century succeeded, if only for a time. Yet the idea and the effort should not be dismissed, in LaFeber's words, as an "illusion" or a "façade that effectively camouflaged what lay beneath it."[54] If they did not actually apply the term "American Century" to their endeavors, policymakers who shared the security ethos tried to bring to life something akin to Luce's vision: an enduring international system based on strategic, political, and economic hegemony. They labored to prevent a return to the dreadful chaos that had cloaked the world in depression and war and to surmount the confusion that marked the initial aftermath of war. That they fell short of their goals highlights the paradox of their efforts. The more secure friends and allies felt, the less accepting they were of American pretensions of hegemony.

Common cause, a hallmark of the free-world society in the immediate postwar years, inexorably gave way to doubt and expressions of national self-interest. Similarly, promises of development under U.S. auspices and tutelage too often went unfulfilled. In fact, the greater the troubles Washington encountered—in the economic realm or, especially, in Indochina—the less likelihood there was that an American Century would take hold abroad. Surely by the fall of 1974, and conceivably six years earlier, it was apparent that Luce's dream had ultimately begat an improbable quest.

Part 1

THE RISE OF THE AMERICAN CENTURY

PURSUING HEGEMONY

Building the American Century commenced as World War II drew to a close. Although the United States aspired to global leadership, how it would lead was not clear. More was needed than military power and economic might. Whether the UN would contribute to stability remained unknown. Moreover, how would the global economy fare under the Bretton Woods system? Was the creation of an international society, one reflective of Washington's interests, even possible? And, after Roosevelt's death, how would the Truman administration engender support for its foreign policy? As they began to consider such questions, policymakers had to figure out, in Acheson's portentous words, how to run the show. In concurrence with Luce's imperative to lead, they chose to pursue hegemony.

Inauspicious Beginnings

What friends and allies wanted from Washington was shared decision-making. Over time, the record of give-and-take in meetings both indicated how well the United States led and helped establish Washington's credibility. The issue of consultation suffused the Inter-American Conference on Problems of War and Peace at Chapúltepec Castle in Mexico City from February 21 to March 8. The early contours of hegemony emerged from the deliberations. Heading the U.S. delegation was Secretary of State Edward R. Stettinius Jr., former vice president of General Motors and chairman of the board at United States Steel. Stettinius, Dean Acheson later acidly wrote, "had gone far with comparatively modest equipment."

Most important to the work of the delegation was Assistant Secretary of State for Economic Affairs William L. (Will) Clayton, cofounder of Anderson, Clayton, and Company, one of the world's leading cotton export firms.[1] The Department of State wanted to use the conference, which began shortly after Roosevelt, Churchill, and Stalin met at Yalta, to get support for the United Nations at its initial meeting, set to begin April 25 in San Francisco. Turning wartime solidarity in the hemisphere, Argentina excepted, into common cause after the war became a major goal of the Latin Americans.[2]

Convening a conference at Chapúltepec Castle was highly symbolic because it was there on September 13, 1847, during the Mexican-American War, that U.S. troops seized the castle from a band of boys and young men, Los Niños Héroes, after defeating the Mexican army under the command of General Antonio López de Santa Anna. Representing his Latin American counterparts, Mexico's foreign minister Ezequiel Padilla worked with the State Department to set the meeting's agenda. Despite agreement on the importance of the UN to peace and collective security, there remained one issue generalities could not finesse: economic relations. Padilla wanted to negotiate arrangements with the United States in order to improve "the economic and social conditions of the people of America for the fundamental purpose of raising their standard of living."[3] Such a sentiment meant pushing for industrialization, which guaranteed a clash with Washington's priorities.

The economic question alarmed U.S. officials, who acknowledged the transition from war to peace would disrupt production and trade. The State Department's Merwin L. Bohan, a member of the U.S. delegation, explained what was at stake. "Our minimum responsibility," he wrote prior to the conference, "is to cooperate in solving current and future problems affecting the well being of this hemisphere." The United States must not abandon Latin America to the vagaries of postwar markets in which foreign exchange surpluses might be rapidly depleted; it should accept commodity agreements for "*essential* exports of Latin America at equitable prices." The alternative meant a return to the economic nationalism and protectionism of the 1930s. Also, wartime procurement programs should continue for a time. The Export-Import Bank, Bohan argued, should see to the need for investment capital. Taken as a whole, these measures should preclude the return of depressed economic conditions.[4] They did not, however, directly address Latin America's major concerns.

That task was left to Will Clayton, who sought to prevent the signature document of the meeting, "An Economic Charter of the Americas," from compromising Washington's interests. Clayton, speaking on February 27, warned about the grave dangers of economic nationalism and the persistence of state-controlled commerce. He made it clear that preferential commodity procurement would stop: "Markets are extremely sensitive to the existence of large surpluses and until such surpluses are absorbed their presence inevitably acts as a depressing influence on prices, on initiative, and on enterprise."[5] Clayton declined to promise that future purchases of security-related commodities, even for the defense of the Americas, would come from Latin America. He did hold out hope that Europe might serve as a market for Latin American goods. As for the prickly issue of foreign-exchange surpluses, he declared that protecting them would be difficult after the war.

Regarding support for economic development, Clayton made a couple of salient points. He noted, "It must be admitted right off that we face an extremely difficult problem." Europe would have first claim on capital goods produced in the United States. The other point emerged from his defense of the Export-Import Bank as the financial institution to which Latin Americans should look for development capital. In practical terms, this meant that Washington would not support the creation, long advocated in Latin America, of an inter-American bank.[6] The Export-Import Bank and the new World Bank would have to suffice.

This turn of events signified the transformation of wartime partnership into a postwar relationship of secondary importance. Clayton explained the inevitability of this change in general terms: "The United States . . . is definitely committed to a postwar policy looking to a substantial expansion in the world economy. . . . It is our intention to work actively for international agreements to remove all discriminations in trade, to reduce tariffs and other barriers to trade. . . ." Simply put, intra-hemispheric consultation was losing its urgency, whereas European recovery was Washington's commercial and financial priority. To think otherwise might jeopardize the economic rationale for an American Century.[7]

If the final version of the economic charter was not as limiting as Clayton, described by one scholar as "an economic ideologue of the first order," desired, it also failed to meet Latin American expectations. Even beyond Clayton's "shock therapy," Chapúltepec—despite initiating the reintegration of Argentina into regional affairs—disappointed Latin American delegates who hoped to sustain the spirit of reciprocity that marked FDR's wartime Good Neighbor policy.[8] The turn outside of the Dominican Republic and part of Central America toward democracy and political participation by organized labor across Latin America in 1944 and 1945 was striking, so much so that many Latin Americans thought relations with Washington were certain to improve. That was not the case, at least in economic terms. Meanwhile, on strategic and political matters Latin American states were expected to follow the U.S. lead. As the traditional forces of order reined in social progressives and leftists after mid-1945, Washington did not actively protest. Stability early in the postwar era, it seems, was preferable to the prospect of radical change.[9]

It is worth noting that Bohan, in words evocative of Luce's 1941 essay, closely linked the outcome of Chapúltepec to U.S. standing in the world. "The conference," he warned, "will not only be a test of the sincerity of the United States with respect to the inter-American system, but a test of the ability of the United States to assume practical and constructive leadership." In that sense, the Act of Chapúltepec, suggesting there were many paths to common goals, papered over critical differences between regionalism and the nascent globalism of U.S. foreign policy.[10]

Latin American endorsement of the UN at Chapúltepec created a problem for those who would build an American Century. The United States was staking out a global economic and political presence in Roosevelt's final months as president, yet the pull of regionalism remained strong. Bohan, who mostly agreed with Clayton, articulated the worrisome dilemma: "It would be a great mistake if the United States failed to meet the practical problems of Latin America because of vague fears that such action might complicate plans for economic cooperation on a world-wide scale."[11] Try as he might, Bohan could not bridge the gap between Pan Americanism and globalism. He later lamented, "We were going to have this one beautiful world. They [sic] had great doubts that regionalism had any importance whatsoever." Bohan, however, seemed to acknowledge that European reconstruction might help Latin American development, though his thinking on the issue lacked clarity.[12]

Indications of the limits to substantive consultation with friends and allies also came through in Thomas C. Mann's assessment of Chapúltepec. Mann, then a young State Department official who would later serve as assistant secretary for inter-American affairs (most famously under Lyndon Johnson), attended the conference as a technical adviser. He recalled in 1974 the vexing presence of the regionalism-globalism divide at the conference but downplayed the gulf between U.S. officials and Latin Americans over economic issues. Maybe Mann forgot that in a plenary session Ezequiel Padilla had defined economic growth as "vital," asserting that Latin America would not revert to a state of economic "semi-colonialism."[13] His words reflected in part the frustration Latin Americans were feeling about condescension by U.S. delegates.[14]

The founding conference of the United Nations did not assuage the worries of Latin Americans about their place in the postwar world. True, Article 51 recognized the importance of regional interests to major powers, especially the United States and the Soviet Union. Delegates from Latin America realized, though, that the veto power held by the five permanent members of the Security Council could trump their concerns. An effort to place a permanent Latin American representative on the Security Council failed. Stettinius, whatever his limitations, was carrying on FDR's work in bringing to life an organization in which the United

States expected to play the dominant role.[15] At the same time, the hubris present in the early construction of Luce's project was increasingly evident.

Beyond the Americas, building an American Century began in Europe in mid-1945. Allied forces had vanquished Nazi Germany; with the defeat of Imperial Japan a matter of time, a new internationalism seemed to be at hand. The Truman-Molotov contretemps of April at the White House aside, disputes among the Big Three allies appeared to be manageable.[16] A test of that assumption came with discussions about Germany's fate at the Potsdam Conference in July. There, Harry Truman and James F. Byrnes, Stettinius's successor, began to reassess relations with Moscow after Winston Churchill's departure at mid-conference following his government's electoral loss to the Labour Party and Clement Attlee.[17]

Social decay and economic chaos loomed over Europe as Truman and Joseph Stalin were meeting. The resuscitation of Germany's coal production might help fix such conditions even though reneging on FDR's pledge to internationalize the Ruhr would raise suspicions in Moscow about U.S. and British intentions. As the Potsdam Conference began, the economic rehabilitation of Germany's western zones was already under way. Although the touchy issues of unification and remilitarization would arise later, this development constituted a major step on the road to building a free-world society. Industrial recovery in areas of Western occupation was nonnegotiable by August, making Stalin's hope for a unified, left-leaning Germany unrealizable.[18]

American leadership depended on a strong world economy, one in which industrial and agricultural production, extraction of subsoil resources, and the relatively unfettered movement of capital fostered a trading regime that rejected prior nationalist tendencies. Simply put, markets were the key to leadership and global prosperity. At Freedom House in New York City on April 30, 1944, Will Clayton set forth the dangers of a world devoid of growing markets: "That kind of world is a world of fear, of restriction, of isolationism, of low living standards, and, in the end, of war and destruction."[19]

Liberalized trade would have to await the genuine give-and-take of negotiations that distinguished the General Agreement on Tariffs and Trade (GATT) from previous trade pacts. "GATT," notes Thomas W. Zeiler, "was designed to ensure American values and security, not just profits." Yet the GATT did not formally get under way until the Geneva round of talks in 1947.[20] In the meantime, policymakers began to assert American hegemony in response to demands for capital. The early postwar months witnessed calls for loans to prime the economic pump of war-ravaged Europe.[21] The most important requests came from Moscow and London.

These two cases had striking similarities. First, the USSR and Britain thought in terms of multibillion-dollar amounts. Moscow had proposed a $6 billion loan in January 1945, an increase of $5 billion from a figure discussed in 1943, whereas officials in London believed that FDR promised Churchill $6.5 billion in reconstruction aid at the Quebec Conference of September 1944.[22] For Washington, two issues stood out in deciding whether to negotiate a loan: the terms of the loan and how a given loan advanced the cause of multilateralism, that is, the Bretton Woods system. Administration officials doubted that Congress would approve a $6 billion loan, no matter who was the recipient, accept a lengthy repayment schedule, or extend low rates of interest. Also, nations remaining outside the Bretton Woods system were less likely to have their loan requests favorably considered.

The terms of loans were negotiable. Clayton revealed that more was at stake in the Soviet request than reconstruction: "It would seem harmful to us to offer such a large credit at this time and thus lose what appears to be the only concrete bargaining lever for use in connection with many other political and economic problems."[23] When Stalin lowered the amount to $1 billion on favorable terms after Potsdam, U.S. officials scrambled to identify concessions in return for granting the loan. Members of Congress wanted to alter the status quo in Eastern Europe, which meant partly undoing the Yalta accords. There was little to discuss, even though the request was not formally rejected. It was "lost," the State Department later claimed. The USSR reopened the issue in March 1946 to no avail; by then events extraneous to the loan had rendered the matter moot.[24]

Meanwhile, Anglo-American negotiations over postwar aid had quickened. Here, U.S. officials had to tread carefully. The nature of consultation was more important in talks with the British than with the Soviets or even with Latin Americans. Clayton explained: "The British financial problem is admittedly the greatest barrier to rapid progress towards free multilateral payments and relaxation of barriers to trade. It threatens not only delay but, indeed, the ultimate success of our economic foreign program. . . . [We must] accelerate Britain's reconversion to multilateralism."[25] In short, Anglo-American comity was indispensable to the genesis of a free-world society and, beyond that, to the forging of an American Century.

Negotiations resulted in an agreement signed in December 1945 for a $3.75 billion loan. Payments would be interest-free for five years, which Clayton had opposed, and then remain at 2 percent for fifty years. British negotiators knew they had few cards to play, so great was the need for foreign exchange beyond what the sterling bloc was providing. Concessions by London allowed sterling bloc members to convert their reserves into dollars and in essence accepted the ideas of multilateralism and nondiscrimination. Congress, with tension with the USSR on the rise as a backdrop, sent a bill funding the loan to Truman for his signature in July 1946.[26]

Assessing the agreement in a speech to the National Farm Institute in Des Moines, Iowa, in February, Clayton echoed Luce on the benefits of freer trade. "We will," he exulted, "pull the world out of the nationalist form of trade which has developed so insidiously and extensively during the last 30 years. . . . This would open the markets of the world to the United States."[27] What negotiations did not do was establish an adequate means for consultation should the loan need adjusting, which was a certainty if British balance-of-payments difficulties persisted.[28]

If troubles with Latin Americans and the British over economic aid and loans were an inauspicious beginning in their effort to exercise postwar leadership, U.S. officials also quickly realized how difficult it was to create a free-world society, let alone something more ambitious. Some combination of persuasion and coercion was necessary to achieve such grand goals. How to bring the Soviet Union into the postwar economic order confounded policymakers who were intent on extracting concessions in exchange for reconstruction aid or loans.

In that regard, it is worth considering the Soviet Union's failure to join the Bretton Woods system. Moscow's decision exemplified the limits of consultation and foreshadowed how the American Century could become an exclusionary project, albeit one with unlimited aspirations. Soviet delegates at Bretton Woods in July 1944 were in over their heads and ill prepared to negotiate the makeup of the IMF and the World Bank. At an organizational meeting, held in Savannah, Georgia, in March 1946, with the Soviets there as observers, the United States made certain its influence over the Bank and Fund would be decisive—to the consternation of the British, who envisioned the two bodies operating as impartial financial institutions. A highly disillusioned John Maynard Keynes, who died on April 21 of that year, lamented, "I went to Savannah expecting to meet the world, and all I met was a tyrant."[29]

The chances for economic multilateralism never approximated what Keynes was seeking. London had played its hand to the fullest and come up short. The Soviets could not open their state-based economy to the degree of scrutiny the Americans required without implicitly also accepting the basic tenets of midcentury capitalism. What transpired at Savannah showed that Washington's leadership style had divisive aspects, which over time caused trouble for those striving to expand America's global influence in quest of Luce's vision.

The American Century Takes Shape

Along with economic issues, important political matters came to the fore in the months after the end of the war. Disappointment over the Council of Foreign

Ministers (CFM) meeting at London in September 1945, where Germany was a nonissue, and the presence of Soviet forces in northern Iran made the quest for hegemony extremely important within the Truman administration. The impasse at London over Eastern Europe, the Balkans, and a peace treaty with Italy deepened fissures in the Grand Alliance.[30] Molotov returned home convinced that his tough stance had made a significant statement about the Soviet Union as a great power, and Byrnes repaired to Washington dismayed that he had failed to extract concessions from the Russians. In December in Moscow for another CFM meeting, Byrnes sought a modus vivendi on Bulgaria and Romania and raised the matter of UN control of atomic energy. Results were disappointing, and little was accomplished vis-à-vis Iran or Turkey, where Soviet interests were on the rise—a development that further eroded the wartime alliance.[31]

Exasperated, Truman told Byrnes in January 1946 that he was "tired [of] babying the Soviets." Similarly, Molotov concluded that American ambitions knew no bounds. As he later put it, "There is no corner of the world in which the USA cannot be seen." The CFM had been critically weakened as a forum for Big Three deliberations.[32]

From his position as chief aide to Ambassador W. Averell Harriman in Moscow, George Frost Kennan found little to applaud in the December CFM meeting, a sentiment his British counterpart Frank Roberts shared.[33] Kennan amplified his thinking in the new year in an essay, "The United States and Russia." After tracing Russia's historical difficulties with its "fierce hostile neighbors," he concluded that "the Russians therefore have no conception of permanent friendly relations between states." The willingness to use power mattered most to Soviet leaders, who perceive enemies "in all that part of the world they do not control." Thus, in responding to the USSR, the United States should follow clear rules of engagement, which for Kennan meant acting cautiously in the face of a presumably implacable foe.[34]

Although Kennan did not send this particular composition to Washington, it served as a prelude to his famous cable of February 22, the Long Telegram. To understand the electrifying effect Kennan's message had on the administration, some context is necessary. Stalin gave a speech on February 9 in advance of elections for the Supreme Soviet. While scarcely mentioning foreign affairs, he indicated that the USSR should increase its prewar industrial production threefold. Coming on the heels of what Kennan saw as the troubling outcome of the December CFM meeting and at a time when Moscow had not decided whether to join the Bretton Woods system, Stalin's speech seemed a challenge to U.S. leadership and a warning that the USSR was prepared to take advantage of a weakened postwar Europe.[35] H. Freemen "Doc" Matthews, head of the State Department's Office of European Affairs, found the speech alarming, a threat to capitalism itself.

"[It] should be given great weight," he advised, "in any plans . . . for extending credits or other forms of economic assistance to the Soviet Union."[36]

The environment in which the Long Telegram was received is also important. In short, the White House and key members of Congress had begun to perceive the USSR as an enemy. Kennan, who was contemplating retirement even as he composed his lengthy cable, soon found his ideas at the center of policy deliberations. Less than a year later when George C. Marshall became secretary of state in January 1947, he asked Kennan to take charge of the department's new Policy Planning Staff (PPS), whose work formally began in May.[37]

Kennan understood that the urgency of his language could be used as a clarion call to arms against the USSR. Looking back in his memoirs on the era of global containment, he wondered whether a government so receptive to such a strong message "should deceive itself into believing that it is capable of conducting a mature, consistent, and discriminating foreign policy."[38] Kennan, never at ease with American culture and his country's political traditions, was a brooding, introspective, brilliant individual who found no comfort in "this thin, tight, lonely American life."[39] That he feared a democracy would be adrift in a world replete with danger occasions no surprise.

Whatever reconsideration the Long Telegram may have later wrested from its author, in the near term it served two purposes. First, it kept the momentum going in the administration to take a harder line against the Soviet Union. This effect received additional impetus on March 6 from Winston Churchill's "Iron Curtain" speech in Fulton, Missouri. On the same day, the State Department demanded an explanation of Soviet actions in, among other places, Iran and Eastern Europe.[40] The Cold War was under way.

Second, Kennan's cable aided the building of the American Century, something he would not wittingly have done. The messianic qualities of Luce's project were alien to his assessment of how the United States should respond to Soviet challenges. Ends should not so exceed means as to render the former meaningless. Pursuing a goal as outsized as an American Century clouded what might happen should Washington fail to counter the Soviet Union where it mattered most—in Europe. For him, containment there was the basic goal of an effective, that is, cautious, foreign policy.[41] Such prudence was on the wane. The Long Telegram paved the way for the policy of containment as seen in the Truman Doctrine and the Marshall Plan; in turn, they composed two essential building blocks for hegemony and, thus, the American Century.[42]

An anguished Kennan, determined to mold a foreign policy focused on the immediate fate of Europe, had to walk a fine line in his new position. To accept the Truman Doctrine as open-ended, meaning the United States logically must counter Soviet actions everywhere, was a recipe for disaster. Yet he feared that ignoring Communist advances in Europe or beyond would damage American credibility. Whether in the Long Telegram or other writings, his words, Frank Costigliola observes, "crackled with emotion even as they claimed the authority of cool reason." It would be clear by mid-1947 that events had outrun Kennan's reservations.[43]

In the terrible winter of 1947, officials at the Foreign Office informed their American counterparts that London could no longer protect Western interests in Greece and Turkey, thus calling into question Great Britain's standing as a great power and deepening its dependence on the United States.[44] The Greek and Turkish governments were seeking some $250 million in military and economic aid. Dean Acheson, then undersecretary of state, foresaw for Greece an "imminent collapse due to mounting guerrilla activity, supplied and directed from the outside." A weak government in Athens, incapable of dealing with "economic chaos," would certainly make things worse. He doubted, too, whether officials in Ankara could "handle the financing of both the modernization and maintenance of the large army that the Russian presence called for and the economic development of Turkey."[45] The situation provided him with an opportunity not to be squandered. "This was my crisis," he declared. Acheson used conditions in Greece to generate support for the Truman Doctrine, which the president announced to a joint session of Congress on March 12; it included a request for $400 million.[46]

Congress soon joined the administration's crusade against feared Communist inroads in the Mediterranean by authorizing assistance. Even so, it took months for aid to reach Greece's conservative regime. Soviet support for leftist partisan forces was never enough to bring them success. Stalin, U.S. officials knew, was not willing to confront the Americans and British over Greece. That position was consistent with his pledge to Churchill at their Moscow meeting in October 1944 that the "Soviet Union [does] not intend to organize a Bolshevik Revolution in Europe."[47] Like Acheson, Kennan worried about a Communist takeover in Greece even though he could not find "*in itself* any immediate and catastrophic setback to the Western world." As for the situation in Turkey, it "afforded no rationale for the mounting of a special aid program. . . . The Soviet threat [had to] be recognized for what it was—primarily a political one and not a threat of a military attack."[48]

Kennan again tried to advocate caution in foreign policy when he drafted PPS/1, "Policy with Respect to American Aid to Western Europe." It reached Acheson on May 23. Kennan's foremost biographer, John Lewis Gaddis, calls it "the most influential" paper ever prepared by the PPS. PPS/1 set the stage for the Marshall Plan. Kennan cast the problem of Europe not primarily as a strategic matter but as an economic and psychological concern, thus disputing those seeing "communist activities as the root of the difficulties of western Europe."[49]

The reception accorded the Truman Doctrine and Marshall Plan imbued them with a boundless importance Kennan could not abide. Luce, for one, applauded the Truman Doctrine's boldness but wondered whether it was too confined in its application. Such thinking horrified Kennan. In turn, the Marshall Plan highlighted differences between universalists, who shared Luce's assumptions about postwar obligations, and those like Kennan, who thought a global crusade anathema to vital American interests.[50] These dueling perspectives, which he and Acheson personified, could not coexist, especially as cold-war policy became the handmaiden of a growing American Century.

The breakdown of the Grand Alliance after Roosevelt died meant trouble for Washington as officials worked to expand American hegemony. Neither Stalin's election speech in February 1946, which had depicted impending splits in the capitalist West, nor Churchill's "Iron Curtain" address in March had generated discernible public support for greater internationalism in foreign policy.[51] In fact, success in the November elections meant the Republican Party might seek to rejuvenate isolationism. As if in response, the Truman administration moved to fortify the Free World. That endeavor began at the Rio Conference in September 1947, which produced the Inter-American Treaty of Reciprocal Assistance, or Rio Pact, a mutual defense agreement proscribing intervention in the Western Hemisphere.[52]

The meeting at Chapúltepec Castle had frustrated Latin American leaders in their quest for regional stability via a special relationship with Washington.[53] The White House was slow to embrace hemispheric solidarity. One reason for delay was Argentina; another was congressional suspicion of military assistance. Juan Perón's election as president in February 1946 in effect solved the first problem; Argentina, which had refused to declare war on the Axis powers until spring 1945, would finally be restored to good standing in the hemisphere. Next, an attempt by the administration to work with Congress, which took the form of the Inter-American Military Cooperation Act, had failed passage in successive years.[54] Only after the Rio gathering, which called for U.S. aid in the training of Latin American military personnel, did officials surmount the second obstacle to strategic cohesion.

The founding of the Organization of American States (OAS) at Bogotá, Colombia, in April 1948, with Secretary of State Marshall in attendance, cemented the emerging cold-war relationship—giving birth to a security-first Pan American Community—but did not address economic issues.[55] U.S. delegates made it clear that nothing like the Marshall Plan was in the cards. Roy R. Rubottom, who later served as assistant secretary of state for inter-American affairs, was working in the U.S. embassy. He was disappointed when Marshall did not couch Export-Import Bank funds for Latin America as a kind of regional Marshall Plan: "We could have gotten all the PR advantages of that."[56] Truman agreed with those opposed to special treatment for Latin America, commenting, "The problems of countries in this Hemisphere are different in nature and cannot be relieved by the same means and the same approaches which are in contemplation for Europe."[57] At most, the Export-Import Bank would increase its lending authority. An economic summit would not take place for another seven years because, Rubottom explained, "Latin America was very much in the economic hegemony of the United States."[58]

These developments in U.S. relations with Latin America were part of a process leading to the creation of the North Atlantic Treaty Organization (NATO). One impetus may have been Marshall's reaction to the assassination on April 9 of Jorge Eliécer Gaitán, an advocate of broad reform in Colombia. Marshall wondered whether Gaitán's murder was the work of "revolutionary movements" with "world-wide implications."[59] By then, the secretary of state and others on Truman's national security team were envisioning mutual security pacts as a key line of defense against Communist subversion in the Americas and elsewhere.

A similar assessment took place in Europe. British military chiefs, the Foreign Office, and Foreign Secretary Ernest Bevin shared what one scholar identifies as a "Cold War mindset" that termed the USSR an ideological adversary. Given its economic weakness, strategic partners, namely, the United States, were essential if Britain was going to survive as a major power.[60] A Franco-British defense accord, the Dunkirk Treaty, signed in March 1947, evolved into the Brussels Treaty after the Communist-backed coup of February 1948 in Czechoslovakia. The signatories at Brussels—Great Britain, France, and the Benelux countries—valued the pact as a way of keeping German revanchism in check. Shortly thereafter, Britain and other nations asked the United States to help found a multilateral security organization.

Acheson and others in the administration believed that, even with U.S. military aid, the signers of the Brussels Treaty stood no chance against a Soviet military offensive, should one eventuate.[61] That such a development was highly unlikely was irrelevant. When the Truman Doctrine was under discussion, Acheson warned about "possible . . . Soviet penetration" of Europe, Asia, and Africa if the United States failed to act.[62] To Acheson, like others for whom the security ethos influenced threat perception, civilization itself was at risk.

As part of its attempt to establish a security perimeter to prevent Western penetration of its presumptive sphere of influence, the USSR created the Cominform in September 1947. Both a reaction to the Truman Doctrine and the Marshall Plan and a move to assert Soviet dominance over the European Left as a challenge to American hegemony, the Cominform fed a growing belief in Western capitals of Moscow's obduracy.[63] Elbridge Durbrow, a U.S. diplomat stationed in Moscow, denounced it as "patently a declaration of political and economic war against [the] US and everything [the] US stands for in world affairs."[64]

The Central Intelligence Agency (CIA), created in the National Security Act of 1947, quickly moved to co-opt French and Italian Communists by relying on cultural diplomacy as well as covert activity to enhance America's image while also protecting its security interests in Europe.[65] Kennan, acknowledging the difficulty of framing a coherent strategy to contend with the USSR, encouraged the CIA to assist forces in Western Europe, left-leaning trade unions chief among them, that were opposed to communism.[66]

For Kennan, political warfare had to offer the prospect of victory in some sense, while preparing the United States for a lengthy struggle. Liberation of people living under the Soviet yoke or attaining decisive influence among the segments of Western societies susceptible to the blandishments of communism might not soon happen, no matter the means employed.[67] Unlike Kennan, neither Acheson nor Truman was disposed to accept such ambiguity. Like the British, theirs was an ideological battle they were fighting with the USSR.

Simply put, the future safety of Western Europe depended on the actions of the United States as the division of Germany became inevitable. Accordingly, the North Atlantic Treaty was signed in Washington on April 4, 1949, and ratified by the end of July.[68] Its European founders envisioned NATO as a political body that presented a unified front to Soviet adventurism and as a means to achieve the larger objective of European unity.[69] Yet should the Federal Republic of Germany, established in Bonn in May, not soon achieve equal status in the incipient free-world society, a transatlantic commitment to mutual security would be of dubious value. Shortly after becoming secretary of state in January 1949, Acheson—more than his counterparts in Paris and London, Robert Schuman and Ernest Bevin, respectively—took a liking to Chancellor Konrad Adenauer and effusively praised the German's "imagination and wisdom" at their meeting in November of that year.[70]

From NATO's inception, Western Europe stood as the first line of defense for the Free World. For many of those who came under its wing, NATO was welcomed as a godsend and a symbol of America's good intentions. They believed that Luce's Good Samaritan possessed a protective and generous spirit. Lawrence Kaplan, the foremost scholar of NATO, writes, "In the American Century, . . . the United States was now the steward of civilization, and Europe, unworthy though it might be, would be a beneficiary of that stewardship."[71]

The embrace of Germany and NATO was not unanimous in Washington. Observing events in Germany to understand how they would affect Europe, Kennan urged a nonmilitary solution to the impasse with the Soviet Union. His assumption that a unified, neutral Germany would lean toward the West earned him few plaudits from fellow policymakers, the builders of the American Century, who by then saw him as akin to a fabulist.[72] Kennan's keen resistance to a North Atlantic alliance and support for a demilitarized zone in Central Europe had negligible effect on his superiors or the White House. He doubted the reality of a Soviet military threat to Western Europe. Those who accepted such a threat as real in the late 1940s pointedly refused to question a policy of military deterrence, which became a central feature of NATO.[73]

As Kennan was settling in at the PPS, the Joint Chiefs of Staff (JCS) were preparing a major assessment, "United States Assistance to Other Countries from the Standpoint of National Security." Starting from the premise that an ideological war with the USSR was under way, JCS 1769/1 devised a hierarchy of need for aid among states crucial to the nation's security. Great Britain and France were indispensable partners. As for Germany, its industrial "resurgence" was "essential for the economic recovery of France," and its economic recovery was "of primary importance from the viewpoint of United States security."[74] Then on July 11, 1947, the State, War, and Navy departments agreed on JCS 1779 for the military governance of Germany. It superseded JCS 1067 of May 1945, which advocated constricting Germany's reconstruction. In stark contrast, the new directive anticipated a politically and economically stable Germany that would "make a maximum contribution to European recovery."[75]

The prospect of American dominance in Germany drove Stalin to a desperate measure, the blockade of Berlin. It began shortly after the introduction of the deutsche mark on June 23, 1948.[76] Stalin's actions revealed more the ineptness of Soviet policymaking than a sophisticated plan to impose Communist domination. Acheson derided the "clumsy diplomacy" by the Soviets. "Theirs is a more primitive form of political method," he averred.[77] Believing the West wanted to exclude it from decision-making about Europe's future, Moscow did not realize that U.S. policy amounted to "double containment" of the West Germans and the Soviets. Stalin's presumption of rifts in the West fostered a policy of aggressive deterrence that soon involved the testing of an atomic bomb and the remobilization of the Red Army.[78]

If Soviet diplomacy was clumsy in American eyes, then U.S. officials were unyielding as the Kremlin saw it—a sentiment Kennan more or less shared.[79] Stalin realized that his options were limited, however, with two prominent reminders being the formation of NATO and the founding of the Federal Republic of Germany on May 23, 1949. The blockade had come to an ignominious end eleven days earlier. Its immediate legacy validated U.S. fears of monolithic communism and assisted both the growth of the free-world society and American hegemony.[80]

The quest for friends and allies to undergird the American Century extended beyond the Americas and Western Europe to the Middle East and East Asia. American hegemony depended substantially on access to oil, the lubricant of free-world dynamism. The salient question in the early Cold War was not whether the United States could meet its oil needs as they multiplied under the pressure of new security commitments. Rather, the issue was whether the United States and its partners could control reserves to the detriment of the Soviet Union and its satellite states. Years before that goal took shape, the Roosevelt administration in 1943 designated Saudi Arabia a strategic partner for the war effort. FDR met with King Abdel Aziz Ibn Saud on his way back to Washington from the Yalta Conference in February 1945 to solidify a security relationship.

The Truman administration moved quickly after Roosevelt's death to bolster U.S.-Saudi ties, acknowledging that the kingdom's "oil resources constitute . . . one of the greatest material prizes in world history."[81] By 1947, the State Department was referring to stability in the greater Middle East—a region where the Foreign Office hoped to maintain a "close affinity" of Anglo-American interests—as "a necessary condition of world peace."[82] Accordingly, U.S. officials initiated a program of military training and aid for Saudi Arabia in exchange for rights at the Dhahran Air Field.[83] The bilateral relationship therefore became nearly as strong as a formal alliance with each partner providing something the other dearly wanted.

The courting of Iran proved to be more problematic in the short term, first, because of the presence of a powerful nationalist movement. Also, as already mentioned, the USSR tried and failed in 1945–1946 to insinuate its influence into Iranian politics. What the Soviets wanted was access to oil in the region of Azerbaijan, which Moscow claimed fell within the USSR's defense perimeter. When the United States and Great Britain threatened to place the matter before the UN, the USSR backed down and averted a crisis.[84] Thereafter, using the leverage provided by military missions, Washington sought to ingratiate itself with the young shah, Mohammed Reza Pahlavi, who had been in power since September 1941, and Prime Minister Ahmad Qavam. By the end of June 1947, the Iranians, who saw an opportunity to forge a network of advantageous ties, were likening their situation to that of Greece. The American response could only have been better had a formal alliance been struck because the Truman administration signed an agreement under which Tehran received a $25 million credit to purchase arms.[85]

U.S.-British oil policy in the Middle East—denial of Soviet bloc access to Iranian or Arab oil—also underwrote the American drive for hegemony. National Security Council (NSC) documents 26 and 26/2, which Truman approved in late 1948 and early 1949, created a division of labor about how to respond should the USSR invade the region. Britain would destroy or disable Iran's and Iraq's reserves, with the United States doing likewise in Bahrain, Kuwait, Qatar, and Saudi Arabia. Moreover, as agreed to in October 1950, the two allies would refrain from consulting local governments until operations commenced.[86]

In East Asia, the rehabilitation of Japan was nearly as important to the young Free World as NATO. Theodore Roosevelt had anticipated in 1905 the convergence of Japanese and U.S. interests, declaring, "My feeling is . . . about the Japanese Nation that they [*sic*] are a wonderful and civilized people."[87] It was essential after the war—in many respects a race war in Asia—for the occupation to emphasize those assumed traits. Bolstering that effort on a people-to-people basis and thus enhancing American prestige were the return of baseball at the professional level and the advent of a revamped educational program in Japanese schools.[88]

The initial phase of the military occupation under General Douglas MacArthur, supreme commander of the Allied powers, lasted three years. Its principal goals, constituting a seismic cultural change, were to demilitarize and democratize Japan. The occupation also sought to transform government and industry and expand political participation, especially by women. Yet as the Cold War was becoming entrenched in Europe in 1948, Washington reconfigured the nature of the occupation with the "Reverse Course." Kennan played a key role in the shift, using a trip to Japan in March to curtail MacArthur's vast authority.[89] The Reverse Course presaged the rearming of Japan, sought to isolate if not eliminate the Marxist Left, allowed purged individuals to reenter politics, and restored to prominence businessmen whose influence the occupation had negated. Postwar Japan was, in John Dower's words, "a client state in all but name."[90] Kennan's report surveyed the changes in general terms. Occupation officials, he wrote on March 25 in PPS/28, should not "press upon the Japanese Government any further reform legislation" but instead "relax pressure on [it] in connection with these reforms."[91] Progressive change evidently was not immediately welcome in parts of the young free-world society.

Even before the founding of the People's Republic of China in October 1949 and the signing of a peace treaty in September 1951, Japan became critical to cold-war strategy and the realization of hegemony. Livingston Merchant, assistant secretary of state for Far Eastern affairs from 1949 to 1951, reinforced the point: "It was essential to our national interest and security that we rebuild bridges to Japan and encourage its rejuvenation as a great power." Acheson, too, recalled, "Our best hope was to make these former enemies willing and strong supporters of a free-world structure." Moreover, Prime Minister Yoshida Shigeru, who presided over Japan's transformation from hated enemy to invaluable partner, "inspired both respect and affection."[92]

Although the Soviet Union was nowhere near as looming a presence in Japan as in Germany, Yoshida still faced a difficult task in rebuilding Japan after taking office in October 1948. While he adamantly opposed anything that betokened remilitarization, his position was at odds with expectations about Japan's future. Tokyo was supposed to advance free-world trade in Asia outside of China, and U.S. officials envisioned a role for Japan in aiding Western security interests. Yoshida focused his attention on domestic matters, including economic reconstruction and a tough policy toward the Left. The White House approved of his antiradicalism yet wanted Yoshida to reconsider Japan's security posture. That desire intensified as the strategic situation across Asia deteriorated after 1949.[93]

A divided Korea did not seem a promising place to implant an outpost of the free-world society. Postwar occupation by Soviet and American forces and division at the 38th parallel on the peninsula did little to curb nationalist passions on the Left and Right. U.S. personnel had refused to deal with the Korean People's Republic (KPR), formed in September 1945 by a leftist coalition in the south. The U.S. command denounced the KPR as Communist and sought to coordinate the occupation with conservative groups, some of which had collaborated in the war with Japanese forces. By the time U.S. troops left Korea in 1948, the Left was in disarray in the south, and chances of moderating a rightward drift there were small. Fledgling attempts to find a basis for reunification failed. With the formation in August 1948 of the South Korean state, the Republic of Korea (ROK), the United States faced limited options. For better or worse, President Syngman Rhee had become Washington's man in Northeast Asia.[94] Rhee moved to create a loyal security apparatus that protected his interests by using force against real and potential political opponents. The most effective device at his disposal was the National Security Law (NSL) of December 1948, which gave him a legal basis to exercise quasi-absolute authority.[95]

Rhee's disdain for the United States was evident when he informed Ambassador John J. Muccio that "twice in 40 years the United States had abandoned Korea"—in Rhee's telling once when Theodore Roosevelt was president and again by Franklin Roosevelt at Yalta. Rhee, of course, was seeking security guarantees from Washington in mid-1949 as cross-border incidents grew in number and severity. A furious Acheson denounced Rhee's "ill-considered statements," calling them a "grave breach [of] ordinary diplomatic courtesy" that "can only redound to [the] disadvantage of [the] ROK."[96] Rhee, Muccio knew, had spent his entire life working for Korean independence. He became so absorbed in that undertaking he could not alter his instinct for self-preservation and actually become an effective head of state. To Muccio, this "determined willful person" was not the Jeffersonian Democrat he imagined himself to be but rather an "autocrat."[97] The testy relationship between Seoul and Washington was poised to become even more so as the Cold War heated up, a development that was sure to affect the reach of U.S. hegemony and the growth of the American Century.

The Political Economy of Hegemony

Luce's 1941 essay offered few practicable ideas about bringing into being the economic side of the American Century. Through his publishing empire, he devoted himself to advancing American influence abroad. *Fortune* magazine played a key role. Luce did not embrace laissez-faire policies as the true path to economic order. His Republicanism had no time for the atavistic philosophy of the likes of Andrew W. Mellon, secretary of the Treasury under Herbert Hoover. To liquidate weak economic sectors, as Mellon had advised, was to deny the need for American leadership if the world was to avoid another depression. *Fortune*, founded in 1930, was not a reflexive champion of unfettered capitalism. Even before the Great Depression began, Luce believed that capital and the nation's industrial elite should draw on the power of the state, albeit sparingly, to construct a modern economic world.

Luce's prescription became more precise after 1945. "Committed to the ethos of the capitalist world," Alan Brinkley writes, Luce used *Fortune* to fashion a new mission for his publications: Fix their gaze on the attributes of "American Business Enterprise."[98] This charge, issued in 1948, complemented the direction of economic policy as the Truman administration asserted U.S. hegemony in shaping European reconstruction under the Marshall Plan. If the West was to counter communism's appeal, an allure that was premised on the uncertainty of the market, it needed to pursue a free-market philosophy responsive to human needs. Thus was born what herein is referred to as containment capitalism. Currency convertibility, relatively free trade, and the promise of growth and development to stave off Communist inroads in Western Europe lay at its heart.

An American-led economic revival seemed improbable in the depths of the Depression. Not only did Roosevelt take the United States off gold in 1933, he undermined the London Economic Conference by refusing to restore an international gold standard, which was intended to promote currency stabilization. These actions, coming in the wake of the Smoot-Hawley Tariff of 1930, reflected economic nationalism's appeal. Unlike Japan and Germany, which found salvation in autarky, the United States under Roosevelt sought the return of domestic prosperity and ways to prevent another financial collapse. The return to the gold standard at $35 per ounce and congressional passage of the Reciprocal Trade Agreements Act, both in 1934, signaled a willingness to assume greater responsibility for the world's economy. (The same held true for the Tripartite Monetary Agreement, signed with Britain and France in 1936.)[99]

That Roosevelt was interested in something grander than a kind of national capitalism via deficit spending, which Britain's John Maynard Keynes advocated, soon became apparent. New Deal economists set out to forge a coalition of industry, investment banks, and internationally inclined commercial banks for the purpose of creating a multinational economy based on free trade.[100] The task for Americans after Bretton Woods was to create a healthy commercial system with trade as the linchpin of peace, prosperity, and hegemony. Keynes's national capitalism would not do. Testifying before Congress in 1944, then assistant secretary of state Dean Acheson remarked, "If you wish to control the entire trade and income of the United States, . . . you could probably fix it so that everything produced here would be consumed here." Yet, "nobody contemplates that," he said. "Therefore, you find you must look to markets and those markets are abroad."[101] Undersecretary of State for Economic Affairs William Clayton added during the drafting of the Marshall Plan, "We need markets—big markets—in which to buy and sell."[102] In sum, there would be no American Century without access to markets.

Europeans needed help buying the range of commodities American businesses wanted to sell. Europe's trade deficit in 1947 exceeded $4.7 billion, more than twice that of 1946.[103] Trying to maintain Britain's status as a great power, Labour Party prime minister Clement Attlee hoped to fashion a modern welfare state at home without sacrificing interests in Europe, the Middle East, or what remained of Britain's overseas empire. It was a daunting task. Policymakers led by Clayton insisted that Britain not discriminate against American commerce. Attlee's government desperately needed the $3.75 billion loan it negotiated in 1945, yet knew the loan, as generous as its terms seemed to the Americans, more served Washington's interests than London's.[104] Simply put, U.S.-directed multilateralism had curbed the worst excesses of national capitalism.

Few British officials judged the Bretton Woods system, which Parliament formally approved in December 1945, an unalloyed success. It had emotional significance and practical consequences that could not be ignored. As for the loan, it was not a grant, and Washington was in position virtually to dictate how the funds should be expended. In addition, funds could not pay off obligations incurred in sterling-area countries.[105] Authorities in London feared that a U.S.-led commercial and financial order, which they acknowledged was vital for national well-being, would constrain their policy options and increase balance-of-payments deficits.[106] In the worst-case scenario, America's economic strength would threaten the welfare state and the very stability of the Labour government.[107]

Conversely, France tried to maintain the franc at an artificial level to prevent American goods from overwhelming domestic markets. The U.S. response raised the prospect of a customs war, which France could ill afford. In meetings with Foreign Minister Georges Bidault in August 1945, Secretary of State Byrnes stressed America's desire to assist France's recovery through loans and trade.[108] As with Britain, the issue soon became whether France possessed sufficient capacity to service loans and generate commercial growth. The payments deficit with the United States exceeded $2 billion in 1946, even as the French people desperately needed food.[109] The two governments reached agreement in May for increased aid. The terms were revealing. France had received postwar credits of $1.2 billion from the Export-Import Bank. In what amounted to a quid-pro-quo, officials issued a statement "expressing . . . full agreement with the principles of the United States' proposals on world trade and employment" and indicating willingness to help secure "general international support for these proposals."[110]

Five months later, Ambassador Jefferson Caffrey described "a profound 'malaise' in France" centered on the slow pace of recovery and accompanied by a belief that democracy there had failed. Many people think that "some form of authoritarian government is needed," Caffrey wrote.[111] If French politics turned in that direction, then building an American Century was certain to fail.[112]

Washington's response was twofold. First, officials had work to do on the edifice of multilateralism. What they came up with, a politicized and limited version of multilateralism, showed how much the world had changed since July 1944. The Bretton Woods agreements had been reached in an optimistic time when major powers assumed postwar amity was feasible. The slide of major powers into cold war undermined that expectation. The World Bank and the IMF were not up to the task facing them; they were neither designed nor sufficiently funded to cope with a crisis of unknowable duration. In fact, the loan to Britain failed beyond the near term to stabilize the pound or strengthen Britain's economy. As Keynes had feared, the IMF and World Bank fell more thoroughly under the sway of the United States.[113]

Second, Washington was particularly interested in a broad agreement on global trade and tariffs. One impediment was the failure of the Truman administration to offer concessions on protected agricultural commodities. The British, in turn, were unwilling to set an early deadline to eliminate import restrictions. Also, a Republican-dominated Congress, acting at the behest of business leaders who disdained statist regulation, refused in 1948 to approve the International Trade Organization (ITO), which had formerly been considered essential to a comprehensive trade regime. (In fact, Congress did not even hold hearings on the ITO's proposed charter until 1950.) Truman was not without recourse, however. The previous October he had used his presidential power to join the GATT, which was originally designated a tariff protocol under the ITO. If less legally binding than the ITO would have been, the GATT presupposed a liberal trade order and promised tariff reduction through a series, or rounds, of negotiations.[114] Yet the GATT at that time held no remedy for anemic international commerce.[115] Therefore, nondiscriminatory, reciprocal trade remained elusive, constraining U.S. economic hegemony.

Notwithstanding the problems policymakers faced in establishing a viable free-trade regime, they drafted plans in the fall of 1948 to extend most-favored-nation (MFN) status to Germany's western zones.[116] U.S. officials, in the face of opposition from London and Paris, abandoned any thought of granting Japan or South Korea comparable treatment. Clayton termed MFN "a cardinal element in our foreign economic policy." His assertion could not break the impasse. The problem—that discrimination against Japan and South Korea amounted to, in the view of the State Department, discrimination against the United States—was not resolvable in the short term because the pace of recovery in Western Europe was impairing acceptance of multilateralism.[117] If hegemony was to fully take root, U.S. officials had to make certain that recovery there succeeded.

Western Europe's vulnerability to communism accelerated planning in the spring of 1947 for what became the Marshall Plan, or European Recovery Program (ERP). Reconstruction aid to Western Europe became the acid test of resolve in the early Cold War. Kennan stressed the need for action: "We had already delayed too long. The hour was late. Time was running out."[118] The next six weeks, until Secretary of State Marshall unveiled plans in his commencement speech in early June at Harvard, were a defining moment for American leadership. Could the White House overcome Republican doubts about funding a peacetime aid program? Would failure to do so embolden Stalin?[119] The principal source of distress was not communism per se but the specter of economic chaos. "The Planning Staff recognizes," Kennan warned, "that the communists are exploiting the European crisis and that further communist successes would create serious danger to American security."[120]

The Marshall Plan was highly successful, whether primary credit is given to the U.S. initiative or to measures participating states took as they moved into the American orbit.[121] A leading scholar of postwar Europe finds the Marshall Plan "contributed, perhaps decisively, to the Americanization of Europe."[122] Economic indicators from gross national product (GNP) to industrial output to agricultural production showed dramatic increases from prewar levels by the time the ERP ended in 1951. Industrial production increased 40 percent and, on average, GNP rose by 30 percent. The ERP also reversed the slight recession experienced by the American economy starting in late 1948. In that sense, a $12.3 billion price tag, reduced from an original proposal of $33 billion, was inexpensive.[123] Acheson, who along with Kennan and Clayton contributed much to the design of Marshall's plan, marveled at its "grandeur." He had insisted that it not look like an American imposition: "Surely the plan should be a European plan and come—or, at any rate, *appear* to come—from Europe."[124]

With bipartisan backing, Congress in April 1948 created the Economic Cooperation Administration (ECA) to orchestrate recovery. The Organization for

European Economic Cooperation (OEEC) handled the European side of operations. The State Department envisioned the ERP as a tool for facilitating a modified multilateralism. The ECA would help individual countries achieve that goal, a key feature of which was intra-European trade.[125] In charge of the ECA was a Republican businessman, Paul G. Hoffman of the Studebaker Corporation. Congress, wanting to emphasize the market-based nature of recovery, rejected Acheson and Clayton as too political for the post. The point was to minimize the influence of State Department planners on the day-to-day activities of the ECA. The naming of a Democrat, W. Averell Harriman, former ambassador to Moscow and Truman's secretary of commerce, as special representative partly vitiated that effort.[126] From the outset of the ECA's operations, Harriman believed that enhancing European security "should be the point of departure of our policy," with economic recovery to follow. The difference in emphasis did not impair his collaboration with Hoffman.[127]

The attempt by Congress to distinguish between foreign-policy planning and business interests was disingenuous. The ERP could not succeed without a blend of planning and free enterprise to rebuild industry, reform finance, liberalize trade and manage payment balances, and draft blueprints for economic growth. The ECA brought into its planning councils experts from finance, business, and labor. Labor's role was noteworthy. The American Federation of Labor and the Congress of Industrial Organizations helped the ECA and the State Department counter the appeal of Communists in the World Federation of Trade Unions.[128] Despite their work and that of the OEEC, progress came slowly from Great Britain to Italy.[129]

Policymakers had no illusions about how crucial the ECA and the OEEC were for U.S. hegemony over intra-European trade, finance, and currency. At a PPS meeting on October 11, 1949, Acheson ominously warned that, without improved planning to finance integration, "the whole structure of the Western World could fall apart in 1952." To the State Department, NATO and the ECA were "keystones" in the struggle against communism even though ECA-funded programs were not supposed to include military aid.[130] In that regard, it is telling that Harriman, who left the ECA in June 1950 to become Truman's foreign-aid coordinator, thereafter led the ECA's successor agency, the Mutual Security Administration (MSA).[131]

The ECA oversaw the fits and starts of recovery, with Great Britain, France, Italy, and West Germany the chief recipients of aid. London's resistance to joining the continent in an economic union dismayed ECA officials. The Foreign Office, which opposed the OEEC, was convinced that Washington wanted to re-create "the American conception of life" in Europe, giving the United States an unassailable advantage in financial and commercial matters.[132] Sir Edmund Hall-Patch, an undersecretary in the Foreign Office and chair of the OEEC's

Executive Committee, knew that, from London's perspective, U.S. influence was the OEEC's best asset and Britain's most serious problem.[133]

Washington did not hold all the cards, however. Of all the economies of Western Europe, Britain's was most reliant on trade and the dollar. ECA dollars were, in fact, maintaining the viability of the sterling area, without which British recovery was impossible. At the same time, ECA funds were not preventing gold and dollar deficits, which reached some $50 million per week on average in July 1949.[134] Attlee told his cabinet on July 21 that "for some time ahead the current heavy [trade] deficit is likely to continue and with it a continued drain on the gold and dollar reserves."[135]

U.S.-British relations were badly strained across the board, pointing out the fragility of hegemony.[136] In August, U.S. officials thought "deterioration of military and general cooperation between the United States and Britain . . . would almost certainly take place if there was a rift in our economic and financial relations."[137] The inevitable ripple effect could weaken the prospects for recovery, question U.S. leadership under the ERP, and leave the American Century in limbo. Officials in London, fearing devaluation of the pound and Britain's place in global finance and commerce, were loath to commit Britain to multilateralism in Europe. They were right, as the pound's devaluation by 30 percent from $4.03 to $2.80 in September 1949 showed.

Discussions over monetary issues saved the day for Washington on all fronts. After meeting with Canadian and U.S. officials in Washington, a defensive Attlee told fellow Britons: "We must either earn more dollars or spend less. . . . Merely to cut down our spending and do nothing to increase our earnings is a policy of desperation. . . . It would deprive us of essential food and raw materials and so reduce our standards of living."[138] Protestations in Attlee's cabinet that devaluation was an unacceptably high price to pay had no effect. The Planning Staff, in advance of the Washington talks, insisted in PPS/62: "We should not accept any conditions with respect to devaluation."[139] Truman, acknowledging the tenuousness of hegemony, declared that without devaluation "our world recovery program is going to smash up and all our post-war efforts will go to pieces."[140] Events did not soon assuage fears on both sides of the Atlantic.

While the State Department and Hoffman at the ECA were trying to limit the impact of a weakened Britain on European recovery, the issue of Germany came to the fore. The ECA made the case for West Germany's participation in the OEEC, which eased security concerns in Paris and London.[141] Kennan captured the essence of the event: "There is no solution of the German problem in terms of Germany; there is only a solution in terms of Europe."[142] In the weeks before the founding of West Germany in May 1949, the ECA was charged with bringing Bonn into Western Europe's economic fold. Paris and London had little say in the matter, which Bevin and Schuman realized during dispiriting talks with Acheson in Washington.[143]

Despite ECA efforts, recovery in Western Europe stalled somewhat by the fall of 1949, raising outsized fears of a prolonged downturn. Economic planning favored austerity in Italy, where tax policy was regressive and, given the scarcity of markets, a currency surplus portended the renewal of recession. The overall situation in France was better, although liberalization of trade and monetary policy was less than what U.S. officials were seeking. Importantly, aid to Austria and Greece limited the influence of local Communists by alleviating widespread hunger and rejuvenating agricultural production.[144]

The question was how to sustain growth, which was essential for securing hegemony and forging an American Century. Hoffman focused the ECA's attention on fiscal, monetary, and credit policy. "Time is running out in many ways," he warned in fall 1949. Problems were many, "not least of which is Soviet possession of [an] atomic bomb so much ahead of schedule."[145] He addressed the OEEC Council at Paris on October 31, urging members to adopt without delay "a far-reaching program to build in Western Europe a more dynamic, expanding economy." His plea resulted in a revitalized commitment by the OEEC to liberalize trade.[146]

One concrete result of his efforts was the creation in July 1950 of the European Payments Union (EPU), an entity designed to bolster trade and ease the payment process. As one analyst has pointed out, national capitalism could well have been the beneficiary of the EPU.[147] Instead, the EPU acted as a catalyst for regional integration, assisted by dollar credits provided by the Bank for International Settlements based in Switzerland. American officials valued the EPU as part of "a step-by-step approach to the progressively closer association, political, military and economic, of the countries of the free world."[148] Once operational, the EPU accelerated recovery in Western Europe and contributed to a dollar glut by the late 1950s.[149]

Hoffman made it clear that British cooperation with the OEEC was necessary for overall recovery. Negotiations in the first half of 1950 improved London's ties with the OEEC. (These talks took place even as the Schuman Plan, which linked the coal and steel production of France and West Germany and placed it under a supranational authority, took shape with the ECA's help.)[150] Compromise centered on general acceptance of the pound sterling as an international currency. That would limit the drain on Britain's gold supply and lead to regulation of the gold supplies of OEEC members, thus helping make the EPU a reality. Hoffman, believing the days of economic nationalism were over, wanted the OEEC to tackle the issue of trade liberalization. Members soon adopted rules setting out ways to curb import discrimination.[151] Paul Hoffman's work at the ECA—as architect of recovery, steward of hegemony, and economic guardian of the young American Century—had paid off.

Credibility, Leadership, and Hegemony

The American Century had come into being and was ably functioning by 1950. Its future health depended on U.S. leadership and credibility. A rocky start on the road to hegemony at Chapúltepec Castle in Mexico in early 1945 provided a cautionary tale even as Latin Americans put aside their economic objectives and acquiesced to Washington's priorities. Similarly, in shaping a new economic order, the Bretton Woods system, officials insisted on arrangements that conformed to their understanding of responsible finance and trade.

The Truman administration fared well in the strategic and political realms. The outcome of the Iran crisis demonstrated Washington's resolve to the Kremlin. Thereafter, the USSR could neither deny nor negate the reality of U.S. leadership in the non-Communist world. That lesson was not lost on America's partners, especially the British. The state of U.S.-British relations after 1945 serves as a barometer for measuring U.S. influence. The overall record was mostly positive, as the response to developments in Greece and Turkey in 1947 showed. George Kennan, in testimony to the importance of credibility for the conduct of foreign policy, later recalled the administration's conundrum, "We had no choice but to accept the challenge and to extend the requisite aid." Unlike others, he discounted threats to Turkey, while knowing how impolitic it would be to dismiss the theoretical possibility of a Soviet advance. "Aid to Greece," he reasoned, "was therefore [as] important as support for stability in Turkey." If the United States did not meet its responsibilities, he warned with an anxious eye to relations with allies, the spillover effect in Europe "could do great damage."[152]

Acheson was also convinced of the need to show resolve in the face of apparent Soviet adventurism. Moscow's influence in Greece "would also carry infection to Africa through Asia Minor and Egypt, and to Europe through Italy and France." Only the United States could prevent such a catastrophe.[153] The rise of containment bolstered U.S. credibility in general and made it easier to act decisively when the USSR blockaded the Western zones of Berlin. Acheson told British officials in the spring of 1949 that Congress demanded "a policy of firmness" toward the USSR. As the crisis ebbed, Acheson worried that a reimposition of the blockade might "be provocative of war or . . . cause us to lose prestige."[154] The founding of NATO lessened his concerns and eased Washington's path to political and economic hegemony in the Free World.[155]

Credibility was also crucial in the conduct of Anglo-American economic diplomacy and, therefore, in London's acceptance of U.S. leadership. Concerning the postwar loan and approval of the Bretton Woods system, the United States—personified by Will Clayton—had driven a hard bargain. Clayton, though, never pushed his British counterparts into an untenable position. Likewise, when Britain devalued the pound in September 1949, the Planning Staff, knowing that Attlee's government had no alternative, counseled: "It would not . . . be advisable to place direct questions about devaluation in the initial stages of the official talks. This should be done in a more private and informal atmosphere."[156]

Deference to U.S. leadership had an uneven record in Asia into 1950. If Syngman Rhee did not overtly resist Washington's policy initiatives, neither did he welcome them with open arms. More receptive to American influence was Japan, because of the transformative nature of the occupation. The Reverse Course afforded Tokyo a degree of autonomy, and the government of Yoshida Shigeru embraced its fate—becoming America's junior partner in East Asia.

The Truman administration essentially made the case for hegemony on a government-to-government basis. Yet much remained to be done to convince the peoples of Western Europe and elsewhere that their daily lives would improve with a powerful American presence. The Marshall Plan and the occupation of Japan suggested what political stability and economic development, that is, nation-building, might resemble given ample resources and time.

Nonetheless, it was clear that Washington's assertion of leadership would not always go smoothly. How, for example, would fellow policymakers reconcile their quest for hegemony with Kennan's fears that an overextended United States could not conduct an effective foreign policy? Were Kennan correct, then maintaining credibility would become a fruitless exercise. Indeed, the presence in Asia, the Middle East, and Western Europe of leftist elements in the body politic offered a sobering reminder that uncertainty lay ahead. What remained unknown was the resilience of U.S. leadership in the face of unexpected challenges like those posed by the USSR's atomic explosion, Communist revolution in China, volatile conditions on the Korean peninsula, and social and political unrest elsewhere across Asia. How Washington responded to its friends and adversaries would define the viability of hegemony and the American Century in the early 1950s.

PROTECTING THE FREE WORLD

In the early years of the Cold War, U.S. officials realized that a secure Free World was possible only in a stable environment. They therefore had to come to terms with the logic of Luce's project: forging the American Century was never to be a finished undertaking but an ongoing, at times contentious, one. In the pursuit of hegemony, waging cold war and expanding the American Century notionally converged. Luce's musings about leadership inexorably led to the making of a grand strategy. Washington's approach to the Cold War, global containment, emerged out of experiences in the late 1940s when policymakers reacted to threats they thought were emanating from the USSR and forces on the Left. They enlarged their goals and worked tirelessly to achieve them. Protecting the Free World meant advancing the American Century. Foremost in that process was generating support for U.S. grand strategy, as embodied in National Security Council document 68 (NSC 68).

The Development of Global Containment

Crafted in early 1950 under the direction of Paul H. Nitze, who replaced George Kennan at the PPS on January 1, and given to the president on April 7, NSC 68 stands among the seminal statements of American foreign policy.[1] Familiar mostly to policymakers and scholars, NSC 68 arguably ranks below only the Declaration of Independence, the Constitution and Bill of Rights, and the Emancipation Proclamation in the nation's history. Why? NSC 68 built on the knowledge, assumptions, and fears about Soviet intentions and made containment global. It set the course of grand strategy for nearly two decades and provided the impetus for ensconcing the American Century abroad.[2]

That Luce's project would become so broad in scope was no sure thing. In a speech at the National Press Club in January 1950, Secretary of State Dean Acheson had essentially placed the strife-ridden Korean peninsula outside the U.S. defense perimeter in Asia. Also, the Truman administration, to the consternation of its political foes, with Luce among the most vocal, had refused in late 1949 to help the Chinese Nationalists as Mao Zedong's forces prevailed in China's civil war.[3] Ever the Atlanticist, Acheson warmed slowly to the idea of an expansive mission for the United States. Yet he was no Kennan—reluctant to use all available resources to counter Soviet ambitions.[4] Acheson believed it was his solemn duty to warn Americans about the grave dangers the USSR posed to security. Although no more trusting than Kennan or Nitze of a democracy's capacity to conduct foreign policy in a troubled world, Acheson hedged his bets by "stretching the truth [about the Soviet threat] in the early days of the Cold War." So wrote Madeleine Albright in a memoir of her years as secretary of state in the 1990s.[5]

The resort to hyperbolic language in service to national security policy preceded the drafting of NSC 68; it began in late 1948 when Truman approved NSC 20/4, "U.S. Objectives with Respect to the USSR to Counter Soviet Threats to U.S. Security." The unreality of NSC 20/4 was evident in its analysis of what would happen after conflict with the Soviet Union: it forecasted the end of "Soviet Russian domination in areas outside the borders of any Russian state *allowed* to exist after the war."[6] Although the Planning Staff had put forth a guide for a self-limiting grand strategy in PPS/13 in November 1947, Kennan's concern about squaring ends and means and differentiating between vital and peripheral interests was largely absent from NSC 20/4. After the Communist victory in China, threat perception did not improve, as seen in NSC 48/2 of December 1949, "The Position of the United States with Respect to Asia."[7]

Kennan, despite his often impassioned tone, insisted on congruence between threat and response. Acheson, eschewing similar restraint, took his case for a proactive foreign policy to Congress and the public. If duly alarmed, he wagered that citizens would accept a call to arms against an ideological foe. Kennan decried maneuvers like Acheson's as an overreaction by those who found it "necessary to oversimplify and to some extent distort the nature of [the Soviet] threat." After Acheson's death years later, Kennan took harsh measure of the man: "He had never lived abroad, knew no foreign languages, knew nothing about the outside world."[8]

Acheson's loathing of the Soviet Union and communism was a well-considered attitude based on his background on Wall Street and his tenure at the Department of State. Acheson's historical legacy, in Michael J. Hogan's words, identifies him as the "master builder of the national security system that took shape in the early Cold War."[9] This ardent cold warrior deemed it his responsibility to create conditions in which the Free World could thrive, and that meant overseeing the growth of the American Century.

The secretary's imperturbable veneer belied the reality of a man who clung fiercely to his convictions. In personal matters, he did not possess his predecessor George C. Marshall's ability to disarm critics. In fact, as Nitze observed, Acheson "could not resist humiliating people whose support he could have used."[10] If he did not humiliate Kennan or treat him, in Kennan's words, like a "court jester, expected to enliven discussion, . . . but not to be taken fully seriously when it came to the final, responsible decisions of policy," he made it obvious that the Soviet expert's talents were not essential for the development of grand strategy. Acheson's psychological makeup helps explain why the Truman administration showed greater concern about communism's potential challenges than did its European allies, which regularly dealt with Socialists, Communists, left-wing intellectuals, and politically strong trade unions.[11] Acheson and other high-level officials disdained those whose perception of the Communist threat significantly differed from their own.

Nitze, unlike Kennan, shared Acheson's concerns about Soviet intentions and, hence, the need for comprehensive preparedness.[12] To Acheson, Nitze "was a joy to work with because of his clear, incisive mind."[13] Nitze's worldview, one scholar finds, gave credence to "a Manichean Universe and . . . [to] American exceptionalism and destiny." This comity with Acheson's beliefs strengthened as the Truman administration was deciding to build a hydrogen bomb and handed Nitze a leading role in the preparation of NSC 68.[14] He seized the opportunity. Had he failed, there would be no West, no Free World, no hegemony for the United States, and, of course, no American Century.[15]

Nitze's document culminated fifty years of thinking about America's proper role in the world. It reflected the security ethos, drew on Wilsonian internationalism, and kept the promise of leadership Franklin Roosevelt had deemed indispensable to national security. Had he been privy to their deliberations, Henry Luce would have welcomed the handiwork of Nitze and his PPS collaborators: NSC 68 was an action-plan for leadership in the American Century. Truman formally approved it as NSC 68/2 on September 30.

A close reading of NSC 68 reveals a protean document, one encompassing political and strategic considerations, economic concerns, and cultural anxieties.[16] Written in a surprisingly affecting tone, NSC 68 transformed containment into a dynamic policy with few limits. "The issues that face us are momentous," it read in language Theodore Roosevelt would have found compelling, "involving the fulfillment or destruction not only of this Republic but of civilization itself."[17] Its authors, referencing the Declaration of Independence, the Constitution, and the Bill of Rights, charged the Soviet Union with seeking to subvert or destroy "the integrity and vitality" of the United States and its core values. Reflecting their fears, they found the Kremlin to be "animated by a peculiarly virulent blend of hatred and fear."[18] To meet so harrowing a threat, in words evocative of Luce's 1941 essay, "we must lead in building a successfully functioning political and economic system in the free world."[19]

Containment as previously conceived, according to Nitze's group, could not thwart Soviet ambitions because the USSR "is developing the military capacity to support its design for world domination." Devoid of hard evidence to support that contention, NSC 68 relied on projections of military capability that were "admittedly . . . incomplete," especially about atomic weaponry.[20] The problem was how to convince the American people and the nation's allies of the urgency of the moment. This was not a minor matter, because dissent from a proactive foreign policy "can become a vulnerability." "Ways must be found," Acheson told Truman, "to enlist public interest and support."[21]

What changed public understanding about how the United States should act in the world was North Korea's attack against South Korea on June 25. In Acheson's telling, acceptance of the mindset behind NSC 68 would have been extremely unlikely "had not the Russians been stupid enough to have instigated the attack against South Korea."[22] Korea made possible the dramatic changes in U.S. foreign policy as set out in NSC 68. The selective containment of the late 1940s with its focus on Europe was obsolete, the status quo unacceptable, and political isolationism out of the question.

The American Century, as reflected in the grand strategy of global containment, reached an early high point in mid-1950. Truman soon requested funds from Congress to implement NSC 68, seeking a "rapid build-up of political, economic, and military strength."[23] The defense budget quadrupled in the second half of the year to some $56 billion. What was later known as military Keynesianism, which is compatible with the concept of containment capitalism, would boost the American economy for an indefinite period of time, while indirectly subsidizing the growth of industrial economies in Germany and Japan.

The benefits and drawbacks of globalism were most evident in Europe. NSC 68 meant nearly free security for the heart of the continent and Great Britain, rendering U.S. leadership attractive in the short term. Fear of a resurgent Germany gave way to finding common ground, notably between West Germany and France. Within a few years, West German remilitarization as part of NATO forces provoked little controversy except among West Germans themselves.[24] France, for its part, profited handsomely from America's turn to globalism. Tellingly, as NSC

68 was being composed, the United States recognized the regime in Saigon of Bao Dai, who had cooperated with occupying Japanese troops during World War II. Lasting through early May 1954 and the battle at Dien Bien Phu in northern Vietnam, Washington supported French efforts in Indochina.[25]

Relations with Great Britain, on which American hegemony relied, exposed limits in U.S. strategy. Despite the disabling costs of the war and the decline of British standing in the world, officials in London clung to the assumption that their nation's stature remained intact. Preserving that illusion had consequences for social policy at home, leading to Labour's defeat in elections in 1951 and the return of Winston Churchill to 10 Downing St.[26] While still in office, Clement Attlee was intent on restoring Great Britain to what he saw as its rightful place in the world; that task entailed turning away from great-power confrontation and toward engagement with the USSR and its allies. Since 1949, this hope, in reality an attempt to safeguard interests in Asia, had reflected London's conciliatory approach toward the People's Republic of China (PRC) and its leader, Mao Zedong.[27]

Differences with Washington were not easy to resolve. Acheson had briefly considered whether Mao might be an Asian equivalent of Yugoslavia's Josep Broz Tito, an inapt if useful analogy. With China's entry into the Korean War on October 27, 1950, and an attack by three hundred thousand Chinese troops one month later, the State Department became convinced that Beijing was doing Moscow's bidding.[28] China's initial sortie was a warning to the United Nations and the United States not to attempt to reunify Korea by force. Acheson warmed to that move after the passage on November 7 by the UN General Assembly of a resolution authorizing forces under General Douglas MacArthur's command to proceed north of the 38th parallel. Acheson saw a chance for political and strategic victory in the Cold War and validation for NSC 68.[29] Attlee and Foreign Secretary Ernest Bevin feared that attempts to reunify Korea would bring China fully into the conflict—prolonging the war, cementing Sino-Soviet ties, and hastening Britain's decline.[30]

Most troubling to British officials and the House of Commons was Truman's comment at a news conference on November 30 suggesting that MacArthur might have the option of using an atomic bomb against China's People's Liberation Army. Attlee rushed to Washington to confer with Truman and his advisers. He was not wrong to ask for clarification of U.S. intentions given Acheson's later description of China's offensive as potentially "an international disaster of the first [order]" for the United States.[31] As the secretary understood, at risk were credibility with European allies, acceptance of U.S. hegemony, and global containment itself.

Acheson acted decisively because he "had long relished risk-taking," Robert J. McMahon contends. After implying that Attlee's plea for a cease-fire (with which

Canada concurred) was wholly contrary to what was "decent and right," Acheson was pleased that China had forced the administration's hand "even though we are fighting the wrong nation. We are fighting the second team, whereas the real enemy is the Soviet Union." Success in the fight would strengthen NATO and hasten implementation of NSC 68 through greater defense spending, or so policymakers expected even as they considered going it alone, if need be, against the USSR.[32]

Attlee's ideas for lessening tensions through a cease-fire never had a chance in five days of talks. He had justly been concerned that Truman would seriously consider using atomic weapons. How to employ the bomb without doing irremediable damage to America's "moral position" was impossible to determine, as the State Department knew.[33] The prime minister was unable to shake the administration from its resolve to either continue the war or keep open the atomic option. Truman did agree to inform Britain and other NATO allies as events warranted. It was a minor concession and showed the pull of hegemony on U.S. officials. Truman, Acheson, and Secretary of Defense Marshall did not agree with Attlee that Beijing and Moscow could be driven apart by altering policy toward Taiwan or reconsidering the denial of a seat to China at the United Nations.[34]

Against this unpromising backdrop, Churchill traveled to Washington in January 1952 to meet with Truman and his advisers. With atypical circumspection, he raised the prickly matter of renewing discussions with the Soviets about global conditions, knowing that a serious proposal for conciliation through negotiation would appear defeatist.[35] He was right. Prior to the visit, Nitze derided Britain's position, saying: "The British are much more concerned than we are to obtain a simple relaxation of tensions."[36] During Churchill's talks with Truman, it became clear that Britain could not fashion a Soviet policy at odds with that of Washington. Offering an olive branch, the prime minister told Truman that London remained desirous of U.S. military aid in the struggle against communism.[37] That political strings would be attached to aid was a given, even for partners in a "special" relationship that appeared to be wounded.[38]

Exasperated with what it deemed the abysmal failure of Britain's China policy, namely, recognition, engagement, and selective trade, on the eve of the Churchill-Truman talks, the State Department declared that "the time has come for the British to accept our viewpoint."[39] This position bolstered Washington's assumption about the need for a strategy like NSC 68. What it also showed was a lack of flexibility, making less certain both deference to U.S. leadership and, thus, the growth of the American Century.

Conversely, developments related to West Germany and France cast a more positive light on the American Century. Churchill had made reference to Germany's importance for Europe's and America's futures as early as September 1946 at Zurich University.[40] When Acheson began to consider German integration into NATO in September 1950, he anticipated few difficulties with London. French concerns were not as easy to mollify, partly because of the influence of the Left in French politics. Working with Schuman and Jean Monnet, an economic adviser to Charles de Gaulle during the war and the godfather of modern Europe, aided U.S. planning for European security. About their plan for Franco-German production of coal and steel, Acheson enthused, "This would end age-old conflicts." Britain nonetheless refused to take part in negotiations for the Schuman Plan in June 1950.[41]

Happily for the Americans and the French, Konrad Adenauer welcomed the Schuman Plan in his campaign to make Bonn a partner in the Western alliance.[42] Along with the Benelux countries and Italy, in April 1951 France and Germany signed the Paris Treaty creating the European Coal and Steel Community (ECSC). London remained on the sidelines, fearing the political consequences of appearing to sanction a French attempt to exert control over West Germany.[43] Ironically, French opportunism—using the ECSC as a way to keep communism at bay in Western Europe—fortified a U.S.-led Free World.

The advent of global containment in Asia initially boded well for the American Century. Five weeks before the start of the Korean War, John Foster Dulles, then working as a consultant to the State Department, told Nitze, "[With] the loss of China to Communists, . . . the situation in Japan may become untenable and possibly that in the Philippines. Indonesia, with its vast natural resources may be lost and the oil of the Middle East will be in jeopardy." Focusing on Japan, the NSC concluded in August 1950, "The lack of Japanese defense forces, and the inadequacy of Japanese police, present a dangerous situation."[44] Accordingly, officials decided that a peace treaty and a mutual security pact were essential for the security of the Free World.

Wanting to end the occupation, Yoshida Shigeru's government aligned itself with U.S. goals more closely than it might otherwise have done.[45] Dulles, who negotiated the peace treaty, pronounced it a "fair and just" agreement giving Japan "a position of equality and dignity in the free world."[46] The signing at a conference in San Francisco nominally restored sovereignty to Japan, for which the payment of reparations to nations occupied in wartime seemed a small price to pay. Acheson painted the larger picture in a memo to Truman: "[A] close association between the United States and Japan . . . will be a tremendous step toward changing . . . the present power situation in the world in favor of the United States and its Allies."[47]

What the peace treaty gave, the Japanese-American security pact, evincing hope and fear, compromised. During negotiations, Prime Minister Yoshida accepted the United States as the guarantor of Japan's security but fought to keep

Tokyo's military expenditures to a minimum. The JCS considered some form of rearmament a high priority.[48] Yoshida's decision opened the door to the presence of U.S. bases and troops on Japanese soil without consultation as part of planning for the defense of Western interests in Asia. The State Department worried that U.S. freedom of action would in time negatively affect the bilateral relationship.[49] As an unequal security partner after 1951, Japan was legally independent but not quite a sovereign state.

Sovereignty became a contentious issue as Japan took its place in the Free World. An agreement providing the details of the security pact left its duration to Washington's discretion, which further impaired Japanese autonomy.[50] Truman's directive regarding relations with Tokyo declared, "The United States can attain its long-range security objectives in the Far East . . . only if Japan . . . fully recognizes its stake in the free world . . . and assumes its fair share of the common burdens."[51] In other words, the status of both U.S. hegemony and the American Century was increasingly linked to their acceptance in Japan, and more broadly in Asia.

U.S.-Taiwanese relations tested that connection. When civil war resumed in China after World War II, Luce placed his faith in Jiang Jieshi (Chiang Kai-shek) and the Guomindang (GMD). The American Century, Luce believed, was in good hands in Asia.[52] U.S. officials knew the truth to be quite different.[53] GMD shortcomings hastened communism's success. Deputy Assistant Secretary of State Livingston Merchant bluntly stated the problem: "There was great corruption in Chiang Kai-shek's political organization. . . . There was no real vitality in the political organization of Chiang Kai-shek, of the Nationalist Party. The vital force, politically, was the Communist Party."[54] The Truman administration distanced itself from Jiang and paid a heavy political price at home, incurring criticism from the Asia-first "China lobby."[55]

The White House decided on isolation of the PRC as the best course of action. Keeping the PRC at arm's length did not resolve the quandary of what to do with Jiang, Taiwan, and the GMD. Placing ships of the Seventh Fleet in the Taiwan Strait in June 1950 was a stop-gap measure. Even so, Taiwan seemed an ideal place from which to monitor events on the mainland; thus, the GMD began to receive military aid by the end of 1950. The hope was that Jiang would accept reform as good politics and beneficial to Taiwan's security. Washington's determination to protect Taiwan fanned the flames of hostility in Beijing, where Taiwan was viewed as an internal Chinese matter.[56]

The rigidity of America's China policy highlighted the difficulty of protecting the Free World. First, Britain thought that isolating China was counterproductive. The U.S. perspective, delivered by an angry Acheson at the meeting with Attlee in December 1950, revealed the cul-de-sac of containment: "This moment for negotiation with the communist movement is the worst since 1917." Failure in the battle against communism in Korea could undermine the French in Indochina, he speculated, and leave the United States holding on in Taiwan against the on-slaught of communism throughout Asia. At a minimum, the security of Japan and the Philippines could be endangered.[57] The presence of Communist-influenced Hukbalahap (Huk) guerrillas in the Philippines had captured Washington's attention, emphasizing the need to build, in Acheson's words, "a stable anti-Commie society," that is, a free-world society.[58]

Such potentially negative developments were not idle scenarios. States across the sweep of Asia that Washington hoped would align with the Free World did not support the succoring of Taiwan. These included Burma, India, Indonesia, and Pakistan; Thailand's leaders would do nothing that might ensnare them in the U.S.-PRC imbroglio.[59] In addition, by supporting the authoritarian Jiang, the United States stood on the wrong side of history, or so Asian nationalists could argue. Bridging the widening gap between U.S. policy and the nationalist aspirations of nonwhite people in Asia would not be easy.

The issue of nationalism also affected the Truman administration's efforts to extend containment to oil-rich nations in the Middle East. In May 1951, Iranian prime minister Mohammed Mosaddeq, not yet one month in office after the as-sassination of General Ali Razmara—in whom the British had placed their hope for a stable partnership—moved to nationalize the Anglo-Iranian Oil Company (AIOC). His objective was to increase to 50 percent Iran's share of AIOC's prof-its, an amount equal to what the Arabian American Oil Company (ARAMCO) had negotiated earlier with Saudi Arabia.[60] Much was at stake for London, which considered the Middle East as "the principal pillar of Great Britain's position in the world."[61] Having a moderate nationalist with whom to do business was cru-cial in the cold-war environment of the early fifties. It was not to be. Attlee and the Foreign Office, following Bevin's death in April, and officials in Washington failed to identify someone to rely on and worried that communism might soon enshroud Iran.[62] Were that to happen, warned the JCS on October 10, "the USSR would be provided with a springboard for domination of the entire Middle East."[63] To allay concerns about such a development and its implications for access to oil, the Truman administration and Attlee's government refined plans for denying Persian Gulf reserves to the Soviet bloc.[64]

The NSC stressed Iran's importance to grand strategy. Without dramatic change, the United States would have to entrust its interests to Mosaddeq, whom Acheson described as "a rich, reactionary feudal-minded Persian." A misstep would probably bring the USSR back into Iran.[65] Even after AIOC personnel were evicted in early October, Acheson did not believe the time was right for interven-tion, covert or otherwise. The NSC foresaw a gloomy future, as it explained a year later in NSC 136/1, "United States Policy Regarding the Present Situation in Iran":

"The United Kingdom no longer possesses the capacity unilaterally to assure stability in the area. If present trends continue unchecked, Iran could be effectively lost to the free world *in advance of* an actual communist takeover."[66] Such pessimism deepened at the end of 1952 as Britain sought Washington's approval for a coup.[67] Importantly, it showed the difficulty in trying to achieve global containment and implant the American Century where political stability was quite tenuous.

The Economics of Global Containment

More than the transformation in strategic thinking that produced global containment was needed to fortify the American Century. Containment capitalism served as a vehicle to assert the economic leadership that was integral to Luce's vision. Chronic instability, which the Marshall Plan alleviated in Western Europe, had to be overcome in order to blunt communism's appeal. As structured, the IMF, the World Bank, and the GATT could not readily promote prosperity or contain communism. Capital would find its way behind the Iron Curtain, East-West trade could not long be curtailed, and the Soviet economy would ultimately recover from the devastation of war.[68] Hence, the Truman administration looked past multilateralism to contend economically with communism. Bilateral trade and aid, private investment, accumulation of resources, and increased defense spending might limit communism's allure. In PPS/23 in 1948, Kennan stressed what was at stake: "We have about 50% of the world's wealth but only 6.3% of its population. Our real task in the coming period is to devise a pattern of relationships which will permit us to maintain this position of disparity without positive detriment to our national security."[69] The actions taken in Washington would be crucial for extending the American Century.

The ECA did more than tend to the ravaged economies of Western Europe. Until it was folded into the MSA, which came into being with the passage of the Mutual Security Act in 1951, the ECA stockpiled strategic materials. In some cases, especially in Africa, this meant providing funds for improving infrastructure. Projects in the Belgian Congo, Southern Rhodesia, Mozambique, the Gold Coast, and French Morocco received priority. For example, from Southern Rhodesia came chromite and from the Belgian Congo, crushing bort, or low-quality diamonds. Other desirable resources included manganese, copper, nickel, lead, cobalt, and tin.[70] War in Korea compelled the State Department to seek resources in Southeast Asia to prevent China from making inroads.[71] Cornering the market on strategic minerals was a commodity counterpart to defense pacts whose purpose was to make the Free World secure. Finding non-Communist markets for resources created comparable economic guarantees.[72]

The United States expanded military assistance beginning in mid-1948; grants provided the basis for defense of areas vital for Western security. Aid would "augment our own military potential by improvement of our armaments industries." In exchange for help, recipient countries should "provide strategic raw materials to the United States," as proposed in an early report of the NSC to Truman.[73] By endorsing military aid as an engine of economic growth, the president and the NSC prefigured the attention in NSC 68 given to military Keynesianism.

The drafters of NSC 68 viewed their handiwork as strategic and economic protection for the Free World. Dissent from the Bureau of the Budget called for a small defense budget in the name of fiscal prudence; to overspend could damage the country's well-being. Truman hesitated before accepting the recommendations of the PPS and others advocating substantial increases in defense spending. The outbreak of the Korean War provided the raison d'être for this change. From a $13 billion request for fiscal year (FY) 1951, Nitze's group estimated the U.S. outlay for security could reach $287 billion through 1955, including projected costs for the war and the funding of 18 army divisions, 397 major combat ships for the navy, and 95 groups for the air force. Truman's supplemental request for FY 1951 brought the numbers to 11 divisions, 282 ships, and 58 air groups. China's entry into the war won the day for military Keynesianism. The requested numbers were met by the end of FY 1952, except by the army, which had already grown to 18 divisions.[74]

What greater spending meant for containment capitalism played out in various ways. First, dollars flowed into countries where U.S. forces were stationed. This influx of capital and the security guarantee that went with it freed local resources to strengthen national and regional economies. The dollar gap would lessen, thereby fostering multilateral growth.[75] In the absence of congressional approval of grant aid, security-based capital allowed predictable economic planning and created a buffer against recession.

The MSA, which in 1952 took over and expanded the activities of the ECA outside Western Europe, helped strengthen America's economic leadership.[76] Its major activities were providing loans for the defense of the Free World, increasing the production of civilian goods, particularly food, and "improv[ing] popular attitudes toward the free world and the U.S."[77] If met, these goals would reinforce the liberal trade and monetary regimes the United States had been nurturing since the conference at Bretton Woods.

There were limits to America's financial largesse, imposed by fiscal conservatives in Congress and by bureaucrats as they put containment capitalism into effect. For instance, even before the ERP ended, European governments, seeking greater access to IMF resources criticized the low level of international liquidity. U.S. authorities made three points in response. Greater liquidity would cast doubt on the efficacy of Marshall Plan aid, tend to restrict deflationary pressures on overvalued currencies and retard intra-European trade, and implicitly question the need for economic and strategic multilateralism. Staff members hoped in vain to double the IMF's resources after 1950, but the negligible draw on funds from Western Europe, which averaged $73 million per year through 1955, delayed an increase.[78]

The United States kept inflation in check and, by controlling the dollar flow, tied liquidity to its cold-war policies. Frank A. Southard Jr., U.S. executive director of the IMF, explained liquidity strategy in April 1951: "The Fund Board (and the U.S.) could give overriding importance to defense considerations in evaluating all proposed adjustments in exchange rates and exchange systems. . . . As long as the ERP continues, the so-called ERP decision in the Fund could be held unchanged, which would make very unlikely any European efforts to draw."[79] Despite pressure to act with greater independence from Washington, the IMF—by deferring to U.S. interests—was bolstering containment capitalism.

Another crucial factor in U.S. strategy to protect the Free World was the revival of West Germany. Multilateralism could not succeed unless Germany became an "economic and political asset to the West," concluded the State Department.[80] The rise in U.S. defense spending in 1950–1951 put West Germany in an enviable position that neither Britain nor France could match. Prohibited from manufacturing arms, West Germany increased steel production from nine million tons in 1949 to nearly fifteen million tons in 1953.[81] With productive capacity booming, U.S. officials envisioned a time when Bonn would bear a large share of Western Europe's security costs. By fall 1952, the Planning Staff was applauding the Federal Republic as "the strongest power in Europe outside the USSR."[82]

Alarm in Paris was palpable. Desperate to keep West Germany (if not German troops) out of NATO, French foreign minister René Pleven proposed a counterpart to the Schuman Plan—a European Defense Community (EDC) equipped with its own forces. Washington and London disliked the idea but were in no position to veto it.[83] They decided to work with the EDC once the May 1952 treaty creating it was ratified. France's National Assembly did not debate ratification; it deemed a remilitarized Germany unthinkable. Also, the French Left and Right charged that the EDC was a stalking horse for U.S. hegemony. The delay did not prevent Washington and Bonn from negotiating the specifics of rearmament; NATO admitted West Germany in 1955, allowing the United States to reduce the costs of containment in Europe.[84]

Japan was no less important than West Germany to security in the Free World. Tying Japan to the West was of paramount importance after the defeat of Jiang Jieshi and the GMD in the Chinese civil war and the start of the Korean War. Although British commercial and financial interests had long been global in scope, the Attlee government realized that a new order was at hand. London, in spite of differences about the timing of a peace treaty, worked with Washington to devise a joint approach to Japan, which essentially entailed following the U.S. lead.[85]

American planners assumed they needed only to stimulate trade and provide sufficient aid to lessen the dollar gap and revive Japan's economy. In turn, a prosperous and grateful Japan would extend the benefits of multilateralism to non-Communist Asia, particularly Southeast Asia. Some officials in the State Department cautioned that it would take five years for Japan to meet expectations. Perhaps as much as any other factor through mid-1950, the vast dollar gap throughout Asia slowed the pace of Japan's economic recovery.[86] Then came the Korean War, bringing the substantial increase in U.S. defense spending.

To assist the American military effort, Prime Minister Yoshida had idle military factories produce arms for the first time since the occupation began. Dollars for security flowed into Japan and, because of the larger U.S. troop presence, the dollar gap closed. At least $125 million per month of war-related spending and exports bolstered Japan's economy.[87] Thus began what was termed "U.S.-Japan economic cooperation." Even so, few in Yoshida's government thought that domestic production and a defense-related influx of dollars would soon make Japan an economic bulwark of the Free World, that is, an agent of the American Century, as Washington desired.

Truman's administration looked to Southeast Asia as a natural market for Japanese goods and as an area where Tokyo could assist with currency stabilization. Led by R. Allen Griffin, a California newspaper publisher who had worked with the ECA in China, the Griffin Mission, after arriving in Southeast Asia in March 1950, reported on the region's centrality to America's objectives. Griffin concluded that local economies would need help if the region was going to play a constructive role in the Cold War. Harland Cleveland of the ECA concurred: "The economic programs contemplated are related intimately to our aim to achieve political stability . . . and encourage the area's continued orientation toward the West."[88] Neither the ECA nor the new Special Technical and Economic Missions could be counted on for the long haul, given doubts about congressional funding. It was unclear whether Japan could step into the breach because of residual animosity from World War II and the inability of some governments to run a modern economy.[89] Just the same, Southeast Asia's importance to U.S. policy increased after war began in Korea. The sale of strategic raw materials to the United States did briefly lessen the dollar gap.[90]

As Japan's economy grew at a modest, yet unsustainable pace, the possibility arose of commercial connections with China. Yoshida admitted that geographic proximity might surpass other considerations, even though he personally supported only nonmilitary trade.[91] His position made the extension of containment capitalism throughout Asia problematic, yet all the more necessary. Tokyo did not, however, rush to establish trade or diplomatic ties with Beijing after signing the peace treaty with the United States and Great Britain, leaving it unclear whether reconciliation with China was imminent.[92]

Further impetus toward Japanese autonomy on trade with the PRC occurred during an economic slump in 1951, which continued into 1953. Although war in Korea had helped bring industrial modernity to Japan, a relative stalemate in 1952 slowed growth and wiped out previous improvements in the dollar gap. Trade lagged behind expectations, and, as a result, the NSC worried that Sino-Japanese commerce, should it eventuate, would impair free-world security interests across Asia and harm the American Century in the process.[93]

Truman and his advisers could not easily make the "U.S.-Japan economic cooperation" regime more responsive to Japan's needs. There were real problems with the concept. It sprang from an American vision about Asia's future that looked to Southeast Asia as a kind of safety valve for the Japanese economy. Despite encouraging the revival of industry in Japan, growth depended heavily on the militarization of foreign policy. This arrangement was formalized with the signing of a mutual security agreement in 1954, which reflected Tokyo's deference to U.S. goals. In sum, the pact constituted an effort to gradually extend containment capitalism to Asia with Japan as its instrument.[94]

As U.S. officials constructed a security-based economic policy for the protection of the Free World, they tried to make it more difficult for the Kremlin to do the same in its sphere of influence. The Export Control Act of 1947 permitted the regulation of exports as a function of supply and national security needs.[95] Washington asked some allies to follow suit in fall 1950. Included in a list agreed to by France and Great Britain were items of strategic value and those readily used for security purposes. Interestingly, the West was then importing copper, nickel, ferromanganese, and lead from Eastern Europe. Differences arose over the identity of proscribed goods; because of the likelihood of disagreements, the State Department did not want NATO members to have decisive authority over the lists.[96]

The Commerce Department favored tough controls without advocating a total embargo on trade with the USSR and its European satellites. While the administration had no trouble embargoing trade with North Korea and China, doing so with the Soviet Union was not feasible. The State Department and the ECA opposed Commerce's position for three reasons: American trade with the USSR had been nominal, getting members of the Atlantic Community to adopt stricter export controls would be to their disadvantage, and trade with Eastern Europe in non-security goods might create strains in the Soviet bloc.[97] What the NSC ultimately decided to do amounted to a compromise of the competing positions.

In any event, the economies of the USSR and the Soviet bloc were mostly self-sustaining. Hence, containment capitalism in Europe reflected more the alliance politics of the West than a concerted attempt to weaken Moscow and its allies. The Office of Intelligence and Research in the State Department summarized the issue: "The effectiveness of economic warfare against the Soviet bloc is limited." The ECA agreed with this assessment.[98] Conversely, the CIA's National Intelligence Estimate (NIE) 22 in February 1951 deemed the bloc quite vulnerable to economic warfare. Agency analysts argued, "A program of economic warfare would add to the internal economic problems of the USSR and its Satellites and would make it virtually impossible to carry out the planned balanced development of their economies."[99] Differences aside, economic containment had become a major component of grand strategy, to both protect the Free World and advance the American Century.

Nation-Building in the Free World

The American Century could not have existed without nation-building, which Luce's call for the United States to serve as an international Good Samaritan implicitly advocated. Harry Truman found a ready guide in the Tennessee Valley Authority (TVA). Led by codirector David E. Lilienthal, the TVA brought electricity to the South during the New Deal. It heralded modernization through state planning by presupposing "systematic intervention in poorer areas of the globe to guide economic and social change," David Ekbladh writes in his superb study, *The Great American Mission*. He convincingly shows that global development owed a considerable debt to Luce's ideas.[100]

Dependent on a malleable workforce, nation-building in practice looked to create bonds between people and their governments and thereby align them with the strategic interests of the United States. Where agriculture dominated economic life—India, Egypt, Indonesia, and Burma come to mind—postcolonial and other nations rejected that outcome in favor of nonalignment in the 1950s. A reluctance to choose sides in the Cold War did not deter modernization experts who thought that planning for development and affiliation with the West were interconnected.[101]

Not only a strategic-cum-political activity, nation-building is also a socioeconomic and cultural endeavor, as evinced by the reconstruction of the South after the American Civil War.[102] Nation-building began to assume its modern guise around 1900 when the Spanish-American-Cuban-Philippine War brought the practice to Cuba and the Philippines. Common in these efforts was a belief that neither the multiracial Cubans nor the ethnically diverse Filipinos possessed the ability to govern themselves without tutelage. Fears of revolt against foreigners made security forces a part of nation-building projects in the Caribbean and across

the Pacific.[103] Public health, educational reform, and the study of English demonstrated self-improvement and the success of U.S. policy.[104] Antiopium campaigns in the Philippines showed that little about modernization would be left to
chance. The presence in Manila of two hundred opium dens impelled reformers
in 1904 to try to cleanse the islands through a program of prohibition; it achieved
modest results.[105]

Henry Luce was too young to be aware of nation-building in Cuba or the Philippines but may have known about efforts to assist China's Nationalist leaders
on the path to parliamentary government after the 1911 Revolution. Luce would
surely have thrilled to the story of how a political scientist, Frank J. Goodenow of
Columbia University, worked with strongman Yuan Shihkai to draft a constitution
for the new China.[106] Whatever Luce knew about such attempts at nation-building,
the genesis of his idea for an American Century may have sprung from them.

Luce wrote that for the American Century to succeed, the United States must
offer an example others could emulate. Scientific research, innovation in manufacturing and agriculture, population growth in the Sunbelt, access to education, the prospect of enduring affluence, social mobility, and increased church
attendance were major aspects of postwar life in America. They were not readily
transferable to peoples lacking comparable advantages. For most people living
in the Free World, they might serve an inspirational function as development
altered patterns of daily life. It remained, however, an open question whether
nation-building would actually help the American Century.

George Kennan, in a PPS paper of July 1947, cast doubt on the broad applicability of the developmental philosophy underlying European recovery aid. He later
recalled, "The congenital American aversion to regional approaches, and the
yearning for universal ones, were too strong to be entirely overcome even by the
success of the Marshall Plan—on the contrary, they were only stimulated by it."[107]
Such reservations aside, private foundation officials, missionaries, and educators,
affected by the deprivation they encountered, drafted blueprints for nongovernmental nation-building, often in coordination with U.S. personnel or under the
auspices of the United Nations.

Truman emphasized America's determination to rebuild the world through
development in his inaugural address in January 1949. He linked the nation's
stature to its support of the UN, recovery in Europe, the vitality of the North
Atlantic and Rio pacts, and, in what became known as Point Four, a program of
development for advanced war-torn nations and postcolonial areas. Truman
called for a grand undertaking: "It must be a world wide effort for the achievement of peace, plenty, and freedom . . . based on the concepts of democratic fair-
dealing."[108] Seen in the context of the global Cold War, nation-building would
bring containment to the local level.

Employment as a precondition of development was an article of faith in postwar Europe. To reduce unemployment, the ECA relied on technical missions and Keynesian economics. Increasing currency reserves would lessen the impact of trade liberalization, just as market integration and export growth promised to close the dollar gap. Thus, the ECA strove to accelerate exports.[109] Gradually, fiscal planning and monetary policy enabled technical missions to produce efficiencies in agriculture and industrial production. Also, labor conditions improved as workers reaped the benefits of growth.[110] Time was running short for the Marshall Plan and the ECA by fall 1950, however. Military aid had provided a cover for economic revival, although Congress was in no mood to pay for guns and butter. That obstacle left Hoffman and Harriman hoping for a rough parity between rearmament and recovery, yet even bringing Canada and the United States into the OEEC as associate members did not achieve that result.[111]

By the end of 1950, Congress had increased the Department of Defense's appropriation by $13 billion for FY 1951, which included $4 billion for military assistance, and cut the ECA's budget by $208 million. Recovery policy, Acheson wrote, was "sweepingly modified by a new sense of danger and urgency."[112] This change resulted in pressure in Western Europe to speed industrial production for the common defense. From Britain to France to West Germany, allies resisted when defense expenditures reached $8 billion in 1951, an 80 percent increase over two years. With the cost of living rising, payment imbalances increasing, and inflation setting in, they feared that remilitarization would kill recovery.[113] That nearly turned out to be true. Frustrated, Acheson later explained: "It made no sense to destroy them in the name of defending them."[114] Ironically, such was a possible result of securitizing recovery.

The Marshall Plan and the ECA came to an end in the waning days of 1951. Congress then appropriated $50 billion to fund America's global military presence. Four divisions, with the prospect of more to come, cemented the U.S. commitment to NATO and, in so doing, bolstered Europe's economy. The kind of aid previously earmarked for recovery through nation-building was soon relegated to a secondary status under the Mutual Security Act as Washington edged its European allies toward defense planning and spending.[115]

Fortunately, there was more in the foundational cement of nation-building than security assistance. One crucial aspect of the Marshall Plan was a focus on women and the youth of Europe. The more they consumed, the more the West produced. The American Century needed consumers. To buy and sell was to become modern in the American style, as Luce had surely understood. If Western Europeans entered the marketplace with their hearts, minds, and wallets and purses, American-led "consumer democracy," to borrow Victoria de Grazia's term, would provide security and prosperity.[116]

At the same time, limited educational opportunity posed a problem for nation-building. The CIA feared as late as fall 1951 that the economic appeal of communism might lead young people to join the Communist Party.[117] That concern was justified. Not even the breadth of the ERP could undo the class basis of access to education in Western Europe. Rarely did children stay in school beyond the age of fourteen. Secondary education was a luxury, particularly in Italy, where less than 5 percent of the population entered and finished secondary school. And, fewer than thirty thousand students in France were graduating from the equivalent of American high schools. In short, the path to university education was closed to a large percentage of young Europeans in the first decade or so of the Cold War.[118]

If access to formal education remained beyond reach, other advantages of modernity were not necessarily out of reach. Certainly, U.S. officials saw modernization taking root in many ways through "the press, radio, motion pictures and like media."[119] Within a short time, "like media" included television. The Truman administration anticipated the benefits that might result from standardized television signals and program-sharing even though neither was then politically or technically feasible. Disregarding British and French concerns, the ECA relied on television in West Germany to inculcate in young people Western values and consumer culture. The dramatic contrast with the lesser technical and programmatic quality of Soviet bloc television in the early 1950s stood out, especially in the cold-war hotspot of divided Berlin.[120]

German youth held the key if new styles of daily life were going to make a contribution to nation-building. Everything that was positive about postwar life in West Germany would be measured against the limits of what existed in East Germany. That thousands of German women married American servicemen and moved to the United States presents one part of the story of acculturation.[121] Crucial to understanding how Western cultural forms took hold was the dance between the old and new playing out in Konrad Adenauer's Germany. To the shock of authorities in Bonn, venerable gender and racial norms vanished after the war. Hypersexuality among young people, influenced by the allure of African American music and popular culture, confounded officials who foresaw a revival of fascism. Similar anxiety about the behavior of the young also existed in the German Democratic Republic (GDR). (Knowing this, in spring 1953 the United States considered encouraging young men to defect from the GDR.) Would youth rebellion inhibit reconstruction in the two Germanys, and, if that occurred, what would it mean for stability in Europe? Indeed, what impact would it have on the strategy of global containment?[122]

What was happening was a class-bound debate over what constituted German identity. Authorities wondered whether German high culture, their path back to respectability, was on trial in some newly politicized way. Yet, what it meant for young people to be political was a matter of dispute. For some, it constituted rejection of cultural mores. For others, being political involved demonstrating against the status quo at Communist-orchestrated rallies. CIA reports on an event in East Berlin in May 1950 pictured "500,000 thoroughly indoctrinated Communist youths" sparking sympathetic demonstrations in West Berlin.[123] West German, French, and Austrian youths subsequently engaged in the planning for a World Youth Festival, scheduled for August 1951 in East Berlin, which young people from eighty nations were expected to attend.[124]

In the short term, Bonn or Washington could do little to change things, so nation-building proceeded at a less than optimal pace. Bonn resisted the entry of American-made consumer and popular culture into German society. More actively, the National Committee for a Free Europe (NCFE), whose membership included luminaries—Good Samaritans in a sense—such as Adolf A. Berle Jr., Lucius D. Clay, Clark M. Clifford, Cecil B. DeMille, Allen W. Dulles, Henry Ford II, Joseph C. Grew, C. D. Jackson, DeWitt Wallace, Darryl Zanuck, and Henry R. Luce, kept U.S. officials informed about its activities in the early to mid 1950s. These included providing new textbooks to replace prewar, pro-Nazi books in West Germany. And, the NCFE brought exceptional students from Eastern Europe to the United States to study how to modernize civil society. Promising students from "the captive countries" also gathered at the Free University in Exile in Strasbourg, France, where teachers from their homelands taught them about their own culture and history.[125]

Starting from a more rudimentary base, nation-building followed a different course in Asia. The ECA got modernization under way there because the agency created to implement Point Four programs, the Technical Cooperation Administration (TCA), did not begin operating until mid-1950. Congressional reluctance to fund the TCA and house it in the State Department prevented an earlier start. Whether in Europe or Asia, the ECA had to work within budgetary confines set by Congress.

After South Korea attained independence in 1948, Truman proposed a multiyear $410 million program; for FY 1950, Congress appropriated $50 million of a $180 million request. The outbreak of war in June 1950 made a more generous program possible.[126] The president differed with a penurious Congress about aid for South Korea, calling it in mid-1949 "a testing ground" for development: "Progress by the young Republic will encourage the peoples of southern and southeast Asia and the islands of the Pacific to resist and reject the communist propaganda with which they are besieged."[127] Truman assumed that aid would spark recovery and growth through the production of coal, electric power, and fertilizer—all vital for economic development and political stability. His claims about South

Korea echoed those made by Paul Hoffman in Seoul, then home to the largest ECA mission anywhere.[128] The South Korean example showed money could not always provide a quick fix, however. The country's export growth remained slow, and uncertain delivery of electricity hampered progress from the late 1940s into the mid-1950s.

As for Japan, recovery depended on relations with Southeast Asia after Washington in March 1950 began aiding the French in Indochina. The ECA opened a field office in Tokyo in mid-1951 after an NSC review of strategy in Asia, NSC 48/5.[129] Evocative of dicta in NSC 68, the NSC warned, "Current Soviet tactics appear to concentrate on bringing the mainland of Eastern Asia and eventually Japan ... under Soviet control, primarily through Soviet exploitation of the resources of communist China." Given so dire a reading of threats to U.S. interests, it was imperative for Japan to become self-reliant under America's security umbrella.[130] But nation-building there could not occur without regard for developments elsewhere in Asia.

As previously mentioned, the Griffin Mission, a team of State, Defense, Treasury, and ECA representatives, visited Indochina, Thailand, Burma, Indonesia, and the Philippines.[131] One goal was to facilitate commerce between Indochina and Japan in order to speed the rebirth of Japanese manufacturing. Development programs would thereafter have to possess economic and military components. R. Allen Griffin, who led the group, suspected the mission had been a hastily devised effort "to satisfy critics of China policy that we were going to do better in the future."[132] His assessment was accurate, even though nonmilitary aid remained an important component of nation-building in Asia.

The Griffin Mission found Thailand more stable than Indochina or Burma, yet in need of technical expertise if it was going to move beyond its long dependence on a rice-based economy. Phibun Songgram's government, even as it reversed a democratic turn in the 1949 constitution, hailed the military and economic aid that folded Thailand into the U.S. orbit. Meanwhile, anger over Washington's support for GMD irregulars in the Golden Triangle soured Burma's attitude about accepting American aid.[133] Rangoon terminated a technical cooperation accord in 1953. Not surprisingly, the CIA found no reason to alter its previous determination that Burma was "the weakest link in the [security] chain" in Asia.[134]

In Indochina, and specifically in Vietnam, where Truman's decision to aid the French and Emperor Bao Dai against Ho Chi Minh and the Vietminh made the region a cold-war theater, Griffin chronicled a need for technical and other aid. Malaria and trachoma were pervasive. Rice exports from the south had declined after 1949, and mineral extraction had stagnated. Rubber production fell below previous levels. Under the auspices of the ECA, repair of roads, rice planting, and treatment of disease dramatized how modernization could complement security objectives.[135] Nonetheless, gains from nation-building were elusive. U.S. minister Donald R. Heath warned in early 1951 that Bao Dai's government "had failed to display any real dynamism and has not yet won confidence of [the] public in its ability to provide security or welfare." It took until September to sign a technical assistance agreement.[136]

Griffin's team concluded that the departure of the Dutch from Indonesia was retarding development. Despite the various obstacles identified by the mission, Griffin insisted that "a small group of good men and expenditure of small amounts of money could accomplish wonders [there]."[137] An evaluation of the ECA's work through 1951 did not support his contention. A lack of technical and administrative expertise undercut any beneficial impact of a currency surplus. Fearing dislocation would accompany the end of the aid program, ECA officials argued that a failure to maintain aid "would be most welcome to the Communists."

John M. Allison of the State Department's Office of Northeast Asian Affairs disagreed, even though rubber and tin were vital for Western security. The United States, he reasoned, did not possess an inexhaustible reservoir of aid, which meant a relatively prosperous and friendly country like Indonesia should not expect further grant aid. And it did not; Djakarta began to chart a nonaligned course in foreign policy. Relations with Western powers increasingly depended on government-to-government loans or agreements with the Export-Import Bank.[138] This turn of events failed to smooth relations. By late 1953, the U.S. intelligence community was worrying about Communist responsibility for Indonesia's leftward drift.[139]

The presence of Communist-influenced Huk guerrillas in the Philippines hastened the development of an aid program, which Washington had tried to avoid. Dealing with President Elpidio Quirino proved to be a headache from the time he took office in March 1948 until Ramon Magsaysay succeeded him six years later. With a low tax base, rampant corruption, and minimal economic diversity, the Philippines could not accumulate sufficient capital to begin modernizing. The persistence of the Huk rebellion into 1950 initiated a reconsideration of aid policy. Daniel Bell, a banker who had served in the Treasury Department, led a mission to the Philippines (the United States Economic Survey Mission) mainly composed of businessmen and economic experts; it arrived in Manila in August.[140]

Bell's initial report, a proposal to extend $250 million in loans, fell in line with the State Department's thinking about the urgency of development. It was left to the ECA administrator, William C. Foster, who would later serve as deputy secretary in the Department of Defense, to negotiate a deal with Quirino. Their talks produced a five-year plan establishing new taxes on corporate activity and currency exchange and a minimum wage for agricultural labor as the country moved to strengthen its industrial sector.[141] Economic conditions improved in 1951 and

1952, a result of U.S. aid and growth sparked by the war in Korea. Trade with Japan doubled in 1951 despite lingering animosity from World War II, capital flight slowed, inflation declined, and foreign investment in joint ventures increased. The Bell Mission and the ECA had made the most of a difficult situation. Yet by the time Magsaysay took office in 1954, what scholars term "cacique democracy" remained intact, evidence of the limits of nation-building by an ally still on the cusp of modernity.[142]

Over time, the delicate balance between technical, nonmilitary assistance and security needs was decided in favor of the latter. Allison was steadfast in his conviction: "Monolithic communism was a reality in 1950."[143] And in contrast to the fairly sanguine evaluation by the Griffin Mission regarding Thailand, Acheson held a similar position. "It is clearly apparent that unless Thailand is given military assistance it cannot hold out against communist pressure," he told Truman.[144] Such concern was the rule rather than the exception as the State Department viewed the entire Asian scene in the early 1950s. The ECA sided with Acheson, describing the U.S. task in Southeast Asia in spring 1951 as "taking the initiative in building a new order and stability . . . firmly oriented to the West."[145] Military, technical, and administrative aid existed as part of a comprehensive package, one binding together nation-building and global containment within the American Century.[146]

Nation-building got off to a poor start in the Americas, where critics equated a greater North American presence with imperialism. ECA activity was limited, and feelings of neglect deepened in the early 1950s, which the CIA blamed on persistent economic nationalism.[147] Although modernization theory was not then well known, the idea of bringing the tools and benefits of modern life to Latin America had pervaded the activities of business, government, and philanthropic organizations there for decades.[148] The Office of the Coordinator of Inter-American Affairs, headed by Nelson A. Rockefeller, created the Institute for Inter-American Affairs (IIAA) in 1942. The IIAA, whose work continued after the war, oversaw government programs that addressed matters of health and sanitation.[149]

The IIAA sought to bridge the gap between expectations of development and the reality of sparse aid. Modern agricultural methods improved public health in Venezuela; health and sanitation projects found their way into Uruguay; and Ecuador initiated programs for nutrition, maternity and child care, and teacher and vocational training. IIAA technicians worried about the "immaturity of political and economic development, the exceedingly low standards of living of the great bulk of the population, and the wide disparity of income between the educated and wealthy groups, and the poor, uncultured classes," which could "provide an opportunity for the growth of Communism or other totalitarian ideology."[150] Clearly, there was much to be done.

Despite a perceived need, there was no Marshall Plan for Latin America. Although gold and dollar reserves were running low, which limited domestically funded development projects, offshore purchases by Europe through the ECA remained the most reliable source of reserves. Congress was reluctant well into the 1950s to fund increases in grant aid, and private investors were not prepared to act on their own. IIAA, ECA, and Point Four programs failed to meet Latin America's needs. Moreover, the World Bank and the Export-Import Bank were slow to process loan applications.[151]

Latin America was the one area of the world where the economics of global containment had made few inroads. The Americas were not covered by grant aid, although leaders associated U.S. aid with development.[152] Assistant Secretary of State for Inter-American Affairs Edward R. Miller Jr. acknowledged the great frustration with Washington, while remaining unsympathetic to pleas for assistance. Miller decried "an exaggerated and extreme sense of self-importance on the part of . . . Latin American Governments." U.S. priorities, he declared, lay elsewhere.[153]

George Kennan, who knew little about Latin America, traveled there in the winter of 1950. He did not think well of America's neighbors. More than a modicum of racially tinted condescension underlay the disdain he felt toward the region and its people.[154] "It seems to me unlikely," he mused, "that there could be any other region of the earth in which nature and human behavior could have combined to produce a more unhappy and hopeless background for the conduct of human life than in Latin America." Washington must pay heed, Kennan conceded, because disaffection with Washington so close to home would harm vital interests elsewhere in times of crisis.[155]

Kennan voiced highly controversial opinions that were pertinent to nation-building and protecting the Free World: "The handicaps to progress are written in human blood and in the tracings of geography; and in neither case are they readily susceptible of obliteration." Hence, it was not up to the United States to transform the "bitter realities" bedeviling Latin Americans. He concluded, "We are a great power; . . . we are by and large much less in need of them than they are in need of us."[156] The dice were cast. Subsequently, in May 1951, the State Department's Louis J. Halle reiterated Washington's fixed belief in "the self-reliance of the Latin American peoples."[157] Grant aid for development would have to wait.

Two examples suggest that nation-building was not necessarily a reliable servant of global containment or a means of broadening the appeal of the American Century. First, cold-war Washington could not ignore Guatemala's "excessive nationalism," its "enigmatic and crusading President [Jacobo Árbenz Guzmán]," his "fuzzy economic and political philosophies," or the "serious penetration by international Communism" there. This perceived radicalism had been growing since Juan José Arévalo's ascent to power in an election after the 1944 revolution.

The CIA had ridiculed his governing philosophy, "spiritual socialism." Árbenz's own election in 1950 as a reform president worsened matters.[158]

The State Department pressured Árbenz with "counter-actions." In practice, this meant no additional Point Four aid. Technical aid under the IIAA was reduced, and U.S. officials refused to support Export-Import Bank and World Bank loans. Ties with Guatemala's military tightened, however, which would become an increasingly important facet of nation-building.[159] In contrast, both Truman and Eisenhower tolerated the government that seized power in Bolivia in April 1952 because the Movimiento Nacionalista Revolucionario (MNR) posed no serious threat to North American corporate interests. In fact, the MNR under President Victor Paz Estenssoro welcomed Point Four aid, even as overall public and private funding from the United States was declining.[160]

The Free World and U.S. Credibility

The Truman administration put U.S. leadership to the test in crafting a strategy of global containment. It was not absurd in 1950 to think that fear of the USSR would lead to a call to arms. Dean Acheson sought to marshal public support for preparedness and an increased defense budget while trying to restrain calls for a military confrontation with the Soviets. It was a fine line to walk, made more difficult by members of Congress who found many of their constituents willing to approve of war against the USSR.[161] In heated language, Acheson asserted in March 1950 that "the Soviet Union has one purpose and that is world domination." A few months later, however, he was afraid that "foolish talk about preventive war, or the inevitability of war, will help make war inevitable. It does not need to be so at all."[162]

Acheson's balancing act set the tone for how the administration tried to muster support for America's burgeoning global role. The problem was that events could outpace Washington's ability to control them. That said, how officials established credibility reflected how they sought to protect the Free World after 1949. That task perhaps was easiest in the economic realm. The founding of the IMF and the World Bank had afforded the United States instant credibility even though neither body performed as well as planned. More positively, the Marshall Plan and the success of the ECA and the TCA through its Point Four programs built a persuasive case for development through American leadership.[163] In Asia, Japan was well on its way to becoming Washington's primary economic partner.

Involvement in the Korean War provided a major test of American credibility. Waging war in Korea provided Washington with an opportunity to make NATO the centerpiece of U.S. security interests in Europe by giving life to extraordinary strategic interdependence. Conversely, the conduct of the war under U.S. command seemed provocative to the British and, at times, to the French and undermined any chances for fruitful exchanges by allies with the Soviets or the Chinese. Fortunately for the architects of global containment, officials in Paris tended to support the war in Korea, particularly as the United States extended the fight against communism in Asia to Indochina. In turn, Clement Attlee and Winston Churchill had little choice but to acquiesce, albeit grudgingly, to the strategic and political hegemony of the United States.[164]

Also, the rebuilding of West Germany occurred at a pace West Europeans initially found alarming, whereas Washington considered Konrad Adenauer's nation something of a tripwire against Soviet adventurism. Neither Paris nor London responded to American plans for West Germany with equanimity, although embarking on a different approach was out of the question. The worrisome implications for U.S. leadership and credibility over the longer term were easy to miss as war dragged on in Korea and the USSR cemented its hold on Eastern Europe.[165]

The aura of beneficence surrounding Point Four programs burnished the image of the United States as a global Good Samaritan. Point Four was no idealistic creation, however; it furthered the securitization of public and private foreign assistance so that nation-building was set to play a key role in expanding and protecting the Free World. Although nation-building proceeded in fits and starts throughout Asia and especially in Latin America, by the time Truman and Acheson left office it had become part of a steadily growing American Century. In the next few years, their successors—adapting global containment to a world in flux—would face novel challenges as caretakers of Luce's vision.

SEEKING ORDER AND STABILITY

Waging cold war provided the necessary predicate for advancement of the American Century; the advent of global containment made it sufficient. Blinded by his utter disdain for Truman and Acheson's focus on Europe, Henry Luce could not make that connection.[1] His Asia-first partisanship diminished his standing in discussions about foreign policy, which his support in the 1952 presidential campaign for Dwight D. Eisenhower could not reverse. What did remain unchanged was the relevance to policymaking of one crucial idea informing Luce's 1941 essay: international order and stability required an American Century.

The uncertainty and turmoil characterizing world affairs from 1953 through 1955 handed U.S. officials what Luce had deemed "the complete opportunity of leadership."[2] Major events included Joseph Stalin's death on March 5, 1953, the Korean War armistice in late July 1953, France's defeat at Dien Bien Phu in Vietnam in May 1954, and the convening in April 1955 of the Afro-Asian Peoples Conference at Bandung, Indonesia.[3] At issue for Eisenhower's national security team was how to create order and stability in such conditions. The means available echoed what officials had drawn on since building the American Century began in early 1945: ensure strategic and political hegemony, foster growth of market-driven economies, and act as a Good Samaritan to the world.

Calibrating Global Containment

Prior to Eisenhower's taking office, Truman's PPS had surveyed the potential effect of a global war on the United States and its allies. Using apocalyptic language, with which Paul Nitze concurred, Louis J. Halle asserted, "Our present conflict with the Soviet Union cannot be definitively ended in our favor short of the elimination of the Soviet regime."[4] Some in the new administration agreed it was imperative to "block further expansion of Soviet power even at [the] grave risk of general war." Diverging from this security-at-all-costs attitude, Eisenhower stressed the need to find a defense posture that would not bankrupt the nation.[5]

Strengthening the case for hegemony soon took on signal importance. Winston Churchill, whose stature remained intact, had a less dire view of world affairs than the Americans. He "is trying to relive the days of World War II," Eisenhower groused privately. Eager to convene a tripartite summit meeting, an implicit challenge to U.S. hegemony, Churchill did not abandon the idea after Stalin's death. Anxious officials criticized Churchill, questioning whether he was sufficiently vigilant about the threat of communism. At a special NSC meeting on March 31, Dulles emphasized that very point when speaking about "ending the peril represented by the Soviet Union."[6]

The Democrats indicated to Churchill in 1952 that they wanted to instill fear in the USSR prior to any change in the bilateral relationship, and Eisenhower and Dulles viewed credibility as a by-product of negotiation from strength. Conditions in Korea, with stalemate on the eve of a round of armistice talks; the brain drain out of East Germany and the June 1953 riots there as Soviet hopes for German reunification evaporated; and the peace feelers of Georgi Malenkov, who as premier and first party secretary wielded the most power in the USSR, all invited a vigorous response from the White House.[7]

Malenkov proved to be a puzzlement.[8] He told the Supreme Soviet in mid-March that the Soviet Union and the United States could settle all matters dividing them without war.[9] If he were serious, would there exist a persuasive rationale for U.S. hegemony, or the American Century for that matter?[10] Furthermore, what would become of NATO if superpower rivalry was waged politically and economically, rather than as a quasi-military confrontation? Ironically, NATO's centrality to U.S. grand strategy and, thus, the American Century had gotten a boost from an unexpected source. Initially unafraid of NATO and its capabilities, the Soviets made it seem more strategically imposing by supporting Kim Il Sung's war plans in Korea.[11] How? Unsettled conditions in Asia raised the question: Did events there foreshadow Soviet military actions in Europe against which NATO was serving as the key line of defense?

The Eisenhower-Dulles response to Malenkov's peace overture was lukewarm at best.[12] Dulles curtly dismissed it: "The current peace offensive is designed by the Soviets to relieve the ever-increasing pressure upon their regime." Melvyn Leffler contends that the administration's reluctance stemmed from two sources: fear and the drive to enhance American power.[13] At stake in 1953 were the very idea of U.S. global leadership and the reach of the American Century. The CIA, on September 30, 1953, in NSC 162, "Review of Basic National Security Policy," termed Malenkov's gambit "a significant move in the master plan designed to negate U.S. psychological warfare capabilities . . . [and] create dissension and confusion among the Western Allies." What the CIA's review meant for peaceful coexistence would play out over time. Meanwhile, belief in the hostility of the USSR toward the Free World remained axiomatic in Washington.[14]

Soviet leaders tried other ways of confounding the United States and its allies. Foreign Minister Vyacheslav M. Molotov informed members of the Presidium in March 1954 that the USSR might seek to join NATO. As outlandish as the idea seems, it was part of a strategy to undermine collective defense. Molotov, desirous of resolving the thorny issue of German reunification to Moscow's advantage, argued that Soviet membership would greatly strengthen NATO. Western powers rejected the idea in May, yet Moscow did not abandon thoughts of pan-European security via NATO until after a meeting in Geneva of foreign ministers, which lasted from October 27 to November 16.[15]

After Geneva, Eisenhower and Dulles minimized the seriousness of Soviet proposals regarding collective security. The president declared, "The results of this conference mean that you can't let down an inch." Echoing Ambassador to Moscow Charles E. Bohlen to the effect that the USSR had not acted in good faith at Geneva, Dulles proclaimed at an NSC meeting that Soviet conduct "derived from the instinctive sentiments of officials who had been brought up under the harsh tenets of Stalinist Communism."[16]

Consistent with his thinking about security and the use of force, Eisenhower acted to put his stamp on grand strategy and strengthen the case for hegemony. First, he and his advisers decided it was not an auspicious time to take risks for peace. The idea of massive retaliation lurked in the shadows of the hydrogen bomb project. Thermonuclear weapons, first tested in January 1953, bolstered the argument for atomic power as vital to national security planning. Although he did not envision using the H-bomb except in truly extraordinary circumstances, Eisenhower was convinced that tactical nuclear weapons had a role to play in security policy. With more than fifteen hundred warheads at his disposal in May 1953, he told the NSC, "We have got to consider the atomic bomb as simply another weapon in our arsenal."[17] What he was seeking was a cost-effective strategy that would neither spark a general conflict with the USSR nor alarm European allies to the point of undermining NATO and crippling U.S. hegemony.[18]

The New Look policy of autumn 1953, although failing to make a convincing case for tactical nuclear weapons as a rough equivalent of conventional weapons, filled the bill. It spurred the growth of America's defense industry with the production of bombs and B-52 warplanes. The brinksmanship of "more bang for the buck" could not solve problems with the USSR, as the president knew, and substantive negotiations with Stalin's successors remained unappealing.[19] The fact that the United States could not prevail in the Cold War without putting the country in mortal danger had the virtue of demonstrating the need for American leadership in a prolonged struggle with communism.[20]

The Cold War remained the servant of the American Century. Despite concerns that the U.S. military was overextended, the NSC concluded, "Any major withdrawal of U.S. forces from Europe or the Far East would be interpreted as a diminution of U.S. interest in the defense of these areas." Indeed, the United States must make evident "its intention to react with military force against any aggression by Soviet bloc armed forces."[21] Eisenhower's New Look clearly presupposed the vital importance of the United States to international order.

As a case in point, doubts about France as a cold-war partner bolstered West Germany, in which, as Eisenhower put it, "we . . . had based our whole political program in Europe."[22] By August 1954, when the National Assembly rejected the EDC Treaty, France had suffered defeat in Vietnam, and Algeria's struggle for liberation was heating up. Before the denouement in Paris, Dulles, on December 14, 1953, displayed his exasperation with France's vacillation, famously observing, "If . . . the European Defense Community should not become effective, if France and Germany should remain apart, . . . that would compel an agonizing reappraisal of basic United States policy."[23] His words were either a bluff or a warning that, without the EDC, the United States was prepared to return to a kind of isolation. The latter was unthinkable, and the bluff not credible. Thus, without French acceptance of the EDC, the only plausible course of action was to end the occupation and usher West Germany into NATO.[24]

Churchill gave voice to what Dulles had downplayed. Without a West German army, "there could be no safety for anyone in Europe."[25] Over time, Adenauer, who deplored the idea of remilitarization, reached a similar conclusion. Cold-war security needs dashed any chance of reunification, which had been unlikely in any event since the Berlin blockade. In exchange for independence, Bonn accepted restrictions on its sovereignty. Its armed forces could not operate outside NATO's command structure nor possess nuclear weapons. An agreement signed in Paris in October 1954 cleared the way for entry into NATO, which took place in

May 1955. The Kremlin at once brought into being the Warsaw Treaty Organization,[26] a relatively mild response that nevertheless reemphasized Washington's centrality to Western Europe's security.[27]

Second, to address Eisenhower's persistent qualms about the defense budget and spread the burden of defending the Free World, the United States moved to extend its alliance structure, thereby expanding the free-world society. Following France's humiliating defeat in Vietnam, the United States brokered the founding of the Southeast Asian Treaty Organization (SEATO) in September 1954. A defense organization designed to contain communism would deter, Dulles told the Overseas Press Club of America, "a grave threat to the whole free community."[28] Few nations from the region other than Thailand joined SEATO, a liability that concerned the White House.[29] Oddly, Pakistan, Great Britain, France, Australia, and New Zealand held membership in SEATO, as did the Philippines. A few years earlier, Washington had also envisioned Indonesia and Burma as part of its regional defense strategy. Their absence from SEATO was as telling as their leadership, along with India's, at Bandung in 1955.[30]

The difficulty of building a comprehensive security community sprung from growing disillusionment with the West by postcolonial people in Asia and, as Deputy Assistant Secretary of State Livingston T. Merchant had put it in September 1950, from "intense nationalism and [a] revolutionary urge for independence as the answer to their problems." Eisenhower's recognition that "nationalism is on the march" was beside the point because U.S. security policy held little appeal for many Asian nationalists, which slowed the advance of the American Century.[31]

Furthermore, under the Geneva accords of July 1954, the government in southern Vietnam was not permitted to sign a defense pact because of plans to reunify Vietnam by election two years hence. Virtually all observers, including U.S. officials, believed that Ho Chi Minh and the Vietminh would rule the country once elections were held. The United States soon moved to undermine the Geneva agreement, an action that drew Washington closer to Ngo Dinh Diem, who became prime minister of South Vietnam in June 1954. (Disregarding Geneva also soon embroiled the United States nearly to the point of war in the thicket of Laotian politics.)[32]

As America's global presence grew, protecting U.S. interests in the Middle East became a focal point for waging cold war and extending hegemony. Maintaining access to the region's most valuable resource, oil, and preventing Arab-Israeli tensions from erupting into hostilities were crucial. Military assistance programs addressed the first goal. In the background loomed NSC 26/2, U.S.-British plans formulated in the late forties to deny oil reserves to the Soviet bloc. The two governments refined the plans for denial in 1953, partly by improving consultation with AIOC and ARAMCO.[33]

In addition, prospects for multilateral help in safeguarding vital oil fields were promising. With the benefits deriving from the August 1953 overthrow of Mo-saddeq's nationalist regime in Iran—abetted by American and British intelligence agencies—and the coming to power of the pro-Western Mohammed Reza Shah Pahlavi, Washington was fashioning a ready-made line of regional containment.[34] As a CIA analysis emphasized in January 1954: "Iran also constitutes a blocking position from which to oppose any Soviet operation aimed at depriving the free world of Middle Eastern oil resources."[35] Iran's transformation helped to usher the American Century into the Persian Gulf. Its long-term presence there, how-ever, depended partly on the shah's acceptance of social and economic reforms.[36]

Providing a measure of regional stability, the Baghdad Pact was operating by October 1955; Britain joined with Turkey, Pakistan, Iran, and Iraq to formalize a security agreement. The United States did not become a member, which perturbed British prime minister Anthony Eden, although U.S. military aid constituted the glue holding the pact together.[37] Its weaknesses soon became evident. Israel op-posed the accord, and domestic instability made Iraq an unreliable member. After nationalists seized power there in July 1958, the Baghdad Pact fell apart.[38] Its de-mise questioned both the feasibility of a system of worldwide alliances against communism and the near-term growth of the American Century.

What neither the New Look nor a beefed-up alliance structure could alter, pol-icymakers feared, was communism's appeal in the Third World.[39] The coup against Mosaddeq inflamed nationalist feelings. Nothing revealed this develop-ment more than the rise to prominence of Gamal Abdel Nasser in Egypt. Nasser skillfully played on East-West rivalries to carve out a position of influence in the Arab world. In the mid-fifties, the Soviets used Nasser to further their own ends, contributing to the radicalization of Arab youth. Washington could not respond in the short run.[40] Meanwhile, the French empire in Indochina was in its death throes, leaving the United States to pick up the pieces. Not until late 1955 would the Eisenhower administration and Diem's regime be in a position to try to counter Communist influence in Vietnam.[41]

Next, Washington looked to Latin America to help prevent the spread of com-munism and buttress hegemony. From debates over recognition of new republics in the 1810s, to the Monroe Doctrine of 1823 and the assertion of U.S. hegemony in the Western Hemisphere, to Secretary of State James G. Blaine's scheme to create a U.S.-dominated inter-American system around 1890, to the advent of economic modernization in the 1920s, and to the signing of the Rio Pact in 1947, Latin America had provided a proving ground for the projection of American power and influence. U.S. policy did not necessarily involve active promotion of democracy. In the late 1940s, CIA analysts worried that military rule, as in Peru or Venezuela, for example, would impair stability. Fulgencio Batista's seizure of power in Cuba in 1952, which the administration did not vigorously protest, belied that concern.[42] To be sure, Truman and Eisenhower viewed stability as a precursor of democracy. In the Caribbean, the OAS in its early years largely shared Washington's goals. As one scholar notes, "The United States placed a premium on stability, preferring obsequious tyrants to nationalistic democrats perceived as 'soft' on communism."[43] Dictators held power in thirteen of twenty Latin American states by 1954, a situation that stayed the same for years.[44]

Early in Eisenhower's presidency, the NSC, having in mind the "heavy psychological significance" of the Western Hemisphere for national security, undertook a policy review.[45] Latin American nationalism, warned NSC 144/1 in March 1953, might precipitate "anti-U.S. prejudices" and also be "exploited by Communists." What was needed was a program of private economic aid, coupled with military assistance. There had been a flurry of activity by midyear, including "training in police methods and anti-subversion techniques," that emphasized Latin America's importance to U.S. strategic interests. The short-term payoff brought no more than "limited successes in combating communism on a local level."[46] Hence, the NSC remained much concerned about "the attractiveness of the Soviet appeal" in the Americas.[47]

Shortly before the coup that overthrew Jacobo Árbenz Guzmán in Guatemala on June 27, 1954, the NSC congratulated itself for "achiev[ing] its primary objective of obtaining a clear-cut policy statement against communism" at an inter-American meeting held in Caracas. The limits of solidarity emerged, however, in contentious debates about intervention.[48] The administration concluded on the eve of the coup that "failure would result in greatly lowered prestige for the U.S. in Latin America."[49]

At the same time, military aid was flowing to friendly states in the greater Caribbean area. Nevertheless, communism "continues to be a threat to the security of the hemisphere." Containing the political aspirations and economic hopes attached to nationalism was "a task of enormous and long-range proportions."[50] Richard M. Bissell Jr., who came to the CIA from the MSA in January 1954 and became CIA deputy director for plans a few years after Árbenz's overthrow, admitted Árbenz was "less of a threat than he appeared at the time." Uncertainty in either waging cold war or expanding the American Century was unacceptable, though. "I would approve the same action today without hesitation," Bissell defiantly proclaimed.[51]

That bluntness highlighted a basic aspect of grand strategy. Success in Iran in 1953 had resulted in a greater appreciation of clandestine activities. Approved by Eisenhower in March 1954, NSC 5412 declared, "In the interests of world peace and U.S. national security, the overt foreign activities of the U.S. Government should be supplemented by covert operations." Also, the CIA must make certain that "if uncovered the U.S. Government can plausibly disclaim any responsibility for them."[52] Covert activity would henceforth cover the globe as necessary. The final form of the directive, NSC 5412/2, was approved in 1955.[53] In retrospect, Árbenz's ouster was a trial run for an operation with fatal liabilities, as the failure of a comparable plan at the Bay of Pigs in Cuba in April 1961 showed.

The response to events in Guatemala impaired the chances of broadening acceptance of U.S. hegemony in the Americas, if not beyond. Students throughout Latin America joined with pro- and non-Communist labor groups to protest U.S. involvement in the coup. At the gate of the U.S. embassy in Mexico City, a black-draped wreath tellingly read: "In memory of the good neighbor policy."[54] The longer-term impact of the protests on the American Century was not knowable, yet they gave officials considerable reason to worry.

Finally, in addition to the New Look policy, alliance building, and the resort to covert operations, the Eisenhower administration adjusted grand strategy in a way that helped set off an arms race. The United States and the Soviet Union could not agree on how to achieve credible disarmament. NATO members complicated the issue, insisting that America's nuclear arsenal protect them from a conventional attack, no matter how unlikely one actually was.[55] Before the July 1955 summit at Geneva, Dulles emphasized that Washington not be seen as "being opposed to disarmament."[56] Afterward, he admitted, "We never wanted to go to Geneva, but the pressure of people of the world forced us to do so."[57] Soviet delegates, surprised by Eisenhower's "Open Skies" proposal for reconnaissance flights, rejected it, forgoing a chance to test U.S. intentions.[58]

The impasse at Geneva troubled the administration but not because of the absence of an arms control agreement. Dulles was concerned about credibility in a changing world. To him, Geneva meant "the blurring of the moral barrier between the Soviet bloc and the free world."[59] A subsequent CIA–State Department analysis echoed his assessment. Asserting that Eisenhower "was brilliantly successful in demonstrating American leadership and convincing the world of America's desire for peace," it cautioned, "Russian leaders accomplished a 'public relations' success of no mean proportions by reducing substantially the unpopularity of the Soviet Union in West European eyes, and the fear of Soviet aggression."[60] If negotiating with Moscow could undermine the very idea of monolithic communism, then global containment itself might face critical scrutiny and diminish the allure of an American Century.

Eisenhower counted on his leadership skills to maintain America's standing throughout the world. In order to lead effectively, he had to shore up existing ties with allies and friends and cultivate new ones. He instinctively knew what Luce had articulated in 1941: propagating an American Century demanded strong leadership. Nowhere was the need to lead any greater than in Asia in the early to mid 1950s.

Japan and South Korea merited special attention from Washington, Japan because of its importance to containment capitalism and South Korea because of its strategic location. Meeting in Tokyo with Japanese officials in March 1956, John Foster Dulles linked America's entry onto the world stage in the 1890s with its contemporary goals. Observing that Admiral Alfred Thayer Mahan had believed "the role of force was to give moral institutions the opportunity to take root and grow," he told his hosts, "United States power act[s] as an umbrella over the Free World and provide[s] an opportunity for free institutions to become strong." In turn, the Japanese reiterated their commitment to work on behalf of the Free World in Asia.[61]

The resurgence of Japan's economy and the country's relative stability offered an example of what leadership in the American Century might produce. Nevertheless, protest on the political Left and Right was raising the possibility that Japan's special place in U.S. strategic policy might not last. Were factionalism to become rife and result in a drastic reduction in purchases of goods for U.S. forces in Japan, a recession would occur and curtail recovery. Yoshida Shigeru's quick fix was to create the Self-Defense Forces in response to demands that Tokyo assist with its own defense. Plans were in the works in October 1953 when Ambassador John M. Allison cabled, "What [a] great step forward this is." Yoshida, hoping for a quid pro quo, urged Washington to reconsider its China policy, but officials refused to do so.[62] They viewed, indeed needed, Japan as "a subject state," concludes John Dower.[63]

The United States anxiously watched events unfold after foes forced Yoshida from power in December 1954. Director of Central Intelligence Allen W. Dulles worried that the Japanese Socialist Party's presence in the Diet made it unlikely that Hatoyama Ichiro's government would "amend the constitution in order to permit the rearmament of Japan."[64] Hatoyama realized how much Japan's wellbeing depended on ties with Washington. Politically, he forged a coalition of parties on the Right to form the Liberal-Democratic Party (LDP) in late 1955. Earlier that year, Tokyo did nothing to anger Washington at the Bandung Afro-Asian Conference of nonaligned states.[65] Secretary of State Dulles, highly pleased by developments in Japan, lauded the decision to form the LDP: "If the Japanese could unify their Government it would undoubtedly be found much easier to get along with us."[66] Despite all that had been achieved since the war, the United States had to pay close attention to relations with Japan in order to project American leadership. That meant ensuring the health of Japan's economy—no sure thing. Crop damage from flooding in 1953 caused a 20 percent drop in rice production and was extensive enough for Allison to refer to it in a cable about budgetary and defense issues.[67] The dependence of the American Century on the growth of prosperity in Japan could not have been clearer.

Efforts to further integrate South Korea into the free-world society showed the limits of American leadership. Syngman Rhee was as deft at consolidating his power as the United States was dependent on South Korea to advance containment. His authoritarian manner had troubled U.S. officials during the political crisis of mid-1952, which Rhee used to extend his presidency by manipulating the constitution. (He would again alter the constitution in 1956, ensuring himself an additional term in office.)[68] There was little Washington could do to chasten Rhee while war raged in his homeland. He grew bolder still with the armistice in 1953, writing an intemperate letter to Eisenhower indicating his dissatisfaction with the United States for not doing more to reunite Korea. "Has not the Armistice arrangement put the communists in an infinitely stronger position than they were?" he asked in describing the fight for Korea as a contest for "freedom and security" in the Free World. Dismayed about the ongoing rehabilitation of Japan, Rhee claimed, "It is becoming quite clear to the Koreans that the United States has no intention of treating the two countries on a just and equal basis."[69]

Rhee believed that his country's losses in war entitled him to exert influence over U.S. national security policy. Therefore, Ambassador Ellis O. Briggs recommended including South Korea in the planning for a Southeast Asian counterpart to NATO. Secretary Dulles disagreed, deriding Rhee as "essentially an Oriental bargainer." An exasperated Eisenhower deemed him a "penny ante dictator" who should be told off. In the cauldron of the Cold War in Asia, however, Rhee had made himself indispensable to the success of U.S. security policy. JCS Chairman Admiral Arthur M. Radford grudgingly admitted as much in February 1956, calling Rhee "the George Washington of Korea." He was, in short, a nuisance who delivered order and stability.[70]

U.S. relations with Taiwan remained unsettled during the 1950s, preventing that strategic ally from serving as a showcase of American leadership. Truman and Eisenhower dared not abandon Jiang and the GMD, yet neither did they give him a free hand and the military resources necessary for undertaking a return to the mainland. Making matters worse, Washington could not forcefully constrain Taiwan without adding fuel to the Asia-first fires burning at home. The CIA stepped into the breach, bolstering Taiwan's shaky place in U.S. policy planning by assisting the GMD with military forays against China in areas far from Beijing. Those endeavors bore little fruit. Instead, they revealed the potential liability of clandestine operations, put on display the GMD's military weaknesses, expanded the role of opium in Asia while abetting the corruption of Thai military and police forces, and indefinitely damaged Burmese-American relations.[71]

In fact, GMD-CIA cooperation aided Mao Zedong's consolidation of power. PRC leaders perceived the U.S. alliance with Taiwan as a gambit to thwart the spread of China's influence in Asia. For Washington, the level of tension with Beijing met certain political needs. Along with Eisenhower's appointment of several pro-Jiang diplomats, it helped keep domestic critics at bay and allowed Dulles to pursue a policy of brinksmanship.[72] Why he did so remains unclear because the potential for miscalculation during a crisis over offshore islands in 1954–1955 was high and raised the possibility of conflict with China.[73] The White House evidently considered using tactical atomic weapons to deter Beijing, if not cripple its hold on the mainland.[74] In U.S. policy toward the two Chinas, waging cold war against the PRC took precedence, which made more difficult creation of a receptive environment in Asia for the American Century.

Also complicating matters, the administration in late 1954 signed a mutual security treaty with Taiwan, one with sufficient ambiguity to make it unclear whether the United States was truly committed to aiding a GMD return to China, prepared to maintain GMD control over the symbolically vital islands of Jinmen (Quemoy) and Mazu (Matsu), or determined to placate Jiang while preventing him from embroiling the United States in conflict with China.[75] What is clear is that Washington acted just as SEATO came into being. Brinksmanship and containment through alliance formation appeared to be mutually reinforcing. The crisis died out when Beijing ceased pressuring the islands at the time of the Bandung conference. Before its denouement, the crisis strained relations with Western allies that wanted the White House to force Jiang to abandon the islands in order to avert a larger conflict.[76]

Spreading the American Century across Asia required diplomatic dexterity, patience, and understanding. Eisenhower's view of Asians added to the difficulty of that undertaking. It seems unlikely he had only the Chinese Communists in mind when he told the NSC during the 1954–1955 offshore island crisis, "We are almost always wrong when we believe that Orientals think logically as we do. . . . Face [is] all-important and . . . Orientals would rather lose everything than lose face."[77] The president's condescension and the deep wellspring of prejudice from which it sprang did not stop his administration from seeking additional allies beyond Japan, South Korea, and Taiwan. Such was the logic of cold-war policy that was also meant to rouse support for U.S. leadership in the Free World.

Perhaps Eisenhower also was thinking about Jiang Jieshi when he made his remarks. Informing the president's attitude as well were the nettlesome relations with Syngman Rhee, the deals Truman and he struck with Thailand's military for its pro-U.S. position, and his concern about finding a reliable partner in southern Vietnam, where Ngo Dinh Diem seemed ill equipped to counter Ho Chi Minh's widespread popularity.[78] Diem, Special Representative General J. Lawton "Lightning Joe" Collins thought, "[had] produced little if anything of a constructive nature." He nevertheless became president of the Republic of Vietnam in October 1955.[79] His ties to Washington, born of the Cold War yet of dubious value, showed how much the American Century in Asia depended on an archipelago of conservative, often authoritarian regimes.

Attempts to influence developments in East and Southeast Asia frustrated Eisenhower. He knew, as Luce implied in his 1941 essay, that problems with leadership would negatively impact the American Century. In Southwest Asia, Pakistan's political soil seemed an unlikely place to satisfy America's cold-war needs. U.S. policymakers wanted help with containment, but Muslim Pakistan, carved out of British India in 1947, was obsessed with Hindu-dominated India and Kashmir. Officials in Karachi desired military aid for their own security goals. Also, after war broke out in Korea, the example of Indian neutralism challenged the urgency of a global cold war in certain parts of the nonwhite, postcolonial world. Despite wanting to treat the two nations evenhandedly, the United States tilted toward Pakistan. That move became necessary, Truman and then Eisenhower concluded, when Britain's power in the Middle East rapidly began to erode.[80] Gradually, that decision paid dividends.

The leaders of a coup in Pakistan in 1953 offered their allegiance to the United States in exchange for military and economic assistance. Dulles, who visited the region in May, welcomed the opportunity even though the British and the JCS were concerned about what effect a security-based relationship between Washington and Karachi would have in New Delhi. In fact, Pakistan wanted to limit American options so that a mutual defense pact would become the next logical step.[81] A decision not to provide aid, officials feared, would invariably "weaken the pro-Western position of the moderate elements now in control [and] . . . strengthen the reactionary religious elements which oppose close ties with the West." The two nations did sign a Mutual Defense Assistance Agreement in May 1954.[82] Including Pakistan in SEATO, despite misgivings in the State Department about the price Karachi would seek to exact, was inevitable. For Karachi, membership in SEATO strengthened Pakistan's security posture.[83]

The arrival of the Cold War in much of Asia did little to help the cause of the American Century. An expanding U.S. presence did not dispose leaders wholly to embrace Washington's leadership, which made it more difficult to incorporate Asians into the free-world society. If conditions in Pakistan seemed more conducive to realizing America's objectives than in other Asian nations, the difference was minimal.

The Contours of Containment Capitalism

Eisenhower's stewardship of the American Century entailed more than crafting strategic policy and handling relations with allies and client states. It also involved economic policy; the administration would bolster trade and growth—to Luce, the essence of "a vital international economy."[84] The early record of containment capitalism remained mixed, however. With the reconstruction of Western Europe and Japan well under way by 1952, economic growth seemed orderly. If overall trade and private investment lagged behind ideal levels, that situation would likely improve.[85]

Some uncertainty remained. Could the West secure resources needed for defense-related purposes? Was a cautious White House prepared to lead in a world of rising expectations? NSC 68 implicitly assumed there were no real contradictions between multilateral prosperity and a security-based economy. Too often, however, that proposition seemed wrong. Modernization, we shall see, offered no guaranteed remedy for poverty and underdevelopment. One major problem was the actual cost of anticommunism. Trying to extend the reach of containment capitalism, which meant greater defense-related costs for friends and allies, "raised doubts about the United States' role as a world economic leader," contends Burton I. Kaufman, a prominent scholar of Eisenhower's economic foreign policy.[86]

Truman and his security bureaucracy had looked to the MSA to win support for economic containment. Eisenhower did not share his predecessor's faith in defense spending as the sine qua non of security; he worried about how more spending would affect the nation's economy and its identity as a land governed by electoral politics and the rule of law. He told an NSC meeting in March 1953, "If we must live in a permanent state of mobilization our whole democratic way of life would be destroyed in the process."[87] In that spirit, Eisenhower proposed a reduction in military and economic aid, hoping to move toward a balanced budget. The State Department, the MSA, and the armed services opposed the cuts. Nonetheless, the projected national security budget for FY 1954 showed a slight reduction.[88]

Secretary Dulles contemplated what would soon be called "the domino theory" in Japan, Indonesia, Indochina, Pakistan, India, Iran, and NATO: "The loss of any one of such positions would produce a chain reaction which would cost us the remainder." Later in the year the White House proposed to spend over $400 million for the security of Indochina. In Latin America, where MSA aid totaled $130 million, Dulles warned, "Anti-American forces [are] on the march . . . and we might well wake up ten years from now to find that our friends . . . had become our enemies."[89] Ever the anti-Communist, Eisenhower did not substantially lessen security-related indebtedness.[90]

Ultimately, the administration did not abandon the MSA or its successor agencies—the Foreign Operations Administration (FOA) (August 1953–June 1955) and the International Cooperation Administration (ICA) (July 1955–November 1961). Instead, it encouraged private funding, long-term commitments, and regional trade accords to make up for lower federal allocations. Primary focus remained on Western Europe and Japan, with South Korea, at some $300 million in aid per year during the decade, receiving special attention because of its strategic importance. Mutual security funding still declined by some $3 billion by FY 1956.[91] In effect, the administration was betting it could protect the Free World on the cheap.

Japan provided an important testing ground in the early 1950s for that assumption, with uneven results. The State Department blamed that outcome on the "primitive economies" of "free Asia" and estimated that $1 billion in aid over ten years was required to address it.[92] Japan ran a trade deficit of $1.3 billion in 1952; reserves in dollars and sterling were declining, possibly to be exhausted by 1955.[93] Also, trade reached only 40 percent of prewar levels. Compounding matters was U.S. tariff policy, which worsened Japan's dollar gap. Agricultural protectionism, tariffs on tuna, and an average impost of 26 percent on Japanese goods impaired economic containment in Asia.[94] A stagnant economy, U.S. officials feared, might hasten a turn toward China as a trading partner. Acting Secretary of State Walter Bedell Smith in April 1953 pledged that if conditions worsened, "we would want to sit down together with [the] Japanese to try [to] consider ways in which we could help."[95]

Two courses of action offered encouragement to Yoshida's government. Negotiations for a mutual security agreement began in July and concluded the following March. Japan agreed to begin rearming when its economy permitted, and the United States agreed to place more defense-related (offshore procurement) orders with Japanese companies.[96] Because Congress approved the security pact too late for Japan to receive aid in FY 1955, the State Department worried about adverse political consequences. Having gotten what it wanted in the accord, though, Washington relaxed its opposition to limited, non-security trade with China.[97] The United States had placed its foremost Asian ally on an aid footing comparable to NATO members, bringing stability to Japan's arms industry and furthering bilateral economic cooperation.[98]

Recommendations of the Commission on Foreign Economic Policy also brought attention to Japan's economy. Clarence B. Randall, the head of Inland Steel, served as the chair of the commission, which operated from September 1953 through January 1954. The Randall Report advocated both freer trade, without calling for an end to protectionism, and terminating grant aid in favor of loans to help close the dollar gap.[99] To assist with the report's implementation, the State

Department wanted the president to have greater authority to reduce tariffs because "Japan needs market opportunities if she is to live. Our own security depends in part on her economic strength."[100] If nothing else, authorities in Tokyo could take heart at the solicitous actions of the executive branch.

Japan's dollar gap still threatened to damage relations. Eisenhower, faced with the power of protectionism in the Buy America Act and his preference for trade or loans over grant aid, was ill positioned to address his concern about the Pacific possibly becoming "a communist lake." Nor was it certain that NATO members and Asian allies would welcome Japan into the GATT. Austerity measures undertaken by Yoshida's government had not had the desired effect on the dollar gap, and Eisenhower feared, as he told his cabinet in August 1954, that barring "all competitive products would result, in the long run, in the disaster of war." Indeed, "if forced too far, Japan would become ripe for Communism."[101] Yoshida arrived in Washington in November after visits to Italy, West Germany, France, Great Britain, and Canada. If he expected substantive change in U.S. policy, he had to be disappointed with the talks. A "Marshall Plan" for Asia was not possible. Nevertheless, Yoshida did not threaten to turn to trade with China to help Japan's economy. On display were Tokyo's lack of full independence and Yoshida's inability to alter a vexing situation. Exhausted and alienated from his party, he resigned on December 7.[102]

In a postmortem on the visit, State Department officials put the issue starkly: "Herein lies the crux of US-Japanese difficulties—the necessity of convincing Japan that its future lies with the United States."[103] The financial benefits of economic alignment with the West evidently lay ahead. Responsibility for the quasi impasse partly resided in the White House. Eisenhower remained adamant about Japan's importance in the Cold War yet declined to use his authority to challenge congressional protectionists and fiscal conservatives. The result was a temporary drift in relations. Fortunately for the United States, neither Moscow nor Beijing was capable of building strong economic ties with Tokyo. Even so, a prominent role for Japan in fostering the free-world society in Asia had to wait until later in the decade.

Japan's dollar gap and trade crises in 1953–1954 typified problems then plaguing the Bretton Woods system and administration efforts to enhance global economic leadership. The executive and legislative branches of the government did not respond with alacrity to Japan's difficulties. Hence, actions of the IMF and the GATT and patterns of trade and investment limned the success of containment capitalism in the mid to late 1950s. The State Department's Bureau of Economic Affairs (BEA) enunciated in mid-May 1954 the goals of economic foreign policy: "We aim to improve our security not only by building the strength and cohesiveness of the free world but also by retarding the build-up of Soviet economic power internally and the extension of Soviet influence beyond the Iron Curtain."[104] The import of this pronouncement connected growth of the American Century to an economic policy in need of revision.

How the IMF would assist containment remained unclear; it had not been active in either Western Europe's reconstruction or Japan's revival. One dilemma was how to promote growth in a dollar-starved world and not spark inflation. Also, the IMF would not deviate from guidelines under which access to the Fund occurred on a case-by-case basis with preference for members in good standing, who had access to an emergency standby fund. The National Advisory Council on International Monetary and Financial Problems reported in August 1952 that "a number of members do not know where they stand with respect to the use of the Fund's resources," which prevented systematic economic planning.[105]

From their vantage point in the economic cold war, Fund members worried about U.S. control of IMF resources; they justly wondered whether funds were sufficient to deal with a recession affecting payment balances and currency convertibility. As late as March 1954, the administration could not legally pledge to increase overall IMF resources without congressional consent.[106] Western European members of the Fund considered using the EPU and the OEEC to hasten convertibility and intra-European trade. Washington viewed those organizations as tools conducive to multilateralism yet worried that this quasi autonomy would trigger bilateralism, which was "a most serious threat [to] progress which has been made in a freer system of trade and payments both globally and within the OEEC area."[107] U.S. dominance of the IMF made it impossible for the Fund to operate effectively. By fall 1956, allies were deriding the IMF as a "do nothing" organization, incapable of facilitating cooperation on trade.[108] That charge, an indirect critique of U.S. leadership, potentially boded ill for the economic American Century.

The GATT did scarcely better for the cause of containment. Contracting parties made numerous exceptions to its operating principles before 1953, notably for members of the ECSC and for many items in American agricultural trade with NATO members, including Belgium, Greece, and Turkey.[109] Protectionism galled other GATT states, leading U.S. delegates at a GATT meeting in October 1953 to wonder whether they could "convince other nations that our intention to accept more imports is real and that whatever steps we do take will be lasting."[110] The issue of agricultural import quotas nearly wrecked the GATT. Policymakers, constrained by an act of Congress, were unable to restrict their usage. And representatives at a GATT meeting in fall 1954 had to admit that U.S. quotas were injurious to potential trading partners.[111] Because of congressional obstruction, this situation persisted into Eisenhower's second term, which limited the GATT's contribution to containment and his efforts to strengthen the American Century.

The Layers of Nation-Building

For Henry Luce, a strong global economy and a moral international order were two sides of the same coin.[112] That neither had been realized did not mean Washington should shy away from helping other nations develop. Nation-building on a local level, especially in the Third World, had the potential to fortify the strategic, political, and economic structures that makers of the American Century had constructed in fighting the Cold War. In policy terms, nation-building deftly blended military, technical, and administrative assistance, as seen in May 1951 in NSC 48/5, "United States Objectives, Policies and Courses of Action in Asia." The State Department concurred, averring that the linkage of security and development was "direct and immediate."[113]

Attitudes about the interdependence of aid programs varied. Critics, including some in the State Department, charged that Point Four worked against "more immediate defense and political goals involved in the short range timetable for strengthening the free world." Point Four was operating with a $50 million budget in thirty-five countries in 1952. TCA officials strongly opposed consolidating their agency, including Point Four, and the MSA into one entity because "it would create a strong impression . . . that the Point 4 Program is part of the 'cold war.'" It was, of course, precisely that. These fears were realized in August 1953, when the FOA combined the TCA, the IIAA, and the MSA to bring bureaucratic order to nation-building while joining security and development.[114]

Luce, harking back to his years in China, took as given the connection among moral order, religious belief, and development. Likewise for cold-war officials, religion often held a major place in their thinking about nation-building. A brief explication of religion and cold-war policymaking therefore seems in order. Lutheran theologian Reinhold Niebuhr, one of the most politically involved ministers in America, muted the social radicalism informing his Depression-era work, *Moral Man and Immoral Society* (1932), after the attack on Pearl Harbor. Niebuhr thereafter concluded that only through unwavering vigilance was security conceivable. Later, as his analysis of the Kremlin's postwar intentions crystallized, his defensive realism morphed into support for Truman's foreign policy. Indicative of his elevated standing in intellectual circles, in January 1947 Niebuhr cofounded the liberal organization Americans for Democratic Action.[115]

At a time when many Americans feared that "Godless, atheistic communism" threatened their way of life, Niebuhr disdained the apocalyptic counsel of Billy Graham and other such evangelicals. Acheson, the son of an Episcopalian minister, and Kennan, who was raised as a Presbyterian, thought well of Niebuhr, who participated in several PPS meetings in 1949. His interaction with officialdom continued throughout Truman's presidency, where he articulated views compatible with containment, thereby infusing religious influences into grand strategy. The Soviets, Niebuhr confided to an acquaintance, "intend to harass us ... all over the world, ... particularly in Asia." "We must," he counseled, "... become concerned about the possibility of [their] carrying on this sort of things [*sic*] for decades to come."[116]

Truman, a lifelong devout Baptist, needed no persuading that the United States had received divine dispensation to lead the world—a perspective Luce shared notwithstanding his disdain for Truman. Speaking to a gathering of Methodist ministers in 1949, Truman exclaimed, "We didn't accept that invitation [in 1920] and the Second World War was the result." He urged Catholics and Protestants to denounce communism, an effort thwarted by doctrinal differences. He did, however, characterize the Cold War as a spiritual conflict, which his State Department heartily endorsed: "Much of our foreign policy cannot be explained, or understood, apart from moral and religions considerations."[117]

John Foster Dulles relied on religious belief in making foreign policy. The Presbyterian policymaker drew on the experiences of his youth in combining the secular and the sacred. Its messianic quality may have been off-putting to men like Kennan and Niebuhr, but the secretary's differences with them, despite revealing sectarian disputes over the theological or philosophical underpinnings of containment, were minor. It is worth noting, William Inboden observes, that Dulles "conflated the ideals of Christianity with the identity of the United States."

Eisenhower, baptized a Presbyterian while in office, did likewise. His resort to religious discourse when mapping out grand strategy was central to his presidential persona. "What is our battle against communism," he asked, "if it is not a fight between anti-God and a belief in the Almighty?" Uttered months before his first election, his sentiments did not change. Eisenhower began his inaugural address in January 1953 by calling attention to the battle raging between "forces of good and evil."[118] His Manichaean message psychologically supported the efforts of the ECA, the TCA, and their successor agencies to provide technical expertise for development activities.

Beyond governmental programs, the importance of religion to development grew during Eisenhower's presidency with Christian missionaries contributing to the task of modernization. Luce would have expected nothing less than for them to be among those whose work made the United States the Good Samaritan of the modern world. Some thirty thousand missionaries were toiling abroad by 1960; providing technical expertise while saving souls made them apostles for Point Four goals. Their ministrations were worldwide in scope, extending to Islamic lands where the prospect of conversion was better than it was in China when Luce's parents toiled there.[119] Latin America also offered hope for tying secular and spiritual development. The Rockefeller family and the Rockefeller Foundation had worked for decades in the northern and Amazonian reaches of South America, importing as a path to modernity a mix of Baptist evangelism, finance capital, resource extraction, and scientific agriculture.[120]

This security-development linkage with religion was not always welcome in places the United States deemed vital to the success of the Cold War and growth of the American Century. To take one example, South Korea's record was mixed in the 1950s. Syngman Rhee believed that Washington's quest for balanced development had enabled Japan to prosper at the expense of his country even as the United Nations Korean Reconstruction Agency, created in December 1950, provided million-dollar block grants to missionaries and nongovernmental organizations (NGOs) for community development. Tensions simmered beneath the surface of South Korean politics, nearly embroiling Catholics and Protestants in electoral intrigue. By 1960, sixty groups from America were involved in projects in agriculture, education, and health.[121] The best U.S. officials could expect, given the turbulent political environment, was that these programs would become "consonant with Free World principles and objectives."[122]

Nation-building needed more than expert advice and religious faith in order to succeed. Acceptance of Washington's leadership depended to a great degree on its reception by young people. Education from elementary school to technical, vocational, and graduate-level training became an important component of modernization and plausibly the bedrock of moral order in the American Century. South Korea again offers a useful example. Divisions in Korea after 1945 brought considerable attention to the state of education in the south. The educational system, a vestige of Japanese colonial rule, lay in shambles, leaving southerners ill prepared for the future. That situation had to change. Newly built schools, in which teachers used textbooks in the Korean language, pervaded the land by 1950, and young South Koreans learned practical skills to help them function in a modern economy. Their education was training them to build a nation receptive to Western institutions and values, including democracy, as evidenced by the many Korean youth who left home after 1953 to study in the United States.[123]

One group involved in this transformation of education was the American Education Mission (AEM), which undertook three separate study missions between 1952 and 1955. Hoping to instill an appreciation for democracy, along with designing curricular reforms, the AEM fell short of its goal. The AEM could neither dictate nor control how educators adapted democracy to the needs of the state. Education emphasized fealty to the nation over the individual. If that approach to reform initially pleased Rhee's regime, whatever satisfaction it brought dissipated as student protests helped force Rhee from power in 1960.[124]

Along with education, popular and material culture also shaped America's standing abroad. In West Germany, for instance, challenges to Bonn's authority persisted, with more than one hundred riots occurring in the mid-1950s. An early one occurred in October 1955 during a Hamburg concert by Louis Armstrong. Initially condemning the riots as threats to the Federal Republic, authorities gradually saw them as displays of youthful ennui that time and maturation would overcome. Aiding this belief was the work of social theorists including David Riesman, whose landmark study *The Lonely Crowd* garnered a wide audience after being translated into German in 1956. German sociologists amplified his theories about mass alienation, youth, and rebellion, thereby quelling fears about revolt and the disintegration of German identity.[125] Ultimately, the return of West Germany to international respectability through membership in NATO and the enjoyment of American popular culture by German youth co-opted their radical potential.

Across Western Europe, the Americanization of culture hastened nation-building and enhanced American prestige. Radio broadcasts by the Voice of America, documentary films, and educational exchanges under the Fulbright program offered Europeans flattering views of life in America. Created at the time of the Marshall Plan, the United States Information Service quickly became controversial, unable to shake the perception that left-wing ideas were contaminating it. Its successor, the United States Information Agency (USIA), enjoyed Eisenhower's support after its creation in June 1953. Within two years, USIA became part of the Operations Coordinating Board, which protected it from conservative critics. With a $77.1 million budget in 1954, USIA undertook a cultural offensive. Jazz legends like Armstrong and Dizzy Gillespie traveled abroad in America's name. Also, television programs in Great Britain extolled the virtues of the United States and its productive capacity.[126] Hollywood did its part to mute leftist artists and portray a resolute anticommunism but could not control how youthful audiences reacted to such films as *The Wild One* (1954) and *Rebel without a Cause* (1955).[127]

Making a cultural cornucopia widely accessible had mixed results. It was positive in that it reflected the distance Western Europeans had come economically and culturally since 1945. The products of popular and material culture were not unattainable luxuries. At the same time, a downside to nation-building through Americanization was that the United States and its various representatives could not exert control over public response to what was available in the cultural marketplace. As a result, the deference to cultural influences that might have helped expand the American Century fell short of what U.S. officials anticipated.

As a case in point, an avid defense of tradition in France had the potential to sidetrack the course of Americanization. The "Coca-Cola affair," commencing in the late 1940s, symbolized the titanic struggle over foreign influence then under way. Communists saw Coke as a cultural Trojan horse, harmful to labor and national beverage interests. The Communist Party newspaper *L'Humanité* denounced the soft drink, asking whether "we will be *coca-colonisés*." Caught up in the controversy, the National Assembly considered banning the manufacture and sale of Coke. The State Department took up Coca-Cola's cause. By 1953, France capitulated and halted legal action against the American company. Ironically, the significance of the battle was less than it seemed because the French public failed to develop a taste for the sugary beverage.[128]

As a coda to the affair, the imprecations of the French Left could not halt the onrush of American consumer culture. The tide turned decisively against the defenders of *civilisation* in October 1956 when the USSR invaded Hungary. Communist intellectuals who did not break ranks with Moscow were thrust to the sidelines of political and cultural debates. Others who had previously framed the battle in broad terms could no longer credibly rail against American-style modernity. After all, American aid had demonstrably improved France's standard of living by the mid-1950s.[129]

Agents of nation-building—private industry, government experts, foundation officials, missionaries, educators, and cultural emissaries—were incredibly adaptive. A popular-culture invasion of Europe ostensibly had little in common, for example, with development in Southeast Asia, which the Griffin Mission had sought to foster. And yet, a larger objective bound these endeavors together as cold-war weapons: stability. Stability was essential if nation-building was to succeed. We have seen how crucial military assistance was to waging the Cold War. Another aspect of that aid, counterinsurgency—or in the case of Guatemala, counterrevolutionary aid—often found a home in day-to-day nation-building. Why? Luce had presciently written that the twentieth century "is also a revolutionary [era]," and the United States cannot long endure unless "we solve for our time the problems of the world revolution."[130]

The lineage of counterinsurgency in modern American history stretches back to conflict in Cuba and the Philippines around 1900.[131] Reliance on counterinsurgency to achieve political stability increased after 1945. In the Greek civil war and the Huk rebellion in the Philippines, U.S. military personnel provided advice and support in campaigns against insurgent forces. The cost of involvement in Greece reached almost $1 billion through 1949 in the struggle with the National People's Liberation Army. By then, the Greek army had grown sevenfold to 140,000 troops.[132] Truman Doctrine aid prevented Greece from hindering recovery in Western Europe, and the use of Marshall Plan funds, via the ECA, helped keep communism at bay.[133]

The Philippines also played a key role in counterinsurgency's evolution. A revolt against President Manuel Roxas began in 1946. His death and the ascent to power of Elpidio Quirino in 1948 temporarily stalled the rebellion. Some fifteen thousand men and women had taken up arms by 1951, reacting against government violence toward peasant communities where the Huks and their sympathizers lived and hid. The rebellion largely ended in May 1954, failing to garner extensive public support in part because inclusion of the general populace in national politics undercut the Huks' appeal.[134]

Before the rebellion died out, U.S. officials became worried about ties between the Huks and the Philippine Communist Party (PKP), which the CIA had initially downplayed. Helping to change attitudes in Washington was the reporting of Lieutenant Colonel Edward Geary Lansdale of the U.S. Army, who was affiliated with the CIA. Lansdale worked with Ramon Magsaysay after he became minister of national defense in September 1950; Lansdale believed that the PKP was controlling the Huks. In response, Washington reorganized Philippine military intelligence, strengthening combat battalions, and increasing the size of the constabulary and army. Joint air missions bombed Huk strongholds and used napalm against crops and rebels. Among the U.S. officers were some who had been present in Greece.[135] Thwarting the Huk rebellion helped to perpetuate cacique democracy and assisted nation-building in service to U.S. political objectives. Counterinsurgency's success seemingly augured well for the prospects of development policy in greater Southeast Asia.

The role of military force in nation-building begs the question of who would control modernization in troubled, mostly nonwhite areas of the Third World. Guatemala is a valuable example in that it shows how important anti-Communist nation-building was to the American Century even close to home. Jacobo Árbenz became suspect in Washington after his election in 1950 because of his connection with Communists through his wife María Vilanova Árbenz's associates and leftists in the government. Decree 900, issued on June 17, 1952, promised the expropriation and redistribution of idle land in a country where 2 percent of all landowners held 70 percent of the land. The prospect of real agrarian reform alarmed the landed elite, corporate landowners, and the hierarchy of the Catholic Church.[136]

Decree 900 moved the CIA and the State Department, at the level of Assistant Secretary Edward Miller, into action. Plans were laid to help Colonel Carlos Castillo Armas destabilize the Árbenz government. With Truman nearing the end of his presidency, the White House and State Department hesitated, fearing the consequences of a covert operation for U.S. credibility.[137] The CIA was adamant about the need to halt Guatemala's radicalization.[138] An increase in private landownership was intolerable because it presaged an upending of Guatemala's power structure and, potentially, a direct challenge to cold-war nation-building.[139]

Agrarian reform substantially decreased after Árbenz's ouster in 1954. Castillo Armas never became the strong leader his administration supporters expected;

his assassination in July 1957 by a disaffected member of the Palace Guard greatly complicated matters. Secretary of the Treasury George Humphrey set out U.S. priorities at an NSC meeting in December 1954: "We should . . . stop talking so much about democracy, and make it clear that we are quite willing to support dictatorships of the right if their policies are pro-American."[140] Eisenhower did not disagree. In support of tough-minded nation-building, a congressional study mission in 1955 envisioned Guatemala, without irony, as a showcase for liberal development.[141]

Neither Castillo Armas nor his successor General Miguel Ydígoras Fuentes, who was elected president in early 1958, was disposed to modernize Guatemala. The consequences of U.S. policy for the people of Guatemala, many of whom were illiterate, were momentous as conservative Democratic senator Allen J. Ellender of Louisiana explained in 1959, "Of the many millions that we have spent in Guatemala, little has trickled down to the 2 million Indians of the country. . . . They are still poor, while the businessmen are prospering."[142] Luce's global Good Samaritan, it seems, had several and contradictory faces.

If stability and order were indispensable to nation-building, internal security programs, the NSC declared in December 1954, were necessary "in order to protect free world countries vulnerable to Communist subversion."[143] Securitized nation-building was not paying expected dividends in South Vietnam, reflecting Diem's inability to build a nation without foreign help. South Vietnam was in chaos. Neither $2.6 billion in aid to France between 1950 and 1954 nor $1 billion for Saigon by 1961 brought stability. Edward Lansdale, twice in the fall of 1954, had to rescue Diem from attempted coups.[144]

Diem, his family, and officials in Saigon ruled in tyrannical, corrupt ways, disrupting the rhythms of daily life in a largely Buddhist land. The loss of local political autonomy, favoritism for Catholics, and repression of the Cao Dai and Hoa Hao sects in 1955 impaired Diem's ability to remake Vietnam.[145] The same can be said for his aversion then to waging counterinsurgency warfare; Diem was reluctant to rely on forces not wholly answerable to him. Worsening his self-created problems and lessening the chances for order and stability were activities of the North Vietnamese and anti-Diem groups in the south that fomented further trouble and precluded the adoption of American-influenced nation-building.[146]

Credibility, Stability, and a "Free" World

If the Eisenhower administration exhibited strong leadership in the Cold War, it followed that its supervision of the American Century should go well. Credibility followed from strong leadership. Waging global cold war put U.S. credibility on the line with allies, client states, and adversaries. Government-to-government relations in Western Europe and East Asia in the main bolstered Washington's image as did the prospect of economic growth, however gradual, and the appeal of American popular culture.

Leadership was not so clear-cut elsewhere. Doubts about credibility crept into relations with Latin America. Attempts to compel Latin Americans to join in pushing aside Guatemala's Jacobo Árbenz conflicted with the sacrosanct principle of nonintervention. Persuasion seemed unlikely, so much so that the Eisenhower administration wondered whether it could rely on OAS members. In fact, a resolution, voted on favorably at Caracas in March 1954, did not mention Árbenz and Guatemala by name; it merely stated that a Communist state in the region threatened the Western Hemisphere as a whole.[147] The resolution was less specific than hoped for, despite a 17–1–2 favorable vote, because Washington had long feared, as Assistant Secretary of State for Inter-American Affairs John Moors Cabot told the NSC in September 1953, that "many [Latin Americans] are essentially native Communists."[148]

Making matters worse, commodity prices for agricultural products and raw materials were not sufficient to provide a modern standard of living. Appeals for a Marshall Plan for the Americas still went unheeded. In practice, this meant White House opposition to grant aid and soft loans.[149] And, repeated requests for a hemisphere-wide economic meeting fell on deaf ears until late 1954. When the Rio Economic Conference finally convened, Dulles warned that U.S. credibility would be harmed if it went badly—and it did. The results of the conference, held in late November and early December, disappointed proponents of development aid.[150]

Southeast Asia also proved problematic for America's image. At an NSC meeting on December 21, 1954, while discussing security policy, John Foster Dulles remarked about "Free Vietnam," Laos, Cambodia, and Indonesia, "These countries are not really of great significance to us, other than from the point of view of prestige, except that they must be regarded as staging grounds for further forward thrusts by the Communist powers." (The same held true for the Middle East, Dulles said; its oil reserves "must be denied to the Soviet bloc.")[151]

Like Dulles, Eisenhower was deeply vested in strengthening the nation's credibility. He had written in his diary on April 27 about conditions in Indochina during the crisis at Dien Bien Phu, "The British government is showing a woeful unawareness of the risks we run in that region."[152] A "woeful unawareness" and the imperative "must be denied" indicate that Dulles and Eisenhower had not persuaded the nation's closest allies to take threats to Western interests in Indochina as seriously as they did. To the extent that was true, it raised serious questions about U.S. leadership of remote outposts in the Free World.

Nothing tested American credibility at mid-decade like Vietnam. Despite seeking a better partner in Saigon than Diem, Eisenhower and Dulles realized that options were few. General J. Lawton Collins had grave doubts about Diem. Nevertheless, while discussing one of Collins's critical reports, the president told Dulles that he was not prepared to abandon Diem "because we bet on him heavily."[153] Eisenhower's risky wager in effect tethered the nation's reputation to an autocratic regime thousands of miles from home. The bonds that joined U.S. credibility and South Vietnam became even tighter with the creation of SEATO in December 1954. SEATO also kept the Communist Chinese acutely aware of American power and resolve. Dulles knew that SEATO was not a counterpart to NATO and expressed misgivings about committing credibility to such an alliance in a place "where the situation was by no means promising." Bringing Indochina under SEATO's protective wing, he told Eisenhower, "would involve a real risk of results which would hurt the prestige of the United States in this area."[154] The logic of a global cold war, despite the troubles Washington was having with South Korea and Taiwan, had impelled the United States deeper into the whole of Asia, resulting in security commitments stretching from Japan to Pakistan.

The breadth of this undertaking affected the expansion of the American Century. It was incumbent on the administration to make the best of the gathering at Bandung in April 1955, whose defining features were neutralism in the Cold War, the emotional appeal of nationalism, and the allure of anticolonialism. India's Jawaharlal Nehru made a spirited defense of neutralism as did Sukarno of Indonesia, who called for unity in the Third World. Nonalignment for Nehru meant "friendly coexistence"; for the Indonesian leader, unity entailed adopting an ideology that encompassed Islam and Marxism.[155]

Two weeks before the conference, Eisenhower told the NSC that he found the rapid growth of nationalism and neutralism "very alarming." Dulles also recognized that Bandung might become "incalculably dangerous" to vital Western interests, which made it imperative for Washington's friends—including Lebanon, Turkey, Iran, Iraq, and Pakistan, which would be present at Bandung—to defend what was positive about the West despite its "regrettable faults," notably the historical sense of racial superiority. As if building on Luce's 1941 essay, Dulles pointed to achievements in "technical and material progress" in the non-Western world. To focus on what was negative about Western dealings with Asia meant "the whole concept of human brotherhood, of equality among men, the fundamental concepts of the United Nations, are in jeopardy."[156]

Dulles thought the results of the conference were encouraging; he did not believe the presence of Chinese foreign minister Zhou Enlai ruined the proceedings. Rather, states friendly to the West had held their own, he told the cabinet on April 29. In fact, "the final communiqué of the conference, except for the mention of the Palestine question, was a document which we ourselves could subscribe to. Even its references to colonialism were in accord with what we feel in our hearts, though we are unable to say them [*sic*] publicly." Lebanon's ambassador, Charles Malik, was less positive about the results at Bandung. Zhou, he told Dulles, "won friends and good will" for China; Nehru solidified his position as a leader of the nonaligned states; and the West did not benefit nearly as much as Dulles believed. As Malik put it, "The emergence of Communist China was a distinct defeat for the West."[157] In fact, four months after Bandung, U.S. officials reluctantly admitted that neutralism boded ill for America's image with youths in North Africa and throughout the Middle East. In response, the USIA gave special attention to Africa, designing programs for students, educators, intellectuals, and labor leaders.[158]

Did developments at Bandung injure the American Century? On the one hand, Dulles and Eisenhower viewed the conference through a cold-war lens. Since Zhou did not obtain a firm commitment from participants to support an aggressive policy toward Taiwan, Washington could claim partial victory. On the other hand, the challenge of neutralism and emergence of a North-South divide in world affairs were undeniable. Dulles considered convening a counter-gathering, one that America's Asian friends would dominate by design, but nothing came of the idea.[159]

Administration officials knew they had to demonstrate leadership on issues affecting more than European allies and Japan. If determining how to do so was not always apparent in mid-1955, Dulles bought time with his relatively positive assessment of Bandung. He may have been conceding, too, that the White House realized the world was in flux and more complex than previously admitted.[160] The United States could not unilaterally produce order and stability in that world. Others, friendly, inimical, and nonaligned, had their own interests and would pursue them. Even so, to the extent Washington's power and influence remained paramount, the future of the American Century seemed bright.

SUSTAINING LEADERSHIP

Luce's call to seize the opportunity of leadership continued to resonate in Washington. What was novel in 1941 had become a shared sentiment among officials by the mid-1950s. Given changing international conditions, they had to wonder how effective American leadership still was. It fell to Dwight D. Eisenhower and his national security team to refine the working of containment, bolster allegiance to Washington within the free-world society, and fulfill the promise of liberal development. In significantly charting the course of foreign policy through 1960, these objectives served as tools for expanding the American Century.

Global Containment and Leadership

As much as anything, the issue of arms control showed how hard it would be to adjust containment strategy and enhance American leadership. The Geneva summit in July 1955 had hinted arms control possibly might supplant the tension of the early Cold War, but the USSR's launching of its Sputnik satellite on October 4, 1957, destroyed any chance of that happening. "The Sputnik effect," Vladislav Zubok writes, "galvanized the United States into launching another costly round in the arms race in order to restore public confidence in American superiority."[1] Sputnik captured the world's imagination. Dismaying to the White House was the impression that the balance of power was shifting in Moscow's direction. Might the Soviets be more dangerous with this novel technology in their hands? Senator Lyndon Johnson (D-Tex.) pictured a grave threat: "Soon they will be dropping bombs on us from space like kids dropping rocks onto cars from freeway over-passes."[2]

Eisenhower downplayed the Russian breakthrough, knowing that an Ameri-can satellite program was under way. The problem, as CIA chief Allen Dulles told the NSC, was Sputnik's effect on credibility. Sensing a psychological advan-tage, Nikita Khrushchev trumpeted the achievement to the underdeveloped world, while Beijing heralded Sputnik as proof of Soviet military and scientific supremacy.[3] In the background was the conviction the United States must not lose a militarized space race. In Eisenhower's terse words, "We must, above all, seek a military posture that the Russians still respect."[4]

What the president could not disclose to the American public was the exact nature of U.S. superiority. Suffice it to say that the United States possessed a nearly ten-to-one advantage in nuclear warheads, which were deliverable by manned bombers. The Strategic Air Command in 1956 had begun compiling a list of pri-ority targets, including East Berlin and Moscow, to be attacked if war broke out.[5] Unfortunately for the White House, classified information could not dispel concerns about U.S. credibility and leadership. Even before Sputnik, the NSC reiterated the centrality of nuclear weapons to defense strategy: America's lead in weapons development must continue. Such was the logic of the 1957 Gaither Report. Composed in part by Paul Nitze and presented to Eisenhower in Novem-ber, it advocated greater spending for the Strategic Air Command and the inter-continental ballistic missile program. The report concluded: "USSR intentions are expansionist, and . . . her great efforts to build military power go beyond any concepts of Soviet defense."[6]

Nitze pushed hard for developing a second-strike nuclear capability and en-hancing conventional forces in order to achieve maximum deterrence. He sub-sequently wrote about Eisenhower and Dulles's failure to adopt his position wholesale, arguing that they believed "a reliant [sic] deterrent capability was not urgent" and "defense against nuclear war was futile."[7] What was really at issue was the president's knowledge, based on evidence provided by U-2 spy planes, that the United States enjoyed a strategic advantage. That superiority grew with the tripling of America's nuclear arsenal from six thousand to eighteen thousand weapons between 1958 and 1960.[8] Meanwhile in March 1958, Khrushchev, aware of the USSR's strategic inferiority, proposed a moratorium on nuclear testing.[9] His bold gambit did not compel Eisenhower to rethink his priorities. The president clung to his belief that tactical nuclear weapons had a place in modern warfare. His conviction reflected a basic assumption guiding U.S. strategic policy: the United States must prevail in the Cold War, even if doing so led to combat with ideo-logical adversaries. Refusing to confront the Communist threat would make the nation appear weak and, in the process, endanger the American Century.

Before the Gaither Report, administration officials considered altering the economics of global containment. Eisenhower, who questioned how duplicative defense systems should be, worried about the report's impact on the federal budget. A projected defense outlay of $40 billion for FY 1959 would adversely affect funding of aid programs for friendly nations, for instance.[10] Moreover, debates over East-West commerce in light of rising defense expenditures raised questions about the utility of economic containment. Eisenhower, like Truman, believed that denying strategic goods to the Communist bloc strengthened containment. Denial depended on the availability of markets for products that friends and allies produced.[11] Analyzing the situation in 1953, Dulles admitted that "as we cut down on our aid, we should let our allies have greater freedom to trade with the [Communist] satellites, while still keeping out top strategic items." Moreover, because of the exchange of "sorely needed dollars and food," some trade with the PRC was likely to continue.[12] And it did.

Beijing's influence grew incrementally after 1954, which made it imperative for South Vietnam, for instance, to reach an agreement with Japan on reparations, investment, and trade.[13] An assessment of the challenges posed by China concluded in 1957, "Asia is impressed by the progress which the Chinese Communists have made in developing their economy and increasing their military power." The CIA and State Department wanted Eisenhower to hold the line in non-Communist Asia, where an American presence "will continue to be the major factor damping down the growth of Peiping's influence." By then it was too late; efforts to curtail trade with the PRC, and the Soviet bloc, had largely failed.[14]

The British, and to an extent the Japanese, succeeded in revamping the lists of proscribed goods. An early revision in August 1954 greatly reduced the items subject to embargo, quota, or surveillance. Great Britain wanted to go further and remove, Ambassador Winthrop W. Aldrich explained, "any extension [of] controls not absolutely [of] clear strategic necessity."[15] Disputes regarding trade with China became rancorous, lingering into mid-1956, when London resumed commerce in disputed items. Secretary of Defense Charles E. Wilson charged London with "undercutting the United States in the field of trade controls and . . . seriously weakening the United States' position in the Far East." Dulles sought to minimize the rift, but common ground was lacking. His dismissal of the China trade as being of "marginal commercial value" did not matter.[16] America's economic leadership was under attack by its most important ally.

A reassessment of trade with the PRC took place in September 1957 during a review of economic defense policy. Challenging aspects of containment capitalism, Clarence Randall, who had become a special assistant to the president and head of the Council on Foreign Economic Policy in July 1956, doubted the United States would sanction its allies for trading strategic goods with China. Dulles knew sanctions were unlikely because they would harm "our weaker brethren" in non-Communist Asia, where "we are holding on . . . only with great difficulty." Wilson became emotional in stating the Defense Department's position: "We don't want to trade with the dirty s.o.b.'s, nor do we want the Free World nations to trade with them either." Vice President Richard Nixon correctly thought that trade with China was a political problem more than an economic issue.[17] Why? For containment to succeed and the American Century to thrive, there had to be broad consensus; but support for American leadership was not what it had previously been.

Containment capitalism in practice also encompassed the GATT's efforts to promote prosperity and involved the interplay of commerce, investment, and aid under the dollar-dominated Bretton Woods system. In July 1956, GATT executive secretary E. Wyndham White told State Department economist John Leddy that progress on tariff reduction was slow, notably in underdeveloped countries. Quantitative restrictions on trade outside of the OEEC were still hurting the GATT. White lamented that "consultations in the GATT are in general meaningless." And, the nations that had not yet become contracting parties were at no disadvantage in their commercial activity. Moreover, political squabbles in Washington were undercutting professed support for a strong GATT.[18]

Congressional refusal to endorse participation in the GATT forced the White House to operate cautiously in negotiating tariff rates both on a bilateral basis and at GATT meetings. The GATT did not become an integral part of containment capitalism even though waivers permitted for Western Europe generally aided economic containment by bolstering regional solidarity.[19] Limited economic containment was all that was possible without a commitment by a majority of GATT members to structural change, that is, to actual multilateralism, in the Free World's economy. Officials followed negotiations in Europe in 1956 about economic integration, which resulted in the founding of the European Economic Community (EEC), or Common Market, on March 25, 1957. Countries belonging to the ECSC composed the initial membership; London did not petition to join the EEC until mid-1961.[20] From Washington, the EEC seemed a small, yet positive step toward multilateralism.

Creating the EEC would have been unthinkable without America's security umbrella. Randall thought that a common market "could contribute significantly to NATO and other United States objectives" through a combination of trade, investment, and aid policy, which was consistent with Luce's thinking about the economic side of the American Century. Accordingly, the adverse tariffs American exporters would face for a time were worth the cost. To be sure, policymakers did not want economic integration to proceed without taking into account cold-war economic policy. Randall noted, "[We] should . . . use our influence to guide the development along lines that seem desirable to us."[21] That turned out to be an elusive goal.

Incorporating other nations into a system of economic containment proved to be difficult, too. Congress would not give Eisenhower the authority to shape a dynamic trading system. He was not free to set tariff rates, and Congress, reluctant to surrender or share its power, closely monitored trade legislation. The restricted lending ability of the Export-Import Bank symbolized the struggle. Congress authorized the bank to make only short-term loans; hence, the World Bank was left to assume responsibility for funding development projects.[22] That did not occur to an appreciable degree during Eisenhower's presidency.

Disputes within the administration and between it and Congress over commercial policy hurt efforts to adjust containment. What the BEA understood as "a mutuality of interest" with crucial partners might be lost if "shaken by economic fears or disputes [affecting trade]."[23] To wit, the dollar value of America's merchandise exports from 1951 to 1958 in the aggregate exceeded imports by one-third. Export values after 1955 ranged from between $18 billion and $20 billion annually, but imports never reached $13 billion per year.[24] Typically, half of all imported goods were semifinished or finished manufactures, with raw materials or foodstuffs making up the other half. Places of origin of trade or the destinations for American goods were primarily Canada, Latin America, and Western Europe.[25] Given this pattern, the unwillingness of some GATT contracting parties to bring Japan into the GATT or extend MFN status to Japanese commerce after Japan became a full member in September 1955 seems like much ado about very little. What was politically and symbolically important to Tokyo and Washington potentially threatened the well-being of these other GATT members.[26] Markets needed to help the free-world economic community develop in Asia scarcely existed, though.

The administration's belief that greater private investment would help achieve its goals went untested during Eisenhower's first term. The Randall Commission had encouraged the government to adopt new devices to spur investment. These included technical aid to create a climate receptive to foreign capital, changes in the tax code so as to promote greater investment, and modifications of antitrust law for similar ends. The State Department also wanted the Export-Import Bank to guarantee some private loans.[27] From 1952 to 1956, yearly private investment abroad by Americans had increased from $22.8 billion to $33 billion. (Government investment rose modestly from $14.4 billion to $16.5 billion.) Canada, Latin America, and Western Europe benefited most from this movement of capital, with mining, petroleum, and manufacturing sectors receiving the majority of corporate America's largesse.[28]

The BEA explained this cautious approach: "[Such] measures may be partially effective but the political hazards of foreign investment will continue to be a strong deterrent."[29] The demonstrable lack of attention to Asia beyond Japan, above all to Southeast Asia, reveals much about foreign economic policy. Patterns of investment (and trade) reflected a pro-Atlantic bias and would not soon change. If nothing else, the difficulty of expanding into areas not well served by American finance capital and commerce was instructive, illustrating the improbability of implanting abroad a market-based economic system premised on thorough-going containment. Even before Eisenhower's reelection, the USSR forced the administration to reconsider its trade and aid policies. In mid-1953, the Soviets began extending their commercial influence into South Asia and the Middle East.[30] Eisenhower viewed these developments with alarm and ordered the CIA to monitor Soviet trade. He also sought increased authority to meet the Kremlin's challenge through the Mutual Security Program. As Dulles explained at the time of the 1956 crises in Suez and Hungary, "The expansion of the Soviet bloc has gone as far as can be tolerated. . . . Our so-called foreign aid program, which is really not foreign aid because it isn't aid to foreigners but aid to us, is an indispensable factor in carrying out our foreign policy."[31]

Some Democrats and Republicans in Congress disagreed. Dissenting Republicans viewed foreign aid as a wasteful enterprise, and Democrats objected to the emphasis on security instead of development. Skirmishing with the White House led to a cut of $1 billion from the requested FY 1957 mutual security budget to $3.8 billion. The president did not receive the flexibility he wanted to dispense funds to Africa and Asia. Nonmilitary assistance survived largely unscathed, a turn of events that better served the cause of containment capitalism than the focus on military aid. At length, Congress and the White House agreed to create the Development Loan Fund (DLF) to complement private investment. Congress, however, again reduced the requested amount for security and development aid by $1 billion for FY 1958.[32] Nevertheless, the DLF set a precedent for long-term aid programs and presaged a greater role for the World Bank in spurring growth in the Third World. The administration saw the DLF as a key part of the battle against the economic threat posed by communism. Dulles still feared, he told Nixon in February 1958, that Soviet economic warfare might overwhelm "our classical free trade [system]." Congress responded with additional congressional support for the DLF.[33]

The dollar remained the regnant international currency at decade's end, but the economic architecture of the American Century was somewhat weaker. Not since the inception of the postwar monetary system in 1944 had authorities felt so compelled to justify U.S. economic leadership, which congressional obstruction complicated. Their defensiveness manifested itself in various ways, particularly as the administration engaged the Third World after 1955.

The Free-World Society in the Third World

Henry Luce wanted the United States to export its values, institutions, and expertise so that others might experience the nation's bounty in an American Century.[34] Pursuing hegemony, waging cold war, and building a free-world society gave concrete form to Luce's ambitions after 1945. In the fluid global environment of the mid-1950s, officials paid increasing attention to the Third World in hopes of strengthening American leadership.

For the American Century to flourish, stability in the Middle East was mandatory. On the positive side of the ledger in Iran, Mohammed Reza Shah Pahlavi presented himself as the antidote to the virus of revolutionary nationalism. U.S. military and emergency economic aid in the amount of $51 million by mid-1954 broke the impasse between Tehran and the AIOC so that oil production could expand.[35] The shah proved to be a worthy client despite concerns about the paucity of domestic reforms.[36] Until he fell from power in 1979, his principal goal was to control reform impulses at home through cautious modernization while making deals—the exchange of oil for arms—with Washington that allowed him to remain Iran's supreme leader.[37] With Iran securely in the camp of the Free World, the American Century seemingly had a stable foothold in the upper Middle East.

Nevertheless, London and Washington maintained their plans to deny oil to the USSR if conditions warranted. The British contemplated using a nuclear strike on oil wells as part of a program of denial in Iran and possibly Iraq, whereas the Americans wanted to plug wells so that oil reserves would not be lost to the West. Evidence is not conclusive, but Washington's position appears to have prevailed. What the role of regional governments was to be should plugging or total destruction take place remains unknown.[38]

During that same time, relations with Egypt and much of the Arab Middle East, perhaps excepting Saudi Arabia, remained unsettled. Especially causing anxiety was the growth of radical nationalism among Arab people, particularly the young. No American client displayed charisma comparable to that of Gamal Abdel Nasser, whose strong advocacy of nonalignment, tilting as he did toward Moscow, frustrated the White House.[39] Eisenhower—demonstrating his own cultural-cum-racial biases as if to counter Nasser's Arab identity—perceived the nationalist Nasser as a "puppet" of the Kremlin who was impeding the attainment of Washington's goals.[40]

The Suez crisis of 1956 and the events leading up to promulgation of the Eisenhower Doctrine in 1957 showed how local developments could affect the stability of the American Century. A major point of contention with Washington was the conviction among pro-Nasser Arab leaders that the United States considered neutralism a sign of political immaturity and cowardice in the Cold War. There was evidence for their belief. The NSC had acknowledged in mid-1953 that Washington should recognize "legitimate aspirations" of Arab states. At the same time, it insisted that Arab leaders must accept their responsibilities "toward the free world."[41]

This perceptual chasm became critical after Nasser nationalized the Suez Canal Company in July 1956. Until then, the United States tended to make policy in concert with London despite the lack of trust by Arabs toward the British. Collusion by London and Paris, in concert with Israel, to return the company to British and French control and terminate Egypt's embargo against Israeli use of the Suez Canal precipitated a major crisis, one that nearly became a cold-war showdown. Working through the UN, to the dismay of British prime minister Anthony Eden, Eisenhower averted a wider war. Even so, some damage had been done to U.S. standing in the Middle East, and the crisis strained Anglo-American relations.[42]

Two months earlier, as tensions mounted, Secretary Dulles blamed Nasser, who "was dreaming of a great buildup of Arab power" that would affect "the balance of power and the future of Western Europe." Dulles also thought that precipitous action by Britain and France would "open fissures between the United States and its allies."[43] He and Eisenhower feared that a lengthy confrontation with NATO allies would gravely damage the Free World's effort to contain communism. An aggrieved Eden, seeing the hand of an opportunistic Soviet Union in the region, agreed: "Alliances cannot be limited geographically in a cold war which is global . . . without danger to the whole structure of the alliance."[44] The prime minister's position reflected Britain's economic interests, which ran counter to Washington's grander plan: advancing the American Century.

As if to demonstrate the vitality of U.S. grand strategy and its applicability to the Middle East, the administration announced the Eisenhower Doctrine in January 1957. Without the Suez crisis, the doctrine might never have been possible.[45] The Eisenhower Doctrine did not exactly supplant the Baghdad Pact yet did suggest British membership in the pact had injured U.S.-Arab relations. The White House, heeding the lesson of Bandung, realized that the United States needed to appeal more to Arab nationalists. Events in 1957 and 1958 showed the unlikelihood of such a profound change. The Eisenhower Doctrine had two objectives: protecting America's allies and clients against Soviet adventurism and containing radical Arab nationalism. To achieve these goals, Washington provided conservative

Arab states with economic and military assistance. Between spring 1957 and fall 1958, the White House responded to crises in Jordan and Lebanon, sending troops into Lebanon; and it failed in a quixotic attempt to dislodge the government of Syria.[46] The latter escapade contributed to the founding in February 1958 of the United Arab Republic (UAR) by Syria and Egypt. Ambassador Charles Yost in Damascus advised caution because Washington "would be wasting its prestige . . . in openly opposing so popular a cause."[47]

The United States attempted to placate Nasser by recognizing the UAR. The promise of military assistance and over $100 million of food aid induced Nasser to tilt toward the West when the Egyptian leader became worried about Soviet meddling in Iraq after its departure from the dormant Baghdad Pact.[48] It was left to Eisenhower's successors to explore the prospects of a rapprochement. Eisenhower, frustrated with the difficulty of achieving either Arab-Israeli peace or his broader goals in the Middle East, angrily inveighed in 1959 against Arab nationalism: "If you go and live with these Arabs, you will find that they simply cannot understand our ideas of freedom or human dignity."[49] Were that true, the American Century had no future in the Arab world, and a free-world society would remain illusory.

Courting Nasser and working through the UAR only went so far. Having discarded the Eisenhower Doctrine by the end of 1958, the administration decided Nasser's fear of Israel might not be a bad thing. The genesis of intimate ties between Washington and the Jewish state, which the Six-Day War in June 1967 would affirm, resided in a program of increased arms sales.[50] Eisenhower tried to implement a policy of evenhandedness toward Arab states and Israel; he assumed that all parties would appreciate his efforts. Anxieties among Arabs came into play, however, as did Israeli ambitions and insecurity, not to mention Soviet interests. Extensive arms sales throughout the region roiled rather than calmed the troubled waters of the Middle East, leading to even deeper U.S. involvement and questions about American leadership.[51]

In the Western Hemisphere, friendly governments had not received as much military or economic assistance as they requested.[52] In late 1952, the CIA had depicted a region verging on crisis: "The immediate political trend of Latin America is toward extremely nationalistic regimes based on demagogic appeal to the depressed masses of the population."[53] Colombia, because of its involvement in the Korean War, could have been helpful. The discord of *la Violencia* after the assassination of Liberal Jorge Eliécer Gaitán in 1948, which cost 250,000 Colombians their lives and displaced 1.5 million others over ten years, precluded that possibility. Unable to help restore democracy there, the Truman administration watched as the regime of Conservative Laureano Gómez Castro alienated Liberal Party members and used the previously nonpartisan military to pursue guerrillas, often disaffected Liberals, denouncing them as Communists. Making matters worse, Gómez urged Roman Catholics to expel Protestant missionaries.[54] Colombia's value as a cold-war partner undercut nominal protests about the abusive treatment of Protestants. The CIA decried the nation's decay. An economically strong country was consuming itself to the extent that "many Liberal partisans now see their only hope in the support of the guerrillas."[55] When the military overthrew Gómez in June 1953 and brought General Gustavo Rojas Pinilla to power, agency analysts did not alter their assessment.[56]

Their concern began to erode, especially as the Rojas government involved the military in modernization activity, which enabled Washington—despite misgivings about Rojas's role in prolonging the persecution of missionaries whom he linked to communism—to mold a patron-client relationship based on anticommunism and nation-building. Ties with Colombia improved through U.S. Army, Navy, and Air Force training missions, the signing of a military aid pact, and $300,000 in internal security assistance in 1957.[57] This common ground solidified when democratic rule returned with the Frente Nacional, or National Front coalition, in 1958.[58] The change was timely. An NIE in April 1956 had noted the inability of Colombia's armed forces to defeat some six thousand guerrillas, reportedly susceptible to Communist influence, and discounted prospects for political stability: "A large proportion [of the population] is poverty stricken and illiterate. Political and economic power is in the hands of a small white elite."[59] In an effort to bring about a change after the Liberal Party's Alberto Lleras Camargo took office in August 1958, the State Department and JCS collaborated with Lleras to thwart communism and combat guerrilla forces then active in the countryside.[60]

The two countries grew closer thanks to the work of a Special Survey Team of guerrilla warfare experts, who had operated in the Philippines, Korea, and Vietnam, sent by Washington in 1959 to assess conditions in guerrilla-dominated regions. The team's report in mid-1960 focused on internal security rather than how to foster political inclusion.[61] Completed at a time when the Eisenhower administration was watching Cuba's growing influence in Latin America, the report ostensibly helped the American Century in two ways. It showed the need for U.S. leadership in the face of a potential Communist threat, namely, Colombia's leftist guerrillas, and emphasized the importance of tying counterinsurgency warfare to stability in the Free World.[62]

As in the Middle East, foreign military sales and grant programs in Latin America also provided a quid pro quo for access to the region's resources. By 1960, twelve nations had received $317 million in grants since 1952; seven others had received $140 million worth of equipment under the Mutual Security Act.[63] The disposition of strategic resources did not always turn out as Washington intended.

In oil-rich Venezuela, aid to military strongman Colonel Marcos Pérez Jiménez had opened access to petroleum reserves. A coup dissolved that cozy relationship in January 1958, soon bringing the centrist Rómolo Betancourt of Acción Democratica to power as Venezuela's duly elected leader.[64] His government returned oil to the fore of relations when the United States decided to diversify its import program because of surplus production and lower demand worldwide. This change meant a reduced market for Venezuelan oil.

Betancourt, whose politics were more progressive than Washington found desirable, saw this untimely development as a threat to his country's interests.[65] He did not directly challenge U.S. hegemony, focusing instead on Cuba's meddling in the region. The White House, with Castro in mind, resolved to work more closely with Caracas. Despite refusing to revise U.S. oil import policy, Eisenhower appreciated the larger political and economic picture, reminding the NSC in March 1960, "[We] must have access to the South American continent . . . [because] we are getting more and more to be a have-not nation as far as raw materials are concerned."[66]

Beyond the government-to-government level, U.S.-Venezuelan relations were in flux, as symbolized by Richard Nixon's stopover in Caracas during a trip to South America in May 1958, whose main purpose was to attend the inauguration of Arturo Frondizi as president in Argentina. Jeopardizing his safety, Nixon ignored warnings about trouble before departing. "Communists came back into the country in force with the overthrow of Perez Jimenez," Allen Dulles told the Senate Foreign Relations Committee on May 19. The State Department blamed anti-Nixon demonstrations at San Marcos University on students, "who appeared to be egged on by older persons." Nixon refused to alter his schedule in Caracas, convinced that giving in to threats from protestors would damage American credibility. His presence emphasized, in John Foster Dulles's words, "the special economic and strategic interests that we have there." Moreover, others in the State Department jumped at an opportunity to "concentrat[e] even more than we already are on students and other intellectual groups in our cultural and information programs." Such efforts to fuse state-to-state relations and cultural influences became highly fraught endeavors.[67]

Except for the rehabilitation of Japan and the recovery of Western Europe, the building of the Free World often lacked a substantial public economic component. Thus, the American Century could grow and prosper only with the intercession of private capital—still an unlikely prospect. This was not welcome news in Latin America, where commodity prices for agricultural products and raw materials were not sufficient to provide a modern standard of living. Nominal grant aid and soft loans from Washington provided no help.[68] Importantly, from

July 1945 to April 1955 the Latin American share of all U.S. grants and credits had not reached 2.5 percent.[69]

Latin Americans once again turned to the idea of a region-wide conference. The 1954 Rio Economic Conference had disappointed advocates of development aid in the hemisphere and in the State Department. A subsequent gathering at Buenos Aires in 1957 fared no better.[70] In fact, Secretary of the Treasury Robert B. Anderson, who led the U.S. delegation, aptly characterized Latin Americans as "feeling [like] stepchildren in the activities of the World Bank."[71] A review by the State Department captured the growing chasm between Latin American expectations and the reality of U.S. policy: "Nothing specific was agreed of any consequence at the conference."[72]

Brazil, whose economy was among the most advanced in the hemisphere, criticized the U.S. position on aid given the acute human needs.[73] In the spirit of solidarity, President Juscelino Kubitschek proposed the two nations undertake a multilateral effort, Operation Pan America, to address the situation. Economic development would be the handmaiden of Pan Americanism and anticommunism. Couched in these terms, the initiative had much to commend it, as its favorable reception in mid-1958 showed. But Brazil's economy was declining, kept afloat by strong coffee prices that were no panacea for structural problems. U.S. officials suggested a remedy of fiscal austerity and negotiations with the IMF to address Brazil's growing balance-of-payments deficit. Such a course of action would entail political difficulty for the government, however.[74]

When it came to specifics, Operation Pan America quickly stalled. At a meeting in Rio de Janeiro, Secretary of State Dulles, Assistant Secretary of State for Inter-American Affairs Roy R. Rubottom Jr., and Assistant Secretary of State for Economic Affairs Thomas C. Mann rejected the linkage between help for underdeveloped nations and U.S. security priorities.[75] Reliance on the free market for aid remained sacrosanct. Mann was blunt in assessing differences in the plans of the two countries: "The United States cannot accept the Brazilian proposals, and the problem is to resolve the issue constructively, with as little discord as possible."[76] Washington's lack of support ultimately killed Kubitschek's initiative.

The rise to power of Fidel Castro in Cuba and pressure in the hemisphere for meliorative action compelled the Eisenhower administration to admit that containing communism depended on economic well-being. Extensive prior reliance on private capital to promote development gradually gave way to recognition of the need for public funds to prime the pump of growth.[77] Although the Inter-American Development Bank (IDB), created in April 1959, did not begin operating until after Eisenhower left office, its founding indicated an awareness of the role of public financing in protecting the free-world society, reaffirming hegemony in the hemisphere, and safeguarding the American Century. In no way, though, was the IDB intended to supplant the role of private capital for development.[78]

In Asia, willing partners were crucial in order to showcase the value of belonging to the Free World under Washington's leadership. As a strategic and economic partner, Japan remained indispensable to the United States. Nonmilitary security aid reached nearly $2.5 million in FY 1958.[79] The Security Treaty of 1951 needed revising to reflect current realities in U.S. security planning. Talks began in 1958 when Kishi Nobosuke, Hatoyama's successor who had overseen economic policy in the 1930s in Manchukuo (part of Japanese-occupied China), attempted to transform the alliance into one of near equals.[80] However improbable this goal, the two nations in January 1960 signed the Mutual Cooperation and Security Treaty containing a secret codicil that permitted U.S. warships to carry nuclear weapons into Japanese ports.[81] The security pact was so disliked that it badly roiled Japanese politics. Kishi resigned in June, and Eisenhower canceled a planned visit. U.S. officials did not doubt the contentious nature of the treaty but defended it in cold-war terms: "[The] basic issue involved in [the] treaty is whether Japan stands with [the] US or is forced into neutralism and eventual absorption by Communists."[82]

The economic relationship between the two allies also experienced some rough patches but was generally positive, troubles with GATT members aside. Trade statistics underline the centrality of Japan to U.S. security policy and the American Century. Exports from the United States to Japan steadily expanded from $416.6 million in FY 1950 to $1.2 billion in FY 1957 before declining; meanwhile, Japanese imports increased from $182 million in FY 1950 to $666.4 million in FY 1958.[83] Commercial intercourse across the Pacific did not exist in a vacuum. Japan's trade with China more than tripled from a value of $19.1 million in 1954 to $67.3 million two years later—more than twice that of any other major American ally and far more than the administration had envisioned in 1954.[84] This situation gave an added urgency to trade disputes. Japan's ambassador Asakai Koichiro saw them as "the most important problems" in bilateral relations. At issue was the disposition of mutual security funds, which Tokyo wanted to use to close its dollar gap. During talks in June 1958, Asakai reminded his hosts that Tokyo was "under constant pressure to increase trade with China."[85] Japan's balance-of-payments deficit, though relatively small, was a real problem because it foretold the outflow of gold and liquid capital and a lack of commercial competitiveness if trends continued.[86] This troubling situation made it harder to expand, let alone protect, the economic side of the American Century.

Grants and credits and nonmilitary aid did buttress the security relationship with South Korea, with aid exceeding $300 million in FY 1956 and FY 1957. (Trade between the two countries, especially Korean exports, remained nominal during the decade.)[87] The NSC knew that caviling about Rhee was pointless because, as Admiral Radford put it in March 1956, "if we shut off Korea we might just as well quit our whole position in the Far East." Even allowing for hyperbole, America's client in Seoul had achieved what he set out to do: He made Washington hostage to the interests of its South Korean client.[88]

Rhee's liberal and independent opponents were dismayed when the United States stayed on the sidelines during a constitutional crisis in 1952. Moreover, the White House was slow to show displeasure when the Korean National Assembly strengthened the NSL in December 1958. The embassy explained the cost: "We run a grave risk of serious loss of influence here if ROK Government persists in enactment . . . and then 'gets away with it.'" Rhee, professing his fidelity to democratic principles, turned aside an expression of concern by Eisenhower. South Korean democracy was in limbo as the assembly unanimously voted for the NSL bill without frightened opponents present. The U.S.-Korean relationship survived, but events had again suggested that growth of the free-world society might not easily occur in troubled areas of the Third World.[89]

There exists a partial caveat to that assessment. Some highly educated students were at the center of protests when Rhee fell from power in April 1960. Their cause encompassed an amalgam of Korean-style democracy, patriotism, and postcolonial nationalism. Importantly, it showed more the lasting influence of the Bandung Conference than any lessons about democracy the AEM had tried to impart throughout the decade.[90]

As for SEATO, its founding did not greatly advance the American Century. The JCS at first opposed the idea of a military pact in Asia. Eisenhower and Dulles disagreed, convinced that SEATO would help contain China. The British wanted a regional organization emphasizing development, but that idea went nowhere.[91] Two military partners, Thailand and Pakistan, found places at SEATO's table. With the Cold War spreading throughout Asia, Washington viewed Thailand with concern. If the Thais were neutral in the struggle or, worse, became Communists, "from Korea to India, there would be no place on the Asian mainland where the United States would have an open friend and ally . . . [or] be [able] to secure such strategic materials as tin, tungsten, and rubber in their present quantities."[92] Military aid, which amounted to more than $140 million by 1956, did the trick, turning Thailand, in Dulles's mind, into the "hub" of U.S. security activities in Southeast Asia.[93] That SEATO headquarters were located in Bangkok was no accident. It was a cold-war outpost and crucial to the growth of the free-world society.

Like many others in Asia, Thai leaders had no natural affinity for democracy. Prime Minister Phibun Songgram, who held power from 1947 until he was overthrown in September 1957, had collaborated with the Japanese in World

War II. Among those with whom he worked closely were Sarit Thanarat, the army commander, and Phao Sriyanon, the national police chief. Phao was termed the "worst man in the history of modern Thailand" by the leader of the Free Thai movement in the United States during the war.[94] Despite his major involvement in the drug trade in the Golden Triangle, in the mid-1950s U.S. officials deemed Phao a dependable security asset. "He has been a strong supporter of U.S. objectives in Thailand [and] cooperated closely with U.S. agencies," insisted the State Department.[95]

The U.S.-Thai security relationship prospered after Phibun's ouster. It also put on display how cold-war priorities were impeding the attainment of goals that Luce had held dear, which included the spread of democratic ideals. In the waning days of Eisenhower's presidency, with Phao in exile and a left-leaning press rendered ineffective, Ambassador U. Alexis Johnson in Bangkok applauded Sarit's ability to temper democratic sentiments among the general populace. "Thailand," he blithely opined, "represents an especially healthy and vigorous plant in the free world garden."[96] Johnson made his remarks in an environment indicative of the tenuous nature of deference to U.S. leadership in Southeast Asia, and beyond.

Pakistan was one place where defending Western interests was inconceivable without greater military aid, which Congress and the White House were reluctant to provide.[97] CENTO, the Central Treaty Organization, established in August 1959 as a replacement for the Baghdad Pact, was no substitute for direct assistance.[98] Plagued from the outset with structural problems and lacking the capacity to become a viable alliance, CENTO could not advance U.S. objectives along the northern tier of the Middle East. America's presence as an associate member failed to rectify that situation.[99] Angered, some officials charged that Washington "treats regional members as if they are children."[100] The demise of the Baghdad Pact and CENTO's weaknesses called into question the feasibility of a system of worldwide alliances as an arm of containment and conduit for a viable free-world society. Only after the development of the U-2 spy plane in the late 1950s—and with it the prospect of using Pakistan, a CENTO member, as a launching site for flights over the USSR—did Pakistan become important to cold-war strategy.[101] Even then, Eisenhower still doubted the benefits of an alliance that precluded close relations with India.

Were Pakistan's feelings ruffled, what would be the impact on American leadership? The NSC feared a "retreat from its present anti-Communist, pro-Western policy." Solicitude for a nation lacking "basic elements of national integrity" and ruled by "an authoritarian regime under army control" bested common sense in an August 1959 policy assessment.[102] With the USSR's downing of the U-2 plane flown by Francis Gary Powers in May 1960, President Mohammad Ayub Khan (who had come to power in October 1958) questioned whether his government's security partnership with Washington was worth the high price of Soviet hostility.[103] Ayub's misgivings gave Pakistan an undeniable geostrategic importance. Less propitiously, a visit by Eisenhower to India at the end of 1959 augured well for improved relations with New Delhi, a change that blossomed after the 1960 presidential election.[104]

The Workings of Development

"America cannot be responsible for the good behavior of the entire world," Henry Luce wrote in 1941. But what was the American Century if not an effort to infuse American influence into world affairs so as to alter the behavior of people and nations?[105] Public and private officials had at their disposal resources to transform a turbulent world. Used well, these tools would bring liberal development not just to Western Europe and Japan but to places where modernity was generally lacking. When successful, development presumably would usher mostly postcolonial, nonwhite people into an American-led present.[106]

Modernization theory flourished during Eisenhower's presidency. Max Millikan and Walt Rostow of the Massachusetts Institute of Technology, its best-known proponents, often weighed in on the trade-versus-aid divide. They thought that many societies in the Third World could not absorb investment capital and that technical aid should prime the pump of development. U.S. officials assumed that what happened in Asia, chiefly Indochina, would determine whether models of liberal development could vanquish communism's appeal. The debate tilted toward aid over trade and private investment after 1956.[107]

A principal figure in this change was Clarence Randall, formerly a vocal advocate of expanding trade. His work as head of the Council on Foreign Economic Policy broadened his outlook. Instructed by Eisenhower to find a "bold new approach" to economic policy, Randall led a fact-finding mission to Asia in December 1956.[108] He concluded that outside of Taiwan and, to a degree, South Korea and Japan, "the economic picture is not bright." "Japan," he believed, "is the key to the economic development of Asia," although trade among America's friends "has not [much] developed." To improve things, trade, private investment, and joint ventures were part of the solution. Importantly, government help in the form of financially backed technical aid "can hasten the process of economic development and lay the foundation for private investment."[109] By mid-March 1957, the contours of development policy were essentially set. What remained undetermined were the immediate goals of development, the source of funds, and how development operated, especially in crucial areas like Indochina.

As the structural foundation of development took shape, Millikan and Rostow worked closely with NGOs to test their ideas. Rostow's subsequent contribution to modernization theory, *The Stages of Economic Growth: A Non-Communist Manifesto* (1960), linked development strategies and security policy. With economic, political, social, and cultural changes at hand, a new battleground in the Cold War was emerging.

President of the World Bank Eugene Black had doubts about uniting development and security. Writing to Randall in March 1957, Black wondered whether justifying aid on security grounds was wise policy: "I am convinced that economic aid can be far more effective if it is divorced from politico-military strategy."[110] Black hoped to use Bank funds to find a balance between aid and security. Echoing Rostow and, indeed, Luce, he thought that only locals imbued with Western values could serve as "apostles of a new life [who wanted] . . . a better material lot for their countrymen."[111] Thus, the Bank had difficulty finding individuals who were prepared philosophically to do its work.

The World Bank, we have seen, did not figure prominently as the administration drafted its economic foreign policy. It therefore could not fulfill its mission unless nations receiving help possessed sufficient liquidity to utilize Bank aid. When local capital complemented Bank funds, chances for development improved. Treasury officials from the United States and Great Britain met in February 1958 and debated that point. Responding to British concerns about a lack of liquidity, Secretary of the Treasury Anderson contended, "Real productive growth was much more important than the level of reserves, or the position of sterling." With the Free World undergoing an economic downturn, Sir Leslie Rowan, Anderson's counterpart, disagreed. A shortage of reserves threatened growth, he countered. Growth demanded both liberal trade by creditor nations and currency reserves sufficient "to support normal functions of the economy." Rowan asked how growth could occur when cash reserves were falling, limiting prospects for trade. Anderson's rejoinder ignored his point, focusing instead on the need to monitor Soviet aid lest it become too extensive and blaming countries, such as India, for overspending.[112]

Currency convertibility helped lessen the liquidity dilemma. The six countries making up the Common Market, plus Great Britain, moved toward convertibility in 1958–1959. Except for Britain, and to some degree France, the 1950s returned prosperity to Western Europe. Aggregate productivity increased 225 percent, exports grew from 10.5 to 15 percent of world trade, and reserve holdings leapt from 6 percent to more than 25 percent of world holdings, with Germany in the strongest position. Also, IMF quotas rose 50 percent for most member countries, and Fund lending to France, Britain, India, and Japan increased. What U.S., IMF, and World Bank officials had hoped for, the growth of regional integration in a multilateral world, verged on becoming a reality.[113] *Time* extolled the inception of limited currency convertibility early in 1959: "When the history of the 20th century is written, last week is likely to prove one of its watersheds."[114] The economic architects of the American Century, including Luce, could not have asked for more.

Unfortunately for U.S. development strategy, evidence for a vibrant American Century beyond Western Europe and Japan was disappointing. In December 1958, Treasury officials denied any responsibility for dollar shortages: "The less-developed areas of the world . . . have import demands in excess of their foreign exchange earnings. . . . The balance-of-payments difficulties of these less-developed countries and of individual developed countries like France, however, are not essentially a dollar problem."[115] Treasury viewed the issue as one of capital shortage and sought to separate mutual security programs and economic assistance from the dollar problems of recipient countries with balance-of-payments shortages.

The relatively limited flow of dollars supporting economic containment and development in less-developed nations had only a nominal impact by the late 1950s. U.S. grants and credits decreased in Southeast Asia from FY 1958 to FY 1959. Net credits fell from $16 million to $3 million in strategically crucial South Vietnam. A similar situation plagued nonmilitary mutual security assistance; South Vietnam's funded outlay slightly rose from $178.4 million to $181 million, barely a 1 percent increase. The new DLF, created to spur development, earmarked 250 percent more for the Philippines, and more for Malaya and Thailand, than for South Vietnam. South Vietnam excelled, though, in the area of military assistance. Aid delivery for FY 1959 was $74.5 million, exceeded in Asia only by funds for South Korea, Taiwan, and Japan. Meanwhile, South Vietnam's export trade, although doubling from FY 1958 to FY 1959, did not reach $11 million.[116] This pattern of aid and trade did little to affect the dollar shortage in Southeast Asia. Eugene Black had lost the argument; development and security were increasingly linked.

The World Bank, hoping to fill the void left by congressional parsimony, endeavored to promote Third World development. In 1956, it created the International Finance Corporation (IFC) to engender private investment. The IFC had thirty-one members and was capitalized at $80 million, including $35 million from Washington. With no guarantee of repayment, the IFC accounted for 3 percent of World Bank lending.[117] The International Development Association (IDA), established in 1960, held out more promise for economic growth in the world's neediest countries, those with low per capita incomes and no credit worthiness. IDA loans were to be mostly interest-free, and repayment, which often could be made in local currency, would not begin for a specified period. The White

House considered the IDA a complement to the DLF and supported the idea of a multilateral agency for extending soft loans.[118] The Senate Banking and Currency Committee applauded the creation of the IDA as a security measure: "In the face of the current Soviet economic offensive, it is more than ever important that nations devoted to liberty and individual dignity work together to help developing countries."[119] Eisenhower also found merit in the IDA because it would "help insure that the economies of the underdeveloped nations progress along with the rest of the free world."[120]

A superstructure for development was in place by the end of Eisenhower's presidency. Multilateralism in free-world trade and finance was largely established, if not fully operational. The IMF, GATT, and World Bank were key components of the American-led system. The appeal of the dollar held the system together, strengthened by the creation of Bank subsidiaries such as the IFC and the IDA. The Mutual Security Program, bilateral defense pacts, and regional alliances contributed to the flow of dollars and stability in balance-of-payments. Though long in coming, currency convertibility was a welcome development. Moreover, in the Americas, the IDB seemed poised to advance U.S. goals. The NSC believed the bank would help "influenc[e] Latin American countries to favor our policies in Cuba."[121]

For development to thrive and Washington to lead, the dollar had to remain the preferred reserve currency. There were indications of future troubles by 1958. The totality of U.S. security and financial commitments had produced a balance-of-payments deficit amounting to $5 billion in 1959, more than double the amount for any prior year in the decade.[122] Growing fears in Western Europe of a chronically weak dollar resulted in speculation against it and an outflow of gold, so much so that concern about the dollar's fate increased in 1959 and 1960.[123]

What the State Department deemed an "adverse trend in [our] balance of payments" had identifiable causes. Through 1957, surpluses in trade and services had offset capital movements and military expenditures abroad. The next year capital outflows increased primarily as a result of military costs, particularly in the NATO countries and Japan. The United States lost $3.4 billion in gold and dollar assets in 1958, whereas Western European nations took in $3.7 billion. A partial solution for the balance-of-payments deficit, which the State Department declared "cannot be permitted to continue for much longer," advocated an increase in long-term capital flows from Western Europe to developing areas.[124] Underwriting modernization was supposed to be more than an American-controlled project. West Germany, for one, was reluctant to invest heavily because the flow of funds back home would likely exacerbate its glut of reserves and therefore spark inflation. To deal with the excess, in 1960 Bonn initiated advance payments for its mutual security obligations. This maneuver did not reduce U.S. imbalances until goods were actually delivered.[125]

Given the dollar's importance, an increase in the price of gold, which remained at $35 per ounce despite climbing above $40 on the open market by November 1960, was unthinkable.[126] Eisenhower was determined to stop the loss of gold from reserves. Much was at stake. Treasury Secretary Anderson warned: "Gold activities can damage our military system and our economy as well as the world economy." And, were John F. Kennedy elected president, the White House feared a run on gold was inevitable. Eisenhower called for a balanced budget for FY 1961 and FY 1962; his advisers knew that was impossible for FY 1961. On November 16, the president issued a directive looking toward a balanced budget. He called for cuts in foreign spending and directed the ICA and DLF to "place primary emphasis on financing good and services of U.S. origin."[127] In effect, he had placed greater importance on fiscal caution than development.

These were small steps, though, that did not address the root causes of America's looming economic woes. In waging cold war, the dollar had become overextended. It alone could not bear the load of development. Moreover, the United States had accepted tariff discrimination against American goods in order to speed recovery. The fate of the multilateral world order, a staple of the American Century, remained unclear. The same can be said of containment capitalism, which had grafted security arrangements onto U.S.-led and U.S.-dominated multilateralism. Officials began to wonder whether friends and allies would take advantage of America's troubles to improve their own places in the global economy. That they did. Even though inflation had sprung from deference to U.S. hegemony, such action seemed ungrateful. Support of an overvalued dollar, officials believed, was a small price to pay for security and prosperity in the Free World. Their reasoning did little to enhance American leadership, however.

Development in practice required much more than beleaguered dollars to bind together governments and the people living under state authority. In short, it required the promise of public safety. The need to protect countries susceptible to subversion moved the ICA, which had responsibility for the Mutual Security Program, to revamp training programs in Asia and Latin America. Over six hundred police officials and twelve thousand officers had received training by the fall of 1956. Washington delivered $2.4 million worth of equipment to buttress the programs, which were often conducted by U.S. contract personnel.[128] Organizational gains resulting from these "civic action" programs were impressive. For example, some remote areas of Laos saw policemen for the first time, and Indonesia added a twenty-thousand-man paramilitary outfit to its national police force.[129]

Commencing in 1956, officials redoubled efforts to convince Latin Americans of threats from communism. The day-to-day task fell to the CIA, the State Department, and the ICA, which at times produced unwarranted perceptions of threat. In Bolivia, for instance, U.S.-sponsored security programs strengthened the military in order to control civilian militias that were doing the work of state authorities. This close connection between nation-building and internal security would be even more fully developed in the 1960s.[130] The idea of political policing as an arm of development took hold as Washington solidified relations with the military and police, despite efforts by leaders like Brazil's Kubitschek to focus on development as the path to modernity and public safety.[131]

Conditions in Indochina also argued for combining development and security. Nation-building in South Vietnam began with establishment of the Army of the Republic of Vietnam (ARVN). That endeavor, through the intercession of a Military Assistance Advisory Group (MAAG), accounted for three-quarters of U.S. foreign aid before 1961. MAAG encountered obstacles as it sought to make the ARVN battle-ready: lack of will in Saigon, minimal officer competency, and a dearth of popular support for Ngo Dinh Diem. Given the need for internal security, it would have been reasonable to focus on paramilitary action instead of conventional warfare. A newly created Civil Guard worried Diem because it promised to be a fighting force not susceptible to his control. It was never adequately prepared to fight a guerrilla war, partly because experts from Michigan State University trained the Civil Guard and national police as though they were urban, American-style police forces rather than mobile paramilitary units.[132]

Diem resisted operational renovation. Ambassador Elbridge Durbrow cabled the State Department on more than one occasion in 1960 about Diem's refusal to fashion "an over-all counter-insurgency plan." His obduracy buoyed southern insurgents, the Vietcong, against whom, Durbrow thought, an expanded Civil Guard would be more effective than conventional forces. MAAG disputed that evaluation.[133] It would be left to Kennedy's administration to try to stabilize the regime in Saigon.

Nation-building in South Vietnam fared better in the economic realm in the late 1950s, despite the modest level of nonmilitary aid. Washington's assistance brought a measure of monetary, fiscal, and commercial integrity to the economy, which helped improve a crumbling infrastructure of roads, railway track, and canals. Also, South Vietnam's agricultural sector was better off than it had been in years.[134] One urgent political and economic question was what to do about the hated agrovilles—agricultural production "regroupment centers" that Diem created in 1958. They were populated by people who had been forced from their ancestral homes to keep them away from revolutionaries. Durbrow worried about the anger of peasants who had no say in what had befallen them in Saigon's quest for security.[135] Bowing to pressure, Diem suspended the agroville experiment in August 1960. By then, the damage was substantial. His standing among the people of South Vietnam and dissident elements in the military was on a downward trajectory, as an attempted coup in November showed. Even Edward Lansdale, Diem's strongest supporter in Washington, thought he needed to "change some of his ways."[136] As bad as things were then in South Vietnam, nation-building was progressing in fits and starts. Whether it could survive Diem, the Vietminh, or the Vietcong remained an open question.

The security situation was less promising in Laos, which had the geographic misfortune of bordering North and South Vietnam. As early as 1953, Washington designated $60 million in an aid package for France to deter a Vietminh incursion into Laos to assist the Pathet Lao.[137] A mountainous land whose economy depended partly on opium, Laos was an unlikely prospect for nation-building. Especially after Prime Minister Prince Souvanna Phouma gravitated toward a neutralist posture in 1956, Laos could not be ignored in the effort to make containment global. Souvanna moved to form a ruling coalition with the Pathet Lao, led by his half-brother Prince Souphanouvong. He also journeyed to Beijing and Moscow in search of assistance.[138]

Souvanna was ultimately too clever for his own good. The Eisenhower administration persuaded him to sign an agreement accepting U.S. funds for the Royal Laotian Army (RLA); the amount totaled $300 million by 1961. In theory, Washington could have promoted nation-building by emphasizing education, road building, and agricultural projects. Instead, internal security became the top priority. Fearing further Communist gains in Indochina, there was no alternative: security came first. Eighty percent of U.S. aid for Laos in the late 1950s went to the RLA, ensuring CIA influence within the military.[139]

Political chaos, which saw one government after another fall from power between 1958 and 1960, led Eisenhower to consider military involvement. The White House lost what little faith it had in Souvanna. Yet on the cold-war battlefield that was Laos, neither superpower held an advantage. Even so, Eisenhower's lament to the NSC in May 1958 in advance of elections spoke volumes about American credibility and the electoral process and less about the virtues of nation-building: "It would be a serious matter if any country such as Laos went Communist by the legal vote of its people." In December 1960, he pondered whether to send in marines attached to the Seventh Fleet or seek international mediation between the rightist government of Phoumi Nosovan and neutralist prime minister Souvanna Phouma along with the leadership of the Pathet Lao. Something had to be done, Eisenhower and top advisers concluded, to keep the Soviets and Chinese from meddling while Washington was propping up conservative elements in the capital of Vientiane.[140] The Laotian situation Kennedy inherited in 1961 was rapidly deteriorating. He had to act decisively if containment and development were to succeed and the American Century were to take root in Indochina and elsewhere.

Power, Influence, and Credibility

American prestige did not escape unscathed between 1956 and 1960. The United States remained strategically supreme, but challenges to its leadership came from friends and allies in the Free World and from places where U.S. power and influence were not predominant. The world of the late 1950s no longer evinced the misleading simplicity of the early Cold War, and the Eisenhower administration was determined to respond accordingly. The harder that became, as exemplified by the dollar's woes and problems related to development, the more policymakers wondered about the status of U.S. leadership. That turn of events put the American Century in a vulnerable position. What had happened?

First of all, global containment lost some support in the Atlantic Community. Differences over the rehabilitation of West Germany produced "blowback" among U.S. allies. "America's political and military weight in Europe," Lawrence Kaplan explains, "stimulated European anger and resentment, which may have been expressed in sublimated form by the Anglo-French Suez invasion of 1956 and, more candidly, by France's posture during Charles de Gaulle's decade in power."[141] When de Gaulle returned to power with the inception of the Fifth French Republic in 1958, he was determined not to play second fiddle to the United States in Europe. His refusal to accept strategic inferiority sparked competition with the United States, prompting the NSC to decry "de Gaulle's intransigence" over NATO.[142] More than de Gaulle's mercurial temperament fueled the Franco-American divide. He doubted Washington's constancy toward NATO allies. Setting off alarm bells was a disagreement over Soviet policy in Berlin.[143] Having learned little from Stalin's humiliation in 1948–1949, Khrushchev issued an ultimatum in November 1958 to the British, French, and Americans. Either they accept West Berlin as a "free city" within six months or Moscow would sign a separate peace treaty with East Germany, which would then control access to West Berlin. The deadline passed and tension within NATO mounted. A clash seemed possible after the U-2 incident in May 1960 and the Eisenhower-Khrushchev summit meeting fell apart.[144]

In November 1959, calling NATO's defense posture a "particularly urgent" matter, the State Department and CIA had admitted "the U.S. balance of payments deficit and budgetary considerations confront the U.S. Government with difficult decisions on the levels of U.S. forces and military aid for NATO." Should NATO members lose their decade-long sense of security, faith in the United States as a strategic partner would decline. Washington had to maintain its contributions to NATO or damage its image. The longer officials did not respond to financial troubles, the more likely it was that changes would be necessary in U.S. defense commitments.[145] At length, the United States did keep its commitment to NATO, and European members of the Atlantic alliance tacitly accepted the costs of a weaker dollar.

Another drag on credibility emanated from South Vietnam, where nation-building had not achieved what Washington expected. Blame for this shortcoming rested with Ngo Dinh Diem and his brother Ngo Dinh Nhu, according to CIA staff historian Thomas L. Ahern Jr. Writing about agency activities in Vietnam between 1954 and 1963, he charged that Diem had "wasted the opportunity [in 1957] to begin urgent economic development programs." By 1959, at which time William Colby was serving as deputy chief of station, Diem remained "preoccupied, even obsessed, with security issues" at the expense of development. One year later, the station and Ambassador Durbrow were pressing Diem to revitalize counterintelligence activities and land reform. He resisted, telling the Americans that "the problem [of subversion] could be solved by military means" if aid increased. An impasse was in the making, with the government in Saigon alienated from its people and the insurgents preparing to take advantage of the situation. After a near mutiny by disaffected officers, George Carver and others at the station and Durbrow argued that Diem had to go. Even the optimistic Colby was disenchanted yet saw no alternative to Diem and his brother.[146] American credibility in Southeast Asia, like it or not, was in their hands.

Credibility was also buffeted in Japan, where the winds of change blew unpredictably. For Washington, Japan was indispensable to the success of the Cold War in Asia; for Tokyo, America's imprimatur meant, along with security and prosperity, revival of Japan's place as an influential player internationally. Unrest in June 1960 over ratification by the Diet of the revised mutual security treaty threatened this symbiotic bond. It also raised doubts about the growth of the Free World. At stake, in the State Department's view, was "[Japan's] future orientation and survival of parliamentary democracy."[147]

Rioting on June 15 by Communists, Socialists, and the radical student federation—the Zengakuren—against the treaty and the conservative ruling LDP made a mockery of hopes for democratization and cultural change. Crafting a strong free-world society was not easy even in a fairly advanced nation like Japan. Zengakuren was founded in September 1948 in opposition to a new educational regime for universities that had been put in place during the Occupation. Fearing a new law would suppress student activism, two hundred thousand students went on strike to protest the proposed changes. Zengakuren was positioned by the late 1950s to play a major role in demonstrations against the treaty.[148] Ambassador Douglas MacArthur II termed Zengakuren "fanatical," whereas coverage in the Japanese press was less damning. MacArthur's subsequent analysis emphasized that much still needed to be done to overcome the growing appeal of nonalignment: "[A] great majority would prefer not to have to join either

[the] free world or Communist blocs in security field and wish they could . . . sit on the sidelines without involvement in [the] superpower struggle."[149] Troubled relations with Japan impaired efforts to expand the American Century in Asia.

Doubts about the United States as a reliable partner also seeped into relations with Latin America. The concern in Washington was that if neutralism spread to the hemisphere it would "constitute a blow to U.S. prestige," so argued a seminal NSC report, NSC 5902/1, "Statement of U.S. Policy toward Latin America." Therein lay the dilemma, which the NSC addressed: What if democracy produced outcomes inimical to U.S. interests? Calls for democracy grew from rising expectations voiced "especially by the leftists and Communists." Many in the anti-Communist Left believed "the United States is, at best, disinterested in the development of democracy . . . [and] on balance favors authoritarian regimes as providing greater stability, greater resistance to Communist penetration, and a better climate for U.S. economic interests."[150]

Hoping to repair the wounds to the Pan American Community, Washington turned to the OAS, believing that it was still supportive of U.S. policy. As had largely been true in the case of Guatemala, it followed the U.S. lead and blocked Venezuela's pleas in 1959 for intervention against the Dominican Republic's Rafael Leonidas Trujillo Molina, who had outlived his usefulness to Washington because of his meddling in Venezuelan affairs. Shocking many leaders in Latin America, the State Department reversed course in August 1960 and proposed the OAS orchestrate Trujillo's peaceful removal. A fallback proposal, the rupture of diplomatic relations, garnered broad support. Some U.S. officials viewed this outcome as a precedent allowing the OAS to endorse a hard line toward Cuba.[151] Less convinced, Eisenhower told the NSC, "Until Trujillo is eliminated, we cannot get our Latin American friends to reach a proper level of indignation in dealing with Castro."[152] Not waiting for Trujillo's fall, which came with his assassination in May 1961, administration planning for Castro's ouster continued apace.

The CIA considered easing Cuba's Fulgencio Batista from power and extending amnesty to Castro and his cadres, to be followed by national elections.[153] When the revolution succeeded at the end of 1958, damage to American credibility was inevitable. The White House failed to persuade Harold Macmillan's government to stop British-owned tankers from carrying petroleum products to Cuba. Treasury Secretary Anderson exclaimed in July 1960, "The Russians are about to secure a base in the Hemisphere. . . . [It] is important for NATO to align itself with us."[154] Anderson's fear of a hostile NATO was exaggerated, but the shadow Castro cast over the Free World was real. "It is my personal opinion," wrote J. C. King, chief of the CIA's Western Hemisphere Division, "that if Castro is successful in consolidating his position and remaining in power for two more years, lasting damage may occur to the United States' already weakened position of leadership in Latin America." From the Caribbean and Central America to Venezuela, Colombia, and Peru, credible evidence indicated that Cuba intended to foment revolution.[155]

Cuba did not pose a threat to U.S. strategic might and could not undermine the power of the dollar. Any political challenge to the Pan American Community was still nothing more than an irritant. What Castro and Cuba could do, as King and others surely realized, was expose the contradictions of liberal development. Nation-building needed time and relied on the police and the armed forces to succeed, which to Cuba invalidated the idea of a "free" world and negated Washington's leadership. The Cuban threat was so alarming because U.S.-led nation-building broadly construed was, at its core, the very essence of the American Century and consequently its surest line of defense.

Importantly, young people began to doubt Washington's ability and right to lead, most ominously in Latin America. Anger had boiled over in May 1958 when Vice President Richard Nixon journeyed across South America after attending President Arturo Frondizi's inauguration in Argentina. Student demonstrators and others protested Nixon's presence in Montevideo, Uruguay; Lima, Peru; and Caracas, Venezuela, where rock-throwing crowds posed a genuine threat to his life. Nixon survived, later blaming what happened on those who were "making a profession of being a student" but were "more often than not . . . Communist functionar[ies]."[156] To be a guardian of the status quo in a world where nuclear war was thinkable and where modernization was often at odds with nationalist sentiments was to lose the battle for the hearts and minds of the young. Radicals and revolutionaries throughout the Americas found inspiration in Cuba's example, which greatly alarmed U.S. officials.[157] Nothing challenged credibility domestically more than revolutionary Cuba. Hundreds of male and female students associated with the Fair Play for Cuba Committee (FPCC) traveled there in late 1960 to show solidarity with the revolution. Moreover, African Americans, who were among the FPCC's founders, had already spent considerable time in Cuba.[158]

The Eisenhower administration sought to fortify American hegemony and expand the free-world society after 1955. Occasionally, this meant angering close allies. U.S. efforts fell short of expectations, especially in the Third World, where pursuing development and security put extensive pressure on the dollar and only partially furthered U.S. interests. That complication clouded the future of the American Century. Doubt crept into the administration's assessment of what it had achieved and fear colored its evaluation of the challenges lying ahead. This is not to argue that Eisenhower failed to sustain America's global position; rather, U.S. credibility and leadership were called into question more than at any time since 1945. If the American Century through liberal development was going to make a real difference in the lives of people beyond Western Europe and Japan and bring greater stability to the Free World as a whole, then it would be up to others to make that happen. Nonetheless, Eisenhower had managed to lead and protect the Free World in a turbulent time. Those were real, albeit limited, accomplishments. Moreover, expansion of the American Century still seemed possible in late 1960. What could not be known was that Luce's project had reached its zenith.[159]

Part 2

THE DECLINE OF THE AMERICAN CENTURY

BEARING BURDENS

John F. Kennedy's lyrical inaugural address evoked prior efforts to expand the American Century. The "celebration of freedom" brooked no limits. It was the duty of all Americans, said the youngest president since Theodore Roosevelt, "to pay any price, bear any burden, meet any hardship, support any friend, oppose any foe to assure the survival and the success of liberty. . . . This much we pledge— and more."[1] Henry Luce probably took great comfort in these stirring words, welcoming Kennedy's approach to foreign policy. As a senator, the Massachusetts Democrat was a staunch defender of the Free World and supporter of South Vietnam. Luce's endorsement of Richard Nixon in the 1960 presidential campaign was lukewarm; whatever bonds they once had were then frayed. To Luce, Kennedy would revitalize a sense of national purpose, placing the American Century in good hands.[2] The task ahead, to rejuvenate hegemony and leadership while appealing to those unconvinced of America's virtues, would be difficult for Kennedy and then Lyndon Johnson. Even so, with the security ethos deeply ingrained, officials heeded Luce's call to lead and acted to fortify the foundations of the American Century. By fall 1964, it was apparent that success was limited at best.

Turmoil and Tribulations

Kennedy's youth belied his toughness in foreign affairs. A cold warrior to the core, he cultivated an aura of being battle-tested, ready for the unexpected. Sharing that mindset, the men of the "New Frontier"—a term Walt Rostow coined—engaged the world. Before Kennedy had served seven months in office, turmoil was the norm, with Laos, the Bay of Pigs, the summit with Nikita Khrushchev at Vienna, and Berlin testing the president's mettle.

Laos seized Kennedy's attention. On the day before his inauguration, Eisenhower told him developments there could decide Indochina's fate.[3] Special assistant Arthur M. Schlesinger Jr. later recalled, because Cuba and Berlin loomed large as festering problems, Kennedy had to defuse the Laotian crisis.[4] How, he wondered, could he send troops into Laos if he was not prepared to commit U.S. forces to the planned invasion against Cuba?[5] Failure at the Bay of Pigs in April broke any impetus toward intervention and opened the door for negotiations.[6] It was not logistically feasible to resist communism in Laos. Though much disparaged, neutralist Souvanna Phouma remained an indispensable man in Vientiane.[7]

The Soviets acted to calm the crisis on April 16, when Foreign Minister Andrei Gromyko gave Britain's ambassador a proposal for a cease-fire.[8] Talks in Geneva proceeded while the Pathet Lao made limited gains. Khrushchev believed that neutrality was in the interest of both superpowers. Laos, he later wrote Kennedy, must not become an "almost permanent source of international tension."[9] After a cease-fire in May, an agreement in July called for a coalition government under Souvanna Phouma and the division of Laos into two zones, with one under Pathet Lao control.[10]

Laos was no longer a flashpoint like Berlin or Cuba. U.S. aid slowed to a trickle and stability seemed at hand until May 1962, when Laotian troops encountered Pathet Lao forces at Nam Tha near the Chinese border. The cease-fire had failed, leaving the United States with a dilemma: intervention throughout Indochina or acceptance of neutralism in Vientiane. Kennedy, mindful of what was at stake in South Vietnam, put the Seventh Fleet on alert and dispatched four thousand U.S. troops to Thailand without a request from Bangkok. He explained his decision to congressional leaders: "We are for a cease-fire now as we were a year ago and a coalition government because military action by the R[oyal] L[ao] G[overnment] seem[s] ineffective and furthermore the British and the French [will] not go along with military action."[11] Secretary of State Dean Rusk backed military action "so that we would not suffer a succession of Dien Bien Phu's [sic]." General Maxwell D. Taylor, the president's military representative, warned that U.S. credibility was at stake.[12] The crisis passed early in June when the Pathet Lao stood down and Souvanna Phouma reiterated his support for a neutralist government.[13]

The location of Castro's Cuba ninety miles from the United States presented the White House with a perilous situation. Plans under way since March 1960 for an invasion by exile forces constrained Kennedy's response.[14] Events at the Bay of Pigs in mid-April were a disaster for the White House, calling into question

Kennedy's judgment, relations with the CIA, and his personal standing in the Western Hemisphere. The State Department's review of the operation concluded: "The complete defeat of the volunteer Cuban liberation force . . . gravely damaged United States prestige."[15]

The appeal of the Cuban Revolution and Castro surged in the Americas after the Bay of Pigs. U.S. intelligence looked with alarm at Cuba's influence on students, agrarian and labor groups, and revolutionary cadres. In early 1962, anxiety about developments favorable to Cuba appeared in reports on leftist activities in Argentina, Bolivia, Brazil, Chile, Colombia, Ecuador, Paraguay, Peru, Uruguay, and Venezuela.[16] Anger about what had happened resulted in pettiness toward regional allies and fed an obsession with Fidel Castro. Brazil and Mexico were singled out for criticism, though little overt retribution occurred.[17] The administration's vendetta against Castro was another matter. Under the supervision of Attorney General Robert Kennedy and Edward Lansdale, the CIA launched a series of covert attempts to remove Castro from power, which continued until Johnson stopped them in 1965.[18]

Reactions among European allies to events in Cuba are revealing. Schlesinger returned home in early May from a trip that included stopovers in Paris and London, where he met with politicians, government officials, and prominent individuals. "I encountered everywhere," he told Kennedy, "what can only be described as a *hunger* for a rational explanation of the Cuban operation. . . . The available stories had left most people baffled and incredulous." Positive feelings toward him and "confidence in the maturity of American judgment and the clarity of American purposes" were giving way to "acute shock and disillusion."[19] Prime Minister Harold Macmillan later described the Bay of Pigs as "a staggering blow" to Kennedy's prestige.[20]

Into the breach leapt Nikita Khrushchev, ready to take advantage of Kennedy's profound sense of humiliation. In a letter to the president on April 22, he excoriated the United States for intervening in Cuba, declaring that "you lack trust in your own system." To him, Kennedy's presumption of leadership rang hollow; he exuded style, not substance.[21] The belief that the president was weak briefly served Khrushchev well, helping him forge a working relationship with Castro. As First Deputy Premier Anastas Mikoyan's son Sergo relates, the Cuban "made Khrushchev feel like a young Bolshevik again."[22]

The leaders of the two superpowers put their credibility on the line when they met in Vienna in June at the White House's invitation, hoping, wrote Ambassador to the Soviet Union Llewellyn E. "Tommy" Thompson Jr., "[the] meeting would strengthen [the] position of [the] US before world opinion."[23] Khrushchev and Kennedy could not find common ground over Berlin, where the West's right of access topped all other concerns; how to manage superpower competition in the Third World; and nuclear weapons. Khrushchev favored moving rapidly toward disarmament rather than creating an arms control regime.[24] Both men evaluated what transpired through the lens of their individual needs and interests. Khrushchev was convinced he had further legitimated the USSR's global standing but found himself enmeshed in a crisis over Berlin. How Kennedy fared depended on developments there, which were likely to intensify the Cold War— as the president, Rusk, and Assistant Secretary of State Foy D. Kohler informed Macmillan, Charles de Gaulle, and Konrad Adenauer, respectively, following the talks.[25]

Berlin exemplified the discord among Western allies. Kennedy refused to alter the nature of the occupation of Berlin, in place since 1945. His position increased Adenauer's anxiety about what Washington might do if the Kremlin and Walter Ulbricht's government in East Germany pressured the West to change Berlin's status. In briefing Kennedy about the many problems he would face, Eisenhower and Secretary of State Christian Herter had described Berlin in stark terms: "*Berlin*—This is acute and dangerous, and Mr. Khrushchev has heavy pressure to get the Berlin question settled and to stop the movement of refugees to the West from behind the Iron Curtain."[26]

The situation worsened in February 1961 when Khrushchev again threatened to sign a separate treaty with East Germany. Not until October did he change his mind; emotions ran high in the interim.[27] From Moscow to Bonn to Paris to London to Washington, officials debated Germany's future, fearing that a misstep meant war. Adenauer clung to his dream of a unified, conservative Christian land. Khrushchev and de Gaulle wanted a kind of containment, the Russian through greater autonomy for East Germany and the Frenchman through predominance in Western Europe. Macmillan desperately wanted to keep Berlin from becoming a tinderbox. He thought that "in certain circumstances" Berlin might become a free city.[28] Conversely, Kennedy and his advisers saw Berlin as a test of wills. The construction in August of the Berlin Wall, however, lessened tensions that had spiked in July when Kennedy responded to a Soviet *aide-mémoire*. Given to him at Vienna, it called for a peace treaty making West Berlin a free city. Were a pact not signed within six months, the note warned, "measures would also be taken to ensure that this status be respected by other countries as well."[29]

Was war in the offing? Kennedy's reply of July 25 was not reassuring. Several advisers including Assistant Secretary of Defense Paul Nitze and Dean Acheson, who had been included in the deliberations, wanted the president to declare a national emergency in conjunction with a military buildup. Instead, Kennedy called up reserve forces, used the draft to expand U.S. troop strength, and asked Congress to increase the defense budget by $3.2 billion. He did not renounce using nuclear weapons to defend West Berlin but made it clear that he preferred negotiation to confrontation. He told the nation on July 25: "The fulfillment of our pledge to [West Berlin] is essential to the morale and security of Western Germany, to the unity of Western Europe, and to the faith of the entire Free World."[30]

The Kremlin was only one audience Kennedy had in mind in his address. The White House did not consult allies about it, merely informing Macmillan, de Gaulle, and Adenauer by letter. Kennedy wanted support, not their advice. De Gaulle charged that talks with the Soviets were "a prelude to the abandonment, at least gradually, of Berlin and as a sort of notice of our surrender."[31] U.S. officials knew de Gaulle's views had to be managed and Macmillan's caution treated with respect. West Germany, personified by West Berlin's dynamic mayor Willy Brandt and the aging Adenauer, held the key to U.S. credibility. Brandt charged in a letter to Kennedy that inaction would convey "[a] crisis of confidence in [the] Western powers" to the advantage of East Germany. A visit by Vice President Lyndon Johnson to Bonn in mid-August papered over differences.[32]

Conflict appeared unavoidable—a point driven home in October when Soviet and U.S. tanks faced off at Checkpoint Charlie separating East and West Berlin. Meanwhile, behind the scenes the superpowers agreed to negotiate.[33] Kennedy had demonstrated sufficient resolve to allay his critics. In letters and meetings with U.S. diplomats, and in the chancellor's case with Kennedy himself, Adenauer and de Gaulle could not conceal their disappointment as the White House engaged the USSR about West Berlin and the access rights of Great Britain, France, and the United States.[34] A brooding Macmillan, who met with Kennedy at Bermuda in December, insisted negotiations precede a return to the crisis atmosphere of July through October.[35]

The year 1961 was a trying time for the administration whose leadership of the Free World remained largely intact. Kennedy learned that leadership had a cost. The price was worth paying, however, if the Free World and the American Century were to remain secure. Kennedy was nevertheless indecisive about how to implement global containment. Threatening massive retaliation was not an option because he and his advisers were unwilling to risk a nuclear exchange. National Security Adviser McGeorge Bundy, Secretary of State Rusk, and Secretary of Defense Robert McNamara opposed the first-use of nuclear weapons.[36] For his part, Rusk desired nuclear weapons in the U.S. arsenal for their deterrent effect, while fearing their deployment in Vietnam, for example, would invite charges of racially motivated usage.[37]

The administration's reluctance to place nuclear weapons at the center of grand strategy nudged it toward arms control. Ultimately, the Limited Test Ban Treaty in August 1963, which prohibited atmospheric testing in peacetime, was one result. The ban was scarcely a halfway measure; the military brass and critics in both superpowers insisted on expanded underground testing as the price for a test ban.[38] Also, efforts to prevent nuclear proliferation took some of the NSC's time that year. As National Security Action Memorandum (NSAM) 231 in March 1963 indicated, Kennedy worried about Israel's small nuclear program and its effect on the Middle East.[39] He was determined to curtail the program.[40] Such concerns made a test ban accord highly desirable; it had the potential to initiate steps toward a broad nonproliferation regime. The test ban agreement also showed that grand strategy need not preclude improved relations between the superpowers, yet Kennedy and the NSC were not prepared to jettison containment for détente.

Walt W. Rostow, who chaired the Policy Planning Council in the State Department, favored innovation in security policy. Addressing graduates from nineteen nations at the U.S. Army Special Warfare School at Fort Bragg, North Carolina, on June 28, 1961, he described the threat of guerrilla warfare to security. "It is on the weakest nations, facing their most difficult transitional moments," he explained to a rapt audience, "that the Communists concentrate their attention. They are the scavengers of the modernization process." "The whole international community [must] begin to accept its responsibility for dealing with this form of aggression," he declared.[41] Whether states would work with U.S. forces to fashion a viable path to modernization remained to be seen. Rostow outlined what was at stake in a memo after the Bay of Pigs. "There is building up a sense of frustration," he wrote, "and a perception that we are up against a game we can't handle."[42]

Rostow's 1962 treatise, "Basic National Security Policy," received extensive criticism among Kennedy's closest security advisers.[43] In fact, it identified the activities—the new flexible response—that would delineate global containment in the 1960s: covert operations, civic action under police and the military, counterinsurgency, better training for law enforcement personnel, and the merger, as needed, of CIA operations and AID programs.[44] This new iteration of global containment had two purposes: to counter Communist interests beyond the Soviet sphere and to safeguard pro-Western societies.[45]

Rostow's worldview somewhat resembled Luce's. Rostow was "deeply imbued with a relatively optimistic view of the sources of human behavior, . . . see[ing] such things as national independence, individual freedom, industrialization, high living standards, social justice, and restraint in foreign policy all fusing into one harmonious whole." So wrote George Kennan, then ambassador to Yugoslavia, in a scathing critique in May 1962. Rusk, in a Lucian manner, told another critic that "if [we] looked at the world country by country, [we] would find that most of the nations [do] in fact share our basic values, . . . that the charter of the United Nations [is] really an expression of our national goals and of the national goals of all countries."[46] What the American Century meant had become so fungible that any direction in foreign policy fell within its purview.

With grand strategy in a state of flux in 1961–1962, it was imperative to nurture the free-world society. The American Century depended on success. With the exception of France, bonds within the Atlantic alliance seemed sturdy. Mutual goals stressed anticommunism and common defense, and economic growth promised to reduce America's balance-of-payments deficits. In practical terms, the issue was whether an alliance of equal partners could exist. The White House promised interdependence, but because of their own interests, often at odds with Washington's, the British, Germans, and French found that pledge dubious. Thus, there arose competing "grand designs" for Western Europe's future, a direct challenge to the American Century.[47] Differences in the Atlantic Community implicitly tested the sinews of the free-world society. Specifically, nuclear weapons, France's place in alliance affairs, and the Cuban missile crisis revealed the limits of interdependence.

Kennedy and McNamara insisted that Washington exercise command and control over nuclear weapons. Great Britain, which previously had used its "special relationship" with the United States to justify its own costly nuclear program, objected.[48] Mindful of British determination to cling to the trappings of a great power, Eisenhower had advocated sale of the Skybolt missile, a U.S.-built air-to-surface missile in the developmental stage.[49] McNamara disagreed. At the North Atlantic Council in May 1962, he disparaged Skybolt as a weapon for which "there is likely to be no effective operational boundary."[50] Later that year, after the Cuban missile crisis and before a summit meeting with Macmillan, he recommended Skybolt's cancellation despite its probable adverse effect on U.S.-British relations.[51] Efforts to save face at Nassau by finding an alternative to Skybolt failed, leaving Macmillan furious and skeptical about Washington's good faith.[52]

McNamara opposed European nuclear programs outside of NATO's command structure, a position de Gaulle abhorred. Franco-American relations were tenuous enough over issues of importance to Paris: the timing of Algerian independence, French nuclear strength and the Multi-Lateral Force (MLF), which challenged the *force de frappe* and French influence in Europe, and Franco-German relations.[53] With de Gaulle's worldview unacceptable to Washington, he and Kennedy disagreed over American plans for the Atlantic Community.[54] Kennedy began 1963 with a review of global relationships, observing that "[some] other states are not carrying their fair share of the burden." De Gaulle, he noted, "[has] tried to restore France to a predominant position in Europe." The MLF would prevent de Gaulle from breaking apart the United States and Europe.[55]

The Cuban missile crisis tested the NATO partnership. Washington treated the crisis as if it primarily concerned the Soviets and the Americans. William J. Perry, a consultant on security issues and subsequently Bill Clinton's secretary of defense, explained what authorities were thinking, à la Luce in 1941: "At stake was civilization itself."[56] The lack of consultation during the crisis perturbed British, Canadian, French, and German leaders. A letter from Kennedy informed them of the blockade of Cuba shortly before it took effect. Prime Minister John Diefenbaker in Ottawa considered a blockade provocative and was reluctant to place his armed forces on heightened alert, having opposed the stationing of U.S. nuclear weapons in Canada. Diefenbaker, under pressure from within his government, had to comply when he learned his defense minister had approved that action.[57]

Allies supported Washington during the crisis, whose outcome earned Kennedy their genuine plaudits. Not all consequences were salutary, though. The foreign policies of France and Germany, and to an extent Great Britain, exhibited greater autonomy than before. (Disputes over Vietnam, China, and trade issues impaired relations with Canada throughout the decade.)[58] This turn of events did not bode well for solidarity in the Atlantic Community, and thus it would be up to Johnson to try to improve relations. The missile crisis was an anomaly in world affairs; the mortal danger marking the early Cold War had largely receded by then.

In East Asia in the early 1960s, Kennedy and his advisers believed that much was at stake for the Free World. They caught a break with Japan. Kishi Nobosuke's fall from power in June 1960 occurred at the outset of an economic boom. Minimizing security and defense issues, Ikeda Hayato pledged to double national income within ten years. U.S.-Japanese relations soon seemed orderly with "no burning issues," as the embassy in Tokyo put it, somehow ignoring the issue of textiles.[59] Relations with Taiwan did not proceed smoothly. To placate Jiang and his followers, Kennedy promised to veto efforts to admit the PRC to the UN, which would have put Beijing on the Security Council in Taipei's place. Nevertheless, an uneasy security relationship continued. Fortunately for Washington, events in China, from the starvation crisis of the early 1960s to the testing of an atomic bomb in 1964 to the onset of the Cultural Revolution in 1966, had the effect of keeping GMD adventurism and PRC provocation in check.[60]

Nor did conditions in South Korea enhance free-world comity. Syngman Rhee's tenure as president of South Korea ended shortly after his party rigged the March 1960 elections, which gave Rhee almost 90 percent of the vote. Student-led protests in support of democracy did not affect Seoul's political course.[61] The new prime minister, Chang Myŏn, a weak leader, could not navigate successfully between conservatives on his right and demands on his left for a rapid democratic transition. U.S. officials welcomed Chang initially but soon realized he could not contribute to stability at home or in the broader Asian region.[62]

Hence, the administration distanced itself from Chang, standing aside when Park Chung Hee led a military coup on May 16, 1961.[63] Park defined relations with Washington by the extent of U.S. aid. His desire to modernize South Korea carried the day. The United States and South Korea were on such good terms by the fall that Park visited Washington in an official capacity. Ambassador Samuel D. Berger declared that Park "represents . . . a most important stabilizing element in the [Korean] situation."[64] Even so, his ruling junta, Berger pointed out in September 1963 in words contrary to the favorable slant of his earlier cable, "is determined [to] perpetuate its power by any means."[65] Park did hold elections, winning a narrow victory. To guard against a determined opposition, he strengthened the Korean CIA, which put his foes on notice that anti-government dissent was impermissible.[66]

Radicalism was on the rise in Latin America despite the creation in 1961 of the Alliance for Progress, about which more later.[67] Beyond Europe and East Asia, the issue of Cuba greatly affected how the Free World and the American Century were faring. By its very existence, Fidel Castro's regime constituted a burden for Washington. The question "Have we determined what we are going to do about Cuba?" reverberated in NSC meetings early in 1961.[68] The State Department, anticipating "grave political dangers . . . in any overt military action not authorized and supported by the [OAS]," wanted to consult members prior to launching an attack. Adolph A. Berle Jr., who had led Kennedy's transition team on Latin American policy, dissented from that position. Berle dismissed the OAS and governments that opposed a hard line.[69] After the invasion began, the OAS could not mount a unified response. At a meeting of foreign ministers held in January 1962 at Punta del Este, Uruguay, U.S. representatives prepared a declaration that won broad support. It decreed communism incompatible with the inter-American system and excluded Cuba from OAS activities.[70] As with Guatemala in 1954, Washington had pointedly ignored the principle of nonintervention in order to shape a brittle consensus.

Kennedy had come to office believing subversion was likely in what he called "the most dangerous area in the world."[71] Rusk worried the Cuban virus would enable "communist parties . . . to establish totalitarian regimes."[72] To prevent such a development, in 1962 the United States housed in the Agency for International Development the Office of Public Safety (OPS) to train local police in internal security tactics. Counterinsurgency programs were active in Guatemala and the Andes; in FY 1963, the Military Assistance Program (MAP) in the region reached $35 million. Yet by late 1963, CIA analysts found unstable conditions in almost half of Latin America.[73] Attempts to roll back Cuban influence remained a mainstay of the defense of the Free World in the Western Hemisphere throughout Kennedy's presidency and beyond.[74]

Kennedy faced considerable obstacles in trying to strengthen the free-world society in Southeast Asia. Officials feared that Laotians were temperamentally unwilling to provide for their own defense.[75] Nevertheless, Dean Rusk wondered whether achieving neutrality in Laos might serve as an example for improving U.S.-Soviet relations elsewhere, though where he did not say.[76] Thailand and Vietnam remained crucial outposts of containment, so Southeast Asia was an unlikely testing ground for détente. Aid to Thailand supplied the majority of that nation's defense needs and met requirements for air bases as the U.S. role in Vietnam deepened. Concern about Laotian neutralism brought U.S. ground forces to Thailand in mid-May 1962, where total aid for FY 1963 exceeded $100 million.[77]

Circumstances did not ordain stability in South Vietnam. Civil war and a political system corrupted by the nepotism of the Ngo family made Saigon a weak bastion of the Free World. Kennedy stood by this difficult ally, setting the stage for escalation in mid-1965. Whether he would have ended the commitment to South Vietnam had he lived is a timeless, misleading question. The logic of containment and the search for allies led Washington to replace France as the dominant foreign power in Indochina after the 1954 Geneva Conference. Long before Diem's overthrow and assassination in November 1963, officials linked credibility to Saigon's fate and the success of containment throughout Southeast Asia. Ensnared in a cul-de-sac of their own making, they carried on.[78] They perceived tangible progress in late 1963 and early 1964, for example, when progress was ephemeral given the fluid political and military situation in South Vietnam.[79] To do otherwise would expose as false their determination to lead, their fidelity to the security ethos.

Although not ready to abandon its Saigon ally, Washington sought a reliable client in Southeast Asia. Indonesia had the potential to fill that role despite its previous neutralism. Relations had become stormy after Bandung when the Eisenhower administration courted Sukarno to little avail.[80] His independence and solicitude for the Indonesian Communist Party (PKI) infuriated the White House. Sukarno was Nasser-like in obtaining aid from both the Americans and the Soviets, which exasperated U.S. authorities. In early 1957, the CIA feared Indonesia was about to sever its ties to the Free World. The upshot was encouragement for anti-Sukarno sentiment among sectors of the military outside of Java.[81] In Kennedy's final year as president, Washington again sought to break the PKI's strong influence in Indonesian politics. The NSC's Robert W. Komer compared Sukarno to Nasser and counseled, "We simply have to sweat him out."[82] That effort to fortify the Free World proved unavailing. A frustrated Kennedy suspended delivery of some financial aid shortly before his assassination.[83]

U.S.-Indian relations reflected Washington's suspicion of nonalignment and its desire to usher New Delhi into the Free World. At the same time, officials could not ignore security ties with Pakistan.[84] Kennedy, who showed an affinity for India while in the Senate, linked prestige to good relations with the world's largest democracy. He proposed an aid package of $500 million for FY 1962, $100 million more than was planned for the rest of the world.[85] If he could not convince Prime Minister Jawaharlal Nehru to forsake nonalignment, he hoped India might adopt anti-Communist neutrality.[86] Nehru refused to do so until war flared with China in October 1962 during the Cuban crisis. Before then, he had turned to the USSR for military aid while looking to the United States for economic help.

Even before the clash with China and India's acceptance of military aid, Komer predicted Ayub Khan will conclude "we are shifting to a pro-Indian stance. . . . [And] we are."[87] Striking a balance between India and Pakistan was difficult despite efforts to convince both that they had a role to play in containing communism. Attempts to broker a settlement of the Kashmir dispute failed, even as efforts to transform India's neutralism persisted.[88] Authorities in Pakistan told Undersecretary of State George Ball in fall 1963 that their strongest weapon against India was to pursue normalization of relations with China. An alarmed Ball reminded his hosts of the U.S. commitment to Pakistan's security despite America's friendship with New Delhi. Were Pakistan to approach China, he warned, "it would inevitably require . . . a very close re-examination of US-Pak [sic] relations."[89] In reality, Washington had few cards to play.

The Middle East offered little fertile ground for the free-world society. In the northern tier, Turkey and Iran were like earthen dams slowing the onrush of communism as radicalism seeped into the area's lower reaches.[90] Kennedy adopted a multilayered approach. He assumed the USSR would not make inroads because its major interests lay elsewhere. Also, Moscow's inconsistent relationship with Nasser and radical Arab states indicated that communism held limited appeal in largely Muslim lands. NIE 36–61 in June 1961 explained: "The inherent incompatibility between ultimate Soviet ambitions in the Middle East and the aspirations of Nasser and the Arab nationalists . . . will become increasingly manifest."[91] This assessment did not necessarily lead to productive policymaking. The White House found itself juggling cold-war security concerns, economic interests, tensions between radical and conservative Arabs, and Arab-Israeli relations. Stability was the watchword, yet stability was a rare commodity that inexorably drew Washington into the vortex of regional events.

Saudi Arabia was not as reliable a strategic partner as Iran, yet both countries clamored after a larger share of U.S. military and economic aid. As King Saud told Kennedy when they met in January 1962, his was "a relatively backward country" badly in need of outside help.[92] Thereafter, the United States monitored Saudi Arabia's progress toward modernization, but at Rusk's behest ceased promoting reform in the kingdom.[93] Had there been a serious Communist threat, the Saudi monarchy likely would have gotten the formal security agreement it desired. Officials, often striking an alarmist tone, warned their American counterparts about what they saw as Communist advances, notably in Egypt after Nasser began meddling in South Yemen in the fall of 1962.[94] The State Department ridiculed as "childish spitefulness" Saudi Arabia's irritation at American attempts to improve relations with Cairo.[95]

In Iran, the administration found no alternative to the shah. A State Department report warned, "Iran's formal alignment with the West is popularly regarded as the Shah's personal venture, and he is judged by its consequences." Washington had reason to doubt the shah's leadership.[96] A political crisis in May 1961 led to the formation of the multiagency Iran Task Force.[97] A policy review in September lamented, "Iran is not in good health. The U.S. will have to slowly nurse it along, but . . . Iran is worth [it]."[98] That endeavor was ongoing as the reformist White Revolution began in early 1963.[99] Ambassador Julius C. Holmes argued from Tehran that not until Iran's military was satisfied with the extent of U.S. aid would nation-building actually take hold.[100]

Holmes's point encapsulated Washington's dilemma: how to transform the interests of individual governments into building blocks of the Free World. Paradoxically, the occupant of the Peacock Throne owed his position to the great diversity of Iranian politics and society. In supporting the shah, Washington gambled on his ability to control dissent, which he did through his intelligence service, SAVAK. A visit by Vice President Johnson in August 1962 evidently sped reform. Johnson advised Kennedy, "We must accept the Shah, with his shortcomings, as a valuable asset."[101] With the free-world society and, thus, the American Century so tightly bound to Tehran, officials were walking a high wire in their client state. Conservative Muslim clerics, including Ayatollah Ruhollah Khomeini, opposed the shah's actions.[102] The State Department and CIA welcomed the White Revolution, praising it as "a reform program which is drastically and irrevocably altering . . . Iran." Their analysis had to hearten proponents of nation-building despite the alienation of traditional religious, landed, and wealthy elites. In 1963 and after, that cost seemed acceptable because opposition to the shah was not cohesive.[103]

Iraq, Syria, and Egypt were unlikely to bolster the cause of the Free World in the Middle East. Colonel Abdel Karim Qassim took over in Iraq in 1958, at times turning to Moscow for aid. Caught off guard when Iraq did not join the UAR, the White House wondered how Qassim would handle foreign concessionaires in the Iraq Petroleum Company and Kuwait after Britain ended its protectorate in 1961; he nationalized oil fields in December. After he tacked leftward again in early 1963, anti-Communist Ba'athist officers overthrew and executed Qassim. The NSC reacted in cold-war terms.[104] Komer called it "almost certainly a net gain for our side." Another coup in late 1963 underlined Iraq's volatility. Washington tried to return Iraq to the Western orbit with economic aid; the results were partly successful until the Six-Day War and the entry in July 1968 of the anti-Western Ba'athist, Saddam Hussein, into Iraqi politics.[105]

Syria was no more inclined than Iraq to align with the Free World despite its defection from the UAR in September 1961. The seizure of power by a right-wing junta "is not necessarily in the U.S. best interest," concluded the State Department, fearing Nasser's embarrassment would harm incipient overtures to Cairo.[106] A patchwork modus vivendi accomplished little because of Saudi fears and distrust of the Egyptian leader.[107] A subsequent change in power in March 1963 turned Syria back toward Egypt, spelling trouble for America's friends including Jordan, Saudi Arabia, and Israel. CIA chief John McCone expressed his concern about Washington's lack of influence to Johnson in early December shortly after Kennedy's assassination.[108]

From early in his presidency, Kennedy reached out to Africa to preserve containment. The best-known example of U.S. interest in independence movements came from Congo, formerly Belgian Congo. The Eisenhower administration became involved in events in January 1961 that resulted in Prime Minister Patrice Lumumba's assassination.[109] Eisenhower desperately wanted to get rid of the man whom he vilified as an African Castro. Revealingly, Khrushchev later insisted to Llewellyn Thompson that "Lumumba was not Communist," nor would he have become one.[110]

The Kennedy White House shared many of the Eisenhower NSC's assumptions about Africa. Newly independent states, thirty of which joined the United Nations between 1957 and 1963, were not to be trusted in international affairs. Coming from a colonial past, they did not see communism as a dire threat, which often led them to embrace nonalignment. Therefore, the continent merited close watching. In practice, Kennedy turned to a kind of engagement and endeavored to establish personal relationships with Africa's nonaligned leaders.[111]

Kennedy believed he understood the complexities of modern Africa. With France the exception, he hoped not to anger NATO allies that wanted to maintain dependency relationships with their subjects or former subjects; he sought to put Washington on the side of nationalism and planned to nudge South Africa, with its abundant natural resources, away from apartheid without resorting to a trade embargo or mandatory sanctions. In fact, he treated South Africa with "constructive engagement," as it became known in the 1980s.[112] The Sharpeville Massacre in March 1960 and South Africa's withdrawal from the British Commonwealth in fall 1961 did not impair relations. Though disdaining apartheid, the United States never seriously considered halting lucrative trade and investment. Moreover, domestic dissent was generally unknown in the West, with leaders of the African National Congress, such as Nelson Mandela, in

jail or under detention.[113] At length, South Africa's strategic value made puni-
tive sanctions unthinkable.

Africa had rarely been important to U.S. security planning. As nationalist
movements emerged after Ghana's independence in 1957, that situation changed.
Sensing communism's growing appeal, Washington overreacted with quasi-
apocalyptic scenarios. In a meeting with British and French officials in April 1959,
the State Department's Robert Murphy declared that Soviet control of North
Africa "would outflank Europe and it was doubtful whether the free world
would survive such a disaster." Because "Africans were on the whole immature,"
it was hard for "leaders who were Western-minded to keep their followers on the
right path."[114] In short, undiluted nationalism left Africans susceptible to Moscow's blandishments. Seeking to keep radicalism at bay, Kennedy expanded economic aid, civic action programs, and selective training of the police and military.
Where feasible, particularly in central Africa, he extended support to antiguerrilla
operations.[115]

Until an assassin's bullet felled him, Kennedy sought to bring stability to the
free-world society and expand it geographically. The job was never going to be
easy, and reluctance to consult with allies during crises made it more difficult.
Beyond Western Europe and East Asia, willingness to follow U.S. leadership in
turbulent times fell short of what Luce had anticipated in 1941 or what policymakers had worked for since 1945. Ascending to the presidency, Lyndon Johnson pledged to continue his predecessor's foreign policy. In so doing, he displayed
the same cold-war mentality and hubris that Luce admired in Kennedy.

Johnson still saw communism as a relatively undifferentiated threat, which
aligned him with Walt Rostow, who in September 1963 had produced an analysis of "the state of the world." Rostow wrote about fissures on both sides of the
Iron Curtain, the easing of tensions with the USSR after the Berlin and Cuban
crises, the Sino-Soviet split, and the general "reduction in fear of communism"
around the globe. Because "the situation poses for us the danger of diluting the
unity of the Free World," the need for vigilance was great. The surest response to
the dangers of communism was to employ U.S. military personnel "in parts of
the world which are inherently explosive if left to themselves." Here Rostow had
in mind Korea, Southeast Asia, the Indian subcontinent, the Middle East, parts
of Africa, Latin America, and Germany.[116] His call to arms was a tall order in a
diffuse world. It was one that Johnson responded to as he sought global stability,
credibility, and a resilient American Century.

The president's perspective on the state of the world reflected how global containment still defined grand strategy. Johnson was no more convinced of the util-
ity of offensive nuclear weapons than Bundy, McNamara, Rusk, or Kennedy.[117]
Like them, he highly valued deterrence. Ironically, the diffusion of national in-

terests, over which Rostow anguished, led Washington to contain, as it were, certain allies. For instance, Johnson sought to monitor British foreign policy so that London's global economic role would endure. He dealt carefully, too, with de Gaulle's threat to NATO unity through France's nuclear arsenal, the *force de frappe*. Also, West Germany earned Johnson's attention because of its ties to Paris and Bonn's concern over what improved Soviet-American relations portended for Europe.[118] In the Middle East, Johnson worried about the destabilizing effect of Israel's nuclear program as he juggled competing U.S. interests.[119]

In October 1964, Johnson was less than one month away from being elected president when two momentous events occurred. The Presidium ousted Nikita Khrushchev from power, and the PRC conducted its first atomic test.[120] As if in reply, Rostow, still at the State Department, perceived a threat to Washington's leadership. "Every region on the planet is now part of a sensitively interacting world community," he argued, seeking to bolster the Free World against communism.[121] Johnson attempted to do just that until Vietnam destroyed his presidency and sealed the fate of the American Century.

Economic Hegemony under Duress

The hegemonic bent of containment capitalism was hard to sustain in the 1960s. As one scholar notes, the "U.S. balance-of-payments position was the dominant issue of international monetary politics from 1958 to 1973."[122] Although doubts arose about America's leadership, economic hegemony essentially held until the gold crisis of spring 1968. The administration crafted its economic policy to spur growth at home and make multilateralism workable globally. Kennedy's underlying assumption was that growth would solve problems ranging from sluggish trade to balance-of-payments deficits. His immediate goals were to slow the movement of capital and retard the outflow of gold. The Trade Expansion Act of 1962, whose tariff reductions to boost agricultural exports were feasible only with Britain in the EEC, and the Kennedy Round at the GATT revived U.S.-led multilateralism. Also, Kennedy proposed a tax cut, which became law in 1964, to hasten domestic growth.[123] What continued to constrain Kennedy's plans was the weak dollar.

The importance of restoring confidence in the dollar was central to Eisenhower's talks with Kennedy in December 1960.[124] Kennedy acted quickly; he urged allies to share the costs of their own security and contribute more to global aid programs, and pushed them to invest dollars in America. Cutting military expenditures was not risk-free. At stake was containment itself. "Unless we do better," Secretary of the Treasury C. Douglas Dillon warned in mid-March 1961, "I fear that public pressure for the reduction of our forces overseas will again emerge."[125] Over the next year, the balance-of-payments situation worsened. Positive change was elusive, based on the prepayment of obligations, or offset payments, by NATO partners and active participation of other currencies in IMF operations. Moreover, American trade did not expand sufficiently to alter the overall payments imbalance. As if in testimony to faltering confidence in U.S. policy, the outflow of gold reserves accelerated.[126]

The flight of gold tore at the fabric of the free-world society, whose raison d'être was stability for Western Europe and other security partners. A leading scholar of gold and the Cold War finds, "The countries that benefited most from American protection—France and West Germany—pursued policies that ran counter to U.S. economic and strategic interests."[127] To address that situation, in February 1963 Kennedy had his national security team monitor the gold- and dollar-related activities of America's allies. William McChesney Martin Jr., chair of the Federal Reserve System, told the president that restricting gold outflows impaired U.S. leadership and the future of multilateralism. Kennedy confidant and ambassador to India John Kenneth Galbraith feared that the United States could maintain credibility only by borrowing, which meant "we will have the economic and political weakness of a debtor nation."[128]

In the short term, the White House protected gold reserves and buoyed confidence in the dollar. An informal gold pool in London ended gold speculation, and borrowing by the United States in foreign currencies slowed conversion of unwanted dollars into gold. Closer cooperation with European financial ministers also lessened pressure on gold. Dillon still felt compelled in December 1963 to tell President Johnson that, for things to improve, "it is essential that the $1 billion annual saving in government spending overseas be achieved as scheduled by the end of next year."[129]

Waging cold war had made American products less competitive. As Japan and Germany modernized their manufacturing sectors, the United States emphasized defense production and fell behind in marketing consumer durables, thus worsening payment imbalances. American firms—intending to take advantage of tax breaks and avoid local tariffs—established branches abroad, especially in Europe. Similarly, American banks expanded foreign operations, which, though profitable, exacerbated the payment troubles. Had the United States in the early to mid 1960s devalued the dollar, governments in Europe and Asia would likely have followed suit.[130]

Dollar devaluation carried the risk of undermining U.S. leadership because a loss of confidence in the dollar would follow devaluation. At a meeting with McGeorge Bundy and Dean Acheson in February 1963, Kennedy discussed limiting private investment abroad through the taxing power or, failing that, by raising interest rates to keep capital at home. The latter stratagem, he worried, might retard domestic growth.[131] Even a revaluation of West Germany's deutsche mark and greater capital exports by Bonn did not guarantee improvement. Dillon identified the crux of the problem as "our non-trade international outlays, and the largest of these were our military expenditures abroad."[132] Germany and, to an extent, Japan and France held the fate of containment capitalism in their hands.[133] The administration attempted in late 1962 and throughout 1963 to foster economic burden-sharing. Discussions with German officials showed reluctance on Bonn's part to spend as much on military preparedness as Washington sought. This hesitation limited the impact of offset arrangements on the dollar. Meanwhile, the gold drain continued, with France among those exchanging the most dollars for gold.[134]

The White House, suspicious of the French and the Germans, watched with unease as the two nations drew closer together. A Franco-German accord could weaken NATO and serve as a quasi alternative to U.S. hegemony. West Germany's economy was thriving, and de Gaulle was prepared to use monetary policy to gain an advantage over Britain and America. At length, the pact, signed in January 1963, was not as divisive as Washington feared. The administration worked with Vice Chancellor Ludwig Erhard to insert in the treaty a preamble in support of the Atlantic Community. When Erhard became chancellor in October, the White House assumed that U.S.–West German relations were better than at any time since the building of the Berlin Wall.[135] Bonn's ongoing concern about the U.S. payments deficit and its less than full commitment to a multilateral order indicates otherwise.[136]

Dillon reminded the president in February 1963, "The sine qua non of all international monetary dealings . . . is that no country can consistently run a large balance-of-payments deficit."[137] A visit by Kennedy to Germany in June improved the chances that Bonn would fulfill its offset obligations and signified changes in the balance-of-payments deficit through an interest equalization tax on capital borrowed in America.[138] What the administration could not surmount was the weak dollar. Allies were betting, erroneously, that Washington would not initiate an inflationary cycle. By mid-decade, though, the costs of involvement in Indochina were stoking inflation and deepening America's payments deficits. Complicating things was the outflow of capital in conjunction with the growing operations of multinational businesses.

Policymakers initially addressed the payments issue by focusing on foreign aid. By mid-March 1962, Dillon was questioning the extent of AID funding to Africa and Latin America.[139] Dillon's conservatism conceivably meant trouble for the Alliance for Progress, Kennedy's signature initiative. He set a goal for growth at 2.5 percent per capita per year, hoping the real figure would be twice that.[140] With private investment not a realistic option, the White House turned to development funds channeled through AID. Kennedy told his economic policy team in February 1962 that "the fate of the whole aid program rests on the success of the Alliance for Progress and that [its] operations and activities . . . should be given the highest priority."[141]

The ever-cautious Dillon warned Kennedy that AID commitments "cannot be allowed to increase . . . if our foreign assistance operations are to bear their fair share of the burden involved in reaching a balance in our payments."[142] Public assistance for Latin America was not extensive compared with European recovery. Also, the projected $20 billion of international and U.S. funds never reached that amount because Latin Americans had to repay pre-1961 loans along with debts incurred during the Alliance decade. At most, the Alliance expended about $4 per Latin American per year.[143] (Bevan Sewell shows that, by the end of Kennedy's presidency, private capital was replacing Alliance-based funding as the primary engine of development.)[144] In any event, officials doubted that Latin Americans possessed adequate financial expertise to oversee local capital disbursements.[145] One of the main issues the IDB, for instance, struggled with was how its activities affected bond ratings in capital markets, where less than a triple-A rating spelled trouble. In fact, maintaining strong credit ratings, one scholar has noted, "militat[ed] against policy changes regarded as desirable from the point of view of development." Soft loans to developing areas, therefore, were often anathema in the financial world.[146]

Such concerns slowed disbursement of IDB funds in 1962, threatening to curtail the reach of the Alliance from the outset.[147] At that time, as Latin American states were slowly becoming integrated into the worldwide economic and financial system, portfolio investment was selective because of corporate fears of more Cuban-style expropriations. Whereas petroleum and mining previously had been the primary targets for investment, trends favored manufacturing in the early 1960s, which accounted for 90 percent of investment.

The World Bank and the IDB did increase lending in the Americas during the 1960s. The former extended nearly $3 billion compared with $1.2 billion from 1945 through 1960; for its part, the IDB loaned nearly $3.5 billion. Moreover, Latin Americans had access, often indirectly, to capital markets in the United States as a result of bonds floated in New York by either the World Bank or the IDB. Also, branch banking grew from 57 outlets in 1960 to about 150 ten years later. First National City Bank and Bank of America led the way, along with Chase Manhattan. Where branches were illegal, so-called representative offices sprang up. The growth of banking closely paralleled the coming of multinationals, which preferred to deal with familiar North American financial institutions than with lesser known local ones.[148]

The role of multinationals as agents of the economic American Century was, in a word, paradoxical. Robert Gilpin contends that official thinking in the 1960s reflected "an enhanced perception of the importance of MNC [multinational corporation] earnings as a means to finance hegemony." Foreign-based businesses, however, were sending home more in profits, royalties, and fees than they invested abroad. (Not surprisingly, Middle Eastern petroleum became the most lucrative and safest investment.) Henry H. Fowler, Johnson's secretary of the treasury, viewed the MNC positively "as an essential instrument of strong and healthy economic progress through the Free World."[149]

However accurate Fowler's assessment, the goals of MNCs were not necessarily compatible with an American-dominated economic order, which put further pressure on the dollar and weakened U.S. leadership. Specifically in Latin America, where the Kennedy administration was willing to incur payments deficits in order to advance development, MNCs were not disposed to become compliant partners.[150] Questions of risk, trust, and self-interest limited their willingness to further hegemony and, by implication, the advance of the American Century. Also, MNCs did not bring a comparative advantage to their host countries; they tended to buy local manufacturing concerns rather than provide capital to create new businesses. In the aggregate, the value of exports declined in the Alliance decade, worsening regional balance-of-payments deficits. External debt doubled, and tax policy, which in effect subsidized a nascent MNC presence, was not really conducive to modernization.

The cost of living rose in Argentina, Brazil, Chile, and Colombia, nations that the United States expected to serve as models of development. Venezuela and Mexico escaped inflationary pressures because foreign exchange earnings facilitated national planning without overreliance on MNCs. Growth was neither predictable nor systematic throughout the decade. Not until the late 1960s would private direct investment begin to reach Latin America in amounts sufficient to attack cycles of debt and dependency.[151]

Devoted more to their own interests than American hegemony, MNCs were risk averse, whereas proponents of hegemony through capital markets and trade liberalization had to take risks if they were to prevail in the economic Cold War. Unfortunately for the administration, the year 1963 was a poor time for risk. Any hope the payments imbalance would soon lessen was fanciful. Suspending capital exports would have altered a basic pillar of economic policy. The same held true for measures affecting trade, particularly with Common Market countries whose tariffs made extensive trade expansion unlikely. A proposed reduction of U.S. troops in NATO countries promised scant change in these conditions.[152] By late 1963, signs of a better future were few, which Dillon detailed in reviewing economic conditions for President Johnson.[153]

Ultimately, Kennedy's economic policies did not substantially advance his mul-tilateral agenda.[154] Frustration in Washington abounded; the government had spent two decades building international economic stability and creating the conditions for long-term prosperity. Yet, those efforts were no longer enough to ensure lasting hegemony. Without the presence of imminent cold-war threats, containment capitalism seemed more like a brake on growth and development than an engine. All of which, including the status of the dollar and its linkage to the price of gold, signaled that trouble lay ahead for U.S. leadership and the American Century.

Lyndon Johnson's options were limited in the early months of his presi-dency. Events turned his attention to Western Europe, where he tried to head off challenges to U.S. monetary policy by proposing that central banks of major participants, including Great Britain, increase their IMF quotas by 50 percent. Doing so would enhance global liquidity and relieve pressure on the dollar. Also, the Fund would be able to increase its activity in the less-developed world, a move consistent with the goals of containment capitalism. An increase in liquid-ity, however, could place undue pressure on existing dollar reserves—hence the need for elevated quotas, especially if the United States reduced its payments imbalances. One nagging fear, expressed by Johnson's Task Force on Foreign Economic Policy in November 1964, was that "large scale conversions of dollars into gold . . . would not only diminish the gold reserves of the U.S.; they would also reduce the total world stock of reserves, since the converted dollars would simply disappear from international use."[155]

The head of the task force, Carl Kaysen, a deputy special assistant to the presi-dent for national security affairs, surmised that the eclipse of the dollar was precisely what France wanted so as to strengthen Paris's financial and commercial standing. In fact, France briefly favored the creation of a Collective Reserve Unit (CRU) that was not susceptible to the needs of the Fund or U.S. monetary policy.[156] French of-ficials would not accept more than a 25 percent increase in IMF quotas, yet by the time de Gaulle in 1965 declared his position on the dollar and gold, the CRU had been all but forgotten.[157] Franco-American bickering did not improve the liquidity, or access to the Fund's reserves, of less-developed countries. Kaysen's group noted: "They will be excluded from the decisions of a rich country's club and from their fruits. . . . The development of monetary institutions in which only rich countries participate has already aroused some suspicion and resentment on the part of the other 92 members of the Fund."[158] The dollar could not change things on its own, which underlined the need for a stable pound to assist the IMF.

The administration courted Labour Party Prime Minister Harold Wilson, who came to power in mid-October 1964. Ambassador David K. E. Bruce warned that, like his Conservative predecessors, Wilson would not curtail Britain's overtures to the Soviet Union, China, and Cuba for cordial relations. He would, however, support "those essential policies requiring agreement between our two countries. . . . We will not find him impervious to reason, but will discover he is skeptical of some of our cherished political, economic, and military beliefs."[159] At the outset of his tenure in office, Wilson attempted to bolster Britain's economy through a series of temporary nationalist measures, including a surcharge on imports other than foodstuffs and basic raw materials. He also moved to shore up the pound by using Britain's drawing rights at the IMF. Cautious and pragmatic, Wilson informed Johnson that "we consider [these measures] essential if we are to have a strong economy as a basis for playing our proper part in international affairs." Johnson accepted Wilson's logic and linked defense of sterling to the well-being of the Free World.[160]

Wilson's defense of the pound quickly failed—as seen in November's run on sterling—and led to an appeal for intervention in order to forestall devaluation. Grudgingly, the Johnson administration put together a $3 billion aid package with the help of West Germany. In effect, the loan was part of what Chairman of the Council of Economic Advisers Gardner H. Ackley had in mind when he informed Johnson during meetings with Wilson in December: "*We should continue to underline to the world our determination to protect the dollar* at all costs."[161] What was unknown was the effect such action would have on Washington's economic leadership.

The Travails of Nation-Building

Authorities thought they could eventually make development democratic, one of Luce's goals, by applying a mix of force and favor. Speaking at the United Nations, Kennedy declared the 1960s a "Decade of Development."[162] Few characterized this hubris as cogently as Senator J. William Fulbright (D-Ark.), who counseled, "We must continue to do what we can . . . to improve the chances of peaceful and democratic social revolution in the underdeveloped world. We would do well, however, to stop deluding ourselves about the likelihood of success."[163] Such cautionary sentiments did not impress the New Frontiersmen, who embraced nation-building as a defense against Communist revolution. Arthur Schlesinger, reporting on his fact-finding mission to Latin America in February and March 1961, informed the president that orderly change would not come easily because of existing economic structures, not because of Cuba's influence. "*Time is running out for the parties of middle-class revolution*," he warned.

Younger intellectuals, Schlesinger found, were impatient with the United States, fearing "that we plan to keep Latin America in perpetual colonial servitude." The key to development was education. Barely 40 percent of Latin Americans were literate; only one-half of school-age children ever attended school, and half of those dropped out. It was impossible to envision social change under those conditions.[164] Influencing the politics and values of students in the near term remained as unlikely as it had been following Nixon's controversial trip in 1958. In Asia, too, prospects for orderly development were unclear, notably in South Vietnam and Laos. Nothing short of dramatic action was called for. Like Henry Luce, administration officials saw the world, writes Michael E. Latham, as "eager to learn the lessons only America could teach."[165]

The ICA had assumed that market forces, along with dollops of U.S. aid, would provide the requisite tools for modernization. The AID advocated a proactive approach to nation-building. As operations began in October 1961, the White House imagined AID as a dynamic arm of foreign policy. AID's mission was more ambitious than the ECA's had been. AID presided over technical aid, lending programs, development projects, and military assistance, which were designed to enable countries to achieve order through growth.[166] Created in August 1962 by NSAM 177, AID's Office of Public Safety would act where there existed a "potential threat of internal subversion" by giving "increased emphasis to the police aspects of existing MAP programs."[167]

Walt Rostow's recommendation about AID's role was blunt: counter neutralism in the developing world by creating "a long-term dependence on the West."[168] AID determined whether recipient countries were attuned "to the vital economic, political and social concerns of [their] people." If not, then emergency aid could be provided only to address "over-riding military or political problems."[169] The New Frontiersmen viewed AID as aligning "the US with the forces for social and economic progress in the less developed countries."[170]

AID, of course, was not the whole story of nation-building under Kennedy. Other major programs included Food for Peace, under the guidance of George McGovern, which derived from Public Law 480 (P.L. 480) as enacted by Congress in 1954; the Peace Corps; and the Alliance for Progress. P.L. 480 formed the heart of food policy in India for several years. While in the Senate, Kennedy saw food aid to India as a means of enhancing U.S. influence.[171] As president, he used agricultural assistance to lessen Prime Minister Jawaharlal Nehru's neutralism. The two men held unproductive talks in November 1961, at which Nehru objected to U.S. policy toward Berlin and Vietnam and disagreed over atmospheric nuclear testing.[172]

Nehru and Kennedy did agree, though, when it came to the Peace Corps and the fourteen hundred Peace Corps volunteers who by 1968 had lived and worked in rural India.[173] Ted Sorensen, a confidant and speechwriter, called the Peace Corps Kennedy's "proudest achievement . . . and an important new instrument to communicate to other countries the best of American values." Schlesinger described the Peace Corps in less altruistic terms. It was a modern iteration of the *"mission civiliatrice [sic]* . . . [that] sent thousands of westerners to the ends of the world in the hope of doing good, from missionaries and administrators in earlier times to the Peace Corps today."[174] Luce doubtless would have concurred with these sentiments.

The Peace Corps enhanced America's global image, unlike the Alliance for Progress. Stephen G. Rabe posits, "The Alliance failed to reach any of its ninety-four numerical goals in health, education, and welfare."[175] Why? As a strategy for nation-building, liberal development faced real limits. Revolution posed a direct challenge, for one. Existing structures of political, military, and economic power would not easily bend to Washington's will.[176] So certain was Cuba of the Alliance's inevitable failure that, at the founding of the Alliance at Punta del Este, Uruguay, in August 1961, Ernesto "Che" Guevara welcomed the Alliance, believing that Latin America's oligarchs and armed forces would never support it.[177]

The future of nation-building was at stake in the conflict with Cuba. Kennedy realized that without popular support, nation-building might be curtailed by a penurious Congress or by the very countries targeted for modernization. Therein lay a dilemma for liberal development. If Washington moved quickly to promote modernization, it ran the risk of alienating entrenched interests; yet if the United States moved slowly, the appeal of revolution would grow. If regional leaders rejected the case for nation-building, the State Department's Policy Planning Council warned that "demands for economic and social reform might even be counterproductive."[178]

A chance to showcase nation-building unexpectedly developed in South Korea. Park Chung Hee, though known to U.S. officials in Seoul, remained a political enigma despite his anti-Communist credentials. Most important to Washington was whether Park could guarantee stability and improve relations with Japan while providing "economic stability, development, and efficient use of U.S. aid."[179] That Park chose development over democracy briefly impaired relations, yet after 1962 he moved toward modernization and earned Washington's approval. He became receptive to aid and advice and acquiesced to Washington's prodding by holding and winning an election in October 1963.[180] To some, his nation epitomized the future of Asian development. William P. Bundy, a Defense Department official, subsequently declared Park's South Korea "a touchstone and partial model for later hopes and plans in South Vietnam."[181] Nation-building did not lead directly to democracy, yet Seoul's progress testified to what development might accomplish over time in the free-world society.

For all the good accomplished under P.L. 480, for all the plaudits the Peace Corps earned, for all the promise of the Alliance for Progress in its early days, the heart of nation-building for Kennedy remained counterinsurgency. As with Eisenhower, the drive to modernity was heavily securitized under Kennedy. His top advisers were drawn to counterinsurgency warfare partly because of Khrushchev's rhetorical support for wars of national liberation. More important were the lessons learned from the prior experiences of British forces in Malaya under the guidance of Sir Robert G. K. Thompson.[182] Kennedy directed the Defense Department on February 3, 1961, in NSAM 2, to find "means for placing more emphasis on the development of counter-guerrilla forces."[183] Thus began a focus on Special Forces that U.S. efforts in Vietnam soon typified.

Kennedy presented his case to the public in a message to Congress and in an appearance at a joint session on March 28 and May 25, 1961, respectively. The Free World was in danger of "being nibbled away at the periphery" by "subversives and saboteurs and insurrectionists, who in some cases control whole areas inside of independent nations."[184] The United States would not stand by with the Free World in danger. Section 501 of the Foreign Assistance Act codified the crucial linkage between internal security and nation-building.[185] JCS Chairman General Lyman L. Lemnitzer told McNamara early in 1962 that civic action would eliminate "some of the causes of national discontent which generate instability and [promote a] closer relationship between the civilian and military communities." Kennedy approved NSAM 124, and the Special Group (CI), or Counterinsurgency, was born.[186]

As early as February 1961, Chief of Naval Operations Admiral Arleigh A. Burke saw a need for civic action in Latin America: "The present governments . . . are afraid of dissident groups in their own countries rising up and taking over the government."[187] Nearly all nations there received CI training and material assistance in FY 1962. Some nine thousand military officers and enlisted personnel partook of the training, at either the School of the Americas in the Panama Canal Zone or the Special Warfare School at Fort Bragg, North Carolina.[188]

The example of Bolivia in the early 1960s illustrates how interconnected were the goals of the Alliance and counterinsurgency. As a leading per capita recipient of U.S. aid, Víctor Paz Estenssoro's government relied heavily on the armed forces to provide stability, which in the early 1960s meant crushing the leftist miners' unions. In line with NSAM 119 of December 1961, the White House expected Bolivia's military to participate fully in development through civic action projects.[189]

Would joining counterinsurgency and development promote stability and democracy?[190] Reports were unenthusiastic about the prospects for modernization. Officials interpreted them as demonstrating the need for the Alliance and civic action. The persistence of structural poverty and oligarchic rule in El Salvador, for example, made that nation susceptible to leftist activity. Also, Venezuela could not escape rumors about a Cuban-inspired *golpe*, and instability in the Dominican Republic was a given. And, U.S. representatives in Chile worried about the power of Marxist Salvador Allende and the political Left in the not-too-distant 1964 elections.[191]

Colombia commanded special attention. However peaceful Colombia seemed, Kennedy knew a drastic decline in coffee prices might set off a cycle of protest and raise fears of a return to *la Violencia*. Should that occur, Colombia's armed forces were ill prepared to respond.[192] Therefore, what emerged in mid-1962 and lasted through 1965 was the convergence of civic action and counterinsurgency. Aided by U.S. advisers, Colombia's military devised Plan Lazo, or Plan Lasso, to curtail guerrilla activity while engaging in military-led nation-building. Results were disappointing.[193] Rivalry between military units and the police and disputes with civilian leaders impeded progress. Moreover, instances of military brutality and fear of guerrillas and bandits left people in targeted areas without protection.[194] Colombia was a nation in trouble.

Then-senator Kennedy proclaimed on June 1, 1956, to the American Friends of Vietnam that the success of American foreign policy depended "in considerable measure upon a strong and free Vietnamese nation. . . . [South Vietnam] is our offspring—we cannot abandon it, we cannot ignore its needs."[195] Determined as president to focus on development and security, Kennedy was moved by the turn of events in Vietnam toward the latter. So enamored was the White House in early 1961 with counterguerrilla activity that officials considered waging campaigns in the north and south against Saigon's foes—even though MAAG favored conventional warfare. In effect, fighting to defend the Free World and the American Century in the cities, hamlets, and jungles of South Vietnam seemed necessary, especially with reports of Vietcong advances.[196]

A plan was in the works by March 1962 to induce officials in Saigon to prepare for counterinsurgency. That development came in the wake of the Taylor-Rostow mission of October 1961. Led by General Maxwell D. Taylor, head of the Special Group (CI), the mission argued for greater involvement in Vietnam in order to enhance political and economic nation-building. Taylor reported in March 1962, "The greatest possible use is being made of South Viet-Nam as a laboratory for technicians and equipment related to the counterinsurgency program."[197] Would the experiment pay off? That largely depended on Diem. AID administrator David E. Bell thought that, though "not yet in a position to make steady progress toward economic growth, [Saigon may] move into that position in not too long a period."[198] Bell's attitude in spring 1963 was overly optimistic in light of the record of the Strategic Hamlet program.

George Herring, perhaps the foremost scholar of U.S. involvement in Vietnam, offers a judicious assessment of the hamlet project. It possessed "deep indigenous roots" and was intended to "revitalize rural South Vietnam and undermine the

NLF [National Liberation Front]." Within the hamlets, local democracy was supposed to emerge, land reform was to take place, and education and health care were to represent Saigon's best efforts. In doing so, Diem and his brother Ngo Dinh Nhu, Diem's security chief, hoped to win over South Vietnam's peasants and extend the Ngos authority to the entire country.[199] Unfortunately for them, the program was poorly implemented. Security was incredibly lax, allowing the Vietcong to infiltrate the hamlets. More damaging was the forcible removal of many peasants from their ancestral lands, especially in the Mekong Delta region, as had occurred under the agroville program. In short, the results were "meager."[200]

Like their allies in Saigon, officials in Washington put much stock in the hamlets. The program's shortcomings were dismissed as administrative problems readily amenable to solution. For every report finding "some of the hamlets are not particularly good," a contrary view was voiced, often in the same report, asserting "in certain areas the reception of the Hamlet program has been very good." McNamara was not immune to such indeterminacy as he worried about the pace of the program and its reception in the United States.[201]

U.S. authorities expected Diem to locate the Strategic Hamlets in regions where the NLF was not entrenched. He initially focused in March 1962 on an area north of Saigon, Binh Duong province, where the Vietcong had a formidable presence. Operation Sunrise, as the undertaking was known, at first fared poorly. Roger Hilsman, head of the State Department's Bureau of Intelligence and Research and on mission to South Vietnam, assumed the Vietcong could easily "discredit the Strategic Village concept." Saigon lacked the resources, if not the will, to carry out campaigns like Operation Sunrise. Unless the Vietcong could be defeated, an unlikely prospect, incremental progress in nation-building was all that could be expected.[202]

Meanwhile, a looming budget deficit in 1962 led Saigon to seek a cash grant to purchase fertilizer and industrial machinery, the basic tools of economic development. In assessing the request, the U.S. embassy questioned whether Diem's government had done enough with tax policy to justify the grant. Ambassador Frederick E. Nolting Jr. feared that delay would endanger the hamlet program and U.S. interests in Southeast Asia. Rusk was reluctant to follow Nolting's advice, and a $25 million deal to support the piaster fell apart in June. Frustrated, McNamara judged the aid to be "of the highest importance." The assistance ultimately provided was less than Diem, Nolting, and McNamara wanted. Diem, George Ball declared, would have "to face up to [his] deficit problem."[203]

The State Department still assumed that good management could foster modernization and security. Meanwhile, discussions continued about what to do if Diem fell from power. As was often the case, proponents of nation-building turned to matters of program organization and management.[204] And, as they had since

January 1961, they asked the ARVN to stabilize South Vietnam. Given the importance of nation-building to the future of the American Century, this was not an absurd request, as the NSC's Robert Komer made clear in a memo to Walt Rostow in mid-1961 entitled "Are We Pushing Hard Enough in South Vietnam?"[205]

ARVN prepared for conventional warfare. Some Americans were pleased with its combat readiness, but Diem, Lansdale, and the JCS knew better.[206] MAAG wanted the troop levels in the Republic of Vietnam Armed Forces (RVNAF) to increase to 270,000 trained personnel, of which 65,000 would be in the Civil Guard. By late July 1961, signs were positive. The RVNAF dedicated its primary mission to counterinsurgency, and MAAG and ARVN had agreed to create a combat test center to train soldiers for guerrilla war. Hilsman knew the numbers could not deter the Vietcong. Leadership by Diem and popular acceptance of the RVNAF were crucial. "The burden on the quality of the government's combat forces is enormous," he observed, doubting that Diem was up to the task.[207]

Civic action was basic to battle plans. Activities included improving village medical care, creating an alarm system to warn of Vietcong penetration of village perimeters, and building roads to improve links to the capital. ARVN units, though, failed to build good relations with villagers. Lansdale lamented in October, "The VC continue to enjoy much popular support, even though this is often obtained through terrorist activities." The head of MAAG, Lieutenant General Lionel C. McGarr, thought that 25 percent of the South Vietnamese backed the Vietcong, with another 25 percent indifferent to Diem's fate.[208]

Nation-building stalled by the end of 1962; the number of U.S. personnel in South Vietnam as "advisers" had tripled to more than nine thousand. They were participating in civic action, fighting alongside ARVN troops in conventional combat against NLF forces, and supervising counterinsurgency operations. ARVN, however, was no match for the Vietcong on the political-psychological-military battlefield, and the Strategic Hamlet program fell short of expectations.[209] Despite wanting to blame the Vietnamese and their U.S. advisers for the problems, in evaluating conditions in late January 1963 Hilsman found that "the Viet Cong continue to be aggressive and . . . extremely effective." General Paul D. Harkins, head of the Military Assistance Command, Vietnam (MACV), which replaced MAAG, agreed: "The VC are still everywhere."[210]

Nation-building had become a fraught endeavor. An artificially favorable exchange rate for the piaster, which Washington accepted, allowed pro-Diem importers to prosper greatly in the resale market. Even had he tried, Diem could not have instituted a modern tax system. And had circumstances been better, Saigon still could not have effectively used the tools for military modernization that Washington was providing. Some sixteen thousand U.S. advisers were in country by late 1963. MACV was determined to exert its influence—all the more so after the Buddhist crisis of spring and early summer and growing military op-position to Diem in late summer.[211]

JCS Special Assistant for Counterinsurgency and Special Activities Major Gen-eral Victor H. Krulak addressed the absence of stability in Saigon when, after a visit in September, he reported on what he saw as positive developments "*irrespective of the grave defects in the ruling regime.*" By late October, the military balance was tilt-ing toward the Vietcong.[212] Diem and Nhu were killed on November 3. At the time of Kennedy's death later that month, it was not clear whether U.S. embassy reports of rejuvenated counterinsurgency operations were accurate.[213]

In any event, the travails of nation-building in South Vietnam persisted. Fol-lowing Diem's death, his successors, ARVN, and Washington all but abandoned the Strategic Hamlet program. Officials still believed peasants' lives could be molded in ways that furthered U.S. interests, but the events of late 1963 cracked the presumptive link between modernization and counterinsurgency warfare.[214]

The ground war was not going well in early 1964; the NLF held over 40 percent of the territory where about one-half of the population lived. Military forays by ARVN throughout the countryside were inconclusive, and rates of desertion rose. Johnson was determined to hold the line. Such was the assessment of NSAM 288 of March 17, 1964, which he saw as "the only realistic alternative."[215] How respon-sive to Saigon's problems was nation-building? Johnson and his advisers did not really examine what had gone wrong, reiterating their commitment to nation-building through civic action in June. Thus, "clear and hold" efforts at pacification would replace Strategic Hamlets. To safeguard them was the task of paramilitary forces, "recruited locally and inspired with the purpose of protecting their own families." Newly deployed personnel would oversee those operations in provinces near Saigon. Step by step, the U.S. government was getting more deeply involved in South Vietnam. Events in the Gulf of Tonkin in August and the year 1965 would show just how deeply.

The Erosion of Credibility

The American Century began to founder during John F. Kennedy's presidency. His administration had to prioritize the political and economic issues it faced without diminishing its credibility. Hemmed in by their hubris and hegemonic aspirations, that was no easy task for the preternaturally confident men of the New Frontier. Two examples—their ill treatment of allies and suspicions of politicized youth—represent their efforts to defend the Free World and salvage their image.

The Cuban crisis illumines the limits of consultation with America's most important partners. Leadership depended on unqualified trust by NATO members. Despite support for Kennedy's response to Soviet missiles in Cuba, the crisis harmed American credibility. Konrad Adenauer blamed Castro, not Khrushchev, for precipitating the crisis because Castro "offered his country to the missiles and thus facilitated the threat against the United States." The chancellor did not want to upset the Soviets. From his vantage point, responsibility for ongoing tensions largely rested with Washington, and the crisis promised further uncertainty over Berlin. In short, the West German leader's trust in the United States was faltering.[216]

Similarly, de Gaulle wondered what the effect on the situation in Berlin would be when Dean Acheson, Kennedy's emissary, informed him about the coming U.S. response to missiles in Cuba. De Gaulle believed that the crisis might make America's security shield less reliable. On November 10 in that same spirit, French foreign minister Maurice Couve d' Murville denounced Washington's treatment of its European allies, declaring that "political consultation between the fifteen [NATO] members does not work well at all."[217]

Global containment as grand strategy was losing its conceptual and practical heft under Kennedy. Tellingly, in his July 25, 1961, address to the American people—an impassioned reply to the Soviet *aide-mémoire* at the Vienna meeting—he had clung to the cold-war verities of the previous fifteen years: "We face a challenge in our own hemisphere, and indeed wherever else the freedom of human beings is at stake."[218] His fascination with counterinsurgency warfare and civic action promised more of the same: grand strategy based on comprehensive globalism. What Kennedy's slowness to change meant for American credibility was evident. One scholar tersely observes, "By the end of 1963 the Atlantic Community had largely ground to a halt."[219] Try as he might, Johnson only partly mitigated the damage.

Luce's Good Samaritan seemed less visible in the early 1960s, the efforts of Peace Corps volunteers aside, as young people became ever more political. The CIA-backed Congress for Cultural Freedom operated in Latin America.[220] Also active there was the Interagency Youth Committee (IYC). A propaganda initiative, it resided in the State Department after its founding in April 1962. Edward Lansdale and Walt Rostow valued the IYC as part of counterinsurgency activity.[221] Dean Rusk explained the need for the IYC: "The phenomenon of youth unrest is worldwide and a serious obstacle to achievement of U.S. objectives."[222] To Rusk, unrest among the young was another burden to bear, a sentiment Johnson doubtless shared. He was the target of protests almost from the outset of his presidency, commencing in Panama in January 1964.[223] The world the United States had made since 1945 was at risk from many sides in the early 1960s. The erosion of credibility, a severe blow to the American Century, inexorably accelerated after the 1964 election.

CONTENDING WITH DECLINE

Henry Luce admired Lyndon Johnson and welcomed his selection as Kennedy's vice presidential candidate in 1960. The two men grew closer after November 22, 1963, so much so that Luce received the "Johnson treatment"—flattery on matters of interest to the publisher. Luce may have voted for Johnson in 1964. Drawing him to Johnson were the Vietnam War and the prospect of a "great society." For Luce, the Great Society epitomized domestic nation-building. "We set our sights on the Great Society," he said in 1965, "where there will be even more good. . . . How to bring joy into the world? . . . It seems impossible, but there are hints of this vision." To reinforce America's reputation as the world's Good Samaritan by building the Great Society at home would take some doing.[1]

Buttressing the Free World?

Johnson could not restore America's global standing merely by opposing communism. Policymakers no longer thought the Soviet Union posed an imminent threat to the Free World. Nonalignment, revolution, and disaffected allies challenged U.S. hegemony. Johnson needed to respond in three ways. He had to restore Washington's preeminent place in the Free World, the global economy had to meet rising expectations about growth, and through liberal development democracy had to blossom in the free-world society—all of which were consistent with Luce's plans for the American Century.

Repairing transatlantic unity took precedence. The CIA reported, "Europeans have had an increasing sense of not being master in their own house."[2] Johnson's political instincts had prepared him to respond. He was comfortable dealing with Western European leaders; in fact, characterizations of him as unprepared to conduct foreign policy are overdrawn. Despite real differences, he skillfully managed relations with Harold Wilson and Charles de Gaulle, even after France's estrangement from NATO in 1966 and when demonstrating students and workers nearly forced de Gaulle from power in May 1968.[3] Johnson turned to Bonn for help. His desire for accommodation maintained cordial relations while prodding Ludwig Erhard, who replaced Adenauer in October 1963, to moderate policy toward the Eastern bloc. Erhard's commitment to reunification precluded a foreign policy based on existing political realities. Officials in Bonn, the U.S. embassy reported, exhibited "a nagging concern about the United States and a fading confidence in the clarity of our purposes in Europe."[4] Fortuitously, Erhard fell from power in October 1966. Unresolved disputes over offset payments for U.S. troops stationed in West Germany hastened his departure.

The Kurt Kiesinger–Willy Brandt Grand Coalition endeavored to improve relations, to which Johnson responded favorably, as it moved toward *Ostpolitik*. Recurring concerns about consultation by Washington persisted, lasting until April 1967, when the president attended Adenauer's funeral.[5] A meeting with Kiesinger set the stage for the Trilateral Agreements with the British and Germans about NATO forces in West Germany and Bonn's offset payments. Washington had smoothed ruffled feathers, leaving NATO temporarily stronger.[6]

Developments in Greece, however, highlighted the difficulty of maintaining a common allied posture. Instability worsened after the ascent to power of George Papandreou in February 1964. Popular with workers and students, Papandreou broadened his support while setting the stage for his son Andreas, an American citizen, to succeed him as prime minister. He appealed to the Left, thereby alienating King Constantine II, elements in the military, and NATO partners. Constantine briefly resolved the crisis by forcing Papandreou to step down in July 1965.[7]

Threats to NATO's integrity emerged as further instability made it impossible to form a ruling coalition in Athens. The king's request to Johnson in November 1965 for aid fell on deaf ears because of defense-related costs in Western Europe and Vietnam.[8] Andreas Papandreou moved to fill the vacuum by proposing an agenda for democracy that scared the military, king, and business elite. The 303 Committee—a covert action review board created in June 1964—asked the NSC to determine whether the CIA should act to check the younger Papandreou's ambitions prior to elections scheduled for May 1967. Ambassador Phillips H.

Talbott, already wary of Papandreou's leftist inclinations, supported the idea, but Dean Rusk, Walt Rostow, and the NSC thought it too risky.[9]

Their reticence did not matter. On April 21, 1967, army officers staged a coup, destroying Greek democracy and instituting a state of emergency.[10] Johnson, concerned about the impact on NATO, adopted a passive approach toward the ruling junta. Blaming Andreas Papandreou for the coup, the administration curtailed military aid and embargoed delivery of crucial equipment in the unwarranted belief the colonels might soon set a date for credible elections. That stratagem contended with the desire for stability as the core of U.S. policy. Stability won.

By August, Rusk and Rostow were urging a partial renewal of aid. "We can't treat our NATO relationship lightly, and we don't want to push Greece in France's direction," warned Rostow.[11] For their part, the colonels reminded Washington of their fealty to NATO and sent supplies to Israel during the Six-Day War. Relations slowly improved, assisted by the Soviet invasion of Czechoslovakia in August 1968.[12] Stability had triumphed over democracy in U.S. policy toward Greece, and the American Century was the poorer for it.

Vietnam, where seeking security outstripped promoting democracy, bedeviled Johnson. With no chance to use nuclear weapons to aid regimes that came to power in Saigon after Diem's death, he had to rely on a mix of conventional warfare and counterinsurgency. But to what end? What could compel North Vietnam's leaders to accept the status quo and abandon efforts to unify their country?[13] Even before Johnson decided in July 1965 to intervene, Saigon remained, in the words of NSAM 314 in September 1964, "the first order of business."[14] Rusk fretted about credibility despite advocating escalation. The administration's response to the Gulf of Tonkin incident of August 1964, which was to fabricate a second incident, had paved the way for future intervention. Decision-making after Tonkin and the November election, William J. Duiker notes, "made further U.S. escalation in Vietnam not only easier but almost inevitable."[15] Joining Rusk in advocating military action were Rostow and Assistant Secretary of State William P. Bundy, McGeorge Bundy's brother.[16]

The North Vietnamese increased aid to the Vietcong, resulting in renewed attacks against Strategic Hamlets at a time when the political situation in Saigon was deteriorating. Conditions in the Mekong Delta, for instance, reflected the dangers facing Saigon and U.S. policy.[17] Johnson reacted cautiously, ordering the bombing of supply lines in Laos.[18] The stakes in Southeast Asia were enormous, admitted the NSC after the 1964 election: "Essentially, the loss of South Vietnam to Communist control, in any form, would be a major blow to our basic policies. US prestige is heavily committed to the maintenance of a non-Communist South Vietnam, and only less heavily so to a neutralized Laos."[19]

The chance to avert disaster came with an attack in February 1965 by NLF forces against U.S. Army barracks at Pleiku in the central highlands. The U.S. response, Operation Rolling Thunder, targeted southern and northern Vietnam; it became the heaviest bombing campaign in the history of warfare to that time.[20] When British prime minister Harold Wilson asked Johnson if he could fly to the United States to discuss the situation in Vietnam, Johnson resisted, arguing that nothing good could come from a visit.[21]

Rolling Thunder served as one track of a strategy of conventional massive retaliation. The other track, ground-based military operations, began after a June-July decision-making process that by year's end sent nearly 150,000 troops into battle. Applied gradually, these approaches to war reached immense proportions. Over 500,000 troops were in Vietnam by mid-1968, and 640,000 tons of bombs, at an estimated cost of $900 million, had been dropped on the north and south. This massive commitment of resources, plus a tractable government in Saigon led by Nguyen Van Thieu and Nguyen Cao Ky, prevented the demise of South Vietnam during Johnson's presidency.

Policymakers realized in July 1965 that America's reputation was under greater scrutiny than it had been in the Cold War. Failure in Indochina would weaken its leadership of the Free World. Hemmed in by the flow of aid to Saigon since 1954, which narrowed his options, Johnson saw no choice but to press on. He plaintively asked Undersecretary of State George W. Ball, "Wouldn't we lose credibility by breaking the word of three presidents?"[22] He likely was right, and the consequences that would plague the American Century were soon to appear.

Lyndon Johnson was not an insensitive man. He did not exude the noblesse oblige of either Franklin Roosevelt or John Kennedy. Though earthy and profane, he cared about less fortunate people and assumed that the strength of his personality and his power as president could fix every problem. He believed that America's and his image were linked to success or failure abroad. "The most important foreign policy problem I faced," Johnson later recalled, "was that of signaling to the world what kind of man I was and what sort of policies I intended to carry out."[23] Awash in his contradictions, he offered Ho Chi Minh's government aid to control flooding of the Mekong River even as he moved to widen the Vietnam War in 1965.[24] Similarly, he had greater faith than Kennedy in the Alliance for Progress to help Latin America's poor yet retained Kennedy's emphasis there on securitized nation-building.[25]

Latin Americans came to doubt Johnson's intentions after an initial positive impression.[26] Would he be as obsessed as Kennedy with Cuba and internal security? Several examples answer this question in the affirmative. The OAS was ill equipped in early 1964 to resolve the rupture of U.S.-Panamanian relations in a dispute about the flying of Panama's flag at Balboa High School in the Canal Zone.[27] President Roberto Chiari wanted to renegotiate the 1903 treaty that gave the United States control over the zone. Johnson, seeing Castro's hand in the student riots, rejected Chiari's request.[28] The OAS could not bring the two countries together. Johnson's contempt for the OAS came through in a discussion about dealing with the Panamanians: "If you squeeze their nuts just a little bit—I think we've been too generous."[29] Washington viewed an ineffective OAS as a disciple, not a partner.

OAS obeisance again manifested itself in July 1964. Venezuela filed a complaint about a cache of arms discovered on a beach the prior November, presumably sent by Cuba and intended for Venezuelan insurgents. In fact, the affair was likely a CIA operation.[30] Whatever the case, the OAS voted overwhelmingly for economic sanctions against Cuba with only Mexico dissenting.[31] The NSC exulted, "The meeting was a success from our point of view."[32] (Success would come again in mid-1967 when Venezuela again took its case against Cuba to the OAS. "On all counts, the OAS Meeting of Foreign Ministers went well, within the limits of what we thought possible," Rostow then informed Johnson.)[33]

In the case of Brazil, neither Kennedy nor Johnson trusted President João Goulart. They had advance knowledge of preparations for a military coup; after his overthrow in April 1964, Johnson recognized Humberto Castelo Branco with unseemly haste. Brazil, one official noted, had stepped back from "the edge of communism."[34] Although evidence for that assertion was inconclusive, a pleased Johnson confided to Assistant Secretary of State for Inter-American Affairs Thomas Mann, "The Brazil thing went all right."[35] (Later that year, when Bolivia's military removed President Víctor Paz Estensorro from office, Washington recognized the new government of General René Barrientos Ortuño just as quickly.)[36]

The Dominican Republic "thing" did not go as well in late April 1965. Johnson justified intervention by claiming it had thwarted Cuban subversion: "The Communist leader in Havana was always alert to any exploitable weakness among his neighbors." The case against Cuba does not hold up.[37] Castro had extended an olive branch of sorts after Johnson became president and hoped for improved relations until U.S. troops landed. Forces operating nominally at the behest of the OAS were present in Santo Domingo to keep the peace until an interim government could take power. Many commentators in the hemisphere, though, looked askance at the display of U.S. force after the removal of the progressive Juan Bosch.[38]

Robert McNamara and McGeorge Bundy doubted Cuba was to blame for events in the Dominican Republic.[39] As for the OAS, Bundy informed Johnson, "We are going to have to use the OAS as a cloak for whatever we're going to do." The OAS arranged a cease-fire between contending forces and facilitated negotiations over the nation's future.[40] The IYC played a minor role. Its report on Dominican youth showed how difficult it was to influence young Latin Americans. People between the ages of thirteen and thirty were "marked by suspicion, immoderation, absolutism and ambivalence." Yet they had to be engaged seriously, if informally, as future political leaders. Over time, the IYC reached out to all but "the hard core on the Left." Results varied, with radical youths often linking IYC activity to the U.S. military presence.[41]

Increasingly, Latin American military officers and their U.S. counterparts worked closely together. The so-called Mann Doctrine, announced by Assistant Secretary of State Thomas Mann in March 1964, indicated the United States would not inquire into the nature of regimes receiving military and economic assistance.[42] Mann wanted aid programs to emphasize "counterinsurgency and internal security capability."[43] Officer training in the Americas or in the Panama Canal Zone at the School of the Americas and OPS grants for police activities amounted to $55 million by FY 1973.[44] These activities, encompassing four thousand personnel per year, bolstered an ideology integral to the region's armed forces, the National Security Doctrine, that provided a cover for the brutal activities related to internal security during periods of counterinsurgency conflict.[45]

In Guatemala, for example, the oligarchy relied on force to prevent a return of Árbenz-era reforms, whereas Washington played a crucial role in bringing state terror to the countryside and cities. Mann's successor, Covey T. Oliver, embraced counterinsurgency, telling Walt Rostow in fall 1967: "The situation in Guatemala continues to improve." Rostow forwarded the report to Johnson.[46] Viron P. Vaky, deputy chief of mission, anguished over U.S. complicity in the terror. On March 29, 1968, two days before a beleaguered Johnson announced that he would not seek reelection, Vaky cabled Washington denouncing what had occurred: "Have our values been so twisted by our adversary concept of politics in the hemisphere? . . . Are we so obsessed with insurgency that we are prepared to rationalize murder as an acceptable counter-insurgency weapon?"[47] For those in the national security bureaucracy who still believed in the ideals of the American Century, developments in 1967–1968 had to be disillusioning. Few were prepared, though, to contemplate the deleterious effects of U.S. policy on America's standing abroad.

In Africa, concern about Soviet and Chinese influence heightened under Johnson.[48] Rusk, harking back to Luce's essay, counseled in fall 1965, "The situation in Africa provides us with a unique opportunity to project American ideas and use American resources in Africa by means which attract attention to and are consistent with our democratic principles, our commitment to an interracial society, and our concern with human welfare."[49] Rusk excluded South Africa from this "unique opportunity" because "we are not the self-elected gendarmes for the political and social problems of other states."[50]

Gendarme or not, the administration constructed its African policy on the foundation of containment. Mindful of commitments elsewhere, Johnson wanted to minimize U.S. expenses and visibility. Following Kennedy's lead, he provided funding for military-based civic action programs. The key, the NSC's Robert W. Komer told him, was not to "get caught on the wrong side of the Rhodesia, Portuguese, and South Africa issues."[51] Komer could have added Ghana, Congo, and Nigeria to his list.

Relations with Ghana's Kwame Nkrumah showed how hard it was to force black Africa into the contours of cold-war policy. Vice President Richard Nixon had attended Nkrumah's installation as president in 1957. Washington wanted to signal its anticolonialism by working with him. The Congo crisis of 1960–1961 tested that position when Nkrumah asked the Soviets to help Patrice Lumumba. Nkrumah leaned toward Moscow, yet Kennedy held out hopes for improved relations and helped fund a major dam project. Nkrumah was neither won over nor isolated.[52] By spring 1965, less than a year before being ousted from power, he was at odds with Washington—angry about the U.S. role in Congo and fearing it might turn into another Vietnam. A trip to Hanoi and publication of a book denouncing Western imperialism impaired relations.[53] It is not known whether the CIA aided in Nkrumah's overthrow in February 1966. Komer termed it "fortuitous," adding, "Nkrumah was doing more than any other black African to undermine our interests."[54] U.S.-Ghanaian relations improved soon thereafter, it is worth noting.

Nkrumah was no Soviet or Chinese puppet. Belief in Washington to the contrary reveals a truth about the resort to containment in the developing world: cold-war tactics were not always a productive response to local conditions. That was true in Congo, where a rebellion broke out in fall 1964 against the U.S.-backed government of Joseph Kasavubu.[55] White mercenaries and CIA-aided Cuban exiles assisted Kasavubu and his premier, Moise Tshombe, a man hated throughout black Africa, reputedly with ties to the CIA. American pilots helped quash the revolt. One year later, Mobutu Sese Seko (Joseph Mobutu) was in charge of the country, which he renamed Zaire; Kasavubu retired from the political scene, and Tshombe went into exile.[56] Just as Kennedy had praised Mobutu for saving Congo from communism in 1961, Johnson viewed him favorably in 1965. U.S. authorities believed they had saved nation-building from ruin by radical nationalists.[57] An ironic coda came in mid-1966 when the NSC denounced Mobutu as "the latest in a series of disastrous Congolese leasers."[58]

One place where Washington expected no trouble was in the Horn of Africa. Relations with Ethiopia's leader Haile Selassie had long been friendly. A mutual defense pact and the lease of a communications base in the 1950s gave the United States access to the Red Sea. Somalia's independence in 1960 threatened Ethiopia's status quo, but military aid averted trouble.[59] NIE 60/70-65, however, warned in April 1965 of future difficulties because a U.S. military presence in Ethiopia was highly unpopular. At the time, Ethiopian students were studying in the West and bringing home lessons they were learning about political activism. An aging Haile Selassie was resisting change, which further radicalized students and enhanced the appeal of Marxism.[60] The administration feared what would happen were he to lose his hold on power. Turmoil intensified within Ethiopia in fall 1967 as a new pro-U.S. regime in Somalia sought to lessen tensions in the Horn.[61] The respite was brief because a military coup turned Somalia leftward in October 1969.

Containment played little role in Southern Rhodesia, where the White House followed London's lead. The rise to power of the racist Ian Smith in late 1965 eliminated any opportunity Washington had to promote self-rule.[62] By rejecting mandatory economic sanctions for almost two years, the United States lost support among black Africans who chafed at America's timid response to efforts by liberation movements to attain democracy.[63] Meanwhile at home, racially conservative whites, including former secretary of state Dean Acheson and business interests, urged Johnson to follow a moderate course.[64] Sanctions, which the State Department discussed, might spark a race war in southern Africa, forcing Washington to choose between "either the 'white settlers' for the sake of stability or the 'black nationalists,' who would probably have Communist backing."[65]

Johnson favored "an orderly, phased, transition program to achieve" self-rule.[66] A former U.S. diplomat in Africa concluded, "In effect, his administration left the American South Africa relationship much as it had been for the previous decade."[67] With no compelling reason to alter established policy, Johnson laid the groundwork for Nixon and Kissinger's approach to black liberation in South Africa, as in National Security Study Memorandum (NSSM) 39 of April 1969: "The whites are here to stay and the only way that constructive change can come about is through them."[68]

Global containment did find a role to play in Portuguese Africa, notably in Mozambique and Angola. Kennedy and Johnson established ties with independence movements, to Lisbon's dismay. A NATO member of the second rank, Portugal bound the nation's identity to its colonial past. The goal was to block inroads by the Soviets, Chinese, and Cubans.[69] Contact with the Mozambique Liberation Front (FRELIMO) and its leader, Eduardo Mondlane, paid dividends, though by the mid-1960s the United States was competing with the USSR and the PRC, which were providing limited aid to FRELIMO.[70]

Covert activity in Angola increased as the decade wore on. The CIA was backing Holden Roberto's National Front for the Liberation of Angola (FNLA); Roberto, whose CIA ties dated to 1955, relied on Mobutu's Zaire for support. His autocratic tendencies weakened U.S. support. Formed in opposition to the FNLA was Antonio Aghostinho Neto's Popular Movement for the Liberation of Angola (MPLA); Neto, an independent Marxist, welcomed Soviet and Cuban help. Finally, Jonas Savimbi, with whom the United States later formed close ties, started the National Union for the Total Liberation of Angola (UNITA). Savimbi cooperated with any government, including that in Lisbon, willing to support him.[71] With no appreciable change in the situation by 1968, the NSC advocated negotiations, backed by a readiness to deny military aid to Portugal if it were "used outside the NATO Defense Area."[72]

Containment ultimately poorly served the White House in Africa. Hopes for peace and plans for social and economic justice, which Johnson and his advisers likened to efforts on behalf of the civil rights movement at home, went unrealized.[73] When a revolt broke out in Zaire in mid-1967, the NSC lamented, "We must keep Mobutu in power because there is no acceptable alternative to him."[74] Worse, though, were conditions in Nigeria, where Washington followed a policy of noninvolvement during the attempt at secession by the Biafra region's Ibo people.[75] Johnson railed at his self-inflicted impotence as the humanitarian crisis worsened in 1968: "Get those nigger babies off my TV set." At length, he had failed to buttress the Free World or advance the American Century in a region where ideological lines were often blurred.[76]

Strengthening the Free World fared somewhat better in East and Southeast Asia outside of Vietnam. Amity between Seoul and Tokyo remained elusive because memories of oppression under imperial Japan haunted the Korean people. After protests led him to impose martial law in June 1964, Park Chung Hee turned toward rapprochement with Japan. Normalization took place on June 22, 1965, amid further protests in South Korean cities.[77] Ratification of the accord soon followed, leaving Japan and South Korea poised to share responsibility for free-world leadership in East Asia. Washington's gamble on Park paid off; Seoul had become a dependable ally.[78]

Incorporating Indonesia and Thailand securely into the Free World entailed a much less straightforward process. Sukarno's hold on power in Indonesia and the influence of the PKI fell apart following an abortive revolt by junior army officers in late September 1965. Over five hundred thousand people lost their lives, and perhaps one million were jailed in related violence as General Suharto restored order. Komer urged Johnson "to give a bit more quiet support to [Suharto's] Army . . . [because] we may at last have Sukarno on the run."[79] Over the next few years, Washington turned its attention to providing economic aid and promoting development to avert political, especially student, dissent. Although the United States did not conclude a formal security pact with Indonesia, senior officials in Jakarta indicated their support for a strong U.S. presence.[80]

Thailand emerged by 1968 as a reliable outpost of the Free World. The JCS deemed Thailand a vital ally in the battle against wars of national liberation.[81] Ties with Bangkok were strong enough for the White House to consider reducing its military aid package to help lower America's balance-of-payments deficit without jeopardizing Thailand's stability.[82] In June 1968, authorities promulgated Thailand's seventh constitution since 1932. The CIA, pleased with a regime that was "autocratic without being despotic, conservative without being reactionary," admitted that the constitution would "perpetuate the rule of the military-civilian establishment."[83] Although the CIA welcomed it as a positive step, such a development hardly helped fortify the Free World and the American Century.

Finding a suitable place for both Pakistan and India in the Free World was no easy task. Johnson pursued Kennedy's initiatives with India, acting as if attention to New Delhi's fragile security situation would inexorably turn India into a staunch ally. Ambassador Chester Bowles abetted this dubious belief when he declared that without more aid for India, the United States would face "the loss of a major opportunity to further [its] interests in Asia."[84] Johnson, growing worried about the Free World's survival without reliable clients in South Asia, thought that the alliance with Pakistan would hold even as he prepared to extend additional military aid to India. The president was wrong. Ayub Khan did not trust the Americans to keep India at bay should a clash occur, particularly over Kashmir.[85]

Operating from a position of relative weakness infuriated Johnson. He and his national security team feared that the Chinese with Pakistan and the Soviets with India might provide assistance that Washington could not displace. "[The] Soviets," Komer told Johnson in February 1964, "are now doing more than we to woo the Indian military establishment. . . . If India goes Communist, it will be a disaster comparable only to the loss of China. Even if India reverts to pro-Soviet neutralism, our policy in Asia will be compromised. These risks are real."[86] So were the costs. Ayub bluntly declared on July 1 that aid to India "imperils the security of Pakistan, your ally." Calling U.S. policy "self-defeating," Ayub warned that, without a major change in policy, "Pakistan would be compelled to reconsider its commitment to her allies."[87]

All parties were upset by the course of events as they unfolded throughout 1964. The White House, having designated one-third of its entire foreign aid budget for the subcontinent, seemingly had few options. Johnson's ire exacerbated the dispute with Karachi. Moreover, Prime Minister Lal Bahadur Shastri, who succeeded Nehru, doubted Washington's readiness to temper Pakistan's actions in the April 1965 clash over the Rann of Kutch, located at the juncture of west India and southeast Pakistan on the Arabian Sea.[88] An NSC intelligence review acknowledged, "Our leverage in both countries is at a low point." McGeorge Bundy cabled Bowles in late April, "These are difficult times."[89] Filling the void, Great Britain brokered a cease-fire at the end of June.

An angry Johnson halted much of the aid to the two countries.[90] This estrangement did not serve American interests when fighting broke out over Kashmir in August. "The psychotic Paks . . . are playing with fire by their continued major infiltration into Kashmir," Komer wrote Bundy. The White House embargoed arms shipments on September 8, having no choice but to work with the UN to prevent Kashmir from becoming an international flashpoint. Rusk feared that "the whole Western power position in Asia may shortly be at stake." Maintaining ties to the two warring states was imperative, he argued.[91] The United States could not accomplish that goal in the short term. Rusk foresaw a "long cold winter in our relationship" with India. Johnson, in turn, welcomed a Soviet offer to help settle the conflict. The parties signed an agreement in the central Asian city of Tashkent in January 1966. Momentarily, Indo-Pakistani enmity was under control.[92]

Less certain, as Johnson, Rusk, and the NSC knew, was the fate of the free-world society, and not just in South Asia. Inability to devise a modus vivendi between the two states did not bode well for the American Century. On a positive note, Moscow's involvement in the Kashmir crisis had the potential to accelerate a Soviet-American détente. Johnson declared in May 1966 that "Americans were pleased with Tashkent."[93] He appreciated Soviet premier Alexei Kosygin's role as mediator. Consequently in June 1967, while meeting in Glassboro, New Jersey, Johnson asked Kosygin to pressure Cuba to curtail its subversive activities.[94] Better cooperation allowed Washington and Moscow to explore areas of mutual interest despite the war in Vietnam.

The Middle East remained a challenge to American leaders and their assumptions about the appeal of the Free World. Saudi Arabia offers a case in point. Vigilance against radicalism by King Saud and his successor King Faisal, who acceded to the throne in November 1964, did not quickly pay off, even though resistance to expanded military sales diminished under Johnson. Komer summed up the U.S. position on such aid in mid-1965, "Our goal is to keep our oil-rich Saudi friends happy and to insure that if they finally do buy anything we get the sale."[95]

The real, if latent, power of the House of Saud was on display in June 1967. Just weeks before the Six-Day War began, the Saudi petroleum minister informed an ARAMCO executive that his company might be nationalized. He also threatened, "If the US does not stay out of this conflict, the US is finished in the Middle East."[96] What then transpired was a short-lived boycott of Western consumers by Arab oil suppliers. Fears of lower revenues, because of a glut of global petroleum reserves, soon outweighed solidarity among producer states. The Saudi boycott ended by September.[97] Yet it was evident Saudi Arabia would be a difficult ally under circumstances increasingly beyond Washington's control.

Conditions in Iran were marginally more predictable. When the shah sent Ayatollah Khomeini into exile in November 1964, the U.S. embassy expressed surprise at the relative leniency of that action given Khomeini's ability to cause trouble for Tehran.[98] Reform continued apace, leaving U.S. authorities impressed with the "Shah's determination to have his nation modernized."[99] At work in policy deliberations was concern about the price of oil and the power of the Organization of Petroleum Exporting Countries (OPEC), which had been created in September 1960, to set prices at odds with U.S. security interests.[100] Despite recurring doubts about the relationship, the CIA by mid-1967 considered the shah "a good friend of the US [who is] . . . heavily dependent on the West for investment, trade, and military equipment."[101]

Egypt and Syria continued to vex Washington. Johnson never found a way to work with Nasser. Differences over Congo, Cuban forces in Africa, and Vietnam, along with Nasser's support for the Palestine Liberation Organization (PLO) and a revival of the USSR's influence in Cairo, brought U.S.-Egyptian relations to a standstill by early 1967.[102] A trip to the Middle East by the NSC's Harold K. Saunders failed to improve relations. Saunders recognized that distrust was mutual: "No amount of logic [is] sufficient [to] persuade Egyptians that everything we do in [the] Near East [is] not directed at them. . . . Unfortunately, there [is] just enough truth [in] their evidence [to] make it difficult to refute."[103] As for Syria, relations were showing extreme strain well before the Six-Day War, a condition that Israel's rapid and total victory magnified. Instability marked what the NSC by late 1968 called "the most radical Arab nation."[104] The administration left office convinced that Syria was serving as an outpost of Soviet meddling.

The Six-Day War also showed that, perhaps other than Iran, Israel had become the best friend of the United States in the Middle East. Kennedy had failed to get Israel to commit to nuclear nonproliferation. Israeli officials valued their nuclear program at Dimona in the Negev Desert for its deterrent effect against an Arab attack. Kennedy's options were few, other than refusing to give Israel a formal security guarantee.[105] Relations warmed under Johnson. Just as determined to bring the free-world society to the Middle East as to Southeast Asia, Johnson saw Israel as a means to that end. The Six-Day War presented an unexpected opportunity to entrench U.S. influence.[106] The issue of land seized during the war dashed that hope, a fact emphasized in UN Security Council Resolution 242 of November 22, 1967, which called for Israel to return occupied territory.[107]

After the war, the White House looked to Israel, Iran, and Saudi Arabia to advance U.S. interests. The cost was predictable: Washington had to meet their security needs with expanded arms sales. Meanwhile, the USSR took advantage of hostility toward Israel by the PLO and radical Arab states to find a place on the Middle East landscape.[108] The saving grace was that Moscow did not want a superpower confrontation, as the Kosygin-Johnson summit made clear despite the lingering issue of arms control. What remained less certain was receptivity to U.S. leadership in the region.[109]

The Ebbing of Containment Capitalism

Less fraught relations with Moscow undercut the rationale for containment capitalism, if not the economic basis of the American Century. Knowing inflation might curtail American power and influence, Johnson tried to preserve the strength of the dollar and the command of gold the United States had enjoyed since 1945. Vietnam, which in FY 1965 cost the American public barely $100 million, became a $6–$14 billion economic drain by 1966.[110] Johnson delayed until 1967 asking for a tax increase to pay for war in Southeast Asia, thereby inviting inflation. Butter and guns were ultimately incompatible, and the costs to multilateralism of an overheated economy became troubling.[111]

The administration turned to capital controls to revitalize hegemony. Efforts proved only partly successful. Gold stocks further declined, falling from about $15.5 billion in 1964—a $7.3 billion decline since 1945 and especially since 1958—to some $10.9 billion in 1968; the overall balance of payments slightly improved by one measure until 1967.[112] Another assessment, based on government outlays, trade balances, private investment, and long-term capital balances, charts a steady decline after 1964.[113]

The primary focus of authorities as they sought to reverse payment imbalances remained on Europe. Nothing showed the precariousness of the situation better than France's attack on U.S. monetary leadership. On February 4, 1965, Charles de Gaulle urged holders of dollars in Western Europe to demand gold in exchange for dollars. He wanted to weaken the dollar and let the exchange rate of $35 per ounce float because the fixed rate did not match monetary reality. The dollar's position as the leading reserve currency allowed Washington to export inflation, forcing allies to pay for, in de Gaulle's view, mismanagement. Officials in Bonn accepted that analysis but were not disposed to jettison the Bretton Woods system.[114] Reporting from Paris, Ambassador Charles E. Bohlen pronounced France's efforts a "significant irritant in our bilateral relations."[115]

Officials believed the dollar's fate and the price of gold were tied to the pound.[116] That bond was evident again in June 1965 when Britain's trade declined and its balance of payments worsened. Johnson seized the occasion to declare, "The Free World [needs] some way of producing the additional liquidity which has been supplied by the payments deficits of the United States." We "should consider what steps the United States could take to arrange for a relief of pressure on sterling [to] sharply reduce the danger of sterling devaluation or exchange controls or British military disengagement East of Suez or on the Rhine."[117] Enumerating the dangers of devaluation, George Ball concurred, "The United States, as the leading Western power, could not engage in economic and financial warfare with other major trading nations of the world and still maintain functioning military alliances—or, in fact, effective cooperation of any kind."[118]

Whatever frustration with Wilson's government underlay Johnson's and Ball's concerns, any animus had to be set aside. Despite a slower outflow of gold and a decrease in the payments imbalance, signaling the short-term success of moral suasion, all was not well with containment capitalism. It seemed frozen in time, with France, Japan, and Germany continuing to worry about Washington's export of inflation. Indicative, too, of uncertainty about U.S. economic leadership, Bonn's reliability as a monetary partner came into question in 1965. Francis M. Bator, a deputy special assistant for national security affairs, feared that a worsening of the payments deficit was likely.[119] Since France and Britain could not be counted on to help, West Germany would have to provide greater support for Washington's priorities. Johnson once described to speechwriter Richard Goodwin how best to handle the Germans: "You keep patting them on the head and then every once in a while you kick them in the balls."[120] Perhaps not. Erhard was reluctant to support U.S. policy in Vietnam or alter his position on offset payments. When they met in December, Johnson argued that Bonn must act so as not "to upset the quarterly balance of US finances and not to weaken the international confidence in the dollar." Results were nominal.[121]

By the time another British crisis was in the offing in mid-1966, the Germans were in the throes of their own unforeseen difficulties. An economic slowdown affected steel production and mining; gross domestic product declined slightly; and the Bundesbank, West Germany's central bank, opted to restrict credit. The result was a cut in government spending in the defense budget and in offset payments to Britain and America.[122]

The decision on offsets threatened the stability of the pound more than the dollar. Britain was experiencing revenue losses of $200 million per week by mid-July, leaving officials there "appropriately scared," as Treasury Secretary Henry Fowler put it. Britain prepared to take drastic action to forestall devaluation. To U.S. officials, a British withdrawal from defense commitments was more symbolic than substantive, yet it would affect U.S. leadership.[123] Indeed, Bator worried about an uncertain future: "The truth is that the present rules of the international money game are stacked against us." He still trusted the power of the dollar: "If the Europeans force a crisis, our economic strength and real bargaining leverage would soon become clear to all concerned."[124] That faith would soon be tested; the Board of Governors of the Federal Reserve System feared the dollar and the price of gold would again face heavy pressure.[125]

Harold Wilson was in a tough spot politically as he moved toward austerity at home and selective disengagement abroad. The latter he carried out by withdrawing from West Germany some British forces that were unsupported by offset payments. Not wanting to further devalue the pound, he adopted a deflationary strategy tying the pound's status as a reserve currency to the dollar's health. "The more the world understands that the dollar and sterling are linked together," Wilson remarked in talks in Washington at the end of July, "the better it will be." Fowler knew that Wilson was correct but focused instead on how the two allies, along with other key powers, could increase global liquidity.[126]

That effort, the creation of a reserve asset—the Special Drawing Rights (SDRs)—to take pressure off the dollar and sterling, had to wait. Erhard's government fell in a political crisis with economic roots. Wilson and Johnson insisted on full offset payments, which the British needed more than the Americans to stave off a run on sterling. An attempt to fashion a tripartite agreement on offsets failed. In late September, Erhard asked Johnson for more time to meet his commitments and also to avoid harming NATO—an underlying theme in the offset discussions. Erhard reminded the president that West Germany had responded to the troubles of the dollar, having not sold dollars or bought gold for four years.[127]

Erhard did not receive the same solicitude as Wilson. Johnson and McNamara doubted the Germans would pay as promised.[128] The chancellor's leadership came under heavy criticism at home, with a proposed tax increase in October the last straw. He resigned in November.[129] Ambassador George C. McGhee's assessment of U.S.-German relations was telling. Erhard had questioned American hegemony. Despite "a large area where our mutual interests are sufficiently close to permit fruitful cooperation," McGhee observed, "the new govt will not proceed from the assumption that there is a virtual identity of US and German interests."[130] In a sense, containment capitalism as signified by multilateralism and common cause in the Free World depended on how Washington and London managed monetary problems in the shadow of West Germany's growing economic power. Their record was not promising.

For U.S. officials, SDRs held out hope for relief from the literal costs of hegemony. Additional runs on sterling were not out of the question; and with the likelihood that West Germany would focus on stabilizing its own economy, Johnson and his top advisers confronted the nagging issue of liquidity. As if payments deficits were not enough of a motivation to act quickly, the increasing costs of involvement in Vietnam were omnipresent. As we have seen, de Gaulle often took

Washington to task for a lack of fiscal and monetary discipline. Even though the dollar had helped non-Communist Europe overcome the ravages of war, by the mid-1960s France saw it as a symbol of systemic inequality. Revising the Bretton Woods system to achieve financial equilibrium was impossible, though.[131]

SDRs offered no panacea for the liquidity crisis.[132] Although a plan for creating SDRs within the IMF was provisionally approved in September 1967, the initial allocation of funds did not take place until January 1970. In theory, the dollar was safe; France had not undermined it as the leading reserve currency. Also, using SDRs would have universal application. Even so, the agreement creating them favored ideas EEC members, especially France and West Germany, put forth on policy and repayment provisions.[133] Washington did not have a good bargaining position because, Treasury officials admitted, "dollar reserves cannot expand as they have in the past."[134]

Impossible to ignore in the debates over SDRs was the crisis afflicting Britain's currency. Devaluation from $2.80 to $2.40 came on November 18, 1967. At the higher rate, Wilson could neither maintain Britain's global financial role in the aftermath of the Six-Day War nor pursue viable domestic economic policies after a strike by dock workers. Sterling's weaknesses had ripple effects beyond the incessant runs on gold that were damaging Washington's monetary leadership.[135] Never before had faith in a durable American Century been so at odds with economic realities.

Johnson, averse to a tax increase, had to change his mind or risk further pressure on the dollar and gold. (Congress had not heeded his call in August for a surcharge on corporate and individual income taxes.)[136] Undersecretary of the Treasury Frederick L. Deming, who consulted nations providing funds to the IMF, the European members of the Group of Ten, found Britain's situation "black."[137] He saw 1967 as a poor year for efforts to lower the balance-of-payments deficit. The president vowed to hold the price of gold at $35 per ounce.[138] Gold reserves still declined; Canada came to the rescue, promising to transfer $100 million in gold to Washington. Among Europeans, only the British, West Germans, and Swiss offered to support U.S. monetary leadership. Chairman of the Federal Reserve Board William McChesney Martin hoped that such collective action would protect the integrity of the Bretton Woods system.[139]

As 1967 turned into 1968, the balance-of-payments problem, whether measured by trade, investment, government expenditures, or tourism, was "grim," in Fowler's view. With no sense of what its words meant for credibility, the Cabinet Committee on Balance of Payments called SDRs "the light at the end of the tunnel."[140] That light was signaling, Francis J. Gavin notes, "the end of Bretton Woods."[141] Compounding things was the fear monetary instability would reverse modest gains made during 1967 in the Kennedy Round of the GATT. Indeed, trade negotiations revealed the difficulty American industry had in competing with Japan, for example. Moreover, attempts to improve trade were similarly troubling by early 1968.[142] And then things worsened.

In a message to Harold Wilson notable for its restraint, Johnson wrote on December 31, 1967, "We are at the end of a difficult year. . . . We have, thus far, met and repelled a serious threat to the foundations of the international monetary system." The United States on January 1, 1968, imposed mandatory controls on foreign direct investment, with an exemption for Canada, looking to stem capital outflows by $1 billion. The Federal Reserve Board also moved to lessen overseas activity of American banks by $500 million.[143] Congress then relented and passed a tax increase, which took effect in June, to slow the nation's economy. These actions paved the way for review of Vietnam policy, a rethinking of what the Great Society might still achieve, and Johnson's decision not to seek reelection. Robert M. Collins concludes that these developments "left . . . the American Century in retreat."[144]

Concerns about global liquidity and inflation persisted as pressure on gold increased.[145] Foreigners held what amounted to an unlimited supply of dollars, whereas the U.S. Treasury controlled a finite quantity of gold. U.S. officials wondered whether Paris would again try to undermine the dollar.[146] The strength or weakness of the dollar was symptomatic of a larger issue—the price of gold and its relation to American hegemony. From March 10 to 14, private gold purchases reached $850 million. After a release of gold from Fort Knox, the White House got the London gold pool to close briefly. The Group of Ten agreed to maintain the fictive price of $35 per ounce, and paper currency could not be exchanged for gold.[147] Fowler feared the worst about Congress: "The attitude on the Hill is one of almost anarchistic willingness to pull down the temple around their ears on the grounds that our budgetary expenditures are out of control."[148] Fortunately, his worries were not put to the test.

In the wake of the gold crisis, a new monetary order, really a quasi order, emerged. The decline of American leadership suffused Johnson's message to Prime Minister Sato Eisake of Japan, in which he beseeched Sato to adopt more liberal trading practices.[149] As sterling came under pressure in money markets, the need for SDRs to maintain stability following the demise of the gold-backed-dollar era became undeniable. It was ironic that pressure on the franc helped the case for monetary diversity. France's economy was among the weakest in the EEC, so much so that devaluation was conceivable. Yet were the franc to fall, the pound might as well. Fowler did not fear a slight devaluation given the extent of French reserves. He did worry, though, about London's ability to resist more pressure on sterling because "there would be repercussions on the dollar and, perhaps, general monetary chaos—with everyone trying to get out of currencies and into gold." If demand for gold were to spike, the fragile monetary system might fail. The Group of Ten, including the United States, subsequently intervened to bolster the pound; the monetary patchwork held.[150]

Concern about the franc's status persisted into November. Johnson implored Chancellor Kiesinger to "promptly contact President de Gaulle and urge no unilateral move until appropriate monetary authorities can convene and act on a multilateral basis." A run on the franc would have been calamitous for de Gaulle. More important to the working of the monetary system, West Germany's farmers, exporters, and bankers did not want to revalue. Bonn did agree to raise taxes on exports and lower them on imports, while Paris vaguely promised to trim its budget by $400 million. A meeting of the Group of Ten in Bonn on November 20 foundered, with Fowler failing to obtain either a French devaluation of 11.1 percent or a German revaluation of 10 percent. He strongly suggested, however, that it was Bonn's responsibility to help stabilize the system.[151]

Postmortems on the Bonn meeting recognized West Germany's imposing position and Washington's inability to maneuver the Group of Ten toward outcomes Fowler and Johnson favored. The White House did not think Kiesinger had assumed a role commensurate with his nation's economic strength. America's resources were not up to the task, so Johnson was relieved not to have to prop up other currencies.[152] That knowledge provided no solace; U.S. economic hegemony was in disarray at the end of 1968, and prospects for the global economy were bleak.

The Allure of Nation-Building

Lyndon Johnson and nation-building were made for each other—all the more so after Walt Rostow replaced McGeorge Bundy as national security adviser on April 1, 1966.[153] Johnson viewed America as the essence of Luce's Good Samaritan—at home and abroad. For Johnson, the American Century had to grow organically to thrive in changing times. This understanding led him to wage war on poverty and support civil rights and voting rights laws. Grand were his plans for nation-building, yet the reality of Vietnam constrained Johnson. Also, reluctance in Congress to fund development weakened its linkage with what his administration saw as the promise of American liberalism.

Nation-building took on a sense of urgency in Vietnam. The "New Life" hamlets and, in late 1966, the Civil Operations and Revolutionary Development Support (CORDS) program testified to the union of modernization and counterinsurgency. While hopes for the New Life program were high, progress came slowly. Trust between villagers and Saigon was elusive. One month after Pleiku, Ambassador

Maxwell D. Taylor reported that "counterinsurgency efforts have been plagued by popular apathy and dwindling morale, consequences of long war with no end in sight. There is no sense of dedication on our side comparable to that instilled into [the] VC."[154] Taylor concluded that to counter Vietcong gains and prevent ARVN's collapse, "it will probably be necessary to commit US ground forces to action." The head of MACV, General William C. Westmoreland, echoed that assessment.[155] Trying to stave off defeat, nearly 200,000 American troops were in Vietnam at the end of 1965 and 536,000 in all before 1969.

Escalation did not speed nation-building. As bombs began falling on the north, Rostow argued that Ho Chi Minh would abandon guerrilla war to protect his industrial base. With the NLF vulnerable, the time seemed right to propose a development scheme in the south. Johnson did so in a speech at Johns Hopkins University on April 7, 1965, where he proposed a project akin to the TVA. Social change was the goal, which he hoped might lead to negotiations to end the war. The project foreshadowed the creation of the Asian Development Bank in December 1966, capitalized at $1 billion. The United States could not meet its $200 million quota because of the costs of the war.[156] Johnson's offer was disingenuous. No high-level policymaker believed that either the North Vietnamese or the NLF would accept his conditions, which would have transformed their revolution into a liberal development project. Also, Johnson was not being honest when he told Senator Mike Mansfield (D-Mont.) on April 12, "We have no desire to exercise 'a primacy' over what transpires in South Vietnam."[157]

CORDS attempted to disrupt contacts between villagers and the NLF.[158] At talks in Honolulu in February 1966, Johnson told Prime Minister Nguyen Cao Ky that nation-building depended on real reforms. Ky seemed receptive, but Johnson remained unconvinced, telling India's ambassador B. K. Nehru, "We have tried for two years to get these people to thinking in terms of building a better society there and not just strictly a military operation but a political one, too. And you can't do it unless you can get . . . the Prime Minister to adopt the baby as [his] own."[159]

Revolutionary development, entailing extensive population movement to urban areas from the countryside, became a priority. Robert Komer, a special assistant to the president after March 1966, extolled the virtues of modernization through pacification. By October, he thought MACV ought to supervise pacification because "progress to date in this largely neglected aspect of the war has been negligible."[160] Security in the provinces remained fragile, partly because of the war's effect on rice production; to wit, South Vietnam had to import 1.25 million tons of rice in 1966 and 1967.[161]

Komer pressed on, taking charge of CORDS in May 1967. Former ambassador Taylor, serving as a consultant, had doubts about revolutionary development.

Management problems and ARVN's inability to meet its responsibilities were hurting the program. Komer painted a rosier picture for Rostow: "We are slowly but surely winning [the] war of attrition in [the] South." MACV's West-moreland, he noted, "clearly thinks we are winning [the] military war." Pacifica-tion seemed on target in provinces relatively devoid of conventional warfare.[162] Komer assured Johnson in October, "By mid-1968 at the latest it will be clear to everyone that we are 'winning' the military war. . . . You can depend on it."[163]

Komer could not keep his promise. Modernization primarily depended on de-mand for consumer goods in an urban environment, which broke with tradi-tional ways in Vietnam despite forced relocation. Also, Washington and Saigon never vanquished the appeal of the NLF and the Democratic Republic of Vietnam as credible repositories of nationalism. Ky and his successor, President Nguyen Van Thieu, were at a disadvantage in the battle for hearts and minds. Rostow made this point indirectly when he criticized ARVN forces during a meeting on November 2, 1967, of the "Wise Men" as they sought to bolster public support for the war. The events of 1968, beginning with the Tet Offensive and the psy-chological blow it dealt the war effort, negated whatever progress CORDS had achieved.[164] McNamara's successor, Clark Clifford, had no good news for Johnson in July after a trip to Vietnam. Nor was Komer's pacification program bearing fruit.[165] By then, precious little time remained for liberal development in Vietnam.

The vagaries of nation-building were on display elsewhere in Asia, notably in Indonesia, where binding technical assistance to counterinsurgency and civic ac-tion enhanced what scholars call "military modernization."[166] Despite the endemic hostility between the United States and Sukarno's government, Kennedy had attempted to incorporate Indonesia into the Free World through economic sta-bilization, collaboration on development, and army participation in civic action. Washington planned to use the IMF and trade with Japan to draw Indonesia further into the Western orbit.[167] These plans went awry in 1965, known as "the year of living dangerously," when Sukarno tightened his grip on power by threat-ening foreign interests and taking Indonesia to the brink of war with Malaysia. "Indonesia," Komer concluded, "is quietly slipping out of our hands." Johnson reduced the U.S. presence and covertly tried to weaken Sukarno. When that gambit badly misfired, the White House, Bradley R. Simpson argues, "actively consider[ed] attempts to break up Indonesia."[168]

The failure of the September 30th Movement (a group of military personnel committed to ousting Sukarno) to stage a coup opened new opportunities. Great Britain and the United States covertly urged the army, which Suharto dominated after mid-October, to destroy the PKI, no matter the human cost, and make it impossible for Sukarno to rule. The CIA expressed relief that the army had acted "to crush the PKI" with U.S. help.[169] Destroying the PKI was a prerequisite for establishing military modernization. Widespread resistance derailed Sukarno's efforts to retain his hold on power. With Suharto in charge by mid-March 1967, Komer urged Johnson to exploit the situation "as quickly and as skillfully as possible."[170] And that he did.

No one in Washington was more pleased with this turn of events than Walt Rostow, who saw modernization theory being validated. If a turn to democratic politics lay in the future, that was insignificant compared with the benefits of stability guaranteed by the army. Ambassador Marshall Green cabled from Jakarta, "We believe [the] army's assessment of [the] role it must play is valid and that its formula for [a] 'new order' is essentially [the] right mixture."[171] An intelligence estimate concluded, "The need for foreign economic assistance—which can only be expected to come from the US, Japan, and Western Europe—virtually assures continuation of Indonesia's new Western-leaning foreign policies."[172]

Promises of additional aid were soon forthcoming. Johnson, despondent about the effect of war on development, thought of aid to Indonesia as a model of what might still be possible. "It has great potential," he told the NSC in August 1967. "It is one of the few places in the world that has moved in our direction." On November 21, with Vietnam influencing all policymaking, he confided to Rostow, "I want to do everything I can for Indonesia—as quickly as I can."[173]

Congress approved an aid package of $156 million. Military modernization was the essence of Indonesia's New Order. Economic problems remained, though, because Japan did not meet its aid obligations. U.S. officials in late 1968 were relieved that Suharto "has forsaken Sukarno's conception of Indonesia as the champion of the 'new emerging forces' of the underdeveloped world, and taken a more realistic attitude toward Indonesia's international position."[174]

Johnson hoped for similar results with India. He tilted away from Pakistan, viewing food aid as a way to create markets for American producers and hasten Western-style development. But Indian officials feared that aid meant dependency. Clashes between India and Pakistan over Kashmir in 1965–1966 gave Johnson an opportunity to tie food aid to his overall nation-building strategy. Unfortunately, a weakened dollar, a payments imbalance, and congressional failure to fund aid projects at requested levels thwarted his ambition. Early in the Indo-Pakistani conflict, Johnson decided to use P.L. 480 contracts as leverage by placing them and the disbursement of aid under regular review.[175]

Soon after the signing of a peace agreement with Pakistan in January 1966, the death of Prime Minister Lal Bahudar Shastri brought Nehru's daughter Indira Gandhi to power. Johnson and his top advisers rued the political turmoil accompanying her early months in office, which Rostow feared would impede development aid. Gandhi's Congress Party survived its political test, which buoyed Johnson, who was worried about the famine plaguing India. Secretary of Agriculture Orville L. Freeman thought that India could face food shortages for an indefinite period, so Washington structured an international response to the famine that Gandhi deftly used to her advantage as she began to diversify India's economy.[176]

Once Gandhi won election in February 1967, Congress authorized short-term aid. Getting food to malnourished Indians became Gandhi's priority; industrial development, long a goal of modernizers in India, had to wait. Johnson promised future assistance so long as Indo-Pakistani relations did not erupt into violence; he expended political capital in 1967 and into 1968 to help India, challenging those in Congress who opposed foreign aid as costly and unproductive.[177]

The battle to provide emergency food aid to India had been won, yet the administration did not reap the larger rewards it sought. Rusk, Freeman, and AID administrator William Gaud recommended in September 1968 that Johnson "keep alive the political and economic assets which you had built up." That seemed small consolation given his desire to use food as a major policy lever. That goal eluded him because New Delhi could not count on the timely delivery of food and fertilizer.[178] Development would nevertheless continue in India, if not necessarily along lines Washington preferred.

Nation-building in Africa promised to be unpredictable as well. Johnson had difficulty designing a comprehensive policy. He gradually moved beyond Kennedy's limited military civic-action programs in spring 1965 after the CIA concluded there remained "a desperate shortage of virtually all kinds of technical and managerial skills" that the United States could provide.[179] Two chiefs-of-missions conferences in Addis Ababa, Ethiopia, and Lagos, Nigeria, helped devise plans for programs of graduate study in America, use of the United States Information Agency, and reliance on AID as a political tool. Komer doubted the effectiveness of aid, telling Johnson, "The new African countries are in such a primitive state of development, and are so hipped on internecine quarrels that I doubt whether even a massive US investment now would show a commensurate result." He doubted that, in such circumstances, Congress would boost economic or military aid, which amounted to $300 million in FY 1965.[180]

Komer's caution upset nation-builders. Assistant Secretary of State for African Affairs G. Mennen "Soapy" Williams advocated additional cultural and economic aid. Rusk concurred, finding in Africa "a unique opportunity to project American ideas and use American resources . . . consistent with our democratic principles." As was his wont, Rusk viewed policy initiatives through a prism evocative of Luce's American Century. Johnson, however, found Komer's plea for caution more persuasive.[181]

There matters rested thanks to the volatility of African politics. Between June 1965 and March 1966, military seizures of power occurred from Algeria to the Congo, Dahomey, Central African Republic, Upper Volta, Nigeria, and Ghana. Such sweeping changes did not necessarily favor U.S. interests despite the potential openings for AID, Food for Peace, the IMF and World Bank, and the Peace Corps. Komer once again recommended gradualism and "limiting our own investment in favor of other more critical areas." Johnson agreed. In July 1966, the Task Force on the Review of African Development Policies and Programs affirmed: "Our primary concern with Africa has been . . . to prevent events in the continent from complicating a search, largely conducted elsewhere, for solutions to the problems of war and peace, or from interfering with our central strategic and political preoccupations in other regions." The task force, led by Ambassador to Ethiopia Edward M. Korry, while not dismissing development in Africa, still concluded, "Such a commitment may make sense in Latin America—but not in Africa."[182]

At length, the administration all but turned over nation-building to international financial institutions and allies like France, which wanted to retain influence with its former colonies. Rejecting an infusion of AID funds, Johnson approved Korry's report as NSAM 356 in October. The NSC soon was discussing conditions in Africa as they affected larger strategic and political interests. The State Department fell in line; in March 1968, with no explicit mention of nation-building, it identified "safeguarding of U.S. strategic interests; adoption by African governments of favorable attitudes; [and] fostering U.S. trade and investments" as policy priorities.[183]

Nation-building in the Americas, relying on the Alliance for Progress, also fell short of expectations.[184] Designed as an engine of self-help, economic diversification, social progress, and, in time, democratization, the alliance seemed the perfect vehicle to advance the American Century. In its first two years, it disbursed $762 million under the auspices of AID, $8 million in loans by the Social Progress Trust Fund, $401 million through the Food for Peace program, $18 million in grant assistance, and $848 million in Export-Import Bank loans for a total of about $2 billion.[185] This largesse did not yield the projected 2.5 percent per capita growth in 1963. Debt exceeded $3 billion with Argentina, Brazil, and Chile accounting for nearly half of the total. The NSC admitted that the data "add up to a very unsatisfactory picture," and an AID assessment in October 1965 agreed.[186]

Development produced a mixed record in Brazil, Chile, Colombia, and Venezuela, for example, and it was abysmal in Guatemala, where the need was acute. Adult illiteracy exceeded 60 percent, and 90 percent of the Indian population did not read or write.[187] Despite a bloody struggle between the military and leftist unions and rural peasants, Maryknoll missionaries and AID tried to bring a degree of development to the countryside. Meanwhile, the CIA monitored missionary activity, seeking to learn more about radical activity.[188] Moreover, AID's

Office of Public Safety abetted repression in the provinces in 1966 during the rule of an elected, civilian president, Julio César Méndez Montenegro. Desperate to halt guerrilla activity, the military, with the help of U.S. advisers, initiated Operación Limpieza (Operation Cleanup), setting off a deadly conflict. Within months, at least eight thousand people died, including labor unionists, leftists, and rural, nonpolitical Guatemalans. The State Department's Thomas L. Hughes declared in October 1967 that "the counter-insurgency machine is out of control."[189] Ambassador John Gordon Mein, who died at the hands of rebels in August 1968, was a notable casualty.[190]

Nevertheless, counterinsurgency remained a mainstay of nation-building because, as the CIA warned in April 1964, "the hazards of governing may be increasing rather than lessening in Latin America."[191] Walt Rostow agreed yet knew that development had to offer the prospect of economic improvement. Before becoming national security adviser, he oversaw the preparation of a blueprint for development, "Frontiers of South America." "Opening of the South American frontiers has an important role to play in the region's future," he wrote. "The laying out of roads and organized settlements is a significant element in preventing the possibilities of Communist insurgency." Johnson found merit in Rostow's idea.[192] "Frontiers of South America," it bears noting, was a project predicated on the American Century's relevance to local conditions.

Bolivia, Colombia, and Peru provide instructive case studies illuminating the security-development nexus at the core of nation-building. AID, through OPS, was helping rural Bolivian police fulfill their civic action duties. MAP assistance through FY 1967 amounted to $15 million, with another $2.4 million projected for FY 1968. The Defense Department, AID, and OPS had programs in Colombia. MAP assistance had reached $83 million and another $5.2 million was requested for FY 1968. Over sixty U.S. military personnel were assisting MAP operations. MAP funds amounted to $75 million in Peru, with $3.5 million more planned for FY 1968. Sixty-six officers and enlisted men were supporting counterinsurgency operations and civic action programs.[193] The U.S. government estimated the number of guerrillas in the Andes in the mid-1960s: between sixty and one hundred in Bolivia, perhaps eight hundred in Colombia, and a small number in Peru. Rostow conveyed this information to Johnson, asserting a connection between the guerrillas and Cuba or the Soviet Union.[194]

Bolivia, where General René Barrientos Ortuño had seized power from President Paz Estenssoro in November 1964, was home to an intractable conflict between left-wing unions and the government. Despite reformist proclivities in the ruling MNR, democratic inclusion remained difficult. Breaking the tin miners' unions was essential if U.S.-supported nation-building was to proceed. Paz had sought in August 1963 to curb the power of miners by revoking their oversight of the operation of the state-owned tin mine (Corporación Minera de Bolivia, or COMIBOL). Barrientos clamped down on dissent, and stability became the watchword in La Paz after the July 1966 elections, which he won by appealing to fellow Quechua-speaking peasants.[195]

U.S. reaction to the battle with the COMIBOL miners was swift; Hughes linked military activity to the fate of private investment and nation-building. The CIA, fearing that the situation might embolden the Bolivian Communist Party, rushed emergency aid to the military. The State Department applauded the crackdown on the miners: "This is the first time in more than a decade . . . that a Bolivian government has a chance to bring law and order to the mines."[196] U.S. aid, in the guise of a Political Action Program of the 303 Committee, flowed to Barrientos to help his presidential campaign. U.S.-Bolivian ties strengthened during his subsequent trip to Washington, during which nation-building was discussed.[197] Ambassador Julio Sanjines Goytia sought help for "additional projects . . . to further Bolivia's development." The administration, integrating security policy and nation-building once again, obliged.[198] The stage was set for cooperation in the hunt for Che Guevara and indigenous guerrillas in mid-1967. It succeeded, with U.S.-trained Rangers killing Guevara in October.[199]

In Colombia, where prospects for development seemed brighter, the "erosion of popular support for the National Front coalition" emboldened rebel forces— the Ejército de Liberación Nacional, or ELN, and the Fuerzas Armadas Revolucionarias de Colombia, or FARC.[200] The National Front's exclusionary politics retarded development in what one scholar describes as "a collection of pseudo-feudal city-states, rather than a modern nation-state." With the Liberal Party reluctant to implement real land reform, the advent of the FARC in 1964 was predictable. The ELN, with the guerrilla-priest Camilo Torres its best-known member, was particularly active in the mid-1960s. His death in combat with Colombian armed forces in February 1966 made him a martyr for alienated youth and the Left throughout Latin America.[201]

Ambassador Covey T. Oliver worried that a stagnant economy would badly weaken the government in Bogotá.[202] Colombia's economy was stronger by fall 1966, yet land reform lagged behind expectations. AID negotiated a $100 million program loan premised on progress toward "political stability against extremist student and guerrilla activities."[203] Was that goal attainable? Hughes described Liberal Carlos Lleras Restrepo, who became president in August 1966, as "somewhat authoritarian, short-tempered, and imperious when angered." The prospect of more dysfunction led the CIA to question the army's effectiveness.[204] In any event, nation-building proceeded slowly in Colombia.

In Peru, where President Fernando Belaúnde Terry sought to maintain cordial ties with Washington after his election in June 1963, agrarian and educational reform continued despite differences over the place of the International Petroleum Company (IPC) in national affairs. The CIA worried that rural unrest swirling around the land question might develop into guerrilla warfare. Moreover, "arbitrary" settlement of the IPC case, that is, seizure or settlement without fair compensation, "could have widespread adverse repercussions in the business community as well as on the U.S. aid program."[205] Such was the context affecting development.

Importantly, the guerrilla threat did not rival that faced by Bolivia, Colombia, Guatemala, or even Venezuela, although peasant uprisings involved over three hundred thousand people during the 1960s. Groups like the Movimiento de Izquierda Revolucionario, or MIR, linked the fight for land to the struggle for indigenous rights—a constant theme in twentieth-century Peru. The military, with the help of AID, struck back, decimating the MIR by early 1966 and leaving eight thousand people dead and twenty thousand homeless. The grim reality of hacienda-like living and working conditions persisted, giving rise to even more radical guerrilla forces. (The most notorious became known as Sendero Luminoso, or Shining Path.) To the extent that insurgents had influence with campesinos in the countryside, it was uncertain whether extensive development was possible.[206]

At issue was who would set the contours of nation-building, the Peruvian government or international financial institutions and officials in Washington. Impeding a U.S.-style path to development was the IPC affair. The dispute centered on subsoil rights and payment of back taxes. The 303 Committee began monitoring the situation in January 1966. Expropriation of foreign holdings without fair compensation meant that aid to Peru would cease under the 1962 Hickenlooper Amendment. To speed negotiations Washington applied pressure; AID loans were disbursed slowly, which in turn reduced the flow of foreign capital.[207]

As inflation mounted and foreign exchange drained away, AID exacted a price for aid: Peru had to put its economic policy on a liberal-developmental track. This meant new taxation, cuts in government spending, denial of equipment to the military, and an agreement with the IMF. The IPC issue still went unresolved, so Johnson reserved for himself the final say over disbursement of AID loans.[208] By July 1967, thinking he had gone too far, Johnson told McNamara, Rusk, and Rostow that without help "there will be many other Cubas in Latin America."[209]

Meanwhile, Belaúnde's popularity declined, and the possibility of a military takeover grew. Rostow warned Johnson that the Alliance for Progress itself could be at risk. His fears, voiced in October 1967, proved to be premature by a year. On October 3, 1968, Peru's military ousted Belaúnde, two months after a tentative, much maligned, settlement in principle with the IPC.[210] Placed in charge was General Juan Velasco Alvarado, whom the U.S. embassy viewed as "highly nationalistic and suspicious of U.S. policies." His saving grace was that he was a "strong anti-Communist." Washington wanted Velasco to use counterinsurgency tactics to hasten nation-building, especially when fissures within leftist groups in 1968 resulted in the formation of a new faction of the Peruvian Communist Party.[211] Nation-building in Peru by then was no more a reality than elsewhere in the Andes.

Liberal development would not soon bring democratic governance to the Third World or mitigate poverty. With modernization and counterinsurgency so inter-woven, did nation-building really reflect Luce's vision of America as a Good Sa-maritan? Answering that query soon fell to Richard Nixon, who was skeptical of his nation's conceit that it was entitled to remake the world.

Johnson and the Credibility Trap

John F. Kennedy had avoided the credibility trap in Southeast Asia; Lyndon John-son was not so lucky. The impulse to defend credibility there proved irresistible. Ambassador Maxwell Taylor cabled Dean Rusk from Saigon in September 1964, "If we leave Vietnam with our tail between our legs, the consequences of this defeat in the rest of Asia, Africa, and Latin America would be disastrous." John-son shared Taylor's apocalyptic view: "Our allies not just in Asia but throughout the world would conclude that our word was worth little or nothing."[212] His words reflected what a Vietnam study group reported to him on July 8, 1965. If South Vietnam fell, Thailand could not be held, and the effects would be felt in Japan and India. Also, "the effect in Europe might also be most serious, and . . . de Gaulle would find many takers for his argument that the US could not now be counted on to defend Europe." In short, the world would question "whether US commitments could be relied on."[213]

As the administration made its fateful decision to choose war in Indochina, the reactions of allies increasingly mattered. George Ball cautioned, "On balance I believe we would more seriously undermine the effectiveness of our world lead-ership by continuing the war . . . than by pursuing a carefully plotted course toward a compromise solution." During the policymaking battle on July 21, Ball argued that allies were more concerned about the effect on their security of events in Berlin, for example, than about developments in Vietnam. De Gaulle, who sup-ported neutralization for Southeast Asia, would have agreed. To him, the United States had no primacy of place within the Atlantic Community.[214] Britain's gen-eral support of U.S. war policy did not extend to bombing that affected the civilian population of North Vietnam. Officials in Bonn rhetorically supported Johnson, while hoping that U.S. commitments to Western Europe would endure.[215] Meet-ing in late December with Ambassador to the United Nations Arthur J. Goldberg, de Gaulle called again for a rapid end to the war, which he thought impossible because "the honor and prestige of America as a great and powerful nation was involved by its commitments."[216]

As Washington struggled to preserve its credibility in 1965, U.S. and Soviet authorities found it difficult to strengthen the trust they had developed after the missile crisis and the signing of the Test Ban Treaty. The greatest impediment was Vietnam. Moscow would not put relations with Washington at risk, but neither would the Kremlin reward behavior it opposed. After the bombing of North Vietnam had begun in February, Soviet ambassador Anatoly Dobrynin informed Ambassador-at-Large Llewellyn Thompson, "[If the] present policy continued, our relations would be adversely affected."[217] To gauge the chance for negotiations, Johnson sent Averell Harriman to Moscow in July as he and his advisers were deciding on war. "Kosygin was completely negative, in fact at times insulting though occasionally with a smile," Harriman reported.[218]

Other blows to American credibility came from within. Johnson's relations with Senate Foreign Relations Committee Chairman J. William Fulbright had soured. By the time of the Tet Offensive, Fulbright despaired: "I am at a loss for words to describe the idiocy of what we are doing." A similar break had occurred earlier with Walter Lippmann, the dean of the nation's journalists. Lippmann, who was close to McGeorge Bundy, advocated a negotiated settlement. His newspaper columns became more critical in 1965 when he wrote that Johnson and his national security advisers were intent on war. He opined in his Today and Tomorrow column of December 21, 1965, "Only those who suffer from delusions of omnipotence will think that this country . . . can fight a major war in Asia, and can police the world from Berlin to Korea from Central Asia to South America."[219]

The buildup of U.S. forces in South Vietnam gave life to an antiwar movement at home. Critics scoffed when the president held out the prospect of negotiations without conditions in his speech at Johns Hopkins University. Explaining why American forces were in Vietnam, he said, "*We are there because we have a promise to keep.*"[220] Ten days later twenty thousand people, many of whom were students, gathered in Washington to protest the war. A battle for the hearts and minds of the American people had been joined. Administration truth squads defended the propriety of the war in the same college classrooms and auditoriums where antiwar teach-ins occurred. At a rally in November with the Washington Monument as a backdrop, Carl Oglesby of the Students for a Democratic Society denounced both the war and the cold-war liberalism that it represented. Preceding Oglesby were luminaries including Arthur Miller, Coretta Scott King, Norman Thomas, Albert Sabin, and Benjamin Spock.[221]

Doing nothing in the face of youthful dissent at home or abroad was not acceptable to Johnson. Debates over war in Indochina sparked denunciations of U.S.

foreign policy and covert operations by the CIA, which likely included infiltration of European student groups. Alliances sprung up between black and white radicals in America and Europe's Left. Frustration within the IYC boiled over before 1968; one official lamented in August 1966, "This is a difficult time. . . . Vietnam casts its shadow over foreign and domestic policy."[222]

To understand what was happening, the IYC commissioned a study of youth in Western Europe, with results presented at a conference in May 1967. Historian Fritz Stern of Columbia University reported on Germany, political scientist Paul E. Sigmund of Princeton University on Great Britain, and Anton W. DePorte of the State Department on France. The IYC asked in the report's preface, "Twenty years after initiation of the Fulbright program, why have we a problem in relationships with the young elites of Europe?" Had the scholars interviewed German and French radicals, which they did not, they would have learned the New Left in Western Europe, Italy included, had pledged solidarity with the Third World in rejecting the status quo.[223]

The global confrontation between young men and women and officialdom in 1968 led to further reviews.[224] The State Department in effect declared militancy a threat to the American Century, specifically to "the objectives of U.S. foreign policy, our relations with the country concerned, the worldwide functioning of our business interests, and our free enterprise economic system." Extremism was growing in Europe, the United States, and parts of Latin America; in Japan students protested the scheduled 1970 renewal of the U.S.-Japan Security Treaty.[225]

The CIA produced a report, "Restless Youth," examining dissent in nineteen countries. Widespread access to higher education emerged as a common explanation for unrest. "A student in the US, France, Brazil, or Japan probably does identify with his peers in other countries," the authors found. The effects on U.S. prestige were not salutary: "Many of today's students—far more than are directly involved in protest—share the activists' disillusionment with the political process." Johnson, feeling betrayed by African Americans and antiwar protestors, lashed out in a cabinet meeting on September 18, 1968; he blamed Communists for their actions. CIA Director Richard Helms disagreed, saying there was "no evidence of Communist control, manipulation, or support of student dissidents."[226] Dissent was more than Johnson could bear by then.

In truth, he had set off the debate over Vietnam following the Gulf of Tonkin incident in August 1964 when he promised a national audience in a late-night address, "We still seek no wider war."[227] The eminent political scientist Hans J. Morgenthau, who debated the war with McGeorge Bundy on television in June 1965, used the occasion of a book review in August 1966 to denounce the president's "deviousness and impetuosity." "This 'credibility gap' has become a persistent aspect of Johnson's conduct of American foreign policy," he declared.[228]

Throughout the remainder of his presidency, Johnson could not change this perception. Opposition to the war intensified on October 21, 1967, when one hundred thousand people marched on the Pentagon, and became even more pronounced after the Tet Offensive.[229]

If allies in the Atlantic Community did not break with Johnson over Vietnam, neither did they discard their reservations. Britain remained a reliable supporter of the administration despite Harold Wilson's own doubts and strong differences with Washington concerning British defense policy.[230] In Bonn, Ludwig Erhard and Kurt Kiesinger, aware of widespread antiwar sentiment in their country, endeavored to keep Vietnam from injuring German-U.S. relations; their visions of German reunification and quest for European security overcame other major concerns.[231]

Less positively, Lester Pearson's doubts strengthened resolve in Ottawa to distance Canada from the United States over Vietnam. Canadian Secretary of State for External Affairs Paul Martin angered Washington in October 1967, declaring that "the onus is on the US to explain its position to the people of the world." French opposition to U.S. policy did not abate.[232] When departing his post as ambassador in January 1968, Charles E. Bohlen admonished officials in Paris, charging that the cool state of bilateral relations, Vietnam aside, derived largely from France's obsession with American power and its alleged misuse.[233] Be that as it may, Johnson's personal trustworthiness and America's credibility were waning.

Also contributing to the credibility trap was the gold crisis of March 1968. Since July 1965, when Johnson's national security team made its fateful decision for war, the United States had been overextended militarily and financially. In financial terms, the United States faced a balance-of-payments deficit and a run on gold that existed because of obligations taken on in pursuit of global containment. Dollar devaluation was consistently rejected as counterproductive, especially after London devalued the pound in November 1967. Washington resisted pressure to raise the price of gold above $35 per ounce, fearing that, as the NSC put it, "dollars therefore could no longer be relied on for international liquidity."[234]

Gold losses spiked after January 1968, reaching $400 million on March 14 and forcing Johnson to close the gold window to keep reserves from falling below the legal requirement of $10 billion. France and West Germany watched to see whether he would act to ease the crisis. Separating the public and private gold markets averted a catastrophe at the time.[235] Europeans watched in amazement as Congress failed to act through the taxing power. Walt Rostow wrote Johnson in mid-March, "[The crisis] obviously goes to the heart of our nation's capacity to carry its external commitments; maintain the world trade and monetary system; and avoid a serious domestic breakdown in our economy."[236] The world's economic powers had stepped back from the abyss; that did not constitute an endorsement of U.S. leadership.

American supremacy in world affairs was not what it once had been. Henry Luce's death on February 28, 1967, kept him from watching his brainchild fall apart. Johnson had been a capable steward of the American Century in various ways. He kept NATO together by juggling U.S., West German, and French political interests. Moreover, Soviet-American relations edged toward détente under Johnson's leadership even as the USSR was lessening America's strategic superiority. Also, his administration's faith in nation-building was unsurpassed in the cold-war era. Therein lay the seeds of decline, however. With internal security and nation-building joined like a modern Gordian knot, Washington squandered its reputation as a global Good Samaritan. In sum, the war in Vietnam had revealed the limits of liberal development along a North-South divide, exposing the dollar's weakness and the difficulty of sustaining economic hegemony. The decline of the American Century was gathering speed.

ATTAINING PRIMACY

Richard Nixon and Henry Kissinger had no intention of restoring the American Century. Trying to recoup hegemony would further reduce U.S. influence in a complex world and impede attainment of their real objective: primacy.[1] Kissinger rejected hegemony as utopian—a quality he would have ascribed to Luce's American Century. A quest for "perfection and permanence" was intrinsically, in Bruce Kuklick's words, "an attempt to escape history." For Kissinger and Nixon, that was a recipe for instability.[2] Kissinger, ironically, did accept the idea of American uniqueness, to wit: "Only America had both the power and the decency to inspire other peoples who struggled for identity, for progress and dignity."[3] Henry Luce could not have said it better.

What was primacy? Stanley Hoffmann in his magisterial *Primacy or World Order* leaves it undefined. He suggests primacy refers to the status of the United States vis-à-vis other powers, a status marked by negativity in that it does not convey hegemonic authority. Contra Hoffmann, American primacy was not a given; events in the late 1960s had exacted a toll on the nation's standing in the world. That does not imply impotence, yet retrenchment was coming. Selectivity and flexibility, rather than the limitless aspirations of global containment, became attributes of a new grand strategy, strategic globalism, in which major interests were less encompassing than before. Like hegemony, primacy required credibility for validation, and credibility, as always, depended on the conduct of diplomacy and how the United States used its vast resources.

The Contours of Retrenchment

Moscow's longtime ambassador to the United States, Anatoly Dobrynin, well understood U.S. objectives. He admired how Nixon and Kissinger, students of "the global diplomatic game and the imperatives of *realpolitik*," operated despite "not really thinking in terms of bringing about a major breakthrough in Soviet-American relations, and of ending the Cold War and the arms race."[4] Kissinger essentially confirmed Dobrynin's analysis, admitting he and Nixon were seeking to make the Cold War less dangerous. The actual purpose of détente was "to give the Soviets a stake in cooperation even while . . . mak[ing] expansionism too dangerous."[5] Russia was moving in that direction, and through détente China might also. The promise of détente pictured stability and order as shared objectives in a calmer Cold War.

The road to retrenchment was an emotional journey, all the more so given the potential pitfalls. Nixon and Kissinger believed in the limits of power. Accepting the need for restraint in a changing world elicited a lament from Nixon: "[It is] sad but true."[6] A sense of urgency underlay his words, just as Kissinger's efforts to develop close ties with Dobrynin indicate how emotion colored the actions of these archetypal men of realpolitik.[7] They feared that the time for using détente to protect America's global standing was fleeting. Their words convey feelings akin to desperation; that they could effectively portray their actions as realist policy-making indicates how pervasive the security ethos still was for American officials.[8] An abiding fear of failure, for Nixon reelection in 1972 and for Kissinger his place in history, was palpable.

Jeremi Suri writes in a related vein, "Nixon and Kissinger had a dark view of human nature and democratic society, born of their own experiences with social prejudice."[9] For the former Harvard professor, containment prevented the shrewd mixing of limited force with a judicious resort to tough diplomacy. For the ex–vice president, containment precluded innovation in foreign policy. Both men understood global containment as the antithesis of the pragmatism that was mandatory in a dangerous world. Yet pragmatism, value-free though it seems, cannot exist outside of the emotional context that gives it meaning. In short, how Nixon and Kissinger cognitively constructed the world reflected deeply held beliefs about what they perceived as the rightful place of the United States in history and the present.

Kissinger, Suri asserts, was the embodiment of the American Century, particularly in his recognition of the nation's limited capacity to remake the world. Only amid the global torment of the mid to late 1960s does Suri's analysis ring true. Previously, those who birthed, managed, and protected the American Century believed it was predicated on hegemony. Nixon and Kissinger regarded allies and adversaries as pawns on a geopolitical chessboard where moves were highly cal-culated. Negotiating détente was a delicate game because Kissinger thought it "impossible to impose [on Russia and China] an American design."[10]

Revamping grand strategy in pursuit of primacy mandated a new China pol-icy, which Nixon's visit to Beijing in February 1972 signified. Nixon knew he was one of a small number of politicians who had the bona fides to produce dramatic changes in U.S.-PRC relations. Likewise, Mao Zedong, having resuscitated his au-thority and cooled the ardor of the Cultural Revolution, was positioned to tran-scend barriers between Beijing and Washington. Both leaders took risks, yet the reward, stability, was worth the gamble.[11] Getting Nixon to Beijing took some doing. Sino-American relations had largely remained frozen in time since Chi-na's civil war ended in 1949. Occasional meetings in Warsaw, Poland, starting after the 1954 Geneva Conference, were exceptions. Major impediments to progress were America's ties with Taiwan, the Vietnam War, the PRC's denunciation of im-perialism (both Soviet and American), and China's self-imposed isolation dur-ing the Cultural Revolution. Officials did not rule out reconciliation yet assumed change was unlikely before a post-Mao era.[12]

The freeze thawed slightly in the spring of 1969. Border clashes with the Soviets along the Ussuri River helped break China's isolation. By the end of the year, intermediaries had made known to Beijing Nixon's desire to open discussions. "We simply cannot afford to leave China outside the family of nations," he had written in 1967.[13] Four years later, change was at hand. Something more was hap-pening than Nixon's recognition of the limits of power. The Americans wanted to be in position to influence China's reentry onto the world stage. Through dex-terous management of this emerging trilateralism, Nixon and Kissinger were endeavoring to attain primacy and rejuvenate U.S. credibility.[14]

With the help of Pakistan, Kissinger met secretly with Zhou Enlai in July 1971 to prepare Nixon's trip. Addressing fears of possible betrayal, Kissinger told Zhou, "We would continue to deal with Moscow, but . . . we would inform Peking in detail of any understanding affecting Chinese interests that we might consider with the Soviets, and we would take Chinese views into account."[15] With this pledge securely in hand in Beijing, the historic meeting of Mao and Nixon was set for the following February. Yet Pakistan's vital contribution to détente and the shaping of strategic globalism had its own complications, which put the White House's plans at risk.

War between India and Pakistan broke out in December 1971. Aligned on one side were the Soviet Union and India. That their treaty of friendship, signed in August, had not provided Indira Gandhi's government with military aid did not allay U.S. concerns about Soviet power in South Asia. On the other side of the geostrategic equation, China sided with Pakistan but could not prevent East

Pakistan, soon to be Bangladesh, from resisting West Pakistan's control. In line with the secret pledge Kennedy had made in 1962 to support Dacca in the event of conflict with India, Washington tilted toward Pakistan.[16] As that move commenced, U.S. consular officials protested U.S. acquiescence in "selective genocide" by Pakistani officialdom in Bangladesh.[17]

With the onset of war, the openings to Moscow and Beijing seemed in jeopardy.[18] Could Nixon and Kissinger put aside their contempt for the Pakistanis and Indians and resolve the crisis in order to salvage their emerging grand strategy? Talks with Gandhi on November 4 and 5 had gone nowhere. The two Americans reviled her, calling her a "bitch" (Kissinger) and an "old witch" (Nixon).[19] Luck was on their side, however. After dispatching the USS *Enterprise* to the Indian Ocean and urging China to move troops to the border with India, they began to worry about a great power confrontation of unprecedented magnitude. More than détente seemed at risk; global stability itself appeared uncertain. Washington would then find itself in a defensive posture from which it might not recover. Fortunately, with China's intercession, the UN brokered a cease-fire, and the crisis ebbed on December 16. The road to détente still lay open.[20]

Nixon and Kissinger traveled to Moscow in May 1972. Leaders in the Kremlin had their own unease about security, which the U.S.-Chinese *démarche* heightened. Moscow's concerns had lessened after Dobrynin met with Nixon following his trip to Beijing. As Dobrynin recalled, Nixon impressed General Secretary Leonid Brezhnev with "his readiness to agree to strategic parity with the Soviet Union, which had long been a goal of the Soviet leadership."[21] Thus, the Moscow summit took place as scheduled.

With the strategic arms limitation treaty (SALT), commonly known as SALT I, which capped the number of nuclear missiles each side could possess, and the accord to halt production of anti-ballistic missile (ABM) systems, the Soviets got what they wanted, and more. Absent from the negotiations were the multiple independently targeted reentry vehicles (MIRVs) that carried numerous warheads. (The U.S. lead in MIRV capacity would spark another arms race by mid-decade.) A wheat deal, derided in the United States as the "Great Grain Robbery," and the prospect of improved trade with the United States gave a boost to the Soviet economy, which was faltering. Most important to Moscow, the summit underlined the USSR's international importance, leaving China in Soviet calculations as the junior player among the three great powers.[22]

Détente has received excessive praise and misleading criticism. It was merely part of a larger process for all three nations. The USSR had much to gain from détente. Yet greater global engagement turned out to be a double-edged sword, the ultimate cost two decades later was its very existence. China, following the deaths of Zhou and Mao in 1976, moved to establish itself as the preeminent power in Asia. By summer 1972, détente was facing opposition at home. There was, however, no other path to stability should tension between the Kremlin and Washington rise to the levels of the first fifteen years of the Cold War.[23] What the United States achieved through diplomacy in 1972 testified, although briefly, to the vital importance of primacy at the highest level of world politics.

Although clearly committed to defending the Free World, Nixon and Kissinger dismissed nurturing parts of it as irrelevant social work. "Latin America doesn't matter," the president told Donald Rumsfeld, a key adviser. To Kissinger, America's neighbor Canada was a second-rate power of limited strategic importance.[24] He also derided SEATO and CENTO as "moribund . . . instruments of collective action. [They] have become . . . unilateral American guarantees."[25] This perspective dovetailed nicely with the Nixon Doctrine (announced in August 1969 on Guam), which insisted that Asian allies, and implicitly other friends, must defend themselves, albeit with Washington's help if needed. As the NSC put it in early 1970, the United States would act only after assessing the "significance of our interests involved" in any given situation. In Vietnam, though, retrenchment in Nixon's first term took a backseat to preexisting obligations; thanks to the so-called madman strategy, disengaging from the war in Indochina became a means to repair American credibility.[26]

Even Israel could not be certain that it remained an ally of the first rank. That status had seemingly been reaffirmed in the aftermath of the crisis between Syria and Jordan in September 1970 when Israeli forces prevented the likely breakup of Jordan.[27] Yet after meeting with Prime Minister Golda Meir on March 1, 1973, Kissinger and Nixon discussed the limits of support for one of Israel's vital interests. Kissinger observed, "The emigration of Jews from the Soviet Union is not an objective of American foreign policy. And if they put Jews into gas chambers in the Soviet Union, it is not an American concern." Nixon responded as though nuclear war were the only feasible course of action: "I know. We can't blow up the world because of it."[28]

Attaining lasting primacy was impossible if Washington did not demonstrate leadership beyond relations with Russia and China. The United States could lead only if ties with Western Europe were on a solid footing, as Nixon had pointed out when he accepted the 1968 Republican nomination for president.[29] In that sense, members of NATO, especially West Germany, became essential to furthering primacy. What actually was NATO in 1969? It was neither moribund nor subservient to Washington's wishes. Kissinger found it in "disarray"; its European members "on the whole acted like ostriches."[30] Speaking in April 1969 to the North Atlantic Council, Nixon was less critical but much alarmed as NATO members adapted to new circumstances. He viewed arms control as "a test of the ability of the Western nations to shape a common strategy."[31] One thorny dilemma was that some major U.S. and European interests were no longer congruent, a reality that consultation might not alter.[32]

Because European members of NATO were convinced the White House would never accept anything other than a U.S.-led alliance, Nixon's response to *Ostpolitik* spoke volumes about Washington's drive for primacy. Kissinger gives the administration high marks for how it handled both NATO's problems and the potentially divisive matter of Willy Brandt and Egon Bahr's creation.[33] What actually happened was not so straightforward. The decline in America's stature emboldened Brandt and Bahr, who believed that West Germany could not become a full-fledged member of the international community until Bonn pursued its own foreign policy out of the shadow of occupation. Accordingly, they looked to *Ostpolitik* to liberate West Germany from its past. Diplomatic openings to East Germany and the USSR envisioned a reunited Germany and an easing of tension across the continent; it set off alarms in Washington. Although relations with the Christian Democrats had been strained at times, Nixon appreciated Kurt Kiesinger, to whom he said in February 1969, "You are the heart of the alliance. . . . Our devotion bilaterally and multilaterally to your nation is firm." He was less complimentary of Brandt as Kiesinger's successor looked eastward, telling Kissinger in May 1971, "I don't want to hurt our friends in Germany though by catering to that son-of-a-bitch."[34]

Nixon did not have that option, however. *Ostpolitik* eased the way for Soviet-American détente, and West Germany became America's closest partner in NATO. Willy Brandt was no Germanic de Gaulle. He did not disparage U.S. leadership of the Atlantic alliance but wanted Washington to factor European interests into its strategic planning—with West Germany in the forefront. Kissinger thought that Brandt and Bahr would fail because Bonn lacked the one thing to give *Ostpolitik* credibility: military power.[35] He was wrong. The Germans signed agreements that recognized existing borders in Europe, reduced tension over Berlin with a quadripartite accord, laid the basis for unification with East Germany, and stressed diplomacy in relations with the Soviet bloc. Brandt and Bahr made possible a European security conference, which began meeting in Helsinki in July 1973 as the Conference on Security and Cooperation in Europe.[36]

Ostpolitik did not ignore Washington's or, for that matter, Moscow's security concerns. In fact, it exploited the Brezhnev Doctrine and the American desire for superpower engagement by promising order and predictability throughout Europe.[37] *Ostpolitik* and détente thus operated on complementary tracks. Brandt and Bahr focused on continental order, while the two superpowers and China tested one another's political good faith. Given their goals, the Germans succeeded and helped strengthen the European Community, which admitted Great Britain and prodded NATO to modernize its mission. Also, beginning in 1969,

France under de Gaulle's successors showed greater flexibility in foreign policy than it had in years. *Ostpolitik* therefore helped set the contours of American primacy in a time of retrenchment. (At a ceremony in 2003 honoring Brandt and Bahr, Kissinger acknowledged the debt he and Nixon owed the two men for aiding the cause of détente and protecting the Atlantic alliance.)[38]

American influence over NATO was nominally preserved, if not exactly as Nixon and Kissinger had planned. The United States had long desired burden-sharing within NATO; that occurred to an extent. In turn, European powers got what they were after: increased consultation regarding defense policy. These changes took shape beginning in 1973, dubbed by Kissinger as the "Year of Europe." (See this chapter's section on credibility.)

If conflict was less likely in Europe thanks to *Ostpolitik*, the same was not always true elsewhere where major interests of the Communist powers and the United States intersected. The Nixon administration responded as its predecessors had by selling arms to security partners. What differed from earlier arms transfers was the greater selectivity and lower cost of the program under Nixon, a result of both congressional restrictions put in place in 1967–1968 and the strictures of the Nixon Doctrine.[39]

Deterrence had long been the basic goal of security arrangements with allies and clients. Retrenchment led to a modified approach: deterrence through restraint. The majority of arms sales would go to clients in the regions of greatest importance to U.S. security. Nations no longer receiving requested allotments of U.S. arms, whether through credit or sales, would have to turn elsewhere or make do with less. Where U.S. sales persisted, principally in Western Europe and the Middle East, American credibility improved and brought primacy within reach.

Attaining primacy partly depended on access to oil for the United States and its allies and on the absence of war between Israel and its Arab neighbors. A related objective was to limit the Soviet Union's presence and influence in the Middle East. It would take until after the October War in 1973 to break Egypt's security dependence on the USSR and restore diplomatic ties with Cairo, which were severed after the Six-Day War. U.S.-Iranian relations were in comparatively good shape, bolstered by a steady flow of arms for which the shah, described by Kissinger as "a friend of our country and a pillar of stability in a turbulent and vital region," was grateful.[40] During Nixon's presidency, Iran and Israel were the leading recipients of U.S. arms transfers. Also crucial for securing a major U.S. presence in the region was an enduring link with Riyadh; an increase in military sales to Saudi Arabia from $305 million in 1972 to more than $5 billion in 1975 nicely accomplished that goal.[41]

One scholarly assessment of the Nixon-Kissinger era concludes, "In the grand trajectory of 'the American Century,' the 1970s stand out as a curious anomaly . . . [when] for a variety of reasons that all peaked around the same time, America's dominance began to wane."[42] Whether that development commenced in the 1970s is debatable. What is certain is the altered place of allies and clients in U.S. strategic thinking. Their importance to grand strategy by 1974 was not what it once had been. The outdated edifice of containment no longer sufficed to protect vital interests. An unpopular war in Indochina and the evolving interests of America's friends had diminished America's status as world leader and clouded the future of the American Century.

The Demise of Containment Capitalism

With monetary leadership in decline, containment capitalism had lost much of its relevance to U.S. foreign policy by January 1969. Japan and West Germany were economic giants, whereas America's trade balance was in the red, its future gloomy.[43] American-based banks and multinational businesses, on which officials had relied for the private funding of containment capitalism, were pursuing their own interests. Policymakers expected that private direct investment would expand, and it did, primarily fueled by foreign capital markets.[44] The integration of banking and business activities, adrift from their national moorings, loomed large. Competitive capitalism had come to characterize the world economy; whether it aided a form of containment, not to mention primacy, as part of its raison d'être was another matter.

Two other issues conveyed the travail of containment capitalism. First, the United States, unlike Canada, had not fashioned a trade agreement with the Kremlin over wheat, a commodity in great demand in the USSR for political and economic reasons. Differences over Vietnam must not inhibit Soviet-American interchange, argued Ambassador Llewellyn E. Thompson in early 1968. His framing of the issue recognized America's economic weakening: "An improved U.S. commercial image in Moscow would lend support to the President's East-West policies and . . . could help our balance of payments program." Regulations mandating American ships to carry 50 percent of the wheat trade, which the USSR rejected, prevented trade expansion.[45]

Second, monetary multilateralism—a pillar of the Bretton Woods system—was at risk, as seen in the implicit threat of Washington to formally suspend gold convertibility of the dollar. By no quantitative measure was the United States in 1969 the hegemon it had previously been. Thus, refusal to sell gold to central bankers, who in turn might sell it not on the London market but on open markets, compromised the prevailing system. If Washington had no incentive, despite the loss of gold, to address balance-of-payments deficits, then the system was rudderless. Prosperous nations were unlikely to long accept the problems an overvalued dollar forced on them.[46]

Nixon had to concede the limits of U.S. power amid a changing global environment.[47] Multilateralism in defense and economic policy had all but failed. Such was the thinking that underlay his approach to major monetary matters as containment capitalism dissipated. The tactics his administration employed in trying to restore economic dominance amounted to monetary brinksmanship; they did not succeed.[48]

Nixon did not follow economic issues with Johnson's tenacity but still appreciated their importance to the making of foreign policy.[49] Although he told his most trusted associates, "I do not want to be bothered with international monetary matters," he recognized that "we need a new international monetary system and I have so indicated in several meetings." He cared less than his predecessors about balance-of-payments deficits and their effects. Indeed, Nixon loosened controls on foreign direct investment in April 1969, a move that European governments found untimely if not counterproductive to monetary stability. Secretary of the Treasury John Connally, who held that post from February 1971 to May 1972, echoed the president's neo-nationalism when he informed central bankers that the "dollar may be our currency but it's your problem."[50]

Nixon's statements on monetary matters came in March 1970, more than a year after he took the oath of office. Three things were clear by then. First, he did not want economic policy to hurt him in the 1970 off-year elections or impair his chances for winning a second term. Adding to his worries, a mild recession in 1970 that prefigured stagflation—high unemployment along with inflation—limited Republican electoral gains in the fall.[51] Second, the Bretton Woods system was irreparably damaged. Endless disputes over the linkage between the dollar and currency rates, uncontrollable swings in the flow of gold, and the difficulty of incorporating less-developed nations into global trade networks showed the lack of agreement on how to preserve the system. Third, Nixon knew that he could not resort to trade protectionism, which was on the rise, if the United States was going to retain any economic or political standing internationally.[52]

No longer willing to tolerate Washington's exercise of power without monetary discipline or fiscal restraint, European nations and Canada forced the administration's hand. Ottawa, faced with an influx of capital, decided in May 1970 to let the Canadian dollar float. The French and West Germans had already acted to protect their currencies from the uncertainty of the dollar. President Georges Pompidou devalued the franc by 11.1 percent in August 1969 to maintain trading advantages for France. Willy Brandt's coalition government then revalued the mark by 9.3 percent in October, a move followed by an outflow of reserves. When that situation improved early in 1970, Bonn adopted stricter monetary and fiscal policies in order to manage the ensuing economic boom and inflation.[53] French finance minister Valéry Giscard d'Estaing pointedly told Secretary of the Treasury David M. Kennedy in December 1969 that EEC leaders were fearful "we would continue to experience such serious balance-of-payments deficits as to imperil world confidence in the dollar and threaten the international monetary system."[54]

European leaders failed to overcome concerns about exchange rates as they moved to coordinate economic policy. A glut of dollars in early 1971 led Bonn to suggest a joint currency float; Paris demurred, fearing that subsequent inflation would harm export trade. Instead, France suggested a devaluation of the dollar. Still, the dollars flowed, and central bankers ceased dollar operations for five days on May 5. Brandt wrote Nixon, complaining that American inaction had created "great difficulties" for Bonn.[55] At the end of May, Connally responded at a conference of bankers in Munich. He warned of "a clear and present danger to our monetary system. . . . We are not going to devalue. We are not going to change the price of gold."[56] As pressure mounted for Washington to act, the stage was set for the dramatic events of the second half of the year.

Bleakness pervaded meetings about monetary policy and the fate of the dollar. Chairman of the Council of Economic Advisers Paul W. McCracken pronounced the old Bretton Woods system "unworkable." Connally disagreed, arguing the United States could still influence the Eurodollar market. Even so, he was concerned about a possible rise of economic nationalism among the Group of Ten. No matter what the White House decided to do—float the dollar, close the gold window, institute tighter capital or trade controls, or raise the price of gold—major foreign policy consequences would follow.[57]

Nixon knew the stakes were high for America's standing in the world. He told William Safire, a special assistant, in late June, "It's terribly important we be #1 economically because otherwise we can't be #1 diplomatically or militarily." Then he acted, announcing on July 15 that he would travel to Beijing before May 1972. Allies were caught off guard; the lack of notice offended the Japanese.[58] On August 15, after a secret meeting at Camp David with trusted aides and economic advisers, came the second "shock": the New Economic Policy. Nixon pledged to protect the dollar "as a pillar of monetary solidarity around the world."[59] Indefinitely suspending convertibility of dollars into gold, he effectively created a new dollar standard. To curb inflation, he announced a ninety-day freeze on wages and prices and implored corporations to withhold dividends over that time. To improve trade, he imposed a 10 percent import surtax on trading partners. Understandably, Tokyo found this measure provocative. And, in deference to growing isolationism in Congress, he agreed to trim foreign aid by 10 percent.[60]

Nixon went to the brink, courting monetary disaster and commercial conflict, to assert the primacy of American power. It was a dangerous game. Japanese textiles, which had become an increasingly politicized issue between the two allies, were an immediate target. Washington saw the flood of textiles as ingratitude for years of protection under America's security umbrella.[61] In contrast, Sato Eisaku's government saw its place as a crucial ally rapidly eroding and suspected that Washington was treating Western European allies better than it was Japan.[62]

He had acted, Nixon told Willy Brandt in a communiqué sent just after he announced the New Economic Policy, to "improve the international monetary system."[63] At a meeting in London on August 16, Undersecretary of the Treasury Paul A. Volker served notice the United States intended to strengthen the dollar before tending to a new monetary and trading order. Bundesbank director Otmar Emminger feared dollars would flood foreign money markets before conditions stabilized enough in America to allow the convening of a monetary conference, which Nixon then opposed. Volker made it clear in London and Paris that Washington was not going to devalue.[64] Hence, the salient question was whether European countries and Japan would revalue their currencies or let them float. Japan moved toward a float, as did most countries other than France. The resort to exchange controls and intervention by central banks of the Group of Ten to control inflation became common in the late summer and early fall.[65]

Momentum built for action on exchange rates and the price of gold, which inevitably meant devaluation by Washington in recognition of the dollar's weakness and the need to prevent a global recession. There was no agreement on adjusting the price of gold. Ominously, fears of a trade war arose in Japan and Europe, so the White House could not ignore the risk of inaction.[66] With devaluation and realignment again under consideration, a solution was in the offing. During meetings of Group of Ten ministers held at the Smithsonian Institution on December 17–18, the Bretton Woods system died, and several informal arrangements took its place. The United States depreciated the dollar by an average of 12 percent against European currencies whose exchange rates would vary within fixed ranges. Although the price of gold was increased to $38 per ounce, the U.S. gold window remained closed. Washington lifted the import surcharge on December 20. For its part, West Germany was not pleased with the implications of the negotiations for trade policy and feared acrimony would impair monetary relations with France. Only Canada kept a floating rate rather than revalue its dollar. Nixon giddily proclaimed the Smithsonian accord "the most significant monetary agreement in the history of the world."[67]

The president's characterization was excessive; he wanted to convince himself that the demise of Bretton Woods had not affected American primacy. In assessing the Nixon shocks, Kissinger wondered "whether the brutal unilateralism . . . mortgaged relations unnecessarily for many years to come, or whether our allies by their immobilism left us no other option." Not having known in advance about the Camp David gathering in August, he had serious doubts about the wisdom of the president's strategy.[68] C. Fred Bergsten, an NSC staffer who left at midyear for the Brookings Institution, subsequently penned a lucid critique of U.S. monetary policy. With uncertainty about trade, exchange rates, and the role of the dollar, "the world moved perilously close to a breakdown of confidence in the future of international economic cooperation." The upshot was that "the United States will no longer be the balance wheel of the world economy."[69]

The Smithsonian agreement marked the start of a search for a new monetary order. It was not a solution to chronic crises, which intermittently plagued the Group of Ten and lesser powers while Nixon was in office. For example, the dollar again came under pressure in 1973 as a result of a worsening trade balance and Nixon's removal of wage and price controls, which sparked inflation. The United States devalued the dollar by another 10 percent in February, threatening to destabilize foreign money markets. With the price of gold increasing and dollars flooding the market, EEC central banks in March closed exchange markets. Six countries including France and West Germany floated their currencies to protect them against a dollar glut; Bonn elected to peg the mark to SDRs, not dollars or gold.[70] If a workable international monetary system still existed, it was not easy to discern.

Developments at the Smithsonian and afterward illuminated the troubled landscape of containment capitalism. Monetary and commercial multilateralism may not have been on life support at the end of 1971 and after, but neither were they useful political tools. As Nixon and Kissinger turned toward engagement with the Soviet Union and China, they clung to what little remained of containment capitalism—the promise of trade to promote détente and ease the road to primacy. Importantly, Japan had no interest in American economic primacy and was intent on discarding its status as a cold-war dependent. Moving toward autonomy soon became imperative because of reliance on Iran and Arab states for 80 percent of its oil needs. Tokyo thus sought to position itself as favorably as possible as a trading partner with many nations, a course of action exemplified by the volume and price of its exports.[71] The priority relationship with Washington was nearing an end.

Beginning in 1972, U.S. negotiations with the Soviets and Chinese over trade were no longer feasible in a cold-war context. Each power was highly vested in a tripartite relationship of relative strategic and political parity, which the White House promoted in the name of détente. Compounding matters for the administration were members of Congress who often insisted on preconditions that delayed or prevented trade agreements altogether. For détente to be successful, the USSR had to receive MFN trade status. This step would help regularize grain deals like that made at the time of the Moscow summit in 1972.[72] Hard-line Democrats, led by Senator Henry M. Jackson of Washington, joined with conservative Republicans to block MFN status for the USSR until Moscow agreed to improve treatment of Soviet Jews, particularly those wanting to emigrate to Israel. Anatoly Dobrynin rued how authorities at home handled the issue because they "turned it into a test of wills that we eventually lost." That defeat, as exemplified by the Jackson-Vanik amendment of 1973, had the support of seventy-three senators; it tied MFN and trade credits to a liberal emigration policy.[73] Détente through grain deals was not possible. Kissinger observed in March 1974 on the eve of a trip to Moscow that "Jackson has obviously been convinced that I am a hostile country."[74]

The impasse with the USSR is generally well known, whereas efforts to open trade with the PRC are less so. As early as February 1968, the Johnson administration began thinking about reducing tensions with Beijing. At the State Department, Dean Rusk proceeded cautiously. After meeting with the NSC and CIA, Rusk in early January 1969 recommended modifying controls on trade in nonstrategic goods by American subsidiaries.[75] Through National Security Decision Memorandum 17, issued six months later, Nixon decided to probe Chinese intentions. By mid-April 1971, he was willing to consider direct trade in nonstrategic goods.[76]

Nixon and Kissinger never considered trade to be at the heart of U.S.-China relations but saw it as a way to extract concessions from the Soviets in order to advance U.S. objectives in the trilateral relationship. In talks in September 1972 with Huang Hua, China's ambassador to the UN, Kissinger told Huang about the substance of U.S.-Soviet trade talks. Why? As he explained to Mao and Zhou one year after the issuance of the February 1972 Shanghai communiqué, "Our interest in trade with China is not commercial. It is to establish a relationship that is necessary for the political relations we both have." Mao agreed.[77] When the Chinese inquired about obtaining MFN status, Kissinger warned that domestic political concerns could delay it.[78]

Détente was superseding containment capitalism as a viable foreign policy tool and making the world less dangerous. For that, Nixon and Kissinger deserve credit, as do the leaders of China and Russia. Yet had Nixon reflected on what he said to William Safire in June 1971 about economic primacy, he would have been dismayed. Were the United States not the world's economic giant, "something will go out of the American spirit," he had also remarked then.[79]

The events of 1971 showed that something important had been irretrievably lost, namely, the economic underpinning of the American Century. The Bretton Woods system was no longer a system per se. In its place was a conglomeration of monetary policies meant to stave off crises until major powers fashioned a replacement to the dollar-led, gold-backed order. No one nation had the capacity to dominate monetary and commercial affairs, though three—the United States, West Germany, and Japan—possessed the most authority. Unlike in the heyday of containment capitalism, their interests did not necessarily coincide. For the Germans, *Ostpolitik* pointed the way to stability, growth, and security. For the Japanese, whatever reduced resource dependency influenced Tokyo's foreign policy. The oil crisis after the 1973 October War had put the West on notice that its core beliefs about security were invalid.[80] As that realization dawned, the era of containment capitalism was over, and economic primacy seemed beyond Washington's reach.

Retrenchment and Nation-Building

Nixon's foreign policy downplayed nation-building. He and Kissinger put little stock in AID. Controversial in many host countries, AID fell victim to a fiscally frugal Congress. That he considered abolishing AID should not obscure Nixon's belief in aid as an arm of foreign policy. The crucial issue was how he and the NSC could exert greater control over aid decisions. "Otherwise foreign aid is dead," Nixon told a meeting of the Task Force on International Development in February 1970. The White House did not control the foreign aid budget and only partly influenced its disbursement. In fact, the Senate rejected Nixon's funding request in October 1971 for FY 1972.[81]

What Nixon and Kissinger were seeking to do was bring foreign aid within the confines of grand strategy.[82] This approach coincided with the Nixon Doctrine, as Nixon noted in 1970, "America cannot—and will not—conceive *all* the plans, design *all* the programs, execute *all* the decisions and undertake *all* the defense of the free nations of the world. We will help where it makes a real difference and is considered in our interest."[83] Notwithstanding Kissinger's professed admiration for Johnson and Rostow's foreign policy after the 1968 election, liberal development had run its course.[84] Neither Nixon nor Kissinger saw himself as a global Good Samaritan who placed importance on promoting democracy or encouraging nation-building.

Nixon viewed what remained of nation-building as something harking back to the 1950s, when private businesses and foundations worked with the government to devise a development strategy. It was no longer a given by 1970 that elites and experts could produce salutary change in the Third World. South Vietnam and the Alliance for Progress had been the acid tests of that undertaking, and their collective record was disappointing. If AID could not be eliminated, its operations could be trimmed. The agency had over 18,000 employees worldwide in 1968, and less than 8,500 by 1975. Private enterprise and technical assistance came to define a new, streamlined foreign aid initiative.[85] As it turned out, linking grand strategy, security policy, and development in a time of retrenchment was risky, as the following examples show.

Changes in development planning gave rise in 1969 to the Overseas Private Investment Corporation (OPIC), which was intended to promote private investment in the developing world. OPIC's mission was to fold foreign aid into multilateral activities and also a means of inducing corporate growth abroad.[86] When operations began in 1971, it had the authority to insure up to $7.5 billion worth of investments; the initial outlay reached $40 million. OPIC was supposed to charge fees to make itself financially self-sustaining, although concerns existed that the fees were not competitive with private insurance or that companies supported by OPIC would engage in risky behavior.[87]

OPIC became embroiled in efforts to destabilize the government of Salvador Allende Gossens in Chile. Allende had nationalized the Anaconda and Kennecott copper companies and the holdings of International Telephone and Telegraph (ITT). All told, the companies claimed over $500 million in compensation, an amount that would have bankrupted OPIC. The U.S. government paid Kennecott's claims but temporarily denied those of Anaconda and ITT. After the coup of September 11, 1973, the Nixon administration and General Augusto Pinochet Ugarte's regime agreed on compensation. OPIC survived the crisis; Ambassador Nathaniel Davis recalled, "Its activism in U.S. policy toward Chile was considerable."[88] OPIC's overall utility to aid and development was less salutary.

Nationalism in the developing world could run counter to U.S. development and security priorities. Such had long been the case in relations with the shah's Iran. After Mosaddeq's ouster in 1953, the United States played a controversial role in Iran's nation-building. David Lilienthal met with Iranian officials at World Bank meetings in the mid-1950s and encouraged the planning of TVA-like water and power projects. Private and public activities frequently worked at cross-purposes. For those viewing Iran as a strategic asset, liberal development made the shah a model of stability, but private enterprise in Khuzistan, for example, James A. Bill writes, "inevitably became caught up in the web of Iranian politics." In short, conceptual, technical, and political problems slowed nation-building. Tehran favored the growth of agribusiness under centralized control at the expense of local elites and farmers. That meant trouble for the shah in the 1970s.[89]

Iran should have epitomized the potential of liberal development. And yet, the Iranian experience suggests otherwise. To placate Washington, the shah did not take extreme measures against domestic dissidents and critics of U.S. foreign policy—students, clerics, and the press. Shrewdly, he used their protests to demand even more military assistance, yet he failed to win public support for efforts in mid-1970 to get American-based businesses and banks to expand investments in Iran. Two leaders of that effort were James A. Linen of Time, Inc., and David Rockefeller of the Chase Manhattan Bank; also participating were Lilienthal and Eugene Black, former head of the World Bank. Elites welcomed a growing American presence, while the shah's foes denounced, in Ayatollah Khomeini's words, "American capitalists and other imperialists . . . [who act] contrary to the will of the people and the ordinances of Iran."[90]

As in many places under the aegis of the United States in the Cold War, Iran's path to modernity was highly securitized. Even when the Nixon administration acknowledged Iran was an economically developed country, it continued to make available military equipment the shah wanted. This was done both under the Foreign Military Sales Act and through credits provided after Nixon signed a waiver to maintain Iran's access in FY 1971 and FY 1972 to grant aid that otherwise would have been cut off.[91] He did so because military sales and aid were essential for adapting the Nixon Doctrine to the Persian Gulf.

At the same time, Nixon, Kissinger, and the CIA knew that the shah's regime was not inherently stable. The problem was more than the unbridgeable chasm between the government and clerics like Khomeini. CIA Director Richard Helms worried about the lack of economic and social advancement for educated young people.[92] Even a comparatively positive evaluation of developments in Iran, prepared for Nixon's visit at the end of May 1972 after the summit meeting in Moscow, admitted that modernization had limits. The regime needed to foster economic and social equality between the urban and rural populations and create opportunities for meaningful political participation.[93]

The shah was unwilling, though, to take advice from Washington. After Nixon's visit, Secretary of the Treasury John Connally went to Tehran to urge the shah to adopt real reforms. As Kissinger explained, "Iran's stability and progress are too exclusively dependent on the Shah's firm personal leadership."[94] Conditions were deteriorating. The U.S. embassy reported in August 1972 that "terrorist activities in Iran [against the shah] seem to be increasing. . . . [A] vigorous anti-guerrilla campaign on part of Iranian security organizations is . . . unable to bring guerrillas under control and may in fact be hardening attitudes of guerrillas and their sympathizers." Ongoing calls for substantive change from Washington fell on deaf ears.[95]

The administration was desperate to make the Nixon Doctrine work in the Persian Gulf.[96] National Security Decision Memorandum 92 of November 7, 1970, reiterated the importance of Saudi Arabia and Iran to U.S. strategy. Desirous of charting his own path in foreign affairs, the shah found U.S. policy goals constraining. Although development had once been a basis for cordial relations, the same could not be said after 1970 as the shah's sense of nationalism and U.S. interests diverged. In William Bundy's assessment, "[The Shah] was more than a surrogate for U.S. power; he often called the tune."[97] In sum, securitized nation-building in Iran provided little help in Nixon's quest for primacy.

An unruly ally was not the primary problem confronting Washington in Thailand, where strategic matters were paramount. Despite their aversion to nation-building as conducted under Johnson, Nixon and Kissinger pursued both counterinsurgency and modernization there. Doing otherwise would have been to put the Nixon Doctrine at risk even as it was being proclaimed. Thailand's importance as a bulwark against communism steadily increased as the Vietnam War continued without resolution. Accordingly, officials in Washington culti-vated a close security relationship with the Royal Thai Government (RTG). In practice, this meant not only covert assistance but also active participation of AID and OPS in RTG efforts to develop regions of the country outside the effec-tive reach of Bangkok.[98]

RTG officials worried that Thailand might be abandoned as Vietnamization proceeded apace, which set the stage for trade missions to the Soviet Union and efforts to repair relations with China, North Vietnam, and Cambodia.[99] Kissinger wondered what would happen "if the United States was perceived to be abdicat-ing its role in Asia." To head off an unwanted change in the RTG's foreign policy, Nixon approved an AID program for FY 1970 extending assistance for Thai police and "developmental measures to prevent the growth of Communist insur-gency in the North and Northeast," as a State Department report put it. As was often the case with AID, counterinsurgency took precedence over social and eco-nomic development.[100]

By 1971, Nixon thought that "the U.S. was on a razor's edge with respect to the Nixon Doctrine in Southeast Asia." Maintaining a global presence while drawing down active forces seemed problematic. Hence, a strong Thailand was essential. Accelerated disengagement from Vietnam after the signing of the Paris accords in January 1972 reaffirmed this belief.[101] Several factors complicated the RTG's abil-ity to serve as an American surrogate. Market prices for rice, tin, and rubber had stagnated, reducing the extent of nation-building by the RTG. Washington in-creased P.L. 480 aid for FY 1972 and FY 1973, stipulating that the RTG divert half of the $30 million allotment to security needs—as reflected in National Security Decision Memorandum 126 of August 11, 1971. Ambassador Leonard Unger in Bangkok praised this proviso, claiming it would "[prevent] the increased RTG security expenditures from threatening development programs."[102] In places where civic action was unlikely to bear fruit, the government resettled thousands of people in a move similar to the Strategic Hamlet program in South Vietnam.[103]

Success in this venture was not ensured because an insurgency by hill tribes persisted. The Hmong, Yao, Lisu, and Lahu people populated the north of

Thailand, with Hmong and Yao being the most active politically. They were among the insurgents in the Communist Party of Thailand (CPT) who had taken a Maoist line in 1961 and turned to armed insurgency in August 1965. While some Hmong fought with the CPT against Bangkok, others participated in the CIA's covert war in Laos.[104] Permeating the Hmong was a culture of opium growing and trafficking, which the appetite for drugs among U.S. servicemen sustained in the late 1960s and early 1970s. Greatly compounding matters were Chinese Irregular Forces (CIF), composed of troops loyal to the GMD in Taiwan who had long plied the opium trade in Indochina. No longer a threat to Beijing, yet entrenched in the Golden Triangle, CIF remnants would not submit to Bangkok's authority, thus composing a separate insurgency from that of the CPT. Efforts to incorporate them into Thai politics and society met with mixed results.[105]

The growing CPT insurgency concerned Washington and Bangkok because it struck at the stability of the RTG and imperiled the Nixon Doctrine. The RTG responded with a two-track plan developed in talks with U.S. officials. Thai military and police would employ armed force against hardcore CPT forces, while the RTG offered a kind of amnesty if combatants, most notably the Hmong, farmed crops other than opium. A dubious enterprise, the crop-substitution campaign failed because local officials were active in the lucrative narcotics trade.[106]

During the rest of Nixon's time in office, trouble in Thailand's northern reaches did not cease. There was only so much that nation-building with a militarized focus could accomplish against committed adversaries. Nixon and Kissinger promised funding for Thai guerrilla units as they were repatriated from Laos after mid-1973. The CIA downplayed the insurgency: "[It] remains small, vulnerable and, for the most part, limited to the periphery of the Thai nation and society." Perhaps so, but the administration linked the fate of the Nixon Doctrine to Bangkok's ability to curtail the insurgency. Extending additional covert assistance was asking for trouble in the months before Nixon's resignation. Members of Congress were scrutinizing any request for funds that could again embroil the nation in conflict in Asia.[107] Development did not disappear from the Thai landscape, yet what survived did not advance U.S. security policy in Indochina. Nation-building there, in fact, may have stood in the way of attaining primacy.

Nixon, Kissinger, and Credibility

Whether as strategists or tacticians, Nixon and his national security adviser were greatly concerned with credibility. The self-styled underdog from California and the German immigrant stood at the pinnacle of power in January 1969. To maintain that status and, as they saw it, secure their place in history, the United States had to attain primacy. For these two driven men, it was not to be. Theirs would be a fruitless quest for three primary reasons: Vietnam, Watergate, and the lack of trust in Washington throughout the free-world society.

Strategic globalism would falter as grand strategy without the restoration of credibility, which in part meant eliminating Vietnam as the albatross of U.S. foreign policy. Nixon set out his Vietnamization policy on November 3, 1969. Earlier that year in *Foreign Affairs*, Kissinger outlined what was at stake: "For what is involved now is confidence in American promises. However fashionable it is to ridicule the terms 'credibility' or 'prestige' they are not empty phrases; other nations can gear their actions to ours only if they can count on our steadiness."[108] Nixon emphatically agreed. On April 30, 1970, he announced the incursion into Cambodia in a statement from the Oval Office: "If, when the chips are down, the world's most powerful nation, the United States of America, acts like a pitiful, helpless giant, the forces of totalitarianism and anarchy will threaten free nations and free institutions throughout the world."[109] Nixon and Kissinger had two audiences in mind as they disengaged from Vietnam: the American public and the Kremlin. Desperate for an end to the war, many Americans gave the president the benefit of the doubt about his Vietnam policy as the number of troops decreased. Shrewdly, Nixon isolated and denounced the most vehement voices in the antiwar movement, casting them as aggressively un-American in stark contrast to a patriotic, silent majority.[110]

The Soviets were not as easy to co-opt. Nixon and Kissinger came to power assuming Moscow could help extricate the United States from Vietnam by pressuring Hanoi. If the USSR, in effect, did their bidding with North Vietnam, restoring American credibility then hinged on the extent to which the Americans could manipulate Soviet actions. This attempt at linkage did not pay off despite Kissinger's persistent efforts to pressure Dobrynin.[111]

What Soviet-American differences over Vietnam revealed was that American credibility would be incredibly hard to restore. This unhappy reality became magnified as tension mounted between India and Pakistan in the second half of 1971, which bothered Nixon and Kissinger because of the ramifications for relations with the USSR and China. With a cease-fire in mid-December blocking India's and presumably the USSR's expansionary goals, Kissinger crowed to Nixon, "We have come out of this amazingly well and we scared the pants off the Russians." His sense of relief was obvious.[112] Détente could go forward with U.S. credibility apparently intact among the world's three military giants. Yet even as the crisis eased, major economic powers were gathering in Washington to craft dramatic changes in the Bretton Woods system, which underlined credibility's contingent nature and the elusiveness of primacy.

Rejuvenating credibility was a complex operation. The White House had to rebuild and sustain trust with its allies, defend vital interests in the Western Hemisphere, compel Soviet leaders to consider U.S. interests as basic to their own policy calculations, and generate domestic support for its foreign policies. These tasks came to the fore after the 1972 presidential election when the Watergate scandal began to weigh heavily on Nixon.[113]

Addressing the annual meeting of Associated Press editors on April 23, 1973, Kissinger announced the "Year of Europe," which was supposed to refresh U.S. primacy in the Atlantic Community. He declared that "the era that was shaped by the decisions of a generation ago is ending." Yet Europeans "[are] less committed to the unity that made peace possible and to the effort required to maintain it." Such complacency rankled Nixon and Kissinger who acted in the belief that America's allies, including Japan, should "share in the regeneration of our purposes."[114] And there was the rub. Unity and security were not possible unless the Atlantic Community accepted Washington's lead in political and economic matters. Six weeks earlier, Nixon had vividly expressed his fears about what would happen were Europe to become too Left-leaning: "We must act effectively and soon or we will create in Europe a Frankenstein monster which could prove to be highly detrimental to our interests in the years ahead." For the sake of détente and American credibility, the nine members of the EEC—also known by then as the European Community (EC)—had to fulfill their obligations in the free-world society.[115]

Despite some differences, the leading powers among the EC Nine, Great Britain, France, and West Germany, did not react well to Kissinger's overture. They imagined the EC as a global force, albeit one in its infancy. Prime Minister Edward Heath felt much aggrieved, signaling that London had tired of being America's junior partner. Willy Brandt, of course, had little interest in placating Nixon. And, after months of uncertainty, President Georges Pompidou and Foreign Minister Michel Jobert threw in France's lot with their European confrères. Regarding Jobert, Kissinger recalled, "He would do anything except make progress [with us]."[116]

It was apparent by mid-July that there would be no trip by Nixon to Europe reaffirming Atlantic ties under U.S. leadership. Not only was the political impasse formidable, the matter of currency exchange rates also proved nettlesome. Since March, the global currency system had operated on a modified floating basis in order to set rates. A drop in the dollar's value made Europeans reluctant to engage in trade negotiations. With rumors of new exchange controls in the air, the prospects for a new, workable monetary system dimmed. The crisis had not abated by the end of the month. George Schultz, who became secretary of the Treasury in June, moved to ameliorate the situation in talks with European and, subsequently, Japanese counterparts. It took more than two years to reach a comprehensive settlement.[117]

The Year of Europe could not wait that long. Brandt and Nixon exchanged letters in July and August revealing how intractable their differences were. Learning that the EC Nine were sharing bilateral communications, Nixon termed the perceived affront "astonishing." Brandt's rejoinder reminded the president that he had not consulted the Europeans about the idea of a "year of Europe" in advance of Kissinger's speech. It was time for the White House to come to terms with "what the Europeans really want." Kissinger, attempting to explain how the Year of Europe failed, minimized the structural and procedural problems his brainchild encountered and focused instead on Watergate and Nixon's "loss of authority."[118] In any event, his Year of Europe neither aided American primacy nor bolstered credibility.

Latin America did not figure prominently in Nixon's or Kissinger's strategic calculations. Kissinger's personal predilections and intellectual assumptions led him to believe the southern hemisphere lay outside "the axis of history," which ran from Moscow to Berlin to Washington and on to Tokyo, a characterization about humankind that he conveyed to Gabriel Valdés, Chile's foreign minister, in 1969. Also adopting a patronizing tone about Latin America's future, Nixon minimized the role of government aid and advocated the expansion of private investment in a speech to the Inter-American Press Association on October 31, 1969. The president's remarks all but acknowledged a decline in the stature of the United States in the region.[119] Two years later when considering a state visit to Latin America, Nixon had changed his mind about the Western Hemisphere's importance for prestige, telling Secretary of State William P. Rogers, "The Latin American thing concerns me. . . . You've been there and you agree. . . . I have a, I really do have a special feeling for those people. Not only because they're close but also because they're damn good people. I mean, whether they're dictators or whatever they are—they want to be with us."[120]

Fears that emerged in the months before Salvador Allende became president of Chile explain the change in attitude. Not only might Chile democratically elect a Marxist in September 1970, it was also possible that some Latin American governments might try to end Cuba's isolation. The CIA had tried for years to prevent Allende from becoming president.[121] On March 30, the 40 Committee (successor to the 303 Committee), realizing that support for Allende's opponents would fail, authorized the CIA to engage in "spoiling operations" against his Unidad Popular (UP) coalition by funding anti-Allende media and bribing opponents in Chile's congress to reduce the UP vote if no candidate received a majority of the popular vote.[122]

When it became apparent that Allende would win the presidency, the White House, the CIA, and the NSC swung into action. Kissinger told CIA Director Richard Helms, "We will not let Chile go down the drain." A worried Nixon warned, "It's going to go to hell so fast."[123] While maintaining correct diplomatic relations with Santiago, officials began planning to undermine Allende's presidency. One tactic involved turning the business community against Allende; in the fall of 1970, however, businessmen were not yet disposed to oppose him.[124] At an NSC meeting on November 6, Rogers remarked, "If we have to be hostile, we want to do it right and bring him down." Undersecretary of State John N. Irwin II added, "The problem is how to bring about his downfall." Nixon believed U.S. credibility would be jeopardized if Allende succeeded. Building support for Washington's position was essential because "if Chile moves as we expect and is able to get away with it, . . . it gives courage to others who are sitting on the fence in Latin America." New relationships were needed. "Let's not think about what the really democratic countries in Latin America say—the game is in Brazil and Argentina," the president declared.[125]

By mid-1971, Brazil was looking to form an anti-Allende entente in the Southern Cone. Brazilian officials prodded Washington to become more involved. A coup in Bolivia in August, in which Brazil and Argentina intervened, and an election in Uruguay in November in which Brazil played a clandestine role, united Brasilia and Washington in common cause. Their union seemed all the more vital to officials in both capitals because of Fidel Castro's extended visit to Chile in November, which kindled fears of a Cuban-Chilean axis to propagate Chilean-style socialism, known as La Vía Chilena.[126]

When Nixon met in early December with Brazil's president Emilio Garrastazu Médici, they sealed the fate of Chile's experiment with socialism. Kissinger told their visitors that "a major relationship with Latin America was fundamental to our foreign policy concept, and a particularly close relationship with Brazil was also fundamental." As partners, the two nations would be "respected and admired, but not liked."[127] Nixon and Médici agreed to work together to prevent Cuba from rejoining the OAS, bring Paraguay into the anti-Allende fold, and encourage Chilean armed forces to overthrow Allende. Médici told the Americans that Brazil was already "exchanging many officers with the Chileans" to hasten anti-Allende subversion. The two leaders agreed to open a line of communication outside normal diplomatic channels, with Kissinger serving as Nixon's intermediary.[128]

On September 11, 1973, a military coup dashed Allende's dream of a Chilean alternative to U.S. dominance in the hemisphere. Allende died of a self-inflicted gunshot in the presidential palace, La Moneda. Plotters checked with Brazilian intelligence before the coup to ascertain whether they would encounter resistance from neighboring armed forces, namely Peru's. U.S. officials, thankful to have Brazil take the lead, watched events unfold, hoping that their helping hand would not be visible. Nixon, pleased with the developments in Santiago, later asserted that to have done nothing "would have been the height of immorality."[129]

What Allende's fall meant for U.S. credibility was hard to sort out at the time. Nixon's Watergate troubles were ongoing, and Kissinger was in the midst of becoming secretary of state. Kissinger knew that the White House could not dispel allegations of involvement in the coup. "But that's not the worst disaster that could befall [us]," he noted in a meeting of State, Defense, NSC, and CIA officials on September 12. He seemed less sure in a telephone conversation with Nixon on September 16. Angry about the unfavorable response to the coup in the press, he fumed, "I mean instead of celebrating—in the Eisenhower period we would be heroes." Nixon tried to reassure Kissinger, observing, "But listen, as far as people are concerned let me say they aren't going to buy this crap from the Liberals on this one."[130] Nevertheless, their general unease about relying on Latin America for validation of America's global standing persisted. As Nixon had explained to Kissinger in July, "I have yet to see a mission to Latin America that didn't cause more trouble than it was worth."[131]

Credibility's contingent nature was soon on display again. An attack on October 6 by Egyptian and Syrian forces set off the October War with Israel, which lasted for three weeks before a cease-fire halted the fighting. U.S. policy effectively became the sole responsibility of Kissinger because Nixon could escape neither the onslaught of bad news relating to Watergate nor the personal demons that went with it. Nixon identified the nation's credibility with his own image and was convinced that Russia would try to take advantage of his predicament.[132]

In the midst of war, Kissinger had three audiences to whom he wanted to make the case for credibility: Israel, Egypt, and the Soviet Union. First, Kissinger was slow to try to stop the fighting after the Israeli army reversed early losses. Reverting to the 1967 borders was not in Tel Aviv's interest, he concluded, contravening the previous position of the State Department. He also reasoned that occupation of Arab lands would benefit Israel in future negotiations, which did not mean Arab-Israeli differences could easily be resolved. Even so, strengthening America's bona fides with Israel in October 1973 was a major undertaking.[133] He later recalled how fraught that effort had seemed during his visit to Israel on October 22: "I reassured Golda [Meir] and her colleagues that there were no secret deals [with Moscow] . . . [yet] Israel's insecurity was so pervasive that even words were daggers."[134]

Dealing with Egyptian leader Anwar el-Sadat was similarly challenging. In February 1971, Sadat had held out the possibility of peace should Israel accept the1967 borders. That did not happen, but Sadat was tiring of Egypt's dependency on the USSR—the vestige of a 1971 Soviet-Egyptian friendship treaty. He expelled Soviet personnel from Egypt in July 1972 after the Moscow summit. Despite his strong support for Israel, Kissinger hoped to use the October War as an opportunity to restrict the USSR's presence in the Middle East. Sadat lent a hand by asking him to advance the cause of peace when the course of war still favored Egypt and Syria. Hence, Kissinger used his diplomatic skills with Meir's government to prevent the destruction of Egypt's Third Army Corps, which gratified Sadat. "Until this message," he wrote unctuously, "I had not taken Sadat seriously. . . . Now I was beginning to understand . . . that we were dealing with a statesman of the first order."[135] Attaining credibility in Cairo at so small a price was an unanticipated achievement.

Sadat's decision for war threatened Soviet interests in the Middle East. To have stood by while Egypt was defeated would have played into Nixon's and Kissinger's hands and affected Brezhnev's understanding of détente. From the outset of the war, Washington refused to consider a Soviet role in achieving peace, especially after Moscow proposed joint military operations. "We were determined," Kissinger recalled, "to resist by force if necessary the introduction of Soviet troops into the Middle East regardless of the pretext under which they arrived."[136]

To argue that the consequences of Soviet exclusion were not injurious to détente and U.S. credibility in Moscow's view is mistaken.[137] When Kissinger arrived in Moscow on October 20, Brezhnev observed that the situation in the Middle East had the potential to harm relations. The Soviet leader later criticized U.S. support for Israel: "Here, in Moscow, Kissinger behaved in a cunning way. He vowed fidelity to the policy of détente, and then while in Tel-Aviv he made a deal with Golda." Soviet diplomat Victor Israelyan, who worked closely with Foreign Minister Andrei Gromyko during the October War, commented, "I do not think that the policy of détente gained strength during the war either." Brezhnev wrote Nixon on October 28, "There is a credibility crisis . . ." that is "undermining our personal mutual trust."[138]

Kissinger essentially conceded Moscow's position on the war and détente. The American perspective on détente, he subsequently wrote, was that it "defined not friendship but a strategy for a relationship between adversaries." He and Nixon wanted to reduce the Soviet presence in the Middle East; the October War allowed them to do that but at a cost to credibility.[139] The war affected American credibility on two other fronts by straining relations with NATO partners and illuminating the importance of petroleum in world affairs. The divide in NATO that resulted from the "Year of Europe" imbroglio worsened, with the White House paying scant heed to allies as it maneuvered among the contending parties. Discontent boiled over when Kissinger put U.S. forces on worldwide alert on October 24. Two days later, when the possibility of confrontation with the Soviet Union subsided, Kissinger justified going to DefCon 3 to German ambassador Berndt Von Staden, saying, "We think our actions in the Near East are in defense of Western interests generally." West Germans and other European allies were more influenced, however, by Washington's lack of consultation after October 6.[140]

Also shaping reaction to the war in Europe were a 70 percent rise in the price of oil by Arab exporters to $5.10 per barrel, a planned reduction in production of 5 percent per month, and the announcement of an oil embargo against the United States. Nixon and Kissinger failed to realize that Western multinational companies, in effect, were allying with producer nations, and that neither cared about U.S. credibility. Causing additional alarm in Europe and Japan, the price of Persian Gulf crude rose to $11.65 per barrel by year's end.[141]

In the months prior to the outbreak of hostilities, Nixon and Kissinger had a sense that war was possible and that the West's access to petroleum could be curtailed. Richard Helms twice cabled Kissinger in April from his new post as ambassador to Iran. The shah wanted Nixon to intercede with the Israelis and Egyptians to avert a clash and prevent oil prices from reaching unprecedented levels. Then in mid-June, Heath, unaware of the pro-Israel tilt of U.S. policy, implored Nixon to get Israel to the bargaining table with its Arab neighbors. Invoking the support of Pompidou and Brandt, Heath expressed fears about a looming energy crisis, which the Arab-Israeli impasse would worsen. If peace remained elusive, he warned, "our whole [Western] industrial power and progress may be threatened."[142] With its ad hoc, awkward response to the novel problems posed by oil-producing states, tensions in the Middle East, and growing fissures in NATO, the White House diminished its own credibility.

Further trouble came on November 7 when Congress overrode Nixon's veto of the War Powers Act. The genesis of the law lay in disagreement about the war in Indochina and the limited ability of Congress to influence foreign policy. Kissinger showed his disdain for the act by barely mentioning it in his memoirs, whereas Nixon called what Congress did a "tragic and irresponsible action."[143] In an interview with James "Scotty" Reston of the *New York Times* on October 6, 1974, Kissinger spoke about the problem of maintaining credibility:[144]

> The necessity of the measures one takes to avoid the catastrophe can almost never be proved. For that reason you require a great deal, or at least a certain amount of confidence in leadership and that becomes difficult in all societies. But, speaking of the United States, if one looks at the crisis through which America has gone over the last decade—the assassinations, the Vietnam War, Watergate—it is very difficult to establish the relationship of confidence.

These reflections were not per se an epitaph for American credibility but rather a lament about the endless challenges to the United States and what they meant for the nation's international standing. In that, they underscored the difficulty of attaining primacy.

Primacy reflects a nation's standing in the eyes of friends and adversaries. The United States during Nixon's presidency possessed substantial power but could not count on exerting decisive influence in a given situation. Soviet-American relations were conducted on an equal footing as a result of strategic parity. Moreover, détente existed at the sufferance of the USSR and China. NATO had lost its identity as a U.S.-dominated model of political comity. A number of allies, notably Iran, used relations with Washington to boost their own interests, sometimes at America's expense. The chronic weakness of the dollar relegated Washington to a crucial but not determinative global economic role. Moreover, nation-building, to which Nixon turned as local conditions dictated, did nothing to help the White House attain primacy. The "Free World" still existed when Kissinger spoke with Reston. Whether the same held true for a "free-world society" seems less certain. Whatever the case, the world that Henry Luce once imagined—the American Century—had declined further as the United States engaged the world between 1969 and 1974.

AN IMPROBABLE QUEST

To avoid impeachment by the House of Representatives and possible conviction by the Senate for criminal activity, Richard Nixon resigned the presidency on August 9, 1974. In its August 19 issue, which was dedicated to assessing Nixon's presidency and his legacy, *Time* magazine imagined a new phase of American history commencing as Nixon began his political exile. The essayist Hugh Sidey, whom Henry Kissinger had briefed, wrote that foremost in the minds of Nixon's national security team was ensuring a legacy of peace. That meant preserving détente.[1]

Kissinger met with Sidey and others from *Time* on August 13, taking care to identify "two Nixons, one that I knew and one I didn't know."[2] The prospects for an enduring détente were discouraging. Kissinger used the occasion to lambast critics who were calling for greater strategic superiority over the USSR. "These [7,000] missiles," he exclaimed, "are politically useless in a crisis. . . . By 1984 we will conservatively have 17,000 missiles. But what do you do with them?" In response to the implied criticism of détente, he asked, "Where has there been an absence of toughness[?] . . . Nixon was not soft on the Soviets." Here, he was echoing Anatoly Dobrynin's belief that Nixon never abandoned the Cold War, electing instead to fight it on less confrontational terrain—where cooperation was possible—than his predecessors. Kissinger also told his interlocutors relations with Japan were "on the upswing" and asserted that "our relations with Europe are now very strong."[3]

All was not well with the American Century, however, such protestations aside. Aversion to détente at home was real, making smooth implementation of strategic globalism unlikely. If a healthy Atlantic alliance meant NATO's acceptance of U.S. primacy, then the varied interests among alliance members threatened further to weaken NATO. In addition, Washington could not count on deference in the Americas to its Cuba policy or, in some cases, bonds with authoritarian governments. Nixon and Kissinger made no place for human rights in grand strategy, thereby undermining any claim the United States had to being the world's Good Samaritan. Also, the dollar, although still a leading international currency, no longer secured economic hegemony; so state-based a concept was an anachronism as the age of globalized business and finance took shape. What actually remained of credibility, a signature characteristic of the American Century? It was a good thing the men of *Time* did not raise the issue with Kissinger because it would have compelled him to engage in a dispiriting exercise, however honestly he chose to reply.

When a search for the term "American Century" returns few pertinent findings in the *New York Times* and *Washington Post* during the height of the Cold War from 1945 through 1960, it seems fair to ask: Did the American Century really exist? In a book of reflections published three decades after his career in government ended, George F. Kennan denounced the idea as "prattle" about "illusions of unique and superior virtue on our part."[4] Neither Truman and Eisenhower nor their successors mentioned it in public addresses.[5] Yet they did internalize and sought to give life to the charge to lead the world that Henry Luce had put at the center of his 1941 essay.

There is little doubt, though, that Luce's imperative had lost most of its original impact by the early 1970s. Thomas L. Hughes, head of the Carnegie Endowment for International Peace after having served from 1963 to 1969 as director of the Bureau of Intelligence and Research in the State Department, made that point in the April 1972 issue of *Foreign Affairs*. He argued that Luce was right about the twentieth century since 1941 being an American one, especially in a productive-cum-cultural sense:[6]

> In all the unfolding indices of quantitative preeminence, the United States is indeed a new kind of power in the world. Our gross national product, our massive output of the food the world needs, the unequaled scale of our technology, the burgeoning talents that still pour by the millions from our troubled educational system, the qualitative skills of our manpower, the seed money with which for years we have capitalized the new world bank of the social sciences, the manifold horizons of the computerized century—all these and more testify to the steady pulsations from contemporary America which circle and recircle the globe. They evoke demands and cravings for things American. . . . America's great

twentieth-century technological revolution sweeps across sovereignties, beats against Walls, and eats away at Iron Curtains.

This, of course, is not precisely what Luce and U.S. policymakers had in mind as they endeavored to project a commanding American presence in world affairs. Yet Hughes was not wrong to downplay the traditional markers of power and, hence, leadership. The modern world possessed crosscurrents of centuries past that were evident in evolving political, military, and economic arrangements. "[The] familiar intergovernmental world is crumbling," he declared, "beginning in the West where it itself began."[7] War in Vietnam and the rise of the multinational corporation testified to what Hughes saw as the ephemeral nature of American hegemony. The consequence of that condition, if seen through a traditional geopolitical lens, was difficult for him to contemplate: "Governments devoid of credibility confront citizens devoid of patriotism."[8]

Few scholars have been as quick as Hughes to write off the Luce-inspired American Century.[9] In an interpretation compatible with this book, historian Walter LaFeber has written that Franklin Roosevelt "planned to make the world safe for American power. If that effort translated into democracy the president would happily accept it." Without ever explicitly saying so, LaFeber implies that the American Century, if it existed, plausibly began no later than 1898. He is not alone in that regard.[10] That proposition seems dubious. The effort to make the twentieth century an American Century prior to 1941 constituted an ill-defined enterprise at best and, more accurately, a circumscribed undertaking.[11]

Hughes's reservations about the durable nature of Luce's project sharply depart from some scholarly assessments about its lasting, widespread appeal. What Luce envisioned and what U.S. officials brought to life in the early Cold War are not the same thing that some analysts see as Luce's principal legacy. Roberto Giorgio Rabel, for example, contended in 2002 that "it would be premature to declare the American Century complete in either its narrow or broader sense" because "the idea of an American Century has never simply involved being the world's dominant power but has implied progress toward the building of a wider liberal world order."[12] The salient question is, therefore, what were Luce and cold-war policymakers trying to do as they forged the American Century.

Fealty to progress and liberal order was in short supply globally from 1945 through 1974. Convinced of an imminent Communist threat until after the 1962 Cuban missile crisis, officials clung to global containment as the safest way to respond to the Soviet Union and its allies. Thereafter, when alarmist rhetoric was no longer credible, the United States, as a direct result of entanglement in Vietnam and growing financial duress, was ill positioned to promote social progress and political stability, as the problems associated with nation-building made clear.

Luce and U.S. officials understood that American leadership depended on acceptance of and deference to the United States as the undisputed world leader. Although hubris disposed them to assert leadership, that was not enough. Hence, the idea of crafting a "Free World" took hold. The scope of this imagined community, to borrow Benedict Anderson's apt concept, was perhaps grander than any of history's imperial schemes. That it stretched ordinary understanding of the boundaries of community beyond recognition mattered not to America's cold warriors. That Anderson's insights apply to nations bounded by geography and cultural affinity was also irrelevant. The makers of the American Century, had they known of it, would have summarily rejected Anderson's most important parameter for an imagined community: "No nation imagines itself coterminous with mankind."[13] Predicated on hegemony, the determination to build a free-world society was from the outset an improbable quest, made even more unlikely by external hindrances.

Weighing as heavily as any impediment to the forging of a viable American Century after 1945 was the belief of the existence of profound evil in the world, exemplified by Nazi Germany and soon replaced by the Soviet Union. This defining American attribute, deeply entrenched in religious belief and political life, turned the Cold War into a near-life-and-death struggle—the doubts of George Kennan notwithstanding. As grand strategy, containment had to be indivisible to the extent possible. To brook dissent was to put the Free World at grave risk. Fortunately for the likes of Luce and Niebuhr, Truman and Acheson, and Eisenhower and Dulles, American power—that is, military strength, economic might, and political authority—could be deployed to provide the necessary space and time for a secure global future to grow and prosper.

So Manichaean a worldview could not adapt to the reality of a dynamic international environment, one in which political alignments, human needs, and nationalist sentiments often exceeded Washington's ability to exert influence. Also hovering over the first fifteen years or so of the Cold War was an unasked question: What if containment succeeded as Kennan predicted? What, then, would bind together the free-world society and advance the American Century? Was the United States sufficiently respected and powerful enough to lead the world into a future based on the orderly conduct of human affairs and socioeconomic progress? Those who celebrate the continued vitality of an American Century, despite the travail of the mid-1960s through the early 1970s, would have us believe that so liberal a promise was coming to fruition.

The evidence adduced herein suggests otherwise. Global containment in the main did succeed. The Berlin blockade exposed the limits of Soviet power in Europe's heartland, leading Joseph Stalin recklessly to insert himself into Korean affairs; Georgi Malenkov's genuine overtures for negotiations were a kind of pre-lude to détente; the Sino-Soviet rift was real even if officials in Washington could not readily acknowledge or exploit it; U.S. strategic superiority was a given even in the age of Sputnik; and despite high levels of tension, Moscow did not turn Berlin or Cuba into tests of will and set off a catastrophic superpower conflict.

Nevertheless, even before 1963 the American Century was beginning to split at the seams with Washington's leadership in doubt. Strains within NATO, epit-omized by Washington's lack of consultation, could not be dismissed; authori-ties in Bonn and Paris were pursuing their own political, economic, and—to an extent—strategic interests at odds with those of America. In the Americas, the Alliance for Progress was not meeting its goals for social progress, and Cuba's in-fluence and potential for mischief clearly persisted. Equally important, South-east Asia offered unfertile ground for liberal nation-building. Perhaps worst of all, the vaunted postwar American economy was encountering troubles that were unimaginable when the decision was made to pursue global containment. Post-war leadership was partly the product of economic preeminence, which ongoing budget deficits and runs on gold invariably diminished.

Lyndon Johnson could not right the ship despite a tactical flexibility in for-eign policy for which he has not received sufficient credit.[14] Even had he not cho-sen war in Vietnam, to employ Fredrik Logevall's formulation, he might not have had at his disposal the political or economic tools needed to revitalize the Amer-ican Century.[15] That Johnson and his advisers set the stage for the U.S. contribu-tion to superpower détente is easy to overlook given the impact of Vietnam on the nation's international standing and the shortcomings of policy toward Latin America and Africa. However genuine his willingness to try to adjust grand strategy, Johnson could not depart from the past. He saw the hand of the Soviet Union, specifically, and the threat of communism more generally in Vietnam and other international trouble spots. Unfortunately for him, global containment lost its relevance to world affairs before he could fashion a replacement to bolster U.S. leadership.

Nixon and Kissinger unsuccessfully endeavored to refurbish American lead-ership. Their strategic vision focused on managing tripartite great-power rela-tions, a crucial task but not what Lucian disciples, on the one hand, or domestic critics of détente, on the other, had in mind. The United States was not alone in the world, but its alliances and client relationships were weaker than before. Also, the American economy had lost its hegemonic power over global finance. To conclude that the American Century no longer existed would be an over-statement. It lived on in the minds of those who wanted the United States to lead the world with the power and influence it once had possessed. That it had fallen into and would languish in a state of dormancy seems more accurate. Whether it would ever reemerge and what it would then look like were matters for conjecture in August 1974.

What had befallen the American Century? In short, as envisioned since the 1940s it had become an anachronism. Its existence had been a balm in the face of Soviet challenges during the thorny cold-war environment of the 1950s. The avid pursuit of global containment, which European allies never fully embraced,[16] inevitably fell out of favor as superpower tensions eased. This is not to argue that strategic miscalculation was impossible as disputes over the status of Berlin and the Cuban missile crisis reminded Washington and its allies. Nevertheless, crisis no longer seemed to define the daily international order. As the prospect of conflict receded, what was overkill but an economic millstone? And in regard to America's economic might, the more the dollar enabled novel forms of economic activity, the less sway the United States had over the world's finance and trade. In short, U.S. power and influence were waning.

Moreover, under any conditions other than actual warfare between East and West, the free-world society as a kind of supranationalist entity would have been virtually impossible to sustain. National interests, whether strategic, political, economic, social, or cultural, impaired the presumed uniformity of Washington's imagined global community. Even during the Korean War, which U.S. officials treated as the nearest thing imaginable to hot war between communism and the Free World, disputes over China policy weakened the facade of Western unity. The economic and political discord that subsequently arose between the United States and its NATO allies over war in Indochina further fractured the cohesion needed for sustaining an American Century.

Ronald Reagan and George H. W. Bush referenced the American Century when it was politically profitable to do so. Their understanding of what it once was only remotely resembled Luce's vision. Reagan devoted his energy to relations with Moscow and exercised military force, notably in Central America, where promoting development and democracy was an afterthought. In economic policy, Reagan espoused quasi multilateralism by favoring deregulation of capital while running up extensive budget deficits.[17] Gone was the pull of fiscal caution that marked containment capitalism in the 1950s and early 1960s. Bush, in accepting the Republican Party's nomination for president in 1988, brought to mind Luce's call for the United States to serve as a Good Samaritan: "I see America as the leader, a unique nation with a special role in the world. . . . [This time] has been called the American Century because, in it, we were the dominant force for good in the world."[18] Neither man endeavored, though, to reconstruct Luce's world in all its complexity. Thus, the idea that military primacy defined the American Century took hold among scholars and the public, and has remained so into the twenty-first century.[19]

A concerted effort to resuscitate the American Century began in the mid-1990s. Designed by neoconservative intellectuals and former policymakers, the Project for the New American Century (PNAC) characterized U.S. foreign and defense policy as "adrift." PNAC's membership declared in a statement of principles on June 3, 1997, "We aim to change this. We aim to make the case and rally support for American global leadership." Strong action was imperative if "the United States is to build on the successes of this past century and to ensure our security and our greatness in the next."[20]

The terrible events of September 11, 2001, kept PNAC's contrivance from being only a curiosity object. The PNAC extended conceptual gravitas to President George W. Bush's war in Iraq, and the American mission in Afghanistan as played out during the presidency of Barack Obama echoed PNAC's concern about the role of American power, influence, and leadership in world affairs. Then in the November 2011 issue of *Foreign Policy*, Secretary of State Hillary Clinton set out the need for an American Century across the Pacific. An expanded presence there was essential if "a more mature security and economic architecture" was going to thrive. "It will help build," she wrote, "that architecture and pay dividends for continued American leadership well into this century, just as our post-World War II commitment to building a comprehensive and lasting transatlantic network of institutions and relationships has paid off many times over—and continues to do so."[21]

Clinton's prescription for the reassertion of U.S. leadership colored the 2012 presidential campaign. Republican Mitt Romney, Obama's opponent, proposed a new American Century—one with a stronger navy and enhanced missile defense system—about a month before Clinton's essay appeared. Obama did likewise during a commencement address in May 2012 at the Air Force Academy. "If we meet our responsibilities," he told graduating cadets, "then—just like the twentieth century—the twenty-first will be another great American Century."[22] Clinton stated the case for leadership: "Our military is by far the strongest, and our economy is by far the largest in the world. Our universities are renowned the world over." Sounding much like Henry Luce seven decades earlier, she asserted, "Our capacity to [lead] ... flows from our model of free democracy and free enterprise, a model that remains the most powerful source of prosperity and progress known to humankind."[23]

Can there actually be a new American Century or is the idea a shibboleth unworthy of serious consideration? So freighted a polarity makes any answer susceptible to contentious, endless dispute. It seems more productive to ask a number of questions in order to ascertain what a new American Century might look like. Can the United States lead through consultation and negotiation? Will an urge for primacy, let alone hegemony, eventuate in order and stability?[24] Despite Clinton's apt reference to military preeminence, does primacy assist or impair prospects for effective leadership? And, in a modern economy that depends on lightning-fast financial transactions, how can the debt-ridden American economy regain a dominant presence globally in view of the deleterious structural effects of the Great Recession of the late 2000s and early 2010s? Can traditional security-based relationships still have a foundational role in world affairs where nonstate actors operate with negligible restraint? Ongoing tensions with Russia and North Korea make that question especially important. Perhaps most crucial is the matter of America's credibility as a putative world leader. Can the United States exert influence, deploy resources, and demonstrate political will to foster social progress and promote democratic governance? In other words, can Luce's Good Samaritan be reborn and engage in nation-building to improve the lot of the world's most at-risk people?

Based on assessments of U.S. conduct and activities in Iraq, a new American Century seems, like the prior one, an improbable quest. In March and April 2013, news sources reported that "U.S. military advisers, with the knowledge and support of many senior officials, including former Secretary of Defense Donald Rumsfeld and disgraced General David Petraeus, oversaw a vast program of torture inside Iraqi prisons."[25] A lengthy report by the Constitution Project, a legal research and advocacy group, evaluated the damage to U.S. credibility resulting from more than a decade of war. The Task Force on Detainee Treatment reached a number of extremely disturbing conclusions: *"Perhaps the most important or notable finding of this panel is that it is indisputable that the United States engaged in the practice of torture."*[26] Not mincing words, the task force blamed George Bush and his advisers for actions taken in the wake of September 11 that violated international legal obligations. The Obama administration did not escape scrutiny, drawing attention for its refusal "as a matter of policy, to undertake or commission an official study of what happened, saying it was unproductive to 'look backwards' rather than forward." Torture, the task force found, had "harmful consequences for the United States' standing in the world."[27] That is, American credibility had a dwindling number of believers.

Obama implicitly addressed on May 23 some of the concerns of the task force in a speech at the National Defense University regarding his administration's controversial drone policy.[28] In language remarkably evocative of Viron P. Vaky's critique in March 1968 of U.S. policy in Guatemala, the president asserted that the Iraq war "carried grave consequences for . . . our standing in the world. . . . And, in some cases, I believe we compromised our basic values—by using torture to interrogate our enemies, and detaining individuals in a way that ran counter to the rule of law."[29] Obama's words made it clear that if the United States was again going to lead, restore its tarnished credibility in the eyes of friends and adversaries by judiciously utilizing its considerable economic and military power, or even attempt to build a new American Century, much remained to be done— no matter how skillful the would-be architects.[30]

The presidency of Donald J. Trump ended speculation about restoration of the American Century anytime soon. Adherents of the security ethos—in Congress, the federal bureaucracy, the military, and the public—took no comfort in the president's forays into foreign affairs. The State Department's diminished role and poor relations with friends and allies from Europe to Mexico to Australia caused great concern. Trump's refusal to rebuke Vladimir Putin for Russia's interference in the 2016 election roiled American politics. Also, his willingness to upend the global trade regime, whether or not to America's advantage, posed a threat to the advances made since 1945. Finally, the president's often contradictory statements raised questions about whether his administration had abandoned even the pretense of international leadership.[31]

Trump's decision on August 21, 2017, indefinitely to wage war in Afghanistan offered no solace for internationalists.[32] Vague promises to defeat the Taliban, while renouncing nation-building, rang hollow; nor did Trump explain how continuing the nation's longest war aided credibility. The allure of an American Century lingered, however. One month earlier, Wendy Sherman, undersecretary of state for political affairs under Obama, remarked in an interview, "We have believed there is a community of nations, . . . we have to create an international order. We want to write the rules . . . that are in our interest and the world's interest." In some altered form, Henry R. Luce's idea of an American Century was surviving but just barely.[33]

Notes

INTRODUCTION

1. Henry R. Luce, "The American Century," *Life*, February 17, 1941; reprinted in *Diplomatic History* 23 (Spring 1999): 159–71 (quotes 164, 165).

2. Joel Isaac and Duncan Bell, eds., *Uncertain Empire: American History and the Idea of the Cold War* (New York: Oxford University Press, 2012).

3. Conceivably, the 1890s marked the dawn of the era of globalization, although its modern period did not start until the 1970s. See Alfred E. Eckes Jr. and Thomas W. Zeiler, *Globalization and the American Century* (New York: Cambridge University Press, 2003); for an analysis of the more than one-hundred-year relationship between American power and globalization, see Frank Ninkovich, *The Global Republic: America's Inadvertent Rise to World Power* (Chicago: University of Chicago Press, 2014).

4. On the origins and evolution of the security ethos, see William O. Walker III, *National Security and Core Values in American History* (New York: Cambridge University Press, 2009).

5. Sarah Watts, *Rough Rider in the White House: Theodore Roosevelt and the Politics of Desire* (Chicago: University of Chicago Press, 2003), 21–25 (quote 23).

6. Alan Brinkley, *The Publisher: Henry Luce and His American Century* (New York: Alfred A. Knopf, 2010), 15.

7. The next two paragraphs draw on Brinkley, *The Publisher*, 3–25 (quote 20).

8. Luce, "American Century," 159, 166.

9. For more on these sometimes competing, sometimes complementary impulses, see John B. Judis, *Grand Illusion: Critics and Champions of the American Century* (New York: Farrar, Straus and Giroux, 1992), 3–21; Perry Anderson, *American Foreign Policy and Its Thinkers* (London: Verso, 2015), 1–12; and Michael Hunt, *The American Ascendancy: How the United States Gained and Wielded Global Dominance* (Chapel Hill: University of North Carolina Press, 2007), 1–9. David Milne creates a fascinating if not always persuasive binary, art versus science, in his explanation of America's rise to world power; David Milne, *Worldmaking: The Art and Science of American Diplomacy* (New York: Farrar, Straus and Giroux, 2015).

10. Erez Manela, *The Wilsonian Moment: Self-Determination and the International Origins of Anticolonial Nationalism* (New York: Oxford University Press, 2007), 22–26.

11. Brinkley, *The Publisher*, 252–65.

12. Generally, see Elizabeth Borgwardt, *A New Deal for the World: America's Vision for Human Rights* (Cambridge, MA: Harvard University Press, 2005).

13. See, for example, Wilson D. Miscamble, *From Roosevelt to Truman: Potsdam, Hiroshima, and the Cold War* (New York: Cambridge University Press, 2006).

14. This assertion derives from David M. Kennedy, "The Origins and Uses of American Hyperpower," in *The Short American Century: A Postmortem*, ed. Andrew J. Bacevich (Cambridge, MA: Harvard University Press, 2012), 17–21.

15. Luce, "American Century," 166, 168, 169. For one scholar, the essence of the American Century came down to the salvation and growth of liberal democracy, a duty for which Franklin Roosevelt's private and public life had thoroughly prepared him. Alonzo L.

Hamby, *Man of Destiny: FDR and the Making of the American Century* (New York: Basic Books, 2015).

16. Luce, "American Century," 169–71 (quotes 170, 171).

17. Ibid., 168.

18. Brinkley, *The Publisher*, 253–60.

19. Luce, "American Century," 161; the earliest use of the term "Free World" in a political sense likely occurred in Frank Capra's series of propaganda films, "Why We Fight," produced during World War II.

20. For differing assessments about how American globalism operated in practice, see Judis, *Grand Illusion*, and Elizabeth Cobbs Hoffman, *American Umpire* (Cambridge, MA: Harvard University Press, 2013). Cobbs Hoffman argues that the United States historically used its unique position in world affairs to turn global trends toward a greater good.

21. Walker, *National Security and Core Values*, 1–71.

22. See the *Washington Post*, February 21, 1941, for Thompson's column, "The American Century," containing her quotation from *The Economist*.

23. *New York Times*, April 5, 1941 (Thomas), and August 31, 1941 (Berle).

24. Melvyn P. Leffler, *For the Soul of Mankind: The United States, the Soviet Union, and the Cold War* (New York: Hill and Wang, 2007), 37–39.

25. Frank Costigliola, *Roosevelt's Lost Alliances: How Personal Politics Helped Start the Cold War* (Princeton, NJ: Princeton University Press, 2012), 319–27.

26. Frank Costigliola, "After Roosevelt's Death: Dangerous Emotions, Divisive Discourses, and the Abandoned Alliance," *Diplomatic History* 34 (January 2010): 1–23. Costigliola observes that the Russians and the British experienced similar disappointment.

27. See, for example, Tim Weiner, *Legacy of Ashes: The History of the CIA* (New York: Doubleday, 2007); Bruce Kuklick, *Blind Oracles: Intellectuals and War from Kennan to Kissinger* (Princeton, NJ: Princeton University Press, 2006), 95.

28. Cabinet Memorandum, "The Proposed United Nations Bank for Reconstruction and Development. Memorandum by the Chancellor of the Exchequer," June 20, 1944, Finance and the Economy, International Monetary Fund and World Bank, Public Record Office, The National Archives, Cabinet Papers, 1915–1964, http://filestore.nationalarchives .gov.uk/ pdfs/small/cab-66-51-wp-44-338–38.pdf (unreliable URL; access document by placing URL in a search engine such as Bing, Google, or Yahoo) (emphasis added).

29. Robert A. Packenham, *Liberal America and the Third World: Political Development Ideas in Foreign Aid and Social Science* (Princeton, NJ: Princeton University Press, 1973); David Ekbladh, *The Great American Mission: Modernization and the Construction of an American World Order* (Princeton, NJ: Princeton University Press, 2009).

30. Perry Anderson provides a similar understanding of hegemony and implicitly refers to a security ethos ("[for U.S. policymakers] central assumptions were widely shared"). He does, however, tend to conflate imperialism and hegemony; Anderson, *American Foreign Policy*, 14, 17, 19, 22, 24 (quote 17).

31. Luce, "American Century," 161, 163, 165.

32. Compare Kennedy, "The Origins and Uses of American Hyperpower," 35–36, for a more positive depiction of American hegemony. Elizabeth Cobbs Hoffman in *American Umpire* (p. 259) writes that the federal government "had been created to stand astride warring contenders and umpire their rivalry. After 1941, however, the states in question were foreign rather than domestic." This depiction of a hegemon as a disinterested observer overlooks the anxieties that officials felt and ignores how much in thrall they were to the security ethos. Frank Ninkovich finds: "At its inception, the American empire was intended to be temporary, pending the restoration of an international society in which cooperation rather than hegemony would be the norm. . . . Luce . . . did not envision an Americanization

of the globe. . . . From the earliest days of the Cold War, [policymakers] recognized that the postwar world was not an American creation." This interpretation is at odds with the one put forward herein. Ninkovich, in fact, admits: "To an amazing extent, Luce's vision was realized in practice." See Ninkovich, *The Global Republic*, 269–70.

33. Despite America's "military preeminence," John W. Dower writes, "postwar US hegemony obviously never extended to more than a portion of the globe." John W. Dower, *The Violent American Century: War and Terror since World War II* (Chicago: Haymarket Books, 2017), xi, 14–15.

34. Melvyn P. Leffler, *A Preponderance of Power: National Security, the Truman Administration, and the Cold War* (Stanford, CA: Stanford University Press, 1992), 19, 16.

35. Melvyn P. Leffler, "The Emergence of an American Grand Strategy, 1945–1952," in *The Cambridge History of the Cold War*, 3 vols., vol. 1, *Origins*, ed. Melvyn P. Leffler and Odd Arne Westad (New York: Cambridge University Press, 2010), 68.

36. For a still relevant critique of primacy and the dilemmas it posed for the conduct of foreign policy, see Stanley Hoffmann, *Primacy or World Order: American Foreign Policy since the Cold War* (New York: McGraw Hill Book Company, 1978), part one, "Thirty Years of Foreign Policy."

37. Influencing my thinking about race and cold-war history is Jason Parker, "Cold War II: The Eisenhower Administration, the Bandung Conference, and the Reperiodization of the Postwar Era," *Diplomatic History* 30 (November 2006): 867–91 (quote 868). See also Thomas Borstlemann, *The Cold War and the Color Line* (Cambridge, MA: Harvard University Press, 2001).

38. Dean Acheson, *Present at the Creation: My Years in the State Department* (New York: W. W. Norton, 1969), 232. Charles Peake, a British official, anticipated this attitude during Winston Churchill's meeting with Roosevelt in August 1941: "FDR has only one clear idea about the peace and that is that America shall emerge . . . as the strongest Power in the world" (quoted in Costigliola, *Roosevelt's Lost Alliances*, 131).

39. Walter LaFeber, "The Tension between Democracy and Capitalism during the American Century," *Diplomatic History* 23 (Spring 1999): 263–72.

40. Ibid., 264.

41. On the politics of productivity, see Charles S. Maier, "The World Economy and the Cold War in the Middle of the Twentieth Century," in Leffler and Westad, *Cambridge History of the Cold War*, 1:44–66.

42. Laura A. Belmonte, *Selling the American Way: U.S. Propaganda and the Cold War* (Philadelphia: University of Pennsylvania Press, 2008); see also the discussion in Andrew J. Falk, *Upstaging the Cold War: American Dissent and Cultural Diplomacy, 1940–1960* (Amherst: University of Massachusetts Press, 2010), 41–43.

43. Luce, "American Century," 169.

44. Robert J. McMahon, "Credibility and World Power: Exploring the Psychological Dimension in Postwar American Diplomacy," *Diplomatic History* 15 (Fall 1991): 455–71 (quotes 455, 458).

45. John W. Dower, *Embracing Defeat: Japan in the Wake of World War II* (New York: W. W. Norton, 1999), especially 547–64.

46. Leslie Bethell and Ian Roxborough, introduction to *Latin America between the Second World War and the Cold War, 1944–1948*, ed. Leslie Bethell and Ian Roxborough (New York: Cambridge University Press, 1992), 24.

47. In general, see Robert J. McMahon, ed., *The Cold War in the Third World* (New York: Oxford University Press, 2013).

48. *Public Papers of the Presidents of the United States: Richard Nixon, 1970* (Washington, DC: Government Printing Office, 1971), 409.

49. See chapter 7 for a discussion of strategic globalism.

50. The most comprehensive study is Donald W. White, *The American Century: The Rise and Decline of the United States as a World Power* (New Haven, CT: Yale University Press, 1996). In a broad narrative reflecting trends throughout American history, White draws on cultural and intellectual history to examine the American Century as a social myth. See also Harold Evans, *The American Century* (New York: Alfred A. Knopf, 1998), which looks at American identity in a sweeping overview of the social, political, and international history of the twentieth century through the prism of democracy's promise, warts and all. Two edited volumes address issues somewhat similar to my concerns: Roberto Giorgio Rabel, ed., *The American Century?: In Retrospect and Prospect* (Westport, CT: Frederick A. Praeger, 2002) and Bacevich, *The Short American Century*. In Rabel's volume, his introduction and Akira Iriye's essay, "The United States and the Making of a Global Community," exemplify how we might usefully think about the origins and implications of the idea of an American Century. Similarly in Bacevich's edited volume, his introduction, "*Life at the Dawn of the American Century*," and essays by David M. Kennedy, "The Origins and Uses of American Hyperpower," and Walter LaFeber, "Illusions of an American Century," are suggestive of major themes in my study. Emily S. Rosenberg's and Jeffrey A. Frieden's chapters on culture and economics, respectively, are important essays whose concerns largely differ from mine.

51. Bruce Cumings, *Dominion from Sea to Sea: Pacific Ascendancy and American Power* (New Haven, CT: Yale University Press, 2009), 477. Emphasizing the limits of, or constraints on, the American Century are Michael Adas, *Dominance by Design: Technological Imperatives and America's Civilizing Mission* (Cambridge, MA: Belknap Press of Harvard University Press, 2006), 214–16, 409–15; Hunt, *American Ascendancy*, 117–18. Less convinced of the decline or demise of the American Century are Walter L. Hixson, *The Myth of American Diplomacy: National Identity and U.S. Foreign Policy* (New Haven, CT: Yale University Press, 2008), 296, 305; Joan Hoff, *A Faustian Foreign Policy from Woodrow Wilson to George W. Bush: Dreams of Perfectibility* (New York: Cambridge University Press, 2008), 92–95; Martin J. Sklar, *Creating the American Century: The Ideas and Legacies of America's Twentieth-Century Foreign Policy Founders* (New York: Cambridge University Press, 2017), xi–xxiii, 129–71. See the spring and summer 1999 issues of *Diplomatic History* for a retrospective on the American Century and its impact.

52. Mary Nolan, *The Transatlantic Century: Europe and America, 1890–2010* (New York: Cambridge University Press, 2012), 1–9, 267–303 (quote 4).

53. David. F. Schmitz, *Richard Nixon and the Vietnam War: The End of the American Century* (Lanham, MD: Rowman & Littlefield, 2014).

54. LaFeber, "Illusions of an American Century," 159, 161, 163; Sayuri Guthrie-Shimizu, "Japan, the United States, and the Cold War, 1945–1960," in Leffler and Westad, *Cambridge History of the Cold War*, 1:244.

1. PURSUING HEGEMONY

1. Dean Acheson, *Present at the Creation: My Years in the State Department* (New York: W. W. Norton, 1969), 88; see Fredrik J. Dobney, ed., *Selected Papers of Will Clayton* (Baltimore: Johns Hopkins University Press, 1971), 1–9 for information on Clayton's background.

2. See U.S. Department of State, *Foreign Relations of the United States, 1945*, vol. 9, *The American Republics* (*FRUS, year*, volume) (Washington, DC: Government Printing Office [GPO], 1969), 1–153 for documents on the U.S. role in the conference.

3. John S. D. Eisenhower, *So Far from God: The U.S. War with Mexico, 1846–1848* (New York: Random House, 1989), 338–42; *FRUS, 1945*, 9:4.

4. *FRUS, 1945*, 9:64–67 (quote 65).

5. For Clayton's remarks, see "Statement by Assistant Secretary [William L.] Clayton," *Department of State Bulletin*, March 4, 1945, pp. 334–38. See also U.S. Department of State, Conference Series No. 85, *Report of the Delegation of the United States of America to the Inter-American Conference on Problems of War and Peace, Mexico City, February 21-March 8, 1945* (Washington, DC: GPO, 1946).

6. On the inter-American bank, see *FRUS, 1945*, 9:72.

7. Useful assessments of the Chapúltepec conference include Samuel L. Baily, *The United States and the Development of South America, 1945–1975* (New York: New Viewpoints, 1976), 40–48; David Green, *The Containment of Latin America: A History of the Myths and Realities of the Good Neighbor Policy* (Chicago: Quadrangle Books, 1971), 169–208.

8. Dobney, *Selected Papers of Will Clayton*, 1; Bryce Wood, *The Dismantling of the Good Neighbor Policy* (Austin: University of Texas Press, 1985), 80–85. Fredrick B. Pike uses the words "shock therapy" in discussing the conference; see Fredrick B. Pike, *FDR's Good Neighbor Policy: Sixty Years of Generally Gentle Chaos* (Austin: University of Texas Press, 1985), 278–80.

9. Leslie Bethell and Ian Roxborough, "Introduction: The Postwar Conjuncture in Latin America: Democracy, Labor, and the Left," in *Latin America between the Second World War and the Cold War, 1944–1948*, ed. Leslie Bethell and Ian Roxborough (New York: Cambridge University Press, 1992), 1–32.

10. *FRUS, 1945*, 9:68 (quote), 142–43; Mark T. Gilderhus, *The Second Century: U.S.-Latin American Relations since 1889* (Wilmington, DE: Scholarly Resources, 2000), 119.

11. *FRUS, 1945*, 9:99.

12. Merwin L. Bohan Oral History, June 15, 1974, Harry S. Truman Presidential Library (HSTL), Independence, MO, pp. 13–14, 18–19, 59 (quote p. 14), http://www.trumanlibrary.org/oralhist/bohanm.htm.

13. Thomas C. Mann Oral History, June 12, 1974, HSTL, pp. 12–13, 19–20, http://www.trumanlibrary.org/oralhist/mannt.htm#8; *FRUS, 1945*, 9:123.

14. Washington's presumption of superiority in hemispheric affairs is analyzed in Fredrick B. Pike, *The United States and Latin America: Myths and Stereotypes of Civilization and Nature* (Austin: University of Texas Press, 1992).

15. Gilderhus, *Second Century*, 118–19; Bethell and Roxborough, "The Postwar Conjuncture in Latin America," 23–25.

16. Geoffrey Roberts, *Stalin's Wars: From World War to Cold War, 1949–1953* (New Haven, CT: Yale University Press, 2006), 271–72.

17. Melvyn P. Leffler, *A Preponderance of Power: National Security, the Truman Administration, and the Cold War* (Stanford, CA: Stanford University Press, 1992), 37–38.

18. Ibid., 63–68; Roberts, *Stalin's Wars*, 350–52.

19. Dobney, *Selected Papers of Will Clayton*, 81–84 (quote 84).

20. Thomas W. Zeiler, *Free Trade, Free World: The Advent of GATT* (Chapel Hill: University of North Carolina Press, 1999), 2.

21. Sweden and Canada were the first recipients of aid. Paul H. Nitze Oral History, August 4, 1975, HSTL, pp. 143–47, https://www.trumanlibrary.org/oralhist/nitzeph2.htm#oh3.

22. Thomas G. Paterson, *Soviet-American Confrontation: Postwar Reconstruction and the Origins of the Cold War* (Baltimore: Johns Hopkins University Press, 1973), 33–56, 159–73, is still useful on the politics of loan diplomacy.

23. *FRUS, 1945*, vol. 5, *Europe* (Washington, DC: GPO, 1967), 966.

24. Once the question of a loan to the Soviet Union was off the table, the administration worked with the Export-Import Bank to provide France with a $650 million loan in

order to influence national elections there. *FRUS, 1945*, vol. 1, *General; The United Nations* (Washington, DC: GPO, 1972), 1430–36.

25. *FRUS, 1945*, vol. 6, *The British Commonwealth, the Far East* (Washington, DC: GPO, 1969), 54, 56.

26. Richard N. Gardner, *Sterling-Dollar Diplomacy: The Origins and Prospects of Our International Economic Order*, expanded ed. (New York: McGraw Hill, 1969), chapters 10 and 11; Paterson, *Soviet-American Confrontation*, 162–63.

27. Dobney, *Selected Papers of Will Clayton*, 156.

28. Gardner, *Sterling-Dollar Diplomacy*, 223.

29. Ibid., 257–68; Paterson, *Soviet-American Confrontation*, 147–58 (Keynes quote 153); *New York Times*, March 9 (Soviet observers) and March 30 (British displeasure), 1946.

30. The CFM had been established at Potsdam to draft peace treaties formally bringing World War II to an end. It became a forum where the Big Three discussed issues that ultimately fractured the wartime coalition.

31. Regarding tensions with the USSR over the situation in northern Iran and its place in the early Cold War, see Acheson, *Present at the Creation*, 196–98.

32. Leffler, *Preponderance of Power*, 38–40, 46–49 (Truman quote 48); Roberts, *Stalin's Wars*, 296–305 (Molotov quote 305).

33. George F. Kennan, *Memoirs*, vol. 1, *1925–1950* (Boston: Little, Brown, 1967), 283–88; John Lewis Gaddis, *George F. Kennan: An American Life* (New York: Penguin Press, 2011), 209–10.

34. Kennan, *Memoirs*, 1:560–65 (quotes 560, 561).

35. This assessment builds on Gaddis, *Kennan*, 216, and Leffler, *Preponderance of Power*, 107–8.

36. *FRUS, 1946*, vol. 6, *Eastern Europe; the Soviet Union* (Washington, DC: GPO, 1969), 695 n. 39.

37. See *FRUS, 1946*, 6:696–709 for the text of the Long Telegram; Leffler, *Preponderance of Power*, 108–9; Gaddis, *Kennan*, 216–19, 252–53, 266.

38. Kennan, *Memoirs*, 1:295.

39. Kennan quoted in Gaddis, *Kennan*, 514.

40. Roberts, *Stalin's Wars*, 305–6; Leffler, *Preponderance of Power*, 109–10.

41. Kennan, *Memoirs*, 1:464.

42. For Kennan's worry that the Truman Doctrine could ensnare the United States in commitments that would leave it overextended, see Leffler, *Preponderance of Power*, 142–51, and Gaddis, *Kennan*, 261–70.

43. Frank Costigliola, "'I React Intensely to Everything': Russia and the Frustrated Emotions of George F. Kennan, 1933–1958," *Journal of American History* 102 (March 2016): 1075–1101 (quote 1078).

44. Wm. Roger Louis, *The British Empire in the Middle East, 1945–1951: Arab Nationalism, the United States, and Postwar Imperialism* (New York: Oxford University Press, 1984), 73–102.

45. Acheson, *Present at the Creation*, 217.

46. Ibid., 219.

47. Roberts, *Stalin's Wars*, 218–22, 233, 299 (quote 222).

48. Kennan, *Memoirs*, 1:316, 317; Gaddis, *Kennan*, 262.

49. *FRUS, 1947*, vol. 3, *The British Commonwealth, Europe* (Washington, DC: GPO, 1972), 223–30 (quote 224); Gaddis, *Kennan*, 267.

50. Alan Brinkley, *The Publisher: Henry Luce and His American Century* (New York: Alfred A. Knopf, 2010), 362–64; John Lewis Gaddis, *Strategies of Containment: A Critical Appraisal of American National Security Policy during the Cold War*, rev. and expanded ed. (New York: Oxford University Press, 2005), 54–59.

51. Frank Costigliola, *Roosevelt's Lost Alliances: How Personal Politics Helped Start the Cold War* (Princeton, NJ: Princeton University Press, 2012), 406.

52. J. Lloyd Mecham, *The United States and Inter-American Security, 1889–1960* (Austin: University of Texas Press, 1961), 284–86.

53. David Green, "The Cold War Comes to Latin America," in *Politics and Policies of the Truman Administration*, ed. Barton J. Bernstein (Chicago: Quadrangle Books, 1970), 149–95; Roger R. Trask, "The Impact of the Cold War on United States-Latin American Relations, 1945–1949," *Diplomatic History* 1 (July 1977): 271–84.

54. *FRUS, 1948*, vol. 9, *The Western Hemisphere* (Washington, DC: GPO, 1972), 218–25.

55. On the political and economic context of the meeting in Bogotá, see Greg Grandin, "What Was Containment?: Short and Long Answers from the Americas," in *The Cold War in the Third World*, ed. Robert J. McMahon (New York: Oxford University Press, 2013), especially 29–39.

56. Roy R. Rubottom Jr. interview, February 13, 1990, p. 5, Library of Congress, Frontline Diplomacy: The Foreign Affairs Oral History Collection of the Association for Diplomatic Studies and Training, https://www.loc.gov/item/mfdipbib001001/.

57. Quoted in Trask, "Impact of the Cold War," 278.

58. Stephen G. Rabe, *Eisenhower and Latin America: The Foreign Policy of Anticommunism* (Chapel Hill: University of North Carolina Press, 1988), 70–72, 76–77; Rubottom interview, p. 6.

59. *FRUS, 1948*, 9:40. The State Department found that Communists were active in Colombia but could not link them to Gaitán's killing; Department of State, "Communist Involvement in the Colombian Riots of April 9, 1948," O[ffice of] I[ntelligence] R[esearch] Report No. 4686, October 14, 1948, pp. 14–17, CK2349422750, Declassified Documents Reference System, Gale, Cengage Learning, Farmington Hills, MI.

60. On Britain's cold-war mindset, see Anne Deighton, "Britain and the Cold War, 1945–1955," in *The Cambridge History of the Cold War*, 3 vols., vol. 1, *Origins*, ed. Melvyn P. Leffler and Odd Arne Westad (New York: Cambridge University Press, 2010), 112–32 (quote 119).

61. Robert J. McMahon, *Dean Acheson and the Creation of an American World Order* (Washington, DC: Potomac Books, 2009), 68.

62. Acheson, *Present at the Creation*, 219.

63. Tony Judt, *Postwar: A History of Europe since 1945* (New York: Penguin Press, 2005), 143; Vladislav M. Zubok, *A Failed Empire: The Soviet Union in the Cold War from Stalin to Gorbachev* (Chapel Hill: University of North Carolina Press, 2007), 73.

64. *FRUS, 1947*, vol. 4, *Eastern Europe; the Soviet Union* (Washington, DC: GPO, 1972), 596.

65. Alessandro Brogi, *Confronting America: The Cold War between the United States and the Communists in France and Italy* (Chapel Hill: University of North Carolina Press, 2011), 87–121, 157–86; Richard F. Kuisel, *Seducing the French: The Dilemmas of Americanization* (Berkeley: University of California Press, 1993), 24–36.

66. Tim Weiner, *Legacy of Ashes: The History of the CIA* (New York: Doubleday, 2007), 26–27, 35–36; Brogi, *Confronting America*, 74–78.

67. Scott Lucas and Kaeten Mistry, "Illusions of Coherence: George F. Kennan, U.S. Strategy and Political Warfare in the Early Cold War, 1946–1950," *Diplomatic History* 33 (January 2009): 39–66; Gaddis, *Kennan*, 293–95, 316–19; Brogi, *Confronting America*, chapters 1–4.

68. Campbell Craig and Fredrik Logevall, *America's Cold War: The Politics of Insecurity* (Cambridge, MA: Belknap Press of Harvard University Press, 2009), 96–99.

69. Richard J. Barnet, *The Alliance: America, Europe, Japan: Makers of the Postwar World* (New York: Simon and Schuster, 1983), 128–30.

70. Acheson, *Present at the Creation*, 341.

71. Lawrence S. Kaplan, *The United States and NATO: The Formative Years* (Lexington: University Press of Kentucky, 1984), 178.

72. Carolyn Woods Eisenberg, *Drawing the Line: The American Decision to Divide Germany, 1944–1949* (New York: Cambridge University Press, 1996), 439–40, 478–83; Costigliola, "'I React Intensely to Everything,'" 1078, employs the term "emotional mystic."

73. Kennan, *Memoirs*, 1:403–4, 464; Gaddis, *Kennan*, 326–51.

74. *FRUS, 1947*, vol. 1, *General; the United Nations* (Washington, DC: GPO, 1973), 734–41 (quote 740).

75. "Military Government of Germany," *Department of State Bulletin*, July 27, 1947, pp. 186–93 (quote 186).

76. Zubok, *Failed Empire*, 73–74; see Eisenberg, *Drawing the Line*, 380–83, 410 on currency issues and the division of Germany.

77. Acheson, *Present at the Creation*, 274–75.

78. Roberts, *Stalin's Wars*, 350–59, 361, 363.

79. Judt, *Postwar*, 87–88.

80. Marc J. Selverstone, *Constructing the Monolith: The United States, Great Britain, and International Communism, 1945–1950* (Cambridge, MA: Harvard University Press, 2009).

81. Peter L. Hahn, *Crisis and Crossfire: The United States and the Middle East since 1945* (Washington, DC: Potomac Books, 2005), 9–10; *FRUS, 1945*, vol. 8, *The Near East and Africa* (Washington, DC: GPO, 1969), 45.

82. *FRUS, 1947*, vol. 5, *The Near East and Africa* (Washington, DC: GPO, 1971), 614–20 (Foreign Office quote 616, State Department quote, 615).

83. See, for example, *FRUS, 1952–1954*, vol. 9, *The Near and Middle East* (in two parts) (Washington, DC: GPO, 1986), pt. 2: 2413.

84. Zubok, *Failed Empire*, 40–46; Louis, *British Empire in the Middle East*, 62–73.

85. Regarding military aid for Iran, see *FRUS, 1946*, vol. 7, *The Near East and Africa* (Washington, DC: GPO, 1969), 209–13, 225–26, 372–73; *FRUS, 1947*, 5: 901–2, 905–10, 914–16.

86. Steve Everly, ed., *U.S., Britain Developed Plans to Disable or Destroy Middle Eastern Oil Facilities from Late 1940s to Early 1960s in the Event of a Soviet Invasion*, June 23, 2016, National Security Archive, Electronic Briefing Book No. 477, Documents 1 and 2, http:// nsarchive.gwu.edu/NSAEBB/NSAEBB552-US-and-Britain-planned-to-destroy-Middle -East-oil-facilities-in-case-of-Soviet-invasion-from-1940s-1960s/. And see National Security Council Progress Report on NSC Series 26, "Removal and Demolition of Oil Facilities, Equipment and Supplies in the Middle East," March 9, 1953, Declassified Documents - Fiscal Year 2011, The Middle East, Dwight D. Eisenhower Presidential Library, Abilene, KS, https://www.eisenhower.archives.gov/research/online_documents/declassified/fy_2011 /1953_03_09.pdf.

87. Quoted in Howard K. Beale, *Theodore Roosevelt and the Rise of America to World Power* (Baltimore: Johns Hopkins University Press, 1956), 268.

88. Michael Schaller, *The American Occupation of Japan: The Origins of the Cold War in Asia* (New York: Oxford University Press, 1985), chapters 2 and 7; Sayuri Guthrie-Shimizu, *Transpacific Field of Dreams: How Baseball Linked the United States and Japan in Peace and World War II* (Chapel Hill: University of North Carolina Press, 2012), 198–223.

89. Kennan, *Memoirs*: 1:368–93; Gaddis, *Kennan*, 300–303.

90. John W. Dower, *Embracing Defeat: Japan in the Wake of World War II* (New York: W. W. Norton, 1999), 23, 239, 270–72, 525–26, 551–52 (quote 552).

91. *FRUS, 1948*, vol. 6, *The Far East and Australasia* (Washington, DC: GPO, 1974), 691–96 (quote 694).

92. Livingston Merchant Oral History, May 27, 1975, HSTL, pp. 38–39, http://www
.trumanlibrary.org/oralhist/merchant.htm#38; Acheson, *Present at the Creation*, 338, 272.

93. J[ohn] W. Dower, *Empire and Aftermath: Yoshida Shigeru and the Japanese Experience, 1878–1954* (Cambridge, MA: Harvard University Press, 1979), 333–414.

94. On the evolution of relations with South Korea, see Gregg Brazinsky, *Nation Building in South Korea: Koreans, Americans, and the Making of a Democracy* (Chapel Hill:
University of North Carolina Press, 2007), 13–18.

95. Ibid., 24–26.

96. *FRUS, 1949*, vol. 7, *The Far East and Australasia* (in two parts) (Washington, DC:
GPO, 1976), pt. 2: 1004, 1014. Muccio served as ambassador from 1949 to 1952.

97. John J. Muccio Oral History, February 10, 1971, HSTL, pp. 13, 14, http://www
.trumanlibrary.org/oralhist/muccio1.htm.

98. Brinkley, *The Publisher*, 148–70, 326–27 (quotes 163, 327).

99. Robert Gilpin, *U.S. Power and the Multinational Corporation: The Political Economy of Foreign Direct Investment* (New York: Basic Books, 1975), 100–101; Diane B.
Kunz, *Butter and Guns: America's Cold War Economic Diplomacy* (New York: Free Press,
1997), 9.

100. Fred L. Block, *The Origins of International Economic Disorder: A Study of United
States International Monetary Policy from World War II to the Present* (Berkeley: University
of California Press, 1977), 25–30; William O. Walker III, *National Security and Core Values in American History* (New York: Cambridge University Press, 2009), 112–13.

101. Quoted in William Appleman Williams, *The Tragedy of American Diplomacy*,
2nd rev. and enlarged ed. (New York: W. W. Norton, 1972), 236.

102. Quoted in Kunz, *Butter and Guns*, 35.

103. Judt, *Postwar*, 91.

104. *FRUS, 1945*, 6:168–204.

105. Conclusions of a Meeting of the Cabinet, "Washington Discussion on Financial
Questions and Commercial Policy," December 3, 1945, Finance and the Economy, Bretton Woods Conference (F & E, BWC), Public Record Office, Cabinet Papers, 1915–1964
(PRO, Cab), http://filestore.nationalarchives.gov.uk/pdfs/small/cab-128-2-cm-45-58-11.
pdf; Gardner, *Sterling-Dollar Diplomacy*, chapters 10–12.

106. See, for example, Cabinet Conclusion 6, "Exchange Control Bill," November 4,
1946, F & E, BWC, PRO, Cab, http://filestore.nationalarchives.gov.uk/pdfs/small/cab-128
-6-cm-46-94-32.pdf.

107. Michael J. Hogan, *The Marshall Plan: America, Britain, and the Reconstruction of
Western Europe, 1947–1952* (New York: Cambridge University Press, 1987), 301, 308.

108. *FRUS, 1945*, vol. 4, *Europe* (Washington, DC: GPO, 1968), 716–17.

109. Judt, *Postwar*, 86–87.

110. *FRUS, 1946*, vol. 5, *The British Commonwealth, Western and Central Europe* (Washington, DC: GPO, 1969), 461–62 (quote 462).

111. Ibid., 469, 470.

112. For a useful overview of the crucial relationship between European economic recovery and U.S. foreign policy objectives, see Report, "The Problem of Future Balance of
Payments of the United States," ca. 1948, Online Documents, The Point Four Program,
HSTL, http://www.trumanlibrary.org/whistlestop/study_collections/pointfourprogram
/index.php.

113. Gardner, *Sterling-Dollar Diplomacy*, 287–99; Alfred E. Eckes Jr. and Thomas W.
Zeiler, *Globalization and the American Century* (New York: Cambridge University Press,
2003), 117, 121, 124–28.

114. Zeiler, *Free Trade, Free World*, 62, 72–74, 135; Gardner, *Sterling-Dollar Diplomacy*,
371–80; Block, *Origins of International Economic Disorder*, 75–76.

115. *FRUS, 1949*, vol. 1, *National Security Affairs, Foreign Economic Policy* (Washington, DC: GPO, 1976), 712–13.

116. *FRUS, 1948*, vol. 1, *General; The United Nations* (in two parts) (Washington, DC: GPO, 1976), pt. 2: 941.

117. Ibid., 918–22 (quote 912).

118. Kennan, *Memoirs*, 1:325.

119. Ibid., 328; Gaddis, *Kennan*, 262–85.

120. *FRUS, 1947*, 3:225.

121. See contrasting interpretations in Hogan, *Marshall Plan*, and Alan S. Milward, *The Reconstruction of Western Europe, 1945–51* (Berkeley: University of California Press, 1984).

122. William I. Hitchcock, "The Marshall Plan and the Creation of the West," in Leffler and Westad, *Cambridge History of the Cold War*, 1:154–74 (quote 172).

123. Kunz, *Butter and Guns*, 52–55; Judt, *Postwar*, 93–96.

124. John W. Snyder Oral History, February 4, 1969, HSTL, pp. 1107–11, http://www.trumanlibrary.org/oralhist/snyder27.htm#1107, and John W. Snyder Oral History for the Oral History Committee of the Treasury Historical Association, March 15, 1980, HSTL, pp. 174–76, http://www.trumanlibrary.org/oralhist/snyderj1.htm#172, in which Snyder, Truman's Treasury secretary, emphasizes Clayton's role in the making of the Marshall Plan. Acheson, *Present at the Creation*, 731, 232 (emphasis added).

125. *FRUS, 1948*, vol. 3, *Western Europe* (Washington, DC: GPO, 1974), 414–17, 432–33, 439; Judt, *Postwar*, 93–94.

126. Richard M. Bissell Jr., with Jonathan E. Lewis and Frances T. Pudlo, *Reflections of a Cold Warrior: From Yalta to the Bay of Pigs* (New Haven, CT: Yale University Press, 1996), 34–40; Hogan, *Marshall Plan*, 102–9, 137–43.

127. Rudy Abramson, *Spanning the Century: The Life of W. Averell Harriman* (New York: William Morrow and Company, 1992), 425; *FRUS, 1949*, vol. 4, *Western Europe* (Washington, DC: GPO, 1975), 494 (quote).

128. Hogan, *Marshall Plan*, 133–51, 201–4; *FRUS, 1948*, 3:673–74, 847 n. 3, 848 n. 4, 867, 1073.

129. *FRUS, 1949*, 4:389, 412–15, 706–11.

130. *FRUS, 1949*, 1:388, 391, 403 (quote 401, Acheson quote 412).

131. Abramson, *Spanning the Century*, 438, 465.

132. *FRUS, 1949*, 4:433–36, 797, 799; Foreign Office quote in Hogan, *Marshall Plan*, 291.

133. Abramson, *Spanning the Century*, 427; Hogan, *Marshall Plan*, 66, 127, 159, 219–20.

134. Conclusions of a Meeting of the Cabinet, "The Economic Situation," July 25, 1949, F & E, Bretton Woods System in Practice (BWS), PRO, Cab, http://filestore.nationalarchives.gov.uk/pdfs/small/cab-128-16-cm-49-48-5.pdf.

135. Cabinet Memorandum, "The Dollar Situation," July 21, 1949, F & E, BWS, PRO, Cab, http://filestore.nationalarchives.gov.uk/pdfs/small/cab-129-36-cp-158.pdf.

136. Cabinet Memorandum, "The Economic Situation," July 21, 1949, F & E, BWS, PRO, Cab, http://filestore.nationalarchives.gov.uk/pdfs/small/cab-129-36-cp-159.pdf.

137. *FRUS, 1949*, 4:805–14 (quote 805–6).

138. Cabinet Conclusion, "The Economic Situation: Washington Talks," September 17, 1949, F & E, BWS, PRO, Cab, http://filestore.nationalarchives.gov.uk/pdfs/small/cab-128-16-cm-49-55-12.pdf.

139. *FRUS, 1949*, 4:822–39 (quote 823).

140. Jeffrey A. Frieden, *Global Capitalism: Its Fall and Rise in the Twentieth Century* (New York: W. W. Norton, 2006), 270; Curt Cardwell, *NSC 68 and the Political Economy of the Early Cold War* (New York: Cambridge University Press, 2011), 151.

141. Hogan, *Marshall Plan*, 137, 174–79, 198–200.

142. *FRUS, 1949*, vol. 3, *Council of Foreign Ministers; Germany and Austria* (Washington, DC: GPO, 1974), 96.

143. Ibid., 174–76.

144. Judt, *Postwar*, 94–98. Auspiciously, during the relatively short life of the Marshall Plan, the combined GNP of Western Europe increased by 30 percent.

145. *FRUS, 1949*, 4:426–29 (quote 429).

146. Ibid., 438–40 (quote 439).

147. Block, *Origins of International Economic Disorder*, 100–102. The idea of a payments union had been under discussion for a couple of years.

148. Judt, *Postwar*, 94; James Ranson, "A Little Marshall Plan: Britain and the Formation of the European Payments Union, 1948–50," *International History Review* 32 (September 2010): 437–54; Cardwell, *NSC 68 and the Political Economy of the Early Cold War*, 251–52; *FRUS, 1950*, vol. 1, *National Security Affairs; Foreign Economic Policy* (Washington, DC: GPO, 1977), 815 (quote).

149. Charles S. Maier, "The World Economy and the Cold War in the Middle of the Twentieth Century," in Leffler and Westad, *Cambridge History of the Cold War*, 1:58.

150. *FRUS, 1950*, vol. 3, *Western Europe* (Washington, DC: GPO, 1977), 740.

151. Hogan, *Marshall Plan*, 320–25; *FRUS, 1950*, 3:655–59, 663.

152. Kennan, *Memoirs*, 1:314, 317, 318.

153. Acheson, *Present at the Creation*, 219.

154. Ibid., 261–63, 274; on the final point, see the discussion in *FRUS, 1949*, 3:705–8, 728–30, 744–48, 749–50, 820, 826–27 (quotes 748, 827).

155. Compare Melvyn P. Leffler, "The Emergence of an American Grand Strategy, 1945–1952," in Leffler and Westad, *Cambridge History of the Cold War*, 1:81.

156. *FRUS, 1949*, 4:825.

2. PROTECTING THE FREE WORLD

1. Others include the Model Treaty or Plan of 1776 and the Monroe Doctrine. Nitze, who came to the PPS in 1949, once entertained the idea of a $20–$25 billion global recovery program; Paul H. Nitze Oral History, August 4, 1975, Harry S. Truman Presidential Library (HSTL), Independence, MO, p. 147, https://www.trumanlibrary.org/oralhist/nitzeph2.htm#oh3.

2. See contrasting discussions of NSC 68 in Melvyn P. Leffler, *A Preponderance of Power: National Security, the Truman Administration, and the Cold War* (Stanford, CA: Stanford University Press, 1992), 312–14, 355–60, and Curt Cardwell, *NSC 68 and the Political Economy of the Early Cold War* (New York: Cambridge University Press, 2011).

3. Alan Brinkley, *The Publisher: Henry Luce and His American Century* (New York: Alfred A. Knopf, 2010), 313–51.

4. John Lewis Gaddis, *George F. Kennan: An American Life* (New York: Penguin Press, 2011), 340–43, 347–51.

5. Madeleine Albright, with Bill Woodward, *Madam Secretary: A Memoir* (New York: Miramax Books, 2003), 659.

6. Leffler, *Preponderance of Power*, 260–65; Christopher Layne, *The Peace of Illusions: American Grand Strategy from 1940 to the Present* (Ithaca, NY: Cornell University Press, 2006), 62–64; for the text, see U.S. Department of State, *Foreign Relations of the United States, 1948*, vol. 1, *General; The United Nations* (in two parts) (*FRUS, year,* volume) (Washington, DC: Government Printing Office [GPO], 1976), pt. 2: 662–69 (quote 669; emphasis added).

7. Gaddis, *Kennan*, 285–87; *FRUS, 1949*, vol. 7, *The Far East and Australasia* (in two parts) (Washington, DC: GPO, 1976), pt. 2: 1215–20.

8. George F. Kennan, *Memoirs*, vol. 2, *1950–1963* (Boston: Little, Brown, 1972), 335–36 (first quote); Gaddis, *Kennan*, 339 (second quote). This harsh assessment gave Kennan no pleasure given the close personal relationship the two enjoyed prior to 1950.

9. Michael J. Hogan, *A Cross of Iron: Harry S. Truman and the Origins of the National Security State, 1945–1954* (New York: Cambridge University Press, 1998), 276; Bruce Cumings, *Dominion from Sea to Sea: Pacific Ascendancy and American Power* (New Haven, CT: Yale University Press, 2009), 390–91.

10. Paul H. Nitze, with Ann M. Smith and Steven L. Rearden, *From Hiroshima to Glasnost: At the Center of Decision: A Memoir* (New York: Grove Weidenfeld, 1989), 66–67 (quote 67).

11. Kennan, *Memoirs*, 2:427; Tony Judt, *Postwar: A History of Europe since 1945* (New York: Penguin Press, 2005), 203–17.

12. Robert J. McMahon, *Dean Acheson and the Creation of an American World Order* (Washington, DC: Potomac Books, 2009), 107–10; David Milne, *Worldmaking: The Art and Science of American Diplomacy* (New York: Farrar, Straus and Giroux, 2015), chapters 5 and 6.

13. Dean Acheson, *Present at the Creation: My Years in the State Department* (New York: W. W. Norton, 1969), 373.

14. Bruce Kuklick, *Blind Oracles: Intellectuals and War from Kennan to Kissinger* (Princeton, NJ: Princeton University Press, 2006), 43–48 (quote 45).

15. This is the implication of Luke Fletcher's fine article, "The Collapse of the Western World: Acheson, Nitze, and the NSC 68/Rearmament Decision," *Diplomatic History* 40 (September 2016): 750–76, which posits West Germany's importance to NSC 68.

16. John Fousek, *To Lead the Free World: American Nationalism and the Cultural Roots of the Cold War* (Chapel Hill: University of North Carolina Press, 2000), 162–65; Layne, *Peace of Illusions*, 62–64.

17. *FRUS, 1950*, vol. 1, *National Security Affairs; Foreign Economic Policy* (Washington, DC: GPO, 1977), 238; Milne, *Worldmaking*, 9, contends, erroneously in my view, that Nitze "excised emotion from his thought process because he believed the circumstances demanded it."

18. *FRUS, 1950*, 1:238, 245–46.

19. Ibid., 241.

20. Ibid., 249, 251.

21. Ibid., 836.

22. Acheson, *Present at the Creation*, 374.

23. *FRUS, 1950*, 1:276–87 (quote 282).

24. Lawrence S. Kaplan, *The United States and NATO: The Formative Years* (Lexington: University Press of Kentucky, 1984), 155–63, 165, 169.

25. George McT. Kahin, *Intervention: How America Became Involved in Vietnam* (New York: Alfred A. Knopf, 1986), 13, 27–28, 34–48.

26. Judt, *Postwar*, 152.

27. *FRUS, 1949*, vol. 9, *The Far East: China* (Washington, DC: GPO, 1974), 1–5; C. R. Attlee, *As It Happened* (New York: Viking Press, 1954), 282.

28. Acheson, *Present at the Creation*, 594.

29. McMahon, *Dean Acheson*, 140–43.

30. *FRUS, 1950*, vol. 7, *Korea* (Washington, DC: GPO, 1976), 396–99, 1032–33, 1138–40; Attlee, *As It Happened*, 281.

31. Acheson, *Present at the Creation*, 447.

32. McMahon, *Dean Acheson*, 144–48 (quote 144); *FRUS, 1950*, 7:1246, 1248, 1324–28, 1335–36, 1339–40 (quotes 1325, 1326).

33. *FRUS, 1950*, 7:1098–99 (quote 1099).

34. Acheson, *Present at the Creation*, 478–85; Leffler, *Preponderance of Power*, 398–400; *FRUS, 1950*, vol. 3, *Western Europe* (Washington, DC: GPO, 1977), 1706–87.

35. Klaus Larres, *Churchill's Cold War: The Politics of Personal Diplomacy* (New Haven, CT: Yale University Press, 2002), 156–66.

36. *FRUS, 1951*, vol. 4, *Europe: Political and Economic Developments* (in two parts) (Washington, DC: GPO, 1985), pt. 1: 987.

37. *FRUS, 1952–1954*, vol. 6, *Western Europe and Canada* (in two parts) (Washington, DC: GPO, 1986), pt. 1: 748.

38. Anne Deighton, "Britain and the Cold War, 1945–1955," in *The Cambridge History of the Cold War*, 3 vols., vol. 1, *Origins*, ed. Melvyn P. Leffler and Odd Arne Westad (New York: Cambridge University Press, 2010), 125–30.

39. *FRUS, 1952–1954*, 6:716.

40. Larres, *Churchill's Cold War*, 141–43.

41. Acheson, *Present at the Creation*, 384, 385.

42. On the Schuman Plan, see Michael J. Hogan, *The Marshall Plan: America, Britain, and the Reconstruction of Western Europe, 1947–1952* (New York: Cambridge University Press, 1987), 364–79.

43. Judt, *Postwar*, 156–59, 164.

44. *FRUS, 1950*, 1:314, 383.

45. *FRUS, 1951*, vol. 6, *Asia and the Pacific* (in two parts) (Washington, DC: GPO, 1977), pt. 1: 1468.

46. Ibid., 1181.

47. Ibid., 1300. The occupation of Japan formally ended in April 1952.

48. Ibid., 1439–40.

49. See, for example, ibid., 1284, 1308.

50. *FRUS, 1952–1954*, vol. 14, *China and Japan* (in two parts) (Washington, DC: GPO, 1985), pt. 2: 1098, 1111–13, 1114, 1155–57.

51. Ibid., 1161.

52. Brinkley, *The Publisher*, 317–19, 335–40.

53. This point draws on James Peck, *Washington's China: The National Security World, the Cold War, and the Origins of Globalism* (Amherst: University of Massachusetts Press, 2006).

54. Livingston Merchant Oral History, May 27, 1975, HSTL, pp. 22–23, http://www.trumanlibrary.org/oralhist/merchant.htm#38.

55. Gaddis, *Kennan*, 353, 357–58.

56. Peck, *Washington's China*, 120–27.

57. *FRUS, 1950*, 3:1712–14 (quote 1714).

58. John F. Melby Oral History, November 14, 1972, HSTL, pp. 181–82, http://www.trumanlibrary.org/oralhist/melby.htm; *FRUS, 1950*, vol. 6, *East Asia and the Pacific* (Washington, DC: GPO, 1976), 1504 (Acheson quote); Nick Cullather, *Illusions of Influence: The Political Economy of United States-Philippine Relations, 1942–1960* (Stanford, CA: Stanford University Press, 1994), 72–87.

59. *FRUS, 1951*, vol. 7, *Korea and China* (in two parts) (Washington, DC: GPO, 1983), pt. 2: 1576–77.

60. Wm. Roger Louis, *The British Empire in the Middle East, 1945–1951: Arab Nationalism, the United States, and Postwar Imperialism* (New York: Oxford University Press, 1984), 640–55.

61. The characterization is that of the historian William Roger Louis; ibid., 5.

62. The British side of the story is best told in Louis, *British Empire in the Middle East*, 632–89.

63. *FRUS, 1952–1954*, vol. 10, *Iran, 1952–1954* (Washington, DC: GPO, 1989), 221.

64. *FRUS, 1950–1955: The Intelligence Community: 1950–1955* (Washington, DC: GPO, 2007), 243–45.

65. Ibid., 881; Acheson, *Present at the Creation*, 504–11 (quote 507).

66. *FRUS, 1952–1954*, 10:529–34 (quote 531; emphasis added).

67. Malcolm Byrne and Mark Gasiorowski, eds., *1953 Iran Coup: New U.S. Documents Confirm British Approached U.S. in Late 1952 about Ousting Mosaddeq*, August 8, 2017, National Security Archive, Electronic Briefing Book No. 601, http://nsarchive.gwu.edu /NSAEBB/NSAEBB601-British-appealed-to-US-in-1952-for-coup-against-Mosaddeq -in-Iran/.

68. Jeffrey A. Frieden, *Global Capitalism: Its Fall and Rise in the Twentieth Century* (New York: W. W. Norton, 2006), 271–76.

69. *FRUS, 1948*, 1, pt. 2: 510–29 (quote 524), PPS/23, February 24, 1948, "Review of Current Trends in U.S. Foreign Policy."

70. Ibid., 580–83.

71. *FRUS, 1950*, 6:131–34.

72. Mats Ingulstad, "The Interdependent Hegemon: The United States and the Quest for Strategic Raw Materials during the Early Cold War," *International History Review* 17 (February 2015): 59–79 (quote 73).

73. *FRUS, 1948*, 1, pt. 2: 585–88 (quotes 586, 588).

74. Hogan, *Cross of Iron*, 302–12.

75. Cardwell, *NSC 68 and the Political Economy of the Early Cold War*, 105–6, 151–52, 174–80.

76. *FRUS, 1951*, vol. 1, *National Security Affairs; Foreign Economic Policy* (Washington, DC: GPO, 1977), 389.

77. Ibid., 392.

78. Fred L. Block, *The Origins of International Economic Disorder: A Study of United States International Monetary Policy from World War II to the Present* (Berkeley: University of California Press, 1977), 109–14; U.S. Bureau of the Census, *Statistical Abstract of the United States, 1953* (Washington, DC: GPO, 1953), 883.

79. *FRUS, 1951*, 1:1626–28 (quote 1614).

80. *FRUS, 1949*, vol. 3, *Council of Foreign Ministers; Germany and Austria* (Washington, DC: GPO, 1974), 299.

81. Judt, *Postwar*, 152.

82. *FRUS, 1952–1954*, vol. 7, *Germany and Austria* (in two parts) (Washington, DC: GPO, 1974), pt. 1: 355–61 (quote 357).

83. Larres, *Churchill's Cold War*, 152–54.

84. Ibid., 265–67.

85. *FRUS, 1948*, vol. 3, *Western Europe* (Washington, DC: GPO, 1974), 1100–1101.

86. William S. Borden, *The Pacific Alliance: United States Foreign Economic Policy and Japanese Trade Recovery, 1947–1955* (Madison: University of Wisconsin Press, 1984), 137–39.

87. J[ohn] W. Dower, *Empire and Aftermath: Yoshida Shigeru and the Japanese Experience, 1878–1954* (Cambridge, MA: Harvard University Press, 1979), 383–84; *FRUS, 1951*, 6, pt. 1: 83–84.

88. *FRUS, 1950*, 6:87–91, 93–94, 104–5 (quote 110–11).

89. Dower, *Empire and Aftermath*, 387.

90. Borden, *Pacific Alliance*, 145.

91. Shigeru Yoshida, "Japan and the Crisis in Asia," *Foreign Affairs* 29 (January 1951): 171–81.

92. *FRUS, 1951*, 6, pt. 1: 1416–21.

93. *FRUS, 1952–1954*, 14, pt. 2: 1307.

94. Dower, *Empire and Aftermath*, 417–18, 424–27.

95. Burton I. Kaufman, *Trade and Aid: Eisenhower's Foreign Economic Policy, 1953–1961* (Baltimore: Johns Hopkins University Press, 1982), 60.

96. *FRUS, 1950*, vol. 4, *Central and Eastern Europe; the Soviet Union* (Washington, DC: GPO, 1980), 187–89, 194.

97. Early trade policy is summarized in "Review of United States Policy in East-West Trade," March 4, 1965, National Security File, Files of Francis M. Bator, East-West Trade Committee - Papers for 1st & 2nd Meetings (1 of 3), Box 4, Lyndon Baines Johnson Presidential Library, Austin, TX.

98. *FRUS, 1951*, 1:1000–12, 1025–44, 1049–52 (quote 1039).

99. Ibid., 1046–48 (quote 1047).

100. David Ekbladh, *The Great American Mission: Modernization and the Construction of an American World Order* (Princeton, NJ: Princeton University Press, 2009), 58–76 (quote 67).

101. For context, see Nick Cullather, *The Hungry World: America's Cold War Battle against Poverty in Asia* (Cambridge, MA: Harvard University Press, 2010), 72–107. "Modernization" and "development" are used interchangeably herein.

102. Jeremi Suri, *Liberty's Surest Guardian: American Nation-Building from the Founders to Obama* (New York: Free Press, 2011).

103. Louis A. Pérez Jr., *Cuba under the Platt Amendment, 1902–1934* (Pittsburgh: University of Pittsburgh Press, 1986), 31–52; Paul A. Kramer, *The Blood of Government: Race, Empire, the United States, and the Philippines* (Chapel Hill: University of North Carolina Press, 2006), 285–89, 305–22.

104. Louis A. Pérez Jr., *On Becoming Cuban: Identity, Nationality, and Culture* (Chapel Hill: University of North Carolina Press, 1999), 148–61; Kramer, *Blood of Government*, 168–70, 198–208; Michael Adas, *Dominance by Design: Technological Imperatives and America's Civilizing Mission* (Cambridge, MA: Belknap Press of Harvard University Press, 2006), 160, 176–78.

105. Arnold H. Taylor, *American Diplomacy and the Narcotics Traffic, 1900–1939: A Study in International Humanitarian Reform* (Durham, NC: Duke University Press, 1969), 31–46.

106. Noel H. Pugach, *Paul S. Reinsch: Open Door Diplomat in Action* (Millwood, NY: KTO Press, 1979), 124–28.

107. George F. Kennan, *Memoirs*, vol. 1, *1925–1950* (Boston: Little, Brown, 1967), 352–53 (quote 353).

108. *Public Papers of the Presidents of the United States (PPP): Harry S. Truman, 1949* (Washington, DC: GPO, 1964), 112–16 (quote 116); Brinkley, *The Publisher*, 349–50, 364–67.

109. Stephanie M. Amerian, "'Buying European': The Marshall Plan and American Department Stores," *Diplomatic History* 39 (January 2015): 45–69.

110. Hogan, *Marshall Plan*, 325–27.

111. Ibid., 311–14, 334–35.

112. Ibid., 337–42; McMahon, *Dean Acheson*, 133–35 (quote 134).

113. Kaplan, *United States and NATO*, 171–72; Hogan, *Marshall Plan*, 393–403.

114. Acheson, *Present at the Creation*, 559–60 (quote 560); *FRUS, 1951*, 1:239; CIA, National Intelligence Digest, November 1, 1952, pp. VI-B-1, VI-C-1, Central Intelligence Agency, Electronic Reading Room (CIA, ERR), https://www.cia.gov/library/readingroom/docs/CIA-RDP86B00269R000300060001-1.pdf.

115. See, for example, *FRUS, 1951*, 1:437–39 on offshore procurement by the United States.

116. Alessandro Brogi, *Confronting America: The Cold War between the United States and the Communists in France and Italy* (Chapel Hill: University of North Carolina Press,

2011), 89, 125, 139; Victoria de Grazia, *Irresistible Empire: America's Advance through Twentieth-Century Europe* (Cambridge, MA: Belknap Press of Harvard University Press, 2005), 4–12; Emily S. Rosenberg, "Consuming the American Century," in *The Short American Century: A Postmortem*, ed. Andrew J. Bacevich (Cambridge, MA: Harvard University Press, 2012), 38, 44.

117. Memorandum by CIA Deputy Director Allen W. Dulles to CIA Director Walter Bedell Smith, September 15, 1951, CIA, ERR, https://www.cia.gov/library/readingroom /docs/DOC_ 0000242325.pdf.

118. Judt, *Postwar*, 390–93.

119. Dulles to Smith, September 15, 1951, CIA, ERR, https://www.cia.gov/library /readingroom/docs/DOC_0000242325.pdf.

120. *FRUS, 1952–1954*, vol. 1, *General: Economic and Political Matters* (in two parts) (Washington, DC: GPO, 1983), pt. 1: 392–95; James Schwoch, *Global TV: New Media and the Cold War, 1946–69* (Urbana: University of Illinois Press, 2009), 27–28, 35–39. Comparable treatment of television as a cultural conduit occurred in Japan and South Korea.

121. Petra Goedde, *GIs and Germans: Culture, Gender, and Foreign Relations, 1945–1949* (New Haven, CT: Yale University Press, 2003).

122. Uta G. Poiger, *Jazz, Rock, and Rebels: Cold War Politics and American Culture in a Divided Germany* (Berkeley: University of California Press, 2000) is helpful on these issues; Walter Bedell Smith memo to George A. Morgan, Acting Director Psychological Strategy Board, March 9, 1953, Declassified Documents - Fiscal Year 2014, Psychological Warfare/Strategy, Dwight D. Eisenhower Presidential Library, Abilene, KS, http://www .eisenhower.archives.gov/research/ online_documents/declassified/fy_2014/083_026.pdf.

123. "The 28 May Communist Youth Rally in Berlin," May 5, 1950, CIA, ERR, https:// www.cia.gov/library/readingroom/docs/DOC_0001117637.pdf.

124. "World Youth Festival in Berlin in August 1951," May 25, 1951, CIA, ERR, https:// www.cia.gov/library/readingroom/docs/DOC_000466276.pdf.

125. Whitney H. Shepardson, President NCFE, to Allen W. Dulles, April 10, 1953, CIA, ERR, https://www.cia.gov/library/readingroom/docs/DOC_0000238877.pdf.

126. Gregg Brazinsky, *Nation Building in South Korea: Koreans, Americans, and the Making of a Democracy* (Chapel Hill: University of North Carolina Press, 2007), 33. Civil war in China cut short ECA operations there; Nancy Bernkopf Tucker, *Taiwan, Hong Kong, and the United States, 1945–1992: Uncertain Friendships* (New York: Twayne, 1994), 19.

127. *PPP: Truman, 1949*, 279.

128. Ekbladh, *Great American Mission*, 114–32.

129. Michael Schaller, *Altered States: The United States and Japan since the Occupation* (New York: Oxford University Press, 1997), 23–24, 51–52.

130. *FRUS, 1951*, 6, pt. 1: 33–34, 36, 38, 54–55 (quote 34).

131. Harry Bayard Price, *The Marshall Plan and Its Meaning* (Ithaca, NY: Cornell University Press, 1955), 204–17.

132. R. Allen Griffin Oral History, February 15, 1974, HSTL, pp. 56–72 (quote p. 51), http://www.trumanlibrary.org/oralhist/griffinr.htm.

133. Robert J. McMahon, *The Limits of Empire: The United States and Southeast Asia since World War II* (New York: Columbia University Press, 1999), 51–56; William O. Walker III, *Opium and Foreign Policy: The Anglo-American Search for Order in Asia, 1912–1954* (Chapel Hill: University of North Carolina Press, 1991), 200–210.

134. Walker, *Opium and Foreign Policy*, 208; *FRUS, 1952–1954*, vol. 12, *East Asia and the Pacific* (in two parts) (Washington, DC: GPO, 1984), pt. 1: 74.

135. Price, *Marshall Plan and Its Meaning*, 210–12; William J. Duiker, *U.S. Containment Policy and the Conflict in Indochina* (Stanford, CA: Stanford University Press, 1994), 95–98.

136. *FRUS, 1951,* 6, pt. 1: 332–38, 490–91, 514 (quote 332).

137. Ibid., 80–81, 87–91 (quote 90).

138. Ibid., 760–62, 771–76 (quote 761).

139. *FRUS, 1952–1954,* 12, pt. 1: 259–61, 291–322, 371–400; Bradley R. Simpson, *Economists with Guns: Authoritarian Development and U.S.-Indonesian Relations, 1960–1968* (Stanford, CA: Stanford University Press, 2008), 13–16.

140. Cullather, *Illusions of Influence,* 72–87.

141. *FRUS, 1950,* 6:1497–502, 1511–13, 1521–23 (quote 1504).

142. Cullather, *Illusions of Influence,* 87–97. On credibility and the Philippines, see *FRUS, 1950,* 6:1515–20.

143. John M. Allison, *Ambassador from the Prairie, or, Allison Wonderland* (Boston: Houghton Mifflin, 1973), 123.

144. Acheson to Truman, March 9, 1950, General Records of the Department of State, Record Group 59, Lot File 57 D 472, National Archives II, College Park, MD.

145. ECA, Office of the Assistant Administrator for Programs, "Economic Aid to Asia," March 27, 1951, Record Group 286, Agency for International Development, Economic Cooperation Administration, Country Subject files, 1950–51, Box 1, Washington National Records Center, Suitland, MD.

146. *FRUS, 1951,* 6, pt. 1: 58–59.

147. *FRUS, 1950,* vol. 2, *The United Nations; the Western Hemisphere* (Washington, DC: GPO, 1976), 590, 639; CIA, National Intelligence Digest, November 1, 1952, pp. VII-A-2 through 4, CIA, ERR, https://www.cia.gov/library/readingroom/docs/CIA-RDP86B00269 R000300060001-1.pdf.

148. Thomas F. O'Brien, *The Revolutionary Mission: American Enterprise in Latin America, 1900–1945* (New York: Cambridge University Press, 1996); William O. Walker III, "Crucible for Peace: Herbert Hoover, Modernization, and Economic Growth in Latin America," *Diplomatic History* 30 (January 2006): 83–117; Elizabeth A. Cobbs, *The Rich Neighbor Policy: Rockefeller and Kaiser in Brazil* (New Haven, CT: Yale University Press, 1992); Darlene Rivas, *Missionary Capitalist: Nelson Rockefeller in Venezuela* (Chapel Hill: University of North Carolina Press, 2002).

149. Irwin F. Gellman, *Good Neighbor Diplomacy: United States Policies in Latin America, 1933–1945* (Baltimore: Johns Hopkins University Press, 1979), 164–66.

150. *FRUS, 1950,* 2:1033, 1014–15, 857–61, 591–93 (quote 857).

151. Ibid., 593–96.

152. Stephen G. Rabe, "The Elusive Conference: United States Economic Relations with Latin America, 1945–1952," *Diplomatic History* 2 (July 1978): 279–94.

153. *FRUS, 1950,* 2:626.

154. Ibid., 598; Stephen G. Rabe, *The Killing Zone: The United States Wages Cold War in Latin America* (New York: Oxford University Press, 2011), 21–35; Kennan, *Memoirs,* 1:476–84.

155. *FRUS, 1950,* 2:598–624 (quote 600); Gaddis, *Kennan,* 381–86.

156. *FRUS, 1950,* 2:601, 602, 622.

157. *FRUS, 1951,* vol. 2, *The United Nations; the Western Hemisphere* (Washington, DC: GPO, 1979), 1062.

158. "Juan Jose AREVALO," March 15, 1954, CIA, ERR, https://www.cia.gov/library/readingroom/docs/DOC_0000917352.pdf; *FRUS, 1951,* 2:1415, 1416; Walter LaFeber, *Inevitable Revolutions: The United States in Central America,* 2nd ed., rev. and expanded (New York: W. W. Norton, 1993), 114–18.

159. *FRUS, 1950,* 2:1423–26, 1438–40, 1451–53.

160. Glenn J. Dorn, *The Truman Administration and Bolivia: Making the World Safe for Liberal Constitutional Oligarchy* (University Park, PA: Penn State University Press, 2011);

Kenneth D. Lehman, *Bolivia and the United States: A Limited Partnership* (Athens: University of Georgia Press, 1999), 115–20, 127.

161. Steven Casey, "Selling NSC-68: The Truman Administration, Public Opinion, and the Politics of Mobilization, 1950–51," *Diplomatic History* 29 (September 2005): 661–65.

162. *FRUS, 1950*, 1:207; Dean Acheson, "Fulfillment of Responsibility in a World in Peril," *Department of State Bulletin*, October 16, 1950, pp. 613–16 (quote 615).

163. Cardwell, *NSC 68 and the Political Economy of the Cold War*, 58–159.

164. On Anglo-American differences over U.S. policy in Asia, see John Baylis, *Anglo-American Defence Relations 1939–1980: The Special Relationship* (New York: St. Martin's Press, 1981), 43–49; on Korea and Franco-American relations, see Irwin M. Wall, *The United States and the Making of Postwar France, 1945–1954* (New York: Cambridge University Press, 1991), 204–5, 212, 224, 233–34, 239–46.

165. Kaplan, *United States and NATO*, 145–73, 186; William W. Stueck, *The Korean War: An International History* (Princeton, NJ: Princeton University Press, 1995), 118, 136–37, 172–78, 188–93, 273, 281, 296–97.

3. SEEKING ORDER AND STABILITY

1. Alan Brinkley, *The Publisher: Henry Luce and His American Century* (New York: Alfred A. Knopf, 2010), 364–79; Henry Luce III Oral History, July 26, 2000, Dwight D. Eisenhower Presidential Library (DDEL), Abilene, KS, p. 17, http://www.eisenhower.archives.gov/research/oral_histories/oral_history_transcripts/Luce_Henry_534.pdf.

2. Henry R. Luce, "The American Century," *Life*, February 17, 1941; reprinted in *Diplomatic History* 23 (Spring 1999): 164.

3. On Bandung's importance, see Jason Parker, "Cold War II: The Eisenhower Administration, the Bandung Conference, and the Reperiodization of the Postwar Era," *Diplomatic History* 30 (November 2006): 867–92.

4. U.S. Department of State, *Foreign Relations of the United States 1952–1954*, vol. 2, *National Security Affairs* (in two parts) (*FRUS, year*, volume) (Washington, DC: Government Printing Office [GPO], 1984), pt. 1: 200–201, 202–5 (quote 200).

5. Ibid., 223–31, 236–37 (quote 224).

6. Robert H. Ferrell, ed., *The Eisenhower Diaries* (New York: W. W. Norton, 1981), 221–24 (quote 223); Klaus Larres, *Churchill's Cold War: The Politics of Personal Diplomacy* (New Haven, CT: Yale University Press, 2002), 182–85; *FRUS, 1952–1954*, 2, pt. 1: 267 (Dulles quote).

7. Vladislav M. Zubok, *A Failed Empire: The Soviet Union in the Cold War from Stalin to Gorbachev* (Chapel Hill: University of North Carolina Press, 2007), 86, 88, 91; Larres, *Churchill's Cold War*, 205; Robert R. Bowie and Richard H. Immerman, *Waging Peace: How Eisenhower Shaped an Enduring Cold War Strategy* (New York: Oxford University Press, 1998), 113, 115.

8. For an assessment of Malenkov, see CIA, "Probable Consequences of the Death of Stalin and of the Elevation of Malenkov to Leadership in the USSR," March 10, 1953, Declassified Documents - Fiscal Year 2012 (DDFY [year]), Intelligence Matters, DDEL, https://www.eisenhower.archives.gov/research/online_documents/declassified/fy_2012/1953_03_10.pdf.

9. *Current Soviet Policies: The Documentary Record of the 19th Communist Party Congress and the Reorganization after Stalin's Death*, ed. and with an introduction by Leo Gruliow (New York: Frederick A. Praeger, 1953), 256–60.

10. CIA Report to Estimate the Significance of Current Communist "Peace" Tactics, April 16, 1953, especially p. 5, DDFY 2012, Intelligence Matters, DDEL, https://www.eisenhower.archives.gov/research/online_documents/declassified/fy_2012/1953_04_16.pdf.

11. Vojtech Mastny, "NATO in the Beholder's Eye: Soviet Perceptions and Policies, 1949–56" (Cold War International History Project Working Paper No. 35, Washington, DC, March 2002).

12. This interpretation, contrary to Eisenhower revisionism, parallels Kenneth A. Osgood, "Form before Substance: Eisenhower's Commitment to Psychological Warfare and Negotiations with the Enemy," *Diplomatic History* 24 (Summer 2000): 405–33 (especially 407–9); Bowie and Immerman, *Waging Peace*, 115–16.

13. *FRUS, 1952–1954*, 2, pt. 1: 268; Melvyn P. Leffler, *For the Soul of Mankind: The United States, the Soviet Union, and the Cold War* (New York: Hill and Wang, 2007), 84–150.

14. CIA, "CIA Report to the Psychological Strategy Board, January-June 1953," July 29, 1953, Central Intelligence Agency, Electronic Reading Room (CIA, ERR), https://www.cia .gov/library/readingroom/docs/DOC_0000196573.pdf; *FRUS, 1952–1954*, 2, pt. 1: 489–514.

15. Geoffrey Roberts, "Introduction," Cold War International History Project, e-Dossier No. 27—Molotov's Proposal That the USSR Join NATO, March 1954, http:// www.wilsoncenter.org/publication/e-dossier-no-27-molotovs-proposal-the-ussr-join -nato-march-1954. For a translation of the document in question, see http://legacy .wilsoncenter.org/va2/index.cfm?topic_id= 1409&fuseaction = home.document&identifier = 9BF64189-5056-9700-03F5FF8ADC31A1A9. Regarding a European security treaty, see *FRUS, 1955–1957*, vol. 5, *Austrian State Treaty; Summit and Foreign Ministers Meetings, 1955* (Washington, DC: GPO, 1988), 576, 640–42, 647–48, 737.

16. *FRUS, 1955–1957*, 5:799 (Eisenhower quote 778, Dulles quote 803).

17. *FRUS, 1952–1954*, vol. 15, *Korea* (in two parts) (Washington, DC: GPO, 1984), pt. 1: 977.

18. Nina Tannenwald, *The Nuclear Taboo: The United States and the Non-Use of Nuclear Weapons since 1945* (New York: Cambridge University Press, 2007), 140–62.

19. *FRUS, 1952–1954*, 2, pt. 1: 594–95.

20. Leffler, *For the Soul of Mankind*, 133–36.

21. *FRUS, 1952–1954*, 2, pt. 1: 593.

22. Eisenhower Diary Notes, October 8, 1853, p. 9, DDFY 2010, Intelligence Matters, DDEL, https://www.eisenhower.archives.gov/research/online_documents/declassified/fy _2010/1953_10_08.pdf.

23. *FRUS, 1952–1954*, vol. 5, *Western European Security* (in two parts) (Washington, DC: GPO, 1983), pt. 1: 463.

24. Irwin M. Wall, *The United States and the Making of Postwar France, 1945–1954* (New York: Cambridge University Press, 1991), 263–75. On the travails of the EDC and U.S. security policy, see Bowie and Immerman, *Waging Peace*, 205–8.

25. *FRUS, 1952–1954*, vol. 5, *Western European Security* (in two parts) (Washington, DC: GPO, 1983), pt. 2: 1802.

26. Richard J. Barnet, *The Alliance: America, Europe, Japan: Makers of the Postwar World* (New York: Simon and Schuster, 1983), 161–63; and see Aleksandr Fursenko and Timothy Naftali, *Khrushchev's Cold War: The Inside Story of an American Adversary* (New York: W. W. Norton, 2006), 33–34.

27. Zubok, *Failed Empire*, 108.

28. John Foster Dulles, "The Threat of a Red Asia," *Department of State Bulletin*, April 12, 1954, pp. 539–42 (quote 540).

29. On Thailand's importance for U.S. security policy in Indochina, see Department of State [?] "Special Report to the National Security Council," July 7, 1954, DDFY 2015, Southeast Asia, DDEL, https://www.eisenhower.archives.gov/research/online_documents /declassified/fy_2015/082_026.pdf.

30. Robert J. McMahon, *The Limits of Empire: The United States and Southeast Asia since World War II* (New York: Columbia University Press, 1999), 49–59; Odd Arne Westad, *The*

Global Cold War: Third World Interventions and the Making of Our Times (New York: Cambridge University Press, 2005), 99–102.

31. Speech at the Naval War College, September 22, 1950, Livingston T. Merchant Papers, Box 1, Mudd Library, Princeton University, Princeton, NJ; Ferrell, *The Eisenhower Diaries*, 223.

32. George Herring, *America's Longest War: The United States and Vietnam, 1950–1975*, 4th ed. (Boston: McGraw Hill, 2002), 45–58; McMahon, *Limits of Empire*, 66, 70, 79–82.

33. National Security Council Progress Report on NSC Series 26, "Removal and Demolition of Oil Facilities, Equipment and Supplies in the Middle East," August 7, 1953, DDFY 2011, The Middle East, DDEL, https://www.eisenhower.archives.gov/research /online_documents/declassified/fy_2011/1953_08_07.pdf. NSC 26/2 became NSC 176, then NSC 5401 and, in May 1957, NSC 5714.

34. Malcolm Byrne, ed., *Iran 1953: US Envoy to Baghdad Suggested to Fleeing Shah He Not Acknowledge Foreign Role in Coup*, July 2, 2014, National Security Archive, Electronic Briefing Book (NSA, EBB) No. 477, http://nsarchive.gwu.edu/NSAEBB/NSAEBB477/; Byrne, ed., *CIA Confirms Role in 1953 Iran Coup*, August 19, 2013, NSA, EBB No. 435, http://nsarchive.gwu.edu/NSAEBB/NSAEBB435/.

35. *FRUS, 1952–1954*, vol. 10, *Iran, 1951–1954* (Washington, DC: GPO, 1989), 881; Eisenhower Diary Notes, October 8, 1853, p. 9, DDFY 2010, Intelligence Matters, DDEL, https://www.eisenhower.archives.gov/research/online_documents/declassified/fy_2010 /1953_10_08.pdf.

36. Ambassador Loy W. Henderson to State Department, March 10, 1954, DDFY 2012, Middle East, DDEL, https://www.eisenhower.archives.gov/research/online_documents /Declassified/fy_2012/1954_03_10.pdf.

37. Anthony Eden, *Full Circle: The Memoirs of Anthony Eden* (Boston: Houghton Mifflin, 1960), 375.

38. Peter L. Hahn, *Crisis and Crossfire: The United States and the Middle East since 1945* (Washington, DC: Potomac Books, 2005), 15–17.

39. Westad, *Global Cold War*, chapters 2 and 3.

40. Douglas Little, *American Orientalism: The United States and the Middle East since 1945*, 3rd ed. (Chapel Hill: University of North Carolina Press, 2008), chapter 5.

41. See especially Fredrik Logevall, *Embers of War: The Fall of an Empire and the Making of America's Vietnam* (New York: Knopf, 2012); William J. Duiker, *Sacred War: Nationalism and Revolution in a Divided Vietnam* (New York: McGraw Hill, 1995), 102–6.

42. Steven Schwartzberg, *Democracy and U.S. Policy in Latin America during the Truman Years* (Gainesville: University Press of Florida, 2003), 196–204.

43. Charles D. Ameringer, *The Caribbean Legion: Patriots, Politicians, Soldiers of Fortune, 1946–1950* (University Park: Pennsylvania State University Press, 1996), 139.

44. Stephen G. Rabe, *Eisenhower and Latin America: The Foreign Policy of Anticommunism* (Chapel Hill: University of North Carolina Press, 1988), 39.

45. *FRUS, 1952–1954*, vol. 4, *The American Republics* (Washington, DC: GPO, 1983), 3.

46. Ibid., 6–26 (quotes 6, 14, 19); Bevan Sewell, *The US and Latin America: Eisenhower, Kennedy and Economic Diplomacy in the Cold War* (London: I. B. Tauris, 2015), 24–34.

47. *FRUS, 1952–1954*, 4:36–37, 41–44 (quote 37).

48. Ibid., 42–54.

49. *FRUS, 1952–1954*, 4:1180.

50. Ibid., 45, 64, 90.

51. Richard M. Bissell Jr., with Jonathan E. Lewis and Frances T. Pudlo, *Reflections of a Cold Warrior: From Yalta to the Bay of Pigs* (New Haven, CT: Yale University Press, 1996), 82, 90; see also Richard M. Bissell Jr., Oral History, November 9, 1976, pp. 13–14, DDEL,

http://www. eisenhower.archives.gov/research/oral_histories/oral_history_transcripts/Bissell_Richard_EL.pdf.

52. *FRUS, 1950–1955: The Intelligence Community, 1950–1955* (Washington, DC: GPO, 2007), 476 (quote 477).

53. Ibid., 746–49.

54. CIA, "Latin American Reactions to the Guatemalan Crisis," *Current Intelligence Weekly*, July 9, 1954, CIA, ERR, https://www.cia.gov/library/readingroom/docs/DOC_0000920294.pdf.

55. Tannenwald, *Nuclear Taboo*, 163–64.

56. *FRUS, 1955–1957*, vol. 20, *Regulation of Armaments; Atomic Energy* (Washington, DC: GPO, 1990), 15.

57. *FRUS, 1955–1957*, 5:535.

58. Geoffrey Roberts, "A Chance for Peace?: The Soviet Campaign to End the Cold War, 1953–1955" (Cold War International History Project Working Paper No. 57, Washington, DC, October 2008), 22–35, 44–60, http://www.wilsoncenter.org/topics/pubs/WP57_WebFinal.pdf.

59. *FRUS, 1955–1957*, 5:534.

60. CIA and Department of State, "Opinion Trends in the Aftermath of Geneva," September 23, 1955, p. 1, CIA, ERR, https://www.cia.gov/library/readingroom/document/CIA-RDP80b0167r 004200110031-2.

61. *FRUS, 1955–1957*, vol. 23 (in two parts), pt. 1, *Japan* (Washington, DC: GPO, 1991), 163–70 (quote 164).

62. William S. Borden, *The Pacific Alliance: United States Foreign Economic Policy and Japanese Trade Recovery, 1947–1955* (Madison: University of Wisconsin Press, 1984), 144–48; J[ohn] W. Dower, *Empire and Aftermath: Yoshida Shigeru and the Japanese Experience, 1878–1954* (Cambridge, MA: Harvard University Press, 1979), 430–36; *FRUS, 1952–1954*, vol. 14, *China and Japan* (in two parts) (Washington, DC: GPO, 1985), pt. 2: 1522.

63. Dower, *Empire and Aftermath*, 434.

64. *FRUS, 1952–1954*, 14, pt. 2: 1796.

65. *FRUS, 1955–1957*, 23, pt. 1:70.

66. Ibid., 96, 139–42.

67. *FRUS, 1952–1954*, 14, pt. 2: 1557, 1574.

68. Gregg Brazinsky, *Nation Building in South Korea: Koreans, Americans, and the Making of a Democracy* (Chapel Hill: University of North Carolina Press, 2007), 28–30.

69. *FRUS, 1952–1954*, vol. 15, *Korea* (in two parts) (Washington, DC: GPO, 1984), pt. 2: 1745, 1746.

70. *FRUS, 1955–1957*, vol. 23 (in two parts), pt. 2, *Korea* (Washington, DC: GPO, 1984), 218 (Radford quote), 348 (Eisenhower quote), 485 (Dulles quote); *FRUS, 1952–54*, 15, pt. 2: 1892.

71. William O. Walker III, *Opium and Foreign Policy: The Anglo-American Search for Order in Asia, 1912–1954* (Chapel Hill: University of North Carolina Press, 1991), 200–213.

72. Nancy Bernkopf Tucker, *Taiwan, Hong Kong, and the United States, 1945–1992: Uncertain Friendships* (New York: Twayne, 1994), 35–46.

73. Gordon H. Chang and He Di, "The Absence of War in the U.S.-Chinese Confrontation over Quemoy and Matsu in 1954–1955: Contingency, Luck, Deterrence," *American Historical Review* 98 (December 1993): 1500–524.

74. Gordon H. Chang, *Friends and Enemies: The United States, China, and the Soviet Union, 1948–1972* (Stanford, CA: Stanford University Press, 1990), 116–42.

75. Hsiao-ting Lin, "U.S.-Taiwan Military Diplomacy Revisited: Chiang Kai-shek, *Baituan*, and the 1954 Mutual Defense Pact," *Diplomatic History* 37 (November 2013): 971–94.

76. *FRUS, 1955–1957*, vol. 2, *China* (Washington, DC: GPO, 1986), 279–86.

77. Ibid., 285.

78. William J. Duiker, *U.S. Containment Policy and the Conflict in Indochina* (Stanford, CA: Stanford University Press, 1994), 194–212.

79. *FRUS, 1955–1957*, vol. 1, *Vietnam* (Washington, DC: GPO, 1985), 169.

80. Robert J. McMahon, *The Cold War on the Periphery: The United States, India and Pakistan* (New York: Columbia University Press, 1994), chapters 1–5.

81. Ibid., 162–72.

82. *FRUS, 1952–1954*, vol. 11, *Africa and South Asia* (in two parts) (Washington, DC: GPO, 1983), pt. 2: 1838–46 (quote 1844).

83. Dennis Kux, *The United States and Pakistan, 1947–2000: Disenchanted Allies* (Baltimore: Johns Hopkins University Press, 2001), 71–74.

84. Luce, "American Century," 166 and passim.

85. This conclusion is drawn from tables in *Statistical Abstract of the United States* for the early to mid 1950s, prepared annually by the U.S. Bureau of the Census.

86. Burton I. Kaufman, *Trade and Aid: Eisenhower's Foreign Economic Policy, 1953–1961* (Baltimore: Johns Hopkins University Press, 1982), 10.

87. *FRUS, 1952–1954*, 2, pt. 1: 261.

88. Michael J. Hogan, *A Cross of Iron: Harry S. Truman and the Origins of the National Security State, 1945–1954* (New York: Cambridge University Press, 1998), 387–99.

89. *FRUS, 1952–1954*, 2, pt. 1: 266 (quote 267). On Indochina, see *FRUS, 1952–1954*, vol. 1, *General: Economic and Political Matters* (in two parts) (Washington, DC: GPO, 1982), pt. 1: 640–41, 649.

90. *FRUS, 1952–1954*, 2, pt. 1: 269–71.

91. Ibid., 283; Brazinsky, *Nation Building in South Korea*, 30.

92. *FRUS, 1952–1954*, 1, pt. 1: 84.

93. Ibid., 650–51.

94. Borden, *Pacific Alliance*, 168–71.

95. *FRUS, 1952–1954*, 14, pt. 2: 1410–11 (quote 1411).

96. Sayuri Guthrie-Shimizu, "Japan, the United States, and the Cold War, 1945–1060," in *The Cambridge History of the Cold War*, 3 vols., vol. 1, *Origins*, ed. Melvyn P. Leffler and Odd Arne Westad (New York: Cambridge University Press, 2010), 251–58.

97. *FRUS, 1952–1954*, 14, pt. 2: 1621, 1630–31.

98. Borden, *Pacific Alliance*, 172–76.

99. Commission on Foreign Economic Policy, "Report to the President and the Congress," January 23, 1954, CIA, ERR, https://www.cia.gov/library/readingroom/docs/CIA-RDP80B01676R004300110002-3.pdf.

100. *FRUS, 1952–1954*, 1, pt. 1: 49–64 (quote 60).

101. *FRUS, 1952–1954*, 14, pt. 2: 1649–50, 1663, 1667–70, 1693–95 (quotes 1662, 1694).

102. Dower, *Empire and Aftermath*, 471–80, 487–92.

103. *FRUS, 1952–1954*, 14, pt. 2: 1789.

104. *FRUS, 1952–1954*, 1, pt. 1: 69.

105. Ibid., 309, 312–20, 338 (quote 315). Secretary of the Treasury John W. Snyder chaired the council.

106. Ibid., 359–63.

107. *FRUS, 1952–1954*, 1, pt. 1: 364–68 (quote 368).

108. *FRUS, 1955–1957*, vol. 9, *Foreign Economic Policy; Foreign Information Program* (Washington, DC: GPO, 1987), 26.

109. *FRUS, 1952–1954*, 1, pt. 1: 120–23.

110. Ibid., 165.

111. Ibid., 216.

112. Luce, "American Century," 166.

113. *FRUS, 1951*, vol. 6, *Asia and the Pacific* (in two parts) (Washington, DC: GPO, 1977), pt. 1: 58–59; *FRUS, 1952–1954*, 1, pt. 1: 51 (quote).

114. *FRUS, 1952–1954*, 1, pt. 1: 249–54, 259–62 (quotes 259, 262). The administration had trouble convincing Congress of the importance of Point Four. Aid to India in 1951 and 1952 remained far below what Ambassador Chester Bowles recommended. As for Pakistan, where the United States sought a close security relationship, Point Four aid was nominal; Dennis Merrill, *Bread and the Ballot: The United States and India's Economic Development, 1947–1963* (Chapel Hill: University of North Carolina Press, 1990), 76–92; McMahon, *Cold War on the Periphery*, 114–20, 143–44.

115. Campbell Craig, *Glimmer of a New Leviathan: Total War in the Realism of Niebuhr, Morgenthau, and Waltz* (New York: Columbia University Press, 2003), 32–53, 73–79. Niebuhr also wrote for *The Nation* magazine and *Christianity and Crisis*.

116. William Inboden, *Religion and American Foreign Policy, 1945–1960: The Soul of Containment* (New York: Cambridge University Press, 2008), 49, 53–54 (quote 53).

117. *Public Papers of the Presidents of the United States* (PPP): *Harry S. Truman, 1951* (Washington, DC: GPO, 1965), 141; Inboden, *Religion and American Foreign Policy*, 121–56; "Development of a Policy for Dealing with Moral and Spiritual Factors and Materials in the United States Information and Education (USIE) Program," June 22, 1951, p. 5, CK3100210894, Declassified Documents Reference System, Gale, Cengage Learning, Farmington Hills, MI.

118. Inboden, *Religion and American Foreign Policy*, 226–32, 254–62 (Dulles quote 256, Eisenhower quote 259); for Eisenhower's inaugural address, see *PPP: Dwight D. Eisenhower, 1953* (Washington, DC: GPO, 1960), 1.

119. David Ekbladh, *The Great American Mission: Modernization and the Construction of an American World Order* (Princeton, NJ: Princeton University Press, 2009), 107–8, 171–76.

120. Elizabeth A. Cobbs, *The Rich Neighbor Policy: Rockefeller and Kaiser in Brazil* (New Haven, CT: Yale University Press, 1992); Darlene Rivas, *Missionary Capitalist: Nelson Rockefeller in Venezuela* (Chapel Hill: University of North Carolina Press, 2002); Gerard Colby, with Charlotte Dennett, *Thy Will Be Done: The Conquest of the Amazon: Nelson Rockefeller and Evangelism in the Age of Oil* (New York: HarperCollins, 1995).

121. Brazinsky, *Nation Building in South Korea*, 33–37; Ekbladh, *Great American Mission*, 134–45.

122. *FRUS, 1958–1960*, vol. 18, *Japan; Korea* (Washington, DC: GPO, 1994), 606–8 (quote 702–3).

123. Ibid., 196; Ekbladh, *Great American Mission*, 117–24, 126–29, 141–43.

124. Jooyoung Lee, "Forming a Democratic Society: South Korean Responses to U.S. Democracy Promotion, 1951–1960," *Diplomatic History* 39 (November 2015): 844–75.

125. Uta G. Poiger, *Jazz, Rock, and Rebels: Cold War Politics and American Culture in a Divided Germany* (Berkeley: University of California Press, 2000), 72–123.

126. Richard F. Kuisel, *Seducing the French: The Dilemmas of Americanization* (Berkeley: University of California Press, 1993), 25–35; Laura A. Belmonte, *Selling the American Way: U.S. Propaganda and the Cold War* (Philadelphia: University of Pennsylvania Press, 2008), 32–72.

127. Poiger, *Jazz, Rock, and Rebels*, 79–82, 97, 106–10; Larry May, *The Big Tomorrow: Hollywood and the Politics of the American Way* (Chicago: University of Chicago Press, 2000), 175–256; Andrew J. Falk, *Upstaging the Cold War: American Dissent and Cultural Diplomacy, 1940–1960* (Amherst: University of Massachusetts Press, 2010), 86–118.

128. Kuisel, *Seducing the French*, 52–69 (quote 55).

129. Ibid., 116–30; Tony Judt, *Postwar: A History of Europe since 1945* (New York: Penguin Press, 2005), 302–6.

130. Luce, "American Century," 166.

131. See John Sayles's film *Amigo* (2011) for a portrayal of counterinsurgency in the Philippines.

132. Michael McClintock, *Instruments of Statecraft: U.S. Guerrilla Warfare, Counterinsurgency, and Counterterrorism, 1940–1990* (New York: Pantheon Books, 1992), 11–15.

133. Harry Bayard Price, *The Marshall Plan and Its Meaning* (Ithaca, NY: Cornell University Press, 1955), 278–79, 314.

134. McClintock, *Instruments of Statecraft*, 100–102.

135. Ibid., 102–26; Jonathan Nashel, *Edward Lansdale's Cold War* (Amherst: University of Massachusetts Press, 2005), 32–33.

136. Stephen G. Rabe, *The Killing Zone: The United States Wages Cold War in Latin America* (New York: Oxford University Press, 2011), 36–43.

137. *FRUS, 1952–1954, Guatemala* (Washington, DC: GPO, 2003), 29–35.

138. Nick Cullather, *Secret History: The CIA's Classified Account of Its Operations in Guatemala, 1952–1954*, 2nd ed. (Stanford, CA: Stanford University Press, 2006), 20–37.

139. Bissell, *Reflections of a Cold Warrior*, 82, 90.

140. *FRUS, 1952–1954*, 2, pt. 1: 838.

141. Stephen M. Streeter, *Managing the Counterrevolution: The United States and Guatemala, 1954–1961* (Athens: Ohio University Press, 2000), 137–63.

142. Ibid., 210–38 (Ellender quote 162).

143. *FRUS, 1952–1954*, 2, pt. 1: 844.

144. Herring, *America's Longest War*, 49–69.

145. Ibid., 63–72; see discussion of a report by General J. Lawton Collins about Diem's liabilities in *FRUS, 1955–1957*, 1:280–87.

146. Duiker, *Sacred War*, chapter 3, "Building the North, Looking to the South."

147. Rabe, *Eisenhower and Latin America*, 37–41.

148. Quoted in Rabe, *Eisenhower and Latin America*, 40.

149. *FRUS, 1955–1957*, vol. 6, *American Republics: Multilateral; Mexico, Caribbean* (Washington, DC: GPO, 1987), 304–10.

150. *FRUS, 1952–1954*, 4:1186; Operations Coordinating Board, "Progress Report on NSC 5432/1: United States Objectives and Courses of Action with Respect to Latin America," January 19, 1955, pp. 2–3, CIA, ERR, https://www.cia.gov/library/readingroom/docs/CIA-RDP80R01731R003000030008-2.pdf. See also Sewell, *US and Latin America*, 57–62, 71, 77.

151. *FRUS, 1952–1954*, 2, pt. 1: 835.

152. Ferrell, *The Eisenhower Diaries*, 280.

153. *FRUS, 1952–1954*, vol. 13, *Indochina* (in two parts) (Washington, DC: GPO, 1982), pt. 2: 2379–82; *FRUS, 1955–1957*, 1:168–71, 175–76 (quote 176).

154. Duiker, *U.S. Containment Policy*, 200–204; *FRUS, 1952–1954*, vol. 12: *East Asia and the Pacific* (in two parts) (Washington, DC: GPO, 1984), pt. 1: 735 (quote).

155. Westad, *Global Cold War*, 99–103 (Nehru quote 103).

156. Parker, "Cold War II," 877 (Eisenhower quote); *FRUS, 1955–1957*, vol. 21, *East Asian Security; Cambodia; Laos* (Washington, DC: GPO, 1990), 83.

157. *FRUS, 1955–1957*, 21:91 (Dulles quote), 96 (Malik quote).

158. Kenneth Osgood, *Total Cold War: Eisenhower's Secret Propaganda Battle at Home and Abroad* (Lawrence: University Press of Kansas, 2006), 126–30.

159. Westad, *Global Cold War*, 103.

160. On Bandung and the U.S. response, see Jason C. Parker, *Hearts, Minds, Voices: US Cold War Public Diplomacy and the Formation of the Third World* (New York: Oxford University Press, 2016), 79–88.

4. SUSTAINING LEADERSHIP

1. Vladislav M. Zubok, *A Failed Empire: The Soviet Union in the Cold War from Stalin to Gorbachev* (Chapel Hill: University of North Carolina Press, 2007), 131.

2. Aleksandr Fursenko and Timothy Naftali, *Khrushchev's Cold War: The Inside Story of an American Adversary* (New York: W. W. Norton, 2006), 149–52 (Johnson quote 151).

3. *FRUS, 1955–1957*, vol. 11, *United Nations and General International Matters* (Washington, DC: GPO, 1988), 757–64.

4. Ibid., 762 (quote); Fursenko and Naftali, *Khrushchev's Cold War*, 248–51.

5. *New York Times*, December 22, 2015; William Burr, ed., *U.S. Cold War Nuclear Target Lists Declassified for the First Time*, December 22, 2015, National Security Archive, Electronic Briefing Book (NSA, EBB) No. 538, http://nsarchive.gwu.edu/nukevault/ebb538 -Cold-War-Nuclear-Target-List-Declassified-First-Ever/.

6. U.S. Congress, Joint Committee on Defense Production, *Deterrence and Survival in the Nuclear Age (The "Gaither Report" of 1957)* (Washington, DC: Government Printing Office [GPO], 1976), 1.

7. Paul H. Nitze, with Ann M. Smith and Steven L. Rearden, *From Hiroshima to Glasnost: At the Center of Decision: A Memoir* (New York: Grove Weidenfeld, 1989), 166–69 (quote 168).

8. Walter LaFeber, *America, Russia, and the Cold War, 1945–2006*, 10th ed. (Boston: McGraw-Hill, 2008), 203; Michael S. Sherry, *In the Shadow of War: The United States since the 1930s* (New Haven, CT: Yale University Press, 1995), 217–19.

9. Matthew Evangelista, *Unarmed Forces: The Transnational Movement to End the Cold War* (Ithaca, NY: Cornell University Press, 1999), 54–57.

10. U.S. Department of State, *Foreign Relations of the United States, 1955–1957*, vol. 19, *National Security Policy (FRUS, year, volume)* (Washington, DC: GPO, 1990), 638–61, 687–88, 703.

11. *FRUS, 1952–1954*, vol. 1, *General: Economic and Political Matters* (in two parts) (Washington, DC: GPO, 1982), pt. 1: 69.

12. *FRUS, 1952–1954*, vol. 1, *General: Economic and Political Matters* (in two parts) (Washington, DC: GPO, 1983), pt. 2: 990 (Dulles quote), 989 (China trade quote).

13. Operations Coordinating Board, "Corrections and Additions to the Text of Outline Plan of Operations on Vietnam," October 24, 1956, pp. 12–13, Declassified Documents - Fiscal Year 2015 (DDFY [year]), Southeast Asia, Dwight D. Eisenhower Presidential Library (DDEL), Abilene, KS, http://www.eisenhower.archives.gov/research/online_doc uments/declassified/fy_2015/082_023.pdf.

14. *FRUS, 1955–1957*, vol. 3, *China* (Washington, DC: GPO, 1986), 649–53 (quotes 649, 652).

15. *FRUS, 1955–1957*, vol. 10, *Foreign Aid and Economic Defense Policy* (Washington, DC: GPO, 1989), 211 (quote 238).

16. Ibid., 361–475 (quotes 371–72, 399).

17. Ibid., 491–98 (quotes 491, 492, 493).

18. *FRUS, 1955–1957*, vol. 9, *Foreign Economic Policy; Foreign Information Program* (Washington, DC: GPO, 1987), 196–203 (quote 198).

19. *FRUS, 1952–1954*, 1, pt. 1: 144–46, 149–50.

20. Tony Judt, *Postwar: A History of Europe since 1945* (New York: Penguin Press, 2005), 303–7.

21. *FRUS, 1955–1957*, 9:24, 25.

22. Burton I. Kaufman, *Trade and Aid: Eisenhower's Foreign Economic Policy, 1953–1961* (Baltimore: Johns Hopkins University Press, 1982), 16–17, 29–33.

23. *FRUS, 1952–1954*, 1, pt. 1: 65–70 (quote 67).

24. U.S. Bureau of the Census, *Statistical Abstract of the United States, 1959* (Washington, DC: GPO, 1960), 884.

25. Ibid., 892, 894–96.

26. William S. Borden, *The Pacific Alliance: United States Foreign Economic Policy and Japanese Trade Recovery, 1947–1955* (Madison: University of Wisconsin Press, 1984), 187; *FRUS, 1952–1954*, 1, pt. 1: 156–58; *FRUS, 1955–1957*, 9:118–20.

27. Kaufman, *Trade and Aid*, 21; *FRUS, 1952–1954*, 1, pt. 1: 52.

28. *Statistical Abstract: 1959*, 871.

29. *FRUS, 1952–1954*, 1, pt. 1: 81.

30. Fursenko and Naftali, *Khrushchev's Cold War*, 56–82; Kaufman, *Trade and Aid*, 63–65.

31. Kaufman, *Trade and Aid*, 66–68; *FRUS, 1955–1957*, 10:118.

32. Kaufman, *Trade and Aid*, 68–73, 95–112.

33. *FRUS, 1958–1960*, vol. 4, *Foreign Economic Policy* (Washington, DC: GPO, 1992), 4 (quote 8).

34. Henry R. Luce, "The American Century," *Life*, February 17, 1941; reprinted in *Diplomatic History* 23 (Spring 1999): 166, 168–69.

35. Operations Coordinating Board, Transmission of Progress Report on NSC 5402, "United States Policy toward Iran," April 14, 1954, Central Intelligence Agency, Electronic Reading Room (CIA, ERR), https://www.cia.gov/library/readingroom/document/CIA -RDP 80R01731 R003000020002-9; Douglas Little, *American Orientalism: The United States and the Middle East since 1945*, 3rd ed. (Chapel Hill: University of North Carolina Press, 2008), 57–58.

36. Operations Coordinating Board Report on Iran (NSC 5703/1), October 8, 1958, DDFY 2012, Middle East, DDEL, https://www.eisenhower.archives.gov/research/online _documents/declassified/fy_2012/1958_10_08.pdf.

37. James A. Bill, *The Eagle and the Lion: The Tragedy of American-Iranian Relations* (New Haven, CT: Yale University Press, 1988), 131–69.

38. Steve Everly, ed., *U.S., Britain Developed Plans to Disable or Destroy Middle Eastern Oil Facilities from Late 1940s to Early 1960s in the Event of a Soviet Invasion*, June 23, 2016, NSA, EBB No. 477, Documents 11A, 11B, 11C, and 12, http://nsarchive.gwu.edu/NSAEBB / NSAEBB552-US-and-Britain-planned-to-destroy-Middle-East-oil-facilities-in-case-of -Soviet-invasion-from-1940s-1960s/.

39. Little, *American Orientalism*, 168–71.

40. *FRUS, 1958–1960*, vol. 11, *Lebanon and Jordan* (Washington, DC: GPO, 1992), 245 (quote); R. Thomas Bobal, "'A Puppet, Even Though He Probably Doesn't Know So': Racial Identity and the Eisenhower Administration's Encounter with Gamal Abdel Nasser and the Arab Nationalist Movement," *International History Review* 35 (October 2013): 943–74.

41. *FRUS, 1952–1954*, vol. 9, *The Near and Middle East* (in two parts) (Washington, DC: GPO, 1986), pt. 1: 401.

42. Little, *American Orientalism*, 179–80; Anthony Eden, *Full Circle: The Memoirs of Anthony Eden* (Boston: Houghton Mifflin, 1960), 604–5, 625–29, 634.

43. *FRUS, 1955–1957*, vol. 14, *Suez Crisis: July 26-December 31, 1956* (Washington, DC: GPO, 1990), 167.

44. Eden, *Full Circle*, 649.

45. Salim Yacub, *Containing Arab Nationalism: The Eisenhower Doctrine and the Middle East* (Chapel Hill: University of North Carolina Press, 2004), 1.

46. In November 1956, Syrian president Shukuri al-Quwatli failed to persuade the Kremlin to send air squadrons and pilots to his country to counter the military aid France and Britain were providing Israel. See Yair Evan, "Two Squadrons and Their Pilots: The First Syrian Request for the Deployment of Soviet Military Forces on Its Terri-

tory, 1956" (Cold War International History Project Working Paper 77, February 2016, https://www.wilsoncenter.org/publication/syrias-1956-request-for-soviet-military -intervention).

47. Peter L. Hahn, *Crisis and Crossfire: The United States and the Middle East since 1945* (Washington, DC: Potomac Books, 2005), 42–43; *FRUS, 1958–1960*, vol. 13, *Arab-Israeli Dispute; United Arab Republic; North Africa* (Washington, DC: GPO, 1992), 408–11, 416 (quote 404).

48. *FRUS, 1958–1960*, 13:521–22; Robert B. Rakove, *Kennedy, Johnson, and the Non-aligned World* (New York: Cambridge University Press, 2013), 24–25.

49. *FRUS, 1958–1960*, vol. 12, *Near East Region; Iraq; Iran; Arabian Peninsula* (Washington, DC: GPO, 1993), 22.

50. Yacub, *Containing Arab Nationalism*, 263–64.

51. *FRUS, 1958–1960*, 13:287–88.

52. *FRUS, 1955–1957*, vol. 7, *American Republics: Central and South America* (Washington, DC: GPO, 1987), 912.

53. CIA, *National Intelligence Digest*, October 6, 1952, pp. VII-A-1, CIA, ERR, https:// www.cia.gov/library/readingroom/document/national-intelligence-digest.

54. Bradley Lynn Coleman, *Colombia and the United States: The Making of an Inter-American Alliance, 1939–1960* (Kent, OH: Kent State University Press, 2008), 122–24.

55. CIA, *National Intelligence Digest*, October 6, 1952, pp. VII-E-1, CIA, ERR, https:// www.cia.gov/library/readingroom/document/national-intelligence-digest.

56. Coleman, *Colombia and the United States*, 126–31, 135–44.

57. The Kennedy administration built on prior antiguerrilla aid to Colombia when it developed its counterinsurgency program. See Viron Peter Vaky interview, January 31, 1991, p. 29, Library of Congress, Frontline Diplomacy: The Foreign Affairs Oral History Collection of the Association for Diplomatic Studies and Training, https://cdn.loc.gov /service/mss/mfdip/2004/2004vak01/2004vak01.pdf.

58. *FRUS, 1955–1957*, 7:909, 928, 932–34; Coleman, *Colombia and the United States*, 148–67; Dennis M. Rempe, "An American Trojan Horse?: Eisenhower, Latin America, and the Development of US Internal Security Policy, 1954–1960," *Small Wars and Insurgencies* 10 (March 1999): 34–64, especially 48–49.

59. NIE 88–56, "Probable Developments in Colombia," April 10, 1956, *FRUS, 1955–1957*, 7:900 (quote 902).

60. *FRUS, 1958–1960*, vol. 5, *American Republics* (Washington, DC: GPO, 1991), 208–13; Dennis M. Rempe, *The Past as Prologue?: A History of U.S. Counterinsurgency Policy in Colombia, 1958–66* (Carlisle, PA: Strategic Studies Institute, March 2002), 1–11.

61. Position Paper: State Visit of Colombian President Lleras, April 5–16, 1960, "U.S. Assistance to Colombia in Combatting Guerrillas," April 5, 1960, CK3100460789, Declassified Documents Reference System (DDRS), Gale, Cengage Learning, Farmington Hills, MI; Rempe, *Past as Prologue?*, 10–11.

62. U.S. Department of State, Staff Summary Supplement, "Colombian Land Reform Project," March 24, 1960, CK3100262640, DDRS; Position Paper: State Visit of President Lleras, April 5–16, 1960, "President Lleras' Interest in Obtaining Assistance for Colombia's Agrarian Reform Program," April 3, 1960, CK3100460778, DDRS.

63. Edwin Lieuwen, *Arms and Politics in Latin America*, rev. ed. (New York: Frederick A. Praeger, 1961), 197–202.

64. Stephen G. Rabe, *The Road to OPEC: United States Relations with Venezuela, 1919–1976* (Chapel Hill: University of North Carolina Press, 1982), 117–43.

65. Acting Secretary of State Christian A. Herter to Secretary of Commerce Lewis L. Strauss, November 21, 1958, CK3100167312, DDRS; Ambassador Edward J. Sparks, Caracas, to Department of State, April 30, 1959, CK3100183678, DDRS; Judith Ewell,

Venezuela and the United States: From Monroe's Hemisphere to Petroleum's Empire (Athens: University of Georgia Press, 1996), 201–2.

66. *FRUS, 1958–1960*, 5:429 (quote), 917–19. For background and contrasting analysis, see Aragorn Storm Miller, *Precarious Paths to Freedom: The United States, Venezuela, and the Latin American Cold War* (Albuquerque: University of New Mexico Press, 2016), 1–31.

67. CIA Memorandum, "Hearing: Senate Foreign Relations Committee," May 23, 1958, CIA, ERR, https://www.cia.gov/library/readingroom/document/CIA-RDP80R01731 R000100160053-0 (CIA and State Department quotes); *FRUS, 1958–1960*, 5:222 (Dulles quote), 237 (State Department quote), 238–46.

68. *FRUS, 1955–1957*, vol. 6, *American Republics: Multilateral; Mexico, Caribbean* (Washington, DC: GPO, 1987), 304–10.

69. CIA, "Psychological Aspects of United States Strategy," November 1955, p. 101, CIA, ERR, https://www.cia.gov/library/readingroom/document/psy-asp-united-states-strat.

70. Stephen G. Rabe, *Eisenhower and Latin America: The Foreign Policy of Anticommunism* (Chapel Hill: University of North Carolina Press, 1988), 70–77, 95; Bevan Sewell, *The US and Latin America: Eisenhower, Kennedy and Economic Diplomacy in the Cold War* (London: I. B. Tauris, 2015), 91–96.

71. *FRUS, 1955–1957*, 6:531.

72. Ibid., 559.

73. The following discussion derives from W. Michael Weis, *Cold Warriors and Coups d'Etat: Brazilian-American Relations, 1945–1964* (Albuquerque: University of New Mexico Press, 1993), 113–26.

74. *FRUS, 1958–1960*, 5:710–20; Sewell, *US and Latin America*, 123–24.

75. *FRUS, 1958–1960*, 5:702 n. 2 and n. 3.

76. Ibid., 709; Sewell, *US and Latin America*, 105–9.

77. For a case study of the convergence of political objectives and economic policy, see Kevin Young, "Purging the Forces of Darkness: The United States, Monetary Stabilization, and the Containment of the Bolivian Revolution," *Diplomatic History* 37 (June 2013): 509–37.

78. *FRUS, 1958–1960*, 5:220–21; Sewell, *US and Latin America*, 105, 121–25.

79. U.S. Bureau of the Census, *Statistical Abstract of the United States: 1958* (Washington, DC: GPO, 1958), 880.

80. John W. Dower, *Embracing Defeat: Japan in the Wake of World War II* (New York: W. W. Norton, 1999), 454.

81. Evidence for the presence of nuclear weapons is presented in Hans M. Kristensen, "Japan under the Nuclear Umbrella: U.S. Nuclear Weapons and Nuclear War Planning in Japan during the Cold War" (Nautilus Institute Working Paper, Berkeley, CA, July 1999).

82. *FRUS, 1958–1960*, vol. 18, *Japan; Korea* (Washington, DC: GPO, 1994), 298–300, 315–16, 329–38, 356–66, 382, 387–88, 398–401 (quote 360).

83. *Statistical Abstract: 1958*, 876, 901.

84. CIA, *Economic Intelligence Report*, "Communist China's Imports and Exports, 1956: Trade and Transport Involved," EIC-R1-86, November 21, 1957, CIA, ERR, https://www .cia.gov/ library/readingroom/CIA-RDP85S00362R00040001-2.

85. *FRUS, 1958–1960*, 4:162–65 (quotes 162, 163).

86. Ibid., 115–17.

87. *Statistical Abstract: 1958*, 876, 880, 901.

88. *FRUS, 1955–1957*, 19:274. Rhee pursued the idea of a military alliance in what he called "Free Asia," hoping to isolate Japan; see Charles Kraus, "'The Danger Is Two-Fold': Decolonisation and Cold War in Anti-Communist Asia, 1955–7," *International History Review* 39 (April 2017): 256–73.

89. *FRUS, 1958–1960*, 18:511–40 (quote 519); David Ekbladh, *The Great American Mission: Modernization and the Construction of an American World Order* (Princeton, NJ: Princeton University Press, 2009), 151–52.

90. Jooyoung Lee, "Forming a Democratic Society: South Korean Responses to U.S. Democracy Promotion, 1951–1960," *Diplomatic History* 39 (November 2015): 844–75, especially 865–75.

91. William J. Duiker, *U.S. Containment Policy and the Conflict in Indochina* (Stanford, CA: Stanford University Press, 1994), 200–204.

92. *FRUS, 1950*, vol. 6, *East Asia and the Pacific* (Washington, DC: GPO, 1976), 43.

93. Robert J. McMahon, *The Limits of Empire: The United States and Southeast Asia since World War II* (New York: Columbia University Press, 1999), 95; *FRUS, 1955–1957*, vol. 22, *Southeast Asia* (Washington, DC: GPO, 1989), 942.

94. Quoted in Denis Warner, *The Last Confucian: Vietnam, Southeast Asia, and the West* (Baltimore: Penguin Books, 1964), 282.

95. *FRUS, 1952–1954*, vol. 12, *East Asia and the Pacific* (in two parts) (Washington, DC: GPO, 1987), pt. 2: 740.

96. *FRUS, 1958–1960*, vol. 15, *South and Southeast Asia* (Washington, DC: GPO, 1992), 1168–73 (quote 1173).

97. Operations Coordinating Board, "Special Status Report on Pakistan," September 13, 1954, pp. 1–2, CIA, ERR, https://www.cia.gov/library/readingroom/sites/default/files/doc ument_ conversions/5829/CIA-RDP 80R01731 R003000070005-1.pdf.

98. Hahn, *Crisis and Crossfire*, 15–17.

99. *FRUS, 1958–1960*, 12:246–48.

100. Ibid., 249.

101. Robert J. McMahon, *The Cold War on the Periphery: The United States, India and Pakistan* (New York: Columbia University Press, 1994), 213, 267–69.

102. *FRUS, 1958–1960*, 15:29–46 (quote 39, 33).

103. Ibid., 818–21; Dennis Kux, *The United States and Pakistan, 1947–2000: Disenchanted Allies* (Baltimore: Johns Hopkins University Press, 2001), 55.

104. McMahon, *Cold War on the Periphery*, 269–304.

105. Luce, "The American Century," 166; Frank Ninkovich, *The Global Republic: America's Inadvertent Rise to World Power* (Chicago: University of Chicago Press, 2014), 269–70 offers a contrary interpretation of Luce's declaration.

106. This assumption included Latin America; Bevan Sewall, "Early Modernisation Theory? The Eisenhower Administration and the Foreign Policy of Development in Brazil," *English Historical Review* 125 (December 2010): 1449–80.

107. *FRUS, 1952–1954*, 1, pt. 1: 83–86; Ekbladh, *Great American Mission*, 173–75, 182–89.

108. *Public Papers of the Presidents of the United States: Dwight D. Eisenhower, 1956* (Washington, DC: GPO, 1957), 594.

109. *FRUS, 1955–1957*, 9:19–43 (quotes 32, 39, 35, 40).

110. Ibid., 142.

111. Catherine Caufield, *Masters of Illusion: The World Bank and the Poverty of Nations* (London: Pan Books, 1998), 61 (Black quote).

112. *FRUS, 1958–1960*, 4:76–80 (quotes 76, 77).

113. Alfred E. Eckes Jr., *A Search for Solvency: Bretton Woods and the International Monetary System, 1941–1971* (Austin: University of Texas Press, 1975), 230–33.

114. "Western Europe: The Fourth Force," *Time*, January 12, 1959.

115. *FRUS, 1958–1960*, 4:95–97 (quote 96).

116. U.S. Bureau of the Census, *Statistical Abstract of the United States: 1960* (Washington, DC: GPO, 1960), 873, 877, 879, 881, 899.

117. Caufield, *Masters of Illusion*, 67–68; *FRUS, 1958–1960*, 4:399.

118. Caufield, *Masters of Illusion*, 66; Kaufman, *Trade and Aid*, 141–45.

119. Quoted in Kaufman, *Trade and Aid*, 145.

120. *FRUS, 1958–1960*, 4:372.

121. *FRUS, 1958–1960*, vol. 6, *Cuba* (Washington, DC: GPO, 1992), 836.

122. *FRUS, 1958–1960*, 4:116.

123. Ibid., 102–4, 112–15.

124. Ibid., 115–18 (quotes 115, 116).

125. Ibid., 126.

126. Ibid., 128.

127. Ibid., 130–33, 139–40 (quote 140).

128. *FRUS, 1955–1957*, 10:107–11.

129. Ibid., 111–15.

130. *FRUS, 1955–1957*, 7:536–40; *FRUS, 1955–1957*, 6:61–89; *FRUS, 1958–1960*, 5:20–27.

131. Martha K. Huggins, *Political Policing: The United States and Latin America* (Durham, NC: Duke University Press, 1998), 80–98. On Brazil, see *FRUS, 1958–1960*, 5:659–63; Jan Knippers Black, *United States Penetration of Brazil* (Philadelphia: University of Pennsylvania Press, 1977), 37–38.

132. George Herring, *America's Longest War: The United States and Vietnam, 1950–1975*, 4th ed. (Boston: McGraw Hill, 2002), 69–72; James M. Carter, *Inventing Vietnam: The United States and State Building, 1954–1968* (New York: Cambridge University Press, 2008), 53–70.

133. *FRUS, 1958–1960*, vol. 1, *Vietnam* (Washington, DC: GPO, 1986), 283–86, 626–29, 701 (quote 626); at Hanoi's direction, these southerners formed the National Liberation Front in December 1960.

134. Ibid., 128, 207–8, 236–38; Herring, *America's Longest War*, 73.

135. *FRUS, 1958–1960*, 1:302, 316, 326–27, 485–89.

136. Ibid., 590–91, 623, 632–53 (quote 653).

137. Irwin M. Wall, *The United States and the Making of Postwar France, 1945–1954* (New York: Cambridge University Press, 1991), 268.

138. McMahon, *Limits of Empire*, 79–82.

139. *FRUS, 1955–1957*, 10:7, 9, 22, 111–12, 180; Len F. Ackland, "No Place for Neutralism: The Eisenhower Administration and Laos," in *Laos: War and Revolution*, ed. Nina S. Adams and Alfred W. McCoy (New York: Harper Colophon Books, 1970), 139–54.

140. *FRUS, 1958–1960*, vol. 16, *East Asia-Pacific Region; Cambodia, Laos* (Washington, DC: GPO, 1992), 441–50, 1024–29 (quote 450).

141. Lawrence S. Kaplan, *The United States and NATO: The Formative Years* (Lexington: University Press of Kentucky, 1984), 173.

142. Judt, *Postwar*, 289–92; *FRUS, 1958–1960*, vol. 3, *National Security Policy; Arms Control and Disarmament* (Washington, DC: GPO, 1996), 189 (quote).

143. On Berlin's importance for the integrity of the Atlantic alliance and U.S. leadership, see Department of State, Memorandum of Conversation, "Germany and Berlin," March 15, 1960, in John A. Calhoun, Director, Executive Secretariat, Department of State, to Allen W. Dulles, March 31, 1960, CIA, ERR, https://www.cia.gov/library/readingroom/sites/default/files/document_conversions/5829/CIA-RDP80B01676R002600130051-6.pdf.

144. *FRUS, 1958–1960*, vol. 9, *Berlin Crisis, 1959–1960; Germany; Austria* (Washington, DC: GPO, 1993), 621–22.

145. Richard M. Bissell Jr., Memorandum for Allen W. Dulles, November 12, 1959, containing Department of State and CIA, "Issue of U.S. Policy Regarding the Defense Policy of NATO," CIA, ERR, https://www.cia.gov/library/readingroom/document/CIA-RDP80B0167R 001100060029-5.

146. Thomas L. Ahern Jr., *CIA and the House of Ngo: Covert Action in South Vietnam, 1954–63 (U)* (CIA History Staff, Center for the Study of Intelligence, n.d.), 121, 129–30, 134–44 (quotes 121, 129, 136), CIA, ERR, https://www.cia.gov/library/readingroom/document/ specialcollectionvietnam2ciaandthehouseofngopdf.

147. *FRUS, 1958–1960*, 18:333.

148. Ikeda Kazuo, "Historical Background," in *Zengakuren: Japan's Revolutionary Students*, ed. Stuart J. Dowsey (Berkeley, CA: Ishi Press, 1970), 40–41; Matsunami Michihiro, "Origins of Zengakuren," ibid., 42–59; Harada Hisato, "The Anti-Ampo Struggle," ibid., 87–95.

149. *FRUS, 1958–1960*, 18:3264–66, 377–84 (quotes 365, 383).

150. *FRUS, 1958–1960*, 5:91–116 (quotes 92, 107, 113); Patrick Iber, *Neither Peace nor Freedom: The Cultural Cold War in Latin America* (Cambridge, MA: Harvard University Press, 2015), 95–101, 115.

151. Rabe, *Eisenhower and Latin America*, 105–6, 155–59; J. Lloyd Mecham, *The United States and Inter-American Security, 1889–1960* (Austin: University of Texas Press, 1961), 472.

152. *FRUS, 1958–1960*, 6:1029.

153. CIA [Jack B. Pfeiffer], *Official History of the Bay of Pigs Operation*, vol. 3, *Evolution of CIA's Anti-Castro Policies, 1959-January 1961* (December 1979) [Released September 26, 1998], p. 4, CIA, ERR, https://www.cia.gov/library/readingroom/docs /bop-vol3.pdf.

154. *FRUS, 1958–1960*, 6:993 (quote 985).

155. J. C. King to Allen W. Dulles, December 11, 1959, CIA, ERR, https://www.cia.gov /library/ readingroom/document/CIA-RDP80R1731R000300250001-5.

156. Alan McPherson, *Yankee No!: Anti-Americanism in U.S.-Latin American Relations* (Cambridge, MA: Harvard University Press, 2003), 9–31; Rabe, *Eisenhower and Latin America*, 100–106; Richard Nixon, *Six Crises* (New York: Doubleday, 1962), 183–234 (quote 190).

157. *FRUS, 1958–1960*, 6: 1064; CIA, Special National Intelligence Estimate 855-4-62: "Castro's Subversive Capabilities in Latin America," November 9, 1962, pp. 6–7: Cuban Crisis, 1962: State Department (2 of 3 folders), Papers of Robert F. Kennedy, Attorney General Papers, John F. Kennedy Presidential Library, Columbia Point, Boston, MA, http:// www.jfklibrary.org/Asset-Viewer/Archives/RFKAG-218–002.aspx.

158. Van Gosse, *Where the Boys Are: Cuba, Cold War America, and the Making of a New Left* (London: Verso, 1993), 155–65; Timothy B. Tyson, *Radio Free Dixie: Robert F. Williams and the Roots of Black Power* (Chapel Hill: University of North Carolina Press, 1999), 220–43; Devyn Spence Benson, "Cuba Calls: African American Tourism, Race, and the Cuban Revolution, 1959–1961," *Hispanic American Historical Review* 93 (May 2013): 259–71.

159. Jeremy Scahill interview with Alfred W. McCoy, July 22, 2017, *The Intercept*, https:// theintercept.com/2017/07/22/donald-trump-and-the-coming-fall-of-american -empire/.

5. BEARING BURDENS

1. John F. Kennedy Inaugural Address, January 20, 1961, John F. Kennedy Presidential Library (JFKL), Columbia Point, Boston, MA, http://www.jfklibrary.org/Research/ Research-Aids/Ready-Reference/JFK-Fast-Facts/Inaugural-Address.aspx.

2. Alan Brinkley, *The Publisher: Henry Luce and His American Century* (New York: Alfred A. Knopf, 2010), 414–27; Roger Morris, *Richard M. Nixon: The Rise of an American Politician* (New York: Henry Holt, 1990), 663 on Luce and Nixon.

3. William J. Rust, *Before the Quagmire: American Intervention in Laos, 1954–1961* (Lexington: University Press of Kentucky, 2012), 256–59; Seth Jacobs, *The Universe Unraveling: American Foreign Policy in Cold War Laos* (Ithaca, NY: Cornell University Press, 2012), 1–4, 239–41; U.S. Department of State, *Foreign Relations of the United States,*

1961–1963, vol. 24, *Laos Crisis* (*FRUS, year*, volume) (Washington, DC: Government Printing Office [GPO], 1994), 19–25, 110–11, 115.

4. Arthur M. Schlesinger Jr., *A Thousand Days: John F. Kennedy in the White House* (Boston: Houghton Mifflin, 1967), 305–8.

5. *FRUS, 1961–1963*, vol. 8: *National Security Policy* (Washington, DC: GPO, 1996), 12, 18.

6. In May, Secretary of State Rusk decried the effect of "the unfortunate Cuban episode" on the administration; *FRUS, 1961–1963*, 24:188.

7. Ibid., 127–29, 143, 147, 795–96; William J. Duiker, *U.S. Containment Policy and the Conflict in Indochina* (Stanford, CA: Stanford University Press, 1994), 304–6.

8. *FRUS, 1961–1963*, 24:135, 137–39; "British Soviet Exchange," *Department of State Bulletin*, April 17, 1961, pp. 545–46; Rust, *Before the Quagmire*, 215–35.

9. *FRUS, 1961–1963*, vol. 6, *Kennedy-Khrushchev Exchanges* (Washington, DC: GPO, 1996), 58–59 (quote 59).

10. Duiker, *U.S. Containment Policy*, 286; Schlesinger, *Thousand Days*, 340. Kennedy's daily intelligence brief regularly covered Laos. CIA, President's Intelligence Checklist, December 14, 1961, p. 3, Central Intelligence Agency, Electronic Reading Room (CIA, ERR), https://www. cia.gov/library/readingroom/docs/DOC_0005992085.pdf; CIA, President's Intelligence Checklist, January 2, 1962, p. 2, CIA, ERR, https://www.cia.gov/library /readingroom/docs/DOC_0005992119.pdf. The briefings began on June 17, two weeks after Kennedy and Khrushchev met at Vienna.

11. *FRUS, 1961–1963*, 24:772; CIA, President's Intelligence Checklist, June 5, 1962, pp. 3–4, CIA, ERR, https://www.cia.gov/library/readingroom/docs/DOC_0005992359.pdf.

12. *FRUS, 1961–1963*, 24:810, 814 (quote 810).

13. Jonathan Mirsky and Stephen E. Stonfeld, "The Nam Tha Crisis: Kennedy and the New Frontier on the Brink," in *Laos: War and Revolution*, ed. Nina S. Adams and Alfred W. McCoy (New York: Harper Colophon Books, 1970), 178; *FRUS, 1961–1963*, 24:734–35, 769, 824–25.

14. National Security File (NSF): Meetings & Memoranda (M &M) Series, National Security Action Memorandum (NSAM) 10, February 6, 1961, Box 328, JFKL; Peter Kornbluh, ed., *Bay of Pigs Declassified: The Secret CIA Report on the Invasion of Cuba* (New York: New Press, 1998), 23–24, 35, 103–5.

15. *FRUS, 1961–1963*, vol. 10, *Cuba, 1961–1962* (Washington, DC: GPO, 1997), 386 (quote 391–92). The defeat was so dispiriting that the CIA delayed until October 25, 2016, the release of its own critique of the operation; Jack B. Pfeiffer, *Official History of the Bay of Pigs Operation*, vol. 5, *CIA's Internal Investigation of the Bay of Pigs* (April 18, 1984), CIA, ERR, https://www.cia.gov/ library/readingroom/docs/bop-vol3.pdf.

16. NSF: M & M Series, NSAM 118, January 13, 1962, Box 333, JFKL; NSF: M & M Series, NSAM 134, February 20, 1962, Box 335, JFKL.

17. *FRUS, 1961–1963*, 10:98, 397, 407 n. 3, 487, 525, 656.

18. Don Bohning, *The Castro Obsession: U.S. Covert Operations against Cuba, 1959–1965* (Washington, DC: Potomac Books, 2005).

19. *FRUS, 1961–1963*, 10:424, 425.

20. Harold Macmillan, *At the End of the Day, 1961–1963* (New York: Harper & Row, 1973), 181. Macmillan worried that failure in Cuba would lead to covert operations in Laos; Harold Macmillan, *Pointing the Way, 1956–1961* (New York: Harper & Row, 1972), 353.

21. *FRUS, 1961–1963*, 6:10–16 (quote 15). On Kennedy's humiliation as a result of the failed invasion, see *FRUS, 1961–1963*, 10:397.

22. Mervyn J. Bain, "Havana and Moscow: The Washington Factor," in *Fifty Years of Revolution: Perspectives on Cuba, the United States, and the World*, ed. Soraya M. Castro Mariño and Ronald W. Pruessen (Gainesville: University Press of Florida, 2012), 73–75;

David A. Welch, "The Kennedy-Castro Years," in Castro Mariño and Pruessen, *Fifty Years of Revolution*, 189 (Sergo Mikoyan quote).

23. *FRUS, 1961–1963*, vol. 5, *Soviet Union* (Washington, DC: GPO, 1998), 130–33 (quote 132).

24. Campbell Craig and Fredrik Logevall, *America's Cold War: The Politics of Insecurity* (Cambridge, MA: Belknap Press of Harvard University Press, 2009), 198–99; Aleksandr Fursenko and Timothy Naftali, *Khrushchev's Cold War: The Inside Story of an American Adversary* (New York: W. W. Norton, 2006), 360–68.

25. Vladislav M. Zubok, *A Failed Empire: The Soviet Union in the Cold War from Stalin to Gorbachev* (Chapel Hill: University of North Carolina Press, 2007), 139–42; *FRUS, 1961–1963*, 5:231.

26. *FRUS, 1958–1960*, vol. 9, *Berlin Crisis, 1959–1960; Germany; Austria* (Washington, DC: GPO, 1993), 621–22 (quote 622).

27. This story is well told in Frank Costigliola, "The Pursuit of Atlantic Community: Nuclear Arms, Dollars, and Berlin," in *Kennedy's Quest for Victory: American Foreign Policy, 1961–1963*, ed. Thomas G. Paterson (New York: Oxford University Press, 1989), 24–56; Fursenko and Naftali, *Khrushchev's Cold War*, 359–408; Anatoly Dobrynin, *In Confidence: Moscow's Ambassador to America's Six Cold War Presidents (1962–1986)* (New York: Crown, 1995), 44–46.

28. *FRUS, 1958–1960*, vol. 8, *Berlin Crisis, 1958–1959* (Washington, DC: GPO, 1993), 520–21; Macmillan, *Pointing the Way*, 390–94, 402, 409; Macmillan, *At the End of the Day* (quote 150).

29. "Soviet Aide Memoire of June 4," *Department of State Bulletin*, August 7, 1961, pp. 231–32 (quote 232).

30. *Public Papers of the Presidents of the United States (PPP): John F. Kennedy, 1961* (Washington, DC: GPO, 1962), 533–40 (quote 534); Costigliola, "The Pursuit of Atlantic Community," 44–45; *FRUS, 1961–1963*, vol. 14, *Berlin Crisis, 1961–1962* (Washington, DC: GPO, 1993), 217–18, 220.

31. *FRUS, 1961–1963*, 14:80–86, 223–26 (quote 377).

32. Ibid., 345–46, 354–58 (quote 345).

33. Tony Judt, *Postwar: A History of Europe since 1945* (New York: Penguin Press, 2005), 252–53; "Soviet Tactics in the Berlin Crisis," August 24, 1961, SNIE 11-10–61, CIA, ERR, https://www.cia.gov/library/readingroom/docs/DOC_0000652295.pdf; *FRUS, 1961–1963*, 14:387.

34. *FRUS, 1961–1963*, 14:389–91, 493–97, 590–95, 636–39.

35. Macmillan, *End of the Day*, 146; *FRUS, 1961–1963*, 14:696–704.

36. On Bundy and first-use, see Nina Tannenwald, *The Nuclear Taboo: The United States and the Non-use of Nuclear Weapons since 1945* (New York: Cambridge University Press, 2007), 283–84; on McNamara, see *FRUS, 1961–1963*, 8:501.

37. Dean Rusk, with Richard Rusk and Daniel S. Papp, *As I Saw It* (New York: W. W. Norton, 1990), 366, 457.

38. Matthew Evangelista, *Unarmed Forces: The Transnational Movement to End the Cold War* (Ithaca, NY: Cornell University Press, 1999), 85–86.

39. NSAM 231, "Middle Eastern Nuclear Capabilities," March 26, 1963, Federation of American Scientists, Intelligence Resource Program (FAS, IRP), http://www.fas.org/irp/offdocs/nsam-jfk/nsam231.gif; Amos Elon, "A Very Special Relationship," *New York Review of Books*, January 15, 2004; Avner Cohen and William Burr, eds., *Kennedy, Dimona and the Nuclear Proliferation Problem: 1961–1962*, April 21, 2016, National Security Archive, Electronic Briefing Book No. 547, http://nsarchive.gwu.edu/nukevault/ebb547-Kennedy-Dimona-and-the-Nuclear-Proliferation-Problem-1961–1962/.

40. Thomas L. Hughes interview, September 1, 1999, pp. 130–31, Library of Congress, Frontline Diplomacy: The Foreign Affairs Oral History Collection of the Association for Diplomatic Studies and Training (FAOHC), https://www.loc.gov/item/mfdipbib001565/.

41. W. W. Rostow, "Guerrilla Warfare in Underdeveloped Areas," *Department of State Bulletin*, August 7, 1961, pp. 233–37 (quotes 234, 236).

42. Memo by W. W. Rostow, April 24, 1961, 71-4-16–26: Cuba - State Department Cables, Section 1, 24 April 1961–26 October 1962, Papers of Robert F. Kennedy, Attorney General Papers, JFKL, http://www.jfklibrary.org/Asset-Viewer/Archives/RFKAG-202–001.aspx.

43. David Milne, *America's Rasputin: Walt Rostow and the Vietnam War* (New York: Hill and Wang, 2008), 110–17.

44. *FRUS, 1961–1963*, 8:216, 236–37, 245–49, 252, 256. Covert operations won the allegiance of liberals in the administration when they were portrayed as undertakings to assist development; Hughes interview, August 25, 1999, p. 74, FAOHC, https://www.loc.gov/item/mfdipbib001565/.

45. NSF, M & M Series, NSAM 114, November 22, 1961, Box 333, JFKL; NSF, M & M Series, NSAM 118, December 5, 1961, Box 333, JFKL; *FRUS, 1961–1963*, 8:236.

46. *FRUS, 1961–1963*, 8:289 (Kennan quote), 252 (Rusk quote).

47. Jeffrey Glen Giauque, *Grand Designs and Visions of Unity: The Atlantic Powers and the Reorganization of Western Europe, 1955–1963* (Chapel Hill: University of North Carolina Press, 2002); Thomas Alan Schwartz, "Victories and Defeats in the Long Twilight Struggle: The United States and Western Europe in the 1960s," in *Diplomacy of the Crucial Decade: American Foreign Relations during the 1960s*, ed. Diane B. Kunz (New York: Columbia University Press, 1994), 115–33.

48. Richard J. Barnet, *The Alliance: America, Europe, Japan: Makers of the Postwar World* (New York: Simon and Schuster, 1983), 208–11.

49. *FRUS, 1958–1960*, vol. 7, pt. 2: *Western Europe* (Washington, DC: GPO, 1993), 860–65.

50. *FRUS, 1961–1963*, 8:279.

51. Ibid., 389–92, 411–13.

52. David N. Schwartz, *NATO's Nuclear Dilemmas* (Washington, DC: Brookings Institution, 1983), 96–105.

53. Eisenhower and Kennedy wanted greater defense cooperation within NATO and considered creating a nuclear force (the MLF) under Washington's control. Giauque, *Grand Designs*, 116–23; Irwin M. Wall, *France, the United Sates, and the Algerian War* (Berkeley: University of California Press, 2001), 193–94.

54. Ibid., 230–33; Giauque, *Grand Designs*, 108–10.

55. *FRUS, 1961–1963*, 8:457–62 (quote 458).

56. William J. Perry, *My Journey at the Nuclear Brink* (Stanford, CA: Stanford University Press, 2015), 1–5 (quote 4).

57. *FRUS, 1961–1963*, 8:147, 149–51; Don Munton and David A. Welch, *The Cuban Missile Crisis: A Concise History* (New York: Oxford University Press, 2007), 60, 66. Macmillan had some advance warning about the blockade, and the White House kept him better informed than other allies during the crisis.

58. *FRUS, 1964–1968*, vol. 12, *Western Europe* (Washington, DC: GPO, 2001), 682, 687, 695, 699–700, 710, 716–17, 721–24; Robert Bothwell, *Canada and the United States: The Politics of Partnership* (New York: Twayne, 1992), 74–100.

59. *FRUS, 1961–1963*, vol. 22, *Northeast Asia* (Washington, DC: GPO, 1996), 696; *FRUS, 1958–1960*, vol. 18, *Japan; Korea* (Washington, DC: GPO, 1994), 422 for the assessment by U.S. diplomats.

60. Nancy Bernkopf Tucker, *Taiwan, Hong Kong, and the United States, 1945–1992: Uncertain Friendships* (New York: Twayne, 1994), 47–50, 72–73, 94–96.

61. Gregg Brazinsky, *Nation Building in South Korea: Koreans, Americans, and the Making of a Democracy* (Chapel Hill: University of North Carolina Press, 2007), 106–10.

62. *FRUS, 1958–1960*, 18:693–96.

63. *FRUS, 1961–1963*, 22:468–71.

64. Ibid., 529–39, 542–48 (quote 543).

65. Ibid., 657–61 (quote 658).

66. Brazinsky, *Nation Building in South Korea*, 130–32.

67. William O. Walker III, "Mixing the Sweet with the Sour: Kennedy, Johnson, and Latin America," in Kunz, *Diplomacy of the Crucial Decade*, 54–59.

68. *FRUS, 1961–1963*, 10:101; NSF, M & M Series, NSAM 10, February 6, 1961, Box 328, JFKL.

69. *FRUS, 1961–1963*, 10:87.

70. Ibid., 775, 841–42, 852.

71. Stephen G. Rabe, *The Most Dangerous Area in the World: John F. Kennedy Confronts Communist Revolution in Latin America* (Chapel Hill: University of North Carolina Press, 1999).

72. Rusk, *As I Saw It*, 370; NSF, Regional Security Series, Latin America, vol. 2, Rusk memorandum, August 31, 1963, Box 216, JFKL.

73. Walker, "Mixing the Sweet with the Sour," 58; NSAM 206, December 4, 1962, Box 339, JFKL; NSF, Country File, "Latin American Situation Report," January 8, 1964, Box 1, Lyndon Baines Johnson Presidential Library (LBJL), Austin, TX.

74. *Alleged Assassination Plots Involving Foreign Leaders: An Interim Report of the United States Senate Select Committee to Study Governmental Operations with Respect to Intelligence Activities* (New York: W. W. Norton, 1977), 176–78.

75. Timothy N. Castle, *At War in the Shadow of Vietnam: U.S. Military Aid to the Royal Lao Government, 1955–1975* (New York: Columbia University Press, 1993); Jacobs, *Universe Unraveling*, 250.

76. *FRUS, 1961–1963*, 6:135–36.

77. Robert J. McMahon, *The Limits of Empire: The United States and Southeast Asia since World War II* (New York: Columbia University Press, 1999), 124–28.

78. The literature on U.S. policy in Indochina and Kennedy's and Johnson's policy options is vast. Still valuable is Ralph Stavins, Richard J. Barnet, and Marcus G. Raskin, *Washington Plans an Aggressive War* (New York: Random House, 1971).

79. The Senator Gravel Edition, *The Pentagon Papers: The Defense Department History of United States Decisionmaking on Vietnam*, 4 vols. (Boston: Beacon Press, 1971), 3:17–32.

80. See especially George McT. Kahin and Audrey R. Kahin, *Subversion as Foreign Policy: The Secret and Eisenhower Debacle in Indonesia* (New York: New Press, 1995).

81. *FRUS, 1958–1960*, vol. 22, *Indonesia* (Washington, DC: GPO, 2000), 192.

82. *FRUS, 1961–1963*, 8:457.

83. McMahon, *Limits of Empire*, 121–22.

84. CIA, President's Intelligence Checklist, June 19, 1961, p. 4, CIA, ERR, https://www.cia.gov/library/readingroom/docs/DOC_0005958912.pdf; ibid., January 8, 1962, p. 4, CIA, ERR, https://www.cia.gov/library/readingroom/docs/DOC_0005992129.pdf.

85. Robert J. McMahon, *The Cold War on the Periphery: The United States, India and Pakistan* (New York: Columbia University Press, 1994), 273–74, 277.

86. *FRUS, 1961–1963*, vol. 19, *South Asia* (Washington, DC: GPO, 1996), 41.

87. Ibid., 312–14 (quote 242).

88. McMahon, *Cold War on the Periphery*, 288–97.

89. *FRUS, 1961–1963*, 19:661–68 (quote 665).

90. *FRUS, 1961–1963*, vol. 17, *Near East, 1961–1962* (Washington, DC: GPO, 1994), 45.

91. Fursenko and Naftali, *Khrushchev's Cold War*, 214–15, 243; *FRUS, 1961–1963*, 17:142–45 (quote 165–66).

92. *FRUS, 1961–1963*, 17:474.

93. *FRUS, 1964–1968*, vol. 21, *Near East Region; Arabian Peninsula* (Washington, DC: GPO, 2000), 449–50, 469–71; Sarah Yizraeli, *Politics and Society in Saudi Arabia: The Crucial Years of Development, 1960–1982* (New York: Columbia University Press, 2012), 28–29, 60–61.

94. Douglas Little, *American Orientalism: The United States and the Middle East since 1945*, 3rd ed. (Chapel Hill: University of North Carolina Press, 2008), 183–85.

95. *FRUS, 1961–1963*, 17:757.

96. Ibid., 7–8, 39–40, 52, 56–65 (quote 59).

97. Ibid., 98–99. For a compelling assessment of Washington's psychology and decision-making about Iran, see Andrew Warne, "Psychoanalyzing Iran: Kennedy's Iran Task Force and the Modernization of Orientalism, 1961–3," *International Historical Review* 35 (April 2013): 396–422.

98. *FRUS, 1961–1963*, 17:245–53 (quote 246).

99. Ibid., 416–27.

100. Ibid., 433–37.

101. *FRUS, 1961–1963*, vol. 18, *Near East, 1962–1963* (Washington, DC: GPO, 1995), 84–88 (quote 72).

102. Little, *American Orientalism*, 219–21.

103. *FRUS, 1961–1963*, 18:311, 464–64.

104. Brandon Wolfe-Hunnicut, "Embracing Regime Change in Iraq: American Foreign Policy and the 1963 Coup d'état in Baghdad," *Diplomatic History* 39 (January 2015): 98–125; Eric Jacobsen, "A Coincidence of Interests: Kennedy, U.S. Assistance, and the 1963 Iraqi Ba'th Regime," *Diplomatic History* 37 (November 2013): 1028–59.

105. *FRUS, 1961–1963*, 18:342 n. 2 (quote); Little, *American Orientalism*, 201–6; *FRUS, 1964–1968*, 21:388.

106. *FRUS, 1961–1963*, 17:271.

107. *FRUS, 1961–1963*, 18:752–53, 852–53.

108. Ibid., 407, 817.

109. Richard M. Bissell Jr., with Jonathan E. Lewis and Frances T. Pudlo, *Reflections of a Cold Warrior: From Yalta to the Bay of Pigs* (New Haven, CT: Yale University Press, 1996), 142–45. See Stephen Weissman's analysis of declassified documents in the *Washington Post*, July 21, 2002; Tim Weiner, *Legacy of Ashes: The History of the CIA* (New York: Doubleday, 2007), 162–63, 583–84.

110. *FRUS, 1961–1963*, 5:116; Lise Namikas, *Battleground Africa: Cold War in the Congo, 1960–1965* (Stanford, CA: Stanford University Press, 2013), 33–46.

111. This story is well told in Philip E. Muehlenbeck, *Betting on the Africans: John F. Kennedy's Courting of African Nationalist Leaders* (New York: Oxford University Press, 2012). The present analysis focuses on cold-war continuities more than the role of personality; *FRUS, 1961–1963*, 8:29; Robert B. Rakove, *Kennedy, Johnson, and the Nonaligned World* (New York: Cambridge University Press, 2013), 31–36.

112. Stephen G. Rabe, *John F. Kennedy: World Leader* (Washington, DC: Potomac Books, 2010), 164–77.

113. National Intelligence Estimate 70-1-67, "The Liberation Movements of Southern Africa," Central Intelligence Agency, November 24, 1967, pp. 3, 8, CK3100295954, Declassified Documents Reference System, Gale, Cengage Learning, Farmington Hills, MI; Daniel Politi, "Former U.S. Spy Says CIA Played Key Role in Nelson Mandela's Arrest," *Slate Magazine*, May 15, 2016, http://www.slate.com/blogs/the_slatest/2016/05/15/former_u_s_spy_says_cia_played_key_role_in_nelson_mandela_arrest.html.

114. *FRUS, 1958–1960*, vol. 14, *Africa* (Washington, DC: GPO, 1992), 8–9, 45–51 (quotes 46, 47).

115. *FRUS, 1961–1963*, vol. 21, *Africa* (Washington, DC: GPO, 1995), 281, 283–84, 289–90, 97–98; *FRUS, 1961–1963*, 8:29.

116. *FRUS, 1961–1963*, 8:507–11 (quotes 509, 510).

117. Ibid., 541.

118. Thomas Alan Schwartz, *Lyndon Johnson and Europe: In the Shadow of Vietnam* (Cambridge, MA: Harvard University Press, 2003), 10–16.

119. Peter L. Hahn, *Crisis and Crossfire: The United States and the Middle East since 1945* (Washington, DC: Potomac Books, 2005), 49; Memorandum by Robert W. Komer, August 10, 1965, National Security File, Name File, Komer Memos, vol. 1 (1 of 3), Box 6 (1 of 2), LBJL.

120. Fursenko and Naftali, *Khrushchev's Cold War*, 531–38; Gordon H. Chang, *Friends and Enemies: The United States, China, and the Soviet Union, 1948–1972* (Stanford, CA: Stanford University Press, 1990), 249–52.

121. *FRUS, 1964–1968*, vol. 10, *National Security Policy* (Washington, DC: GPO, 2002), 225.

122. Robert Gilpin, *U.S. Power and the Multinational Corporation: The Political Economy of Foreign Direct Investment* (New York: Basic Books, 1975), 154–55; Fred L. Block, *The Origins of International Economic Disorder: A Study of United States International Monetary Policy from World War II to the Present* (Berkeley: University of California Press, 1977), 140 (quote).

123. David P. Calleo, *The Imperious Economy* (Cambridge, MA: Harvard University Press, 1982), 9–17, 223–24.

124. *FRUS, 1958–1960*, vol. 4, *Foreign Economic Policy* (Washington, DC: GPO, 1992), 147–51; *FRUS, 1961–1963*, vol. 9, *Foreign Economic Policy* (Washington, DC: GPO, 1995), 1–2 for a meeting held on January 19, 1961.

125. *FRUS, 1961–1963*, 9:2–10 (quote 10).

126. Ibid., 15–18; Block, *Origins of International Economic Disorder*, 145, 160 for trade and payments data.

127. Francis J. Gavin, *Gold, Dollars, and Power: The Politics of International Monetary Relations, 1958–1971* (Chapel Hill: University of North Carolina Press, 2004), 60.

128. *FRUS, 1961–1963*, 9:48, 54 (quote 79).

129. Ibid., 94–104, 318 (quote 103).

130. Block, *Origins of International Economic Disorder*, 136; Benjamin J. Cohen, *In Whose Interest?: International Banking and American Foreign Policy* (New Haven, CT: Yale University Press, 1986), 18–24; Gilpin, *U.S. Power and the Multinational Corporation*, 155.

131. *FRUS, 1961–1963*, 9:45–47.

132. Ibid., 116–19 (quote 117).

133. On Japan, see *FRUS, 1961–1963*, 22:682–87.

134. *FRUS, 1961–1963*, 9:157–60, 169.

135. Giauque, *Grand Designs*, 199–223.

136. *FRUS, 1961–1963*, 9:329–34. U.S. doubts about Japan's embrace of multilateralism persisted in Kennedy's presidency; *FRUS, 1961–1963*, 22:686, 734–35, 746–48, 754–57, 783–86.

137. *FRUS, 1961–1963*, 9:163–64.

138. Ibid., 170–75, 180–81, 184–85, 188.

139. Ibid.,18.

140. Rabe, *Most Dangerous Area in the World*, 148.

141. *FRUS, 1961–1963*, vol. 12, *American Republics* (Washington, DC: GPO, 1996), 95.

142. *FRUS, 1961–1963*, 9:37, 294 (quote 18).

143. Rabe, *Most Dangerous Area in the World*, 155.

144. Bevan Sewell, *The US and Latin America: Eisenhower, Kennedy and Economic Diplomacy in the Cold War* (London: I. B. Tauris, 2015), 136–60; Michael E. Latham, *Modernization as Ideology: American Social Science and "Nation Building" in the Kennedy Era* (Chapel Hill: University of North Carolina Press, 2000), 69–72.

145. Sidney Dell, *The Inter-American Development Bank: A Study in Development Financing* (New York: Frederick A. Praeger, 1972), 26.

146. Ibid., 68–69.

147. *FRUS, 1961–1963*, 12:89, 94–95, 175.

148. Barbara Stallings, *Banker to the World: U.S. Portfolio Investment in Latin America, 1900–1986* (Berkeley: University of California Press, 1987), 84–94.

149. Gilpin, *U.S. Power and the Multinational Corporation*, 156–62 (quotes 156, 161).

150. This conclusion is influenced by Richard J. Barnet and Ronald E. Müller, *Global Reach: The Power of the Multinational Corporations* (New York: Simon and Schuster, 1974), 154–84.

151. Jerome Levinson and Juan de Onís, *The Alliance That Lost Its Way: A Critical Report on the Alliance for Progress* (Chicago: Quadrangle Books, 1972), 132–37, 186–89.

152. See *FRUS, 1961–1963*, 9:78–87 for Galbraith's incisive memo to Kennedy of August 28, 1963.

153. Ibid., 103–4.

154. Block, *Origins of International Economic Disorder*, 159–63.

155. *FRUS, 1964–1968*, vol. 8, *International Monetary and Trade Policy* (Washington, DC: GPO, 1998),44–47 (quote 46).

156. Ibid., 47.

157. Schwartz, *Lyndon Johnson and Europe*, 71–73. Britain supported raising IMF quotas.

158. *FRUS, 1964–1968*, 8:48–49.

159. *FRUS, 1964–1968*, 12:465, 467.

160. *FRUS, 1964–1968*, 8:27–29 (quote 28); on Wilson, see Judt, *Postwar*, 371.

161. Schwartz, *Lyndon Johnson and Europe*, 68–70; Gavin, *Gold, Dollars, and Power*, 130–32; *FRUS, 1964–1968*, 8:62.

162. *PPP: Kennedy, 1961*, 203, 205–6.

163. J. William Fulbright, *The Arrogance of Power* (New York: Vintage Books, 1966), 71.

164. *FRUS, 1961–1963*, 12:10–18 (quotes 13, 15).

165. Latham, *Modernization as Ideology*, 59.

166. Ibid., 57.

167. NSAM 177, "Police Assistance Programs," August 7, 1962, FAS, IRP, http://www.fas.org/irp/offdocs/nsam-jfk/nsam177.htm; NSF, M & M Series, Special Group (CI), August 13, 1962, Box 319, JFKL.

168. *FRUS, 1961–1963*, 9:262.

169. Ibid., 265, 266.

170. Ibid., 272, 283.

171. David Ekbladh, *The Great American Mission: Modernization and the Construction of an American World Order* (Princeton, NJ: Princeton University Press, 2009), 192–97; Nick Cullather, *The Hungry World: America's Cold War Battle against Poverty in Asia* (Cambridge, MA: Harvard University Press, 2010), 142–44, 153.

172. Cullather, *Hungry World*, 156–57; *FRUS, 1961–1963*, 19:128–35; McMahon, *Cold War on the Periphery*, 280–81.

173. Rabe, *Kennedy*, 144–45.

174. Ted Sorensen, *Counselor: A Life at the Edge of History* (New York: Harper, 2008), 329; Arthur M. Schlesinger Jr., *The Cycles of American History* (Boston: Houghton Mifflin, 1986), 119.

175. Elizabeth Cobbs Hoffman, *All You Need Is Love: The Peace Corps and the Spirit of the 1960s* (Cambridge, MA: Harvard University Press, 1998); Rabe, *Kennedy*, 82.

176. Rabe, *Most Dangerous Area in the World*, 148–72; Rabe, *Kennedy*, 82

177. *FRUS, 1961–1963*, 10:642–45; Richard N. Goodwin, *Remembering America: A Voice from the Sixties* (Boston: Little, Brown, 1968), 195–205.

178. *FRUS, 1961–1963*, 9:273.

179. *FRUS, 1961–1963*, 22:459, 468–69 (quote 462 n. 2).

180. Brazinsky, *Nation Building in South Korea*, 127–33.

181. Ekbladh, *Great American Mission*, 197–201 (quote 197).

182. Douglas Blaufarb, *The Counterinsurgency Era: US Doctrine and Performance, 1950 to the Present* (New York: Free Press, 1977), 18; Jeff Goodwin, *No Other Way Out: States and Revolutionary Movements, 1945–1991* (New York: Cambridge University Press, 2001), parts 1 and 2; Robert S. McNamara, with Brian Van DeMark, *In Retrospect: The Tragedy and Lessons of Vietnam* (New York: Crown, 1995), 45.

183. NSAM 2, "Development of Counter Guerrilla Forces," February 3, 1961, FAS, IRP, http://www.fas.org/irp/offdocs/nsam-jfk/nsam2.jpg.

184. *PPP: Kennedy, 1961*, 229, 397 (quotes).

185. Michael McClintock, *Instruments of Statecraft: U.S. Guerrilla Warfare, Counterinsurgency, and Counterterrorism, 1940–1990* (New York: Pantheon Books, 1992), 165.

186. NSF, M & M Series, NSAM 118, January 13, 1962, Box 333, JFKL; NSF, M & M Series, January 18, 1962, Box 333, JFKL; Hughes interview, August 25, 1999, p. 88, https://www.loc.gov/item/mfdipbib001565/.

187. *FRUS, 1961–1963*, 8:51.

188. Rabe, *Most Dangerous Area in the World*, 130–31; NSF, M & M Series, NSAM 118, January 13, 1962, "Appendix B: Military Actions for Latin America, Part 2," Box 333, JFKL; NSF, M & M Series, NSAM 134, February 20, 1962, Box 333, JFKL.

189. Thomas C. Field Jr., "Ideology as Strategy: Military-Led Modernization and the Origins of the Alliance for Progress in Bolivia," *Diplomatic History* 36 (January 2012): 147–83; *FRUS, 1961–1963*, 8:231–32.

190. NSF, M & M Series, NSAM 182, August 24, 1962, Box 338, JFKL presents a thorough look at counterinsurgency doctrine.

191. NSF, Country (CO) Series, El Salvador, Memorandum for McGeorge Bundy, December 16, 1962, Box 69, JFKL; NSF, CO Series, Venezuela, C. Allan Stewart to State Department, August 30, 1962, Box 192, JFKL; NSF, M & M Series, NSAM 153, "Policy Statement on the Dominican Republic," March 15, 1962, Box 336, JFKL.

192. NSF, CO Series, Colombia, John F. Kennedy to President Alberto Lleras Camargo, May 4, 1962, Box 26, JFKL; NSF, CO Series, Colombia, Report on Colombia, June 8, 1962, Box 26, JFKL; NSF, M & M Series, Special Group (CI), Report of a Visit to Colombia, March 12, 1962, Box 319, JFKL; McClintock, *Instruments of Statecraft*, 222–24.

193. Bradley Lynn Coleman, *Colombia and the United States: The Making of an Inter-American Alliance, 1939–1960* (Kent, OH: Kent State University Press, 2008), 199; "Colombia Survey Team Recommendations for U.S. Action," [May 1965?], Collection: Colombia, Item Number: CD00100, Digital National Security Archive; Henry Dearborn to State Department, May 26, 1964, Appendix B, CO File, Latin America, Chile/Colombia, vol. I, Cables, Box 14, LBJL.

194. Richard L. Maullin, *Soldiers, Guerrillas and Politics in Colombia*, R-630-ARPA (Santa Monica, CA: Rand Corporation, December 1971), 52–59.

195. John F. Kennedy, "America's Stake in Vietnam," *Vital Speeches of the Day* 22 (August 1, 1956): 617–19 (quote 618).

196. CIA, President's Intelligence Checklist, November 30, 1961, p. 7, CIA, ERR, https://www.cia.gov/library/readingroom/docs/DOC_0005992060.pdf.

197. Duiker, *U.S. Containment Policy*, 268–81; *FRUS, 1961–1963*, 8:29–30, 49–50, 254–56, 352–55 (quote, 353).

198. *FRUS, 1961–1963*, 9:360.

199. George Herring, *America's Longest War: The United States and Vietnam, 1950–1975*, 4th ed. (Boston: McGraw Hill, 2002), 103.

200. Ibid., 107.

201. *FRUS, 1961–1963*, vol. 2, *Vietnam, 1962* (Washington, DC: GPO, 1990), 546–51 (quote 546).

202. Ibid., 245–50, 303–4, 369, 380, 418 (quote 246).

203. Ibid., 441–45, 454–55, 460–61, 46–68 (quotes 464, 467).

204. Ibid., 459–60, 475–78.

205. *FRUS, 1961–1963*, vol. 1, *Vietnam, 1961* (Washington, DC: GPO, 1990), 234–36.

206. Robert Buzzanco, *Masters of War: Military Dissent and Politics in the Vietnam Era* (New York: Cambridge University Press, 1997), 56–73; *FRUS, 1958–1960*, vol. 1, *Vietnam* (Washington, DC: GPO, 1986), 283–84, 286, 288–90.

207. *FRUS, 1961–1963*, 1:228–29, 236–40, 244–46, 619–28 (quote 622).

208. Ibid., 229, 347–59, 370–72 (quote 423).

209. Herring, *America's Longest War*, 104–9.

210. *FRUS, 1961–1963*, vol. 3, *Vietnam, January-August, 1963* (Washington, DC: GPO, 1991), 3–7, 19–22, 49–62, 118–22 (quotes 50, 118).

211. James M. Carter, *Inventing Vietnam: The United States and State Building, 1954–1968* (New York: Cambridge University Press, 2008), 132–46.

212. *FRUS, 1961–1963*, vol. 4, *Vietnam, August-December, 1963* (Washington, DC: GPO, 1991), 154–55, 418–19.

213. Ibid., 472–73, 554, 566–67, 575–78.

214. Latham, *Modernization as Ideology*, 200–204; *FRUS, 1964–1968*, vol. 1, *Vietnam, 1964* (Washington, DC: GPO, 1992),77.

215. Herring, *America's Longest War*, 138–40; *FRUS, 1964–1968*, 1:153–67, 170–73 (quote 171).

216. *Cold War International History Project Bulletin*, Issue 17/18: *The Global Cuban Missile Crisis at 50: New Evidence from behind the Iron, Bamboo, and Sugarcane Curtains, and Beyond* (Fall 2012), 634 (Adenauer quote).

217. Ibid., 750–52 (quote 756).

218. *PPP: Kennedy, 1961*, 533.

219. Melvyn P. Leffler, *For the Soul of Mankind: The United States, the Soviet Union, and the Cold War* (New York: Hill and Wang, 2007), 182–85; Giauque, *Grand Designs*, 123 (quote).

220. Patrick Iber, *Neither Peace nor Freedom: The Cultural Cold War in Latin America* (Cambridge, MA: Harvard University Press, 2015), chapters 4 and 5.

221. Memoranda by Lansdale, January 22 and February 6, 1964, Peace File, PC 11/22/63-4/30/65, Box 4, LBJL.

222. U.S. Department of State, *Emphasis on Youth: Reaching and Influencing Rising Young Leaders* [1965], 2, Office Files of Harry McPherson, McPherson: Youth Committee (1 of 3), Box 18 [1 of 2], LBJL; Rusk to Chiefs of Mission, April 24, 1962, McPherson Files, McPherson: Youth Committee (2 of 3), ibid.

223. Michael L. Conniff, *Panama and the United States: The Forced Alliance* (Athens: University of Georgia Press, 1992), 120–21.

6. CONTENDING WITH DECLINE

1. Alan Brinkley, *The Publisher: Henry Luce and His American Century* (New York: Alfred A. Knopf, 2010), 444–47 (quote 444).

2. Memorandum (unsigned) for CIA Director Richard Helms, November 8, 1966, National Security File (NSF), Files of Francis M. Bator, Trilaterals - Cables and Miscellaneous, 10/66-5/67 (3 of 4), p. 2, Box 5, Lyndon Baines Johnson Presidential Library (LBJL), Austin, TX.

3. Thomas Alan Schwartz, *Lyndon Johnson and Europe: In the Shadow of Vietnam* (Cambridge, MA: Harvard University Press, 2003), 1–33, 44–50; Randall B. Woods, *LBJ: Architect of American Ambition* (New York: Free Press, 2006), 483–93; Frédéric Bozo, "France, 'Gaullism,' and the Cold War," in *The Cambridge History of the Cold War*, 3 vols., vol. 2, *Crises and Détente*, ed. Melvyn P. Leffler and Odd Arne Westad (New York: Cambridge University Press, 2010), 158–78.

4. U.S. Department of State, *Foreign Relations of the United States, 1964–1968*, vol. 15,: *Germany and Berlin (FRUS, year*, volume) (Washington, DC: Government Printing Office [GPO], 1999), 388–92 (quote 389–90).

5. Johnson to Kurt Kiesinger, March 11, 1967, NSF, Bator Files, Trilaterals - Cables and Miscellaneous, 10/66-5/67 (1 of 4), Box 5, LBJL; *FRUS, 1964–1968*, 15:520; Schwartz, *Lyndon Johnson and Europe*, 152, 169.

6. *FRUS, 1964–1968*, 15:527–40; *FRUS, 1964–1968*, vol. 13, *West Europe Region* (Washington, DC: GPO, 1995): 562–70. Two memos Francis M. Bator, a presidential assistant, wrote when Kiesinger visited Washington in August reveal the upturn in NATO relations; Bator to Johnson, August 11 and 16, 1967, Papers of Francis M. Bator, Subject File, Kiesinger Visit, 8/14-8/16/67, Memoranda for the President, Box 22, LBJL.

7. See James Edward Miller, *The United States and the Making of Modern Greece: History and Power, 1950–1974* (Chapel Hill: University of North Carolina Press, 1974), 106–24 for a survey of major issues from 1963 to 1965; U.S. Embassy, Athens, to State Department, September 5, 1965, NSF, Files of Robert W. Komer, Greece - 1965 Cabinet Crisis (Cables), Box 21, LBJL; Special National Intelligence Estimate (SNIE 29.1-65), "Short-Term Prospects for Greece," September 16, 1965, NSF, National Intelligence Estimates, 29.1 Greece, Box 6, ibid.; Alfred G. Vigderman, U.S. Embassy Counselor, Athens, to State Department, October 8, 1965, NSF, Komer Files, Greece - 1965 Cabinet Crisis (Cables), Box 21, ibid.

8. *FRUS, 1964–1968*, vol. 16, *Cyprus; Greece; Turkey* (Washington, DC: GPO, 2000), 450.

9. Ibid., 528–30, 541–42, 552–55, 611–12; Miller, *United States and the Making of Modern Greece*, 124–32.

10. CIA, President's Daily Brief, April 21, 1967, p. 4, Central Intelligence Agency, Electronic Reading Room (CIA, ERR), https://www.cia.gov/library/readingroom/docs/DOC_0005973762.pdf.

11. John P. Owens, Near Eastern Affairs, State Department, to Harold K. Saunders, NSC Staff, April 27, 1967; Rusk to Johnson, July 21, 1967; and Rostow to Johnson, July 1967; all in NSF, Country (CO) File, Cyprus, Greece, vol. 2: Memos & Misc. (1 of 2), 1/66-7/67, Box 126, LBJL; Miller, *United States and the Making of Modern Greece*, 134–35.

12. Miller, *United States and the Making of Modern Greece*, 151–56; *FRUS, 1964–1968*, 16:751–55.

13. William J. Duiker, *U.S. Containment Policy and the Conflict in Indochina* (Stanford, CA: Stanford University Press, 1994), 249–361.

14. NSAM 314, LBJL, http://www.lbjlib.utexas.edu/johnson/archives.hom/NSAMs/nsam314.asp.

15. Duiker, *U.S. Containment Policy*, 324.

16. The Senator Gravel Edition, *The Pentagon Papers: The Defense Department History of United States Decisionmaking on Vietnam*, 4 vols. (Boston: Beacon Press, 1971), 3: 561–62.

17. David W. P. Elliott, *The Vietnamese War: Revolution and Social Change in the Mekong Delta, 1930–1975*, 2 vols. (Armonk, NY: M. E. Sharp, 2003), 2:736–41.

18. *FRUS, 1964–1968*, vol. 1, *Vietnam, 1964* (Washington, DC: GPO, 1992), 812. Laos became the most heavily bombed nation in history, having had more than two million tons of bombs dropped on it.

19. *FRUS, 1964–1968*, 1:917.

20. George Herring, *America's Longest War: The United States and Vietnam, 1950–1975*, 4th ed. (Boston: McGraw Hill, 2002), 152–65.

21. Harold Wilson, *A Personal Record: The Labour Government, 1964–1970* (Boston: Little, Brown, 1971), 80.

22. Quoted in Robert Buzzanco, *Masters of War: Military Dissent and Politics in the Vietnam Era* (New York: Cambridge University Press, 1996), 223.

23. Lyndon Baines Johnson, *The Vantage Point: Perspectives of the Presidency, 1963–1969* (New York: Holt, Rinehart and Winston, 1971), 22.

24. George McT. Kahin, *Intervention: How America Became Involved in Vietnam* (New York: Alfred A. Knopf, 1986), 324–28. The Mekong River flood-control offer suggests how Johnson perceived the Third World and nonaligned states. As former Senate majority leader, he thought of legislative solutions—like building a dam—to large problems. Such a response, of course, was essentially irrelevant to revolutionary situations. For more on Johnson and nonalignment, see Robert B. Rakove, *Kennedy, Johnson, and the Nonaligned World* (New York: Cambridge University Press, 2013), 55–60.

25. This interpretation differs from those of Jerome Levinson and Juan de Onís, *The Alliance That Lost Its Way: A Critical Report on the Alliance for Progress* (Chicago: Quadrangle Books, 1970), 87–88, and Jeffrey F. Taffet, *Foreign Aid as Foreign Policy: The Alliance for Progress in Latin America* (New York: Routledge, 2007), 47, 59–63.

26. *Public Papers of the Presidents of the United States (PPP): Lyndon Baines Johnson, 1963–1964, Book 1: November 22, 1963 to June 30, 1964* (Washington, DC: GPO, 1964), 6–7; Johnson pledged support for the Alliance for Progress in a meeting on November 26 with Latin American diplomats.

27. Walter LaFeber, *The Panama Canal: The Crisis in Historical Perspective*, updated ed. (New York: Oxford University Press, 1989), 107–13.

28. Woods, *LBJ*, 496–99.

29. *FRUS, 1964–1968*, vol. 31, *South and Central America* (Washington, DC: GPO, 2005), 818–61 (quote 836).

30. Thomas L. Hughes interview, September 7, 1999, p. 183, Library of Congress, Frontline Diplomacy: The Foreign Affairs Oral History Collection of the Association for Diplomatic Studies and Training, https://www.loc.gov/item/mfdipbib001565/. Hughes and the author discussed the Venezuelan matter during an event at the Johnson Library, April 6, 2005.

31. Stephen G. Rabe, *The Most Dangerous Area in the World: John F. Kennedy Confronts Communist Revolution in Latin America* (Chapel Hill: University of North Carolina Press, 1999), 107–8.

32. *FRUS, 1964–1968*, 31:64.

33. Ibid., 153; M. Margaret Ball, *The OAS in Transition* (Durham, NC: Duke University Press, 1969), 480–82.

34. NSF, NSC Meetings, Meeting No. 526, April 3, 1964, Box 1, LBJL; NSF, CO File, Latin America, Thomas Mann to Rusk, May 13, 1964, Box 1, LBJL.

35. *FRUS, 1964–1968*, 31:45. *Time* magazine profiled Mann when Johnson appointed him to his post; see "One Mann and 20 Problems," *Time*, January 31, 1964.

36. Thomas C. Field Jr., *From Development to Dictatorship: Bolivia and the Alliance for Progress in the Kennedy Era* (Ithaca, NY: Cornell University Press, 2014), 159–88.

37. Johnson, *Vantage Point*, 188; CIA Intelligence Memorandum, April 29, 1965, NSF, Gordon Chase Files, Communism in the Dominican Republic, Box 2, LBJL; CIA, Presi-

dent's Daily Brief, April 29, 1965, p. 2, CIA, ERR, https://www.cia.gov/library/readingroom /docs/DOC_0005967651.pdf.

38. Bruce Palmer Jr., *Intervention in the Caribbean: The Dominican Crisis of 1965* (Lexington: University Press of Kentucky, 1989), 69–72.

39. *FRUS, 1964–1968*, vol. 32, *Dominican Republic; Cuba; Haiti; Guyana* (Washington, DC: GPO, 1997), 109–11.

40. Peter Felten, "Yankee, Go Home and Take Me with You: Lyndon Johnson and the Dominican Republic," in *Beyond Vietnam: The Foreign Policies of Lyndon Johnson*, ed. H. W. Brands (College Station: Texas A & M University Press, 1999), 103–15, 118–27; Bundy's comment, 104.

41. "Attitudes of Dominican Youth: A New Political Culture," November 1965, Office Files of Harry McPherson, McPherson: Youth Committee (2 of 3), Box 18 [1 of 2], LBJL; Interagency Youth Committee Meeting, August 31, 1966, ibid.

42. *New York Times*, March 19, 1964. The best study of Mann is Thomas Tunstall Allcock, "Thomas C. Mann and Latin America, 1945–1966" (PhD diss., Sidney Sussex College, University of Cambridge, 2012), chapters 4 and 5; Allcock, "Becoming 'Mr. Latin America': Thomas C. Mann Reconsidered," *Diplomatic History* 38 (November 2014): 1017–45.

43. NSF, CO File, Latin America, Mann to Edwin M. Martin, January 2, 1965, Box 2, LBJL. Covert action and counterinsurgency reflected a mindset built on prior successes in Iran (1953) and Guatemala (1954). Hughes interview, August 25, 1999, p. 91, https://www .loc.gov/item/mfdipbib001565/.

44. Michael T. Klare, *Supplying Repression: U.S. Support for Authoritarian Regimes Abroad* (Washington, DC: Institute for Policy Studies, 1977), 20.

45. Brian Loveman, *For la Patria: Politics and the Armed Forces in Latin America* (Wilmington, DE: Scholarly Resources, 1999), 182–84. Brazil may have originated the National Security Doctrine, though armed forces throughout the Americas had long accepted such a depiction of their role.

46. *FRUS, 1964–1968*, 31:153; Rostow to Johnson, July 6, 1967, NSF, CO File, Latin America, Box 3, LBJL.

47. *FRUS, 1964–1968*, 31:237–41 (quote 240).

48. Gerald E. Thomas, "The Black Revolt: The United States and Africa in the 1960s," in *The Diplomacy of the Crucial Decade: American Foreign Relations during the 1960s*, ed. Diane B. Kunz (New York: Columbia University Press, 1994), 326–27; *FRUS, 1964–1968*, vol. 10, *National Security Policy* (Washington, DC: GPO, 2001), 122–23; *FRUS, 1964–1968*, vol. 24, *Africa* (Washington, DC: GPO, 1999), 274.

49. *FRUS, 1964–1968*, 24:311.

50. *FRUS, 1964–1968*, vol. 21, *Near East Region; Arabian Peninsula* (Washington, DC: GPO, 2000), 635.

51. *FRUS, 1964–1968*, 24:287, 334 (quote 323); Jeremy Kuzmarov, *Modernizing Repression: Police Training and Nation-Building in the American Century* (Amherst: University of Massachusetts Press, 2012), 165–87.

52. Thomas, "The Black Revolt," 335–36; Odd Arne Westad, *The Global Cold War: Third World Interventions and the Making of Our Times* (New York: Cambridge University Press, 2005), 135.

53. *FRUS, 1964–1968*, 24:444–51.

54. Ibid., 457.

55. Lise Namikas, *Battleground Africa: Cold War in the Congo, 1960–1965* (Stanford, CA: Stanford University Press, 2013), 186–217.

56. *FRUS, 1964–1968*, 24:292; Thomas, "The Black Revolt," 332–35.

57. Westad, *Global Cold War*, 140–42.

58. *FRUS, 1964–1968*, 24:328.

59. Thomas, "The Black Revolt," 331.

60. *FRUS, 1964–1968*, 24:297–98, 302; Westad, *Global Cold War*, 254–55.

61. *FRUS, 1964–1968*, 24:590–92, 598–99, 602.

62. Ibid., 819–20.

63. National Intelligence Estimate 70-1-67, Central Intelligence Agency, "The Liberation Movements of Southern Africa," November 24, 1967, p. 15, CK3100295954, Declassified Documents Reference System (DDRS), Gale, Cengage Learning, Farmington Hills, MI.

64. Thomas, "The Black Revolt," 344–45.

65. *FRUS, 1964–1968*, 24:932–37 (quote 937).

66. Ibid., 1101.

67. Thomas, "The Black Revolt," 349.

68. Kenneth Mokoena, ed., *South Africa and the United States: The Declassified History* (New York: New Press, 1993), 198–218 (quote 211).

69. Che Guevara went to Africa in 1965 to revive Cuba's reputation as a model for revolution. His efforts to provide support for liberation movements, notably in Zaire and Angola, were largely unsuccessful. Thomas L. Hughes to Rusk, April 19, 1965, NSF, CO File, Cuba, Personalities, Box 20, LBJL; Piero Gleijeses, *Conflicting Missions: Havana, Washington, and Africa, 1959–1976* (Chapel Hill: University of North Carolina Press, 2002), 133–59.

70. Westad, *Global Cold War*, 134, 210–11; CIA, "Liberation Movements," 8, 13–14; *FRUS, 1964–1968*, 24:741.

71. *FRUS, 1964–1968*, 24:291, 741, 720–21, 770; Westad, *Global Cold War*, 210–13.

72. *FRUS, 1964–1968*, 24:371. Subsequent developments brought little improvement; the climactic struggle for independence began in 1974.

73. Ibid., 378–79.

74. Ibid., 368.

75. Ibid., 372–73.

76. Quoted in Roger Morris, *Uncertain Greatness: Henry Kissinger and American Foreign Policy* (New York: Harper & Row, 1977), 42. Morris was an NSC staff member at the time; he left the NSC after the invasion of Cambodia in April 1970.

77. *FRUS, 1964–1968*, vol. 29, *Korea* (in two parts) (Washington, DC: GPO, 2000), pt. 1: 756, 795.

78. Ibid., 455–58.

79. Ibid., 119–20, 122–24; *FRUS, 1964–1968*, vol. 26, *Indonesia; Malaysia-Singapore; Philippines* (Washington, DC: GPO, 2001), 401–2.

80. *FRUS, 1964–1968*, 26:440–43, 556–57, 564–65.

81. *FRUS, 1964–1968*, vol. 3, *Vietnam, July-December, 1965* (Washington, DC: GPO, 1996), 361, 363.

82. *FRUS, 1964–1968*, vol. 27, *Mainland Southeast Asia; Regional Affairs* (Washington, DC: GPO, 2000), 854–56, 868–69.

83. Ibid., 906.

84. *FRUS, 1961–1963*, vol. 19, *South Asia* (Washington, DC: GPO, 1996), 696–701, 720–30 (quote 730).

85. Dennis Kux, *The United States and Pakistan, 1947–2000: Disenchanted Allies* (Baltimore: Johns Hopkins University Press, 2001), 147–53.

86. *FRUS, 1964–1968*, vol. 25, *South Asia* (Washington, DC: GPO, 2000), 45–46.

87. Ibid., 129. Johnson's briefing on Pakistan for July 1 remains classified; CIA, President's Intelligence Checklist, July 1, 1964, p. 3, CIA, ERR, https://www.cia.gov/library/readingroom/docs/DOC_0005959271.pdf.

88. Robert J. McMahon, *The Cold War on the Periphery: The United States, India and Pakistan* (New York: Columbia University Press, 1994), 317–24.

89. *FRUS, 1964–1968*, 25:227–31, 240–42 (quote 230); Komer to Bundy, May 30, 1965, NSF, Name File, Komer Memos, vol. 1 (2 of 3), Box 6 (1 of 2), LBJL.

90. *FRUS, 1964–1968*, 25:274.

91. Komer to Bundy, August 20, 1965, NSF, Name File, Komer Memos, vol. 1 (1 of 3), Box 6 (1 of 2), LBJL; *FRUS, 1964–1968*, 25:345–46, 372, 375–77 (quote 376).

92. *FRUS, 1964–1968*, 25:461; Kux, *The United States and Pakistan*, 165, 168–69.

93. *FRUS, 1964–1968*, 25:638.

94. William O. Walker III, "The Johnson-Nixon-Castro Years: Superpower Containment of Cuba," in *Fifty Years of Revolution: Perspectives on Cuba, the United States, and the World*, ed. Soraya M. Castro Mariño and Ronald W. Pruessen (Gainesville: University Press of Florida, 2012), 208–9.

95. Komer memo to Johnson, June 16, 1965, NSF, Name File, Komer Memos, vol. 1 (2 of 3), Box 6 (1 of 2), LBJL.

96. *FRUS, 1964–1968*, vol. 34, *Energy Diplomacy and Global Issues* (Washington, DC: GPO, 1999), 419; on ARAMCO and economic development in Saudi Arabia, see Sarah Yizraeli, *Politics and Society in Saudi Arabia: The Crucial Years of Development, 1960–1982* (New York: Columbia University Press, 2012), 31–65.

97. Douglas Little, *American Orientalism: The United States and the Middle East since 1945*, 3rd ed. (Chapel Hill: University of North Carolina Press, 2008), 63–64.

98. *FRUS, 1964–1968*, vol. 22, *Iran* (Washington, DC: GPO, 1999), 113–14.

99. Ibid., 262–65, 283–84, 371–72 (quote 371).

100. Ibid., 262; Little, *American Orientalism*, 60–62.

101. *FRUS, 1964–1968*, 22:384.

102. Little, *American Orientalism*, 185–87.

103. *FRUS, 1964–1968*, 21:44–48; *FRUS, 1964–1968*, vol. 18, *Arab-Israeli Dispute, 1964–1967* (Washington, DC: GPO, 2001), 773 (quote).

104. *FRUS, 1964–1968*, vol. 20, *Arab-Israeli Dispute, 1967–1968* (Washington, DC: GPO, 2001), 463–64 (quote 578).

105. Warren Bass, *Support Any Friend: Kennedy's Middle East and the Making of the U.S.-Israel Alliance* (New York: Oxford University Press, 2003), 186–238.

106. See, for example, *FRUS, 1964–1968*, vol. 19, *Arab-Israeli Crisis and War, 1967* (Washington, DC: GPO, 2004), 456, 478, which lends support to this interpretation.

107. Douglas Little, "A Fool's Errand: America and the Middle East, 1961–1969," in Kunz, *Diplomacy of the Crucial Decade*, 307.

108. Ibid., 307–10.

109. Matthew Evangelista, *Unarmed Forces: The Transnational Movement to End the Cold War* (Ithaca, NY: Cornell University Press, 1999), 212–13, 223–30; Anatoly Dobrynin, *In Confidence: Moscow's Ambassador to America's Six Cold War Presidents (1962–1986)* (New York: Crown, 1995), 162–67.

110. The air war accounts in part for the increasing cost of the Vietnam War. The large gap in cost estimates reflects Washington's ignorance about the actual outlay for the war. Gabriel Kolko, *Anatomy of a War: Vietnam, the United States, and the Modern Historical Experience* (New York: Pantheon, 1985), 283–88.

111. Diane B. Kunz, *Butter and Guns: America's Cold War Economic Diplomacy* (New York: Free Press, 1997), 108–10; David P. Calleo, *The Imperious Economy* (Cambridge, MA: Harvard University Press, 1982), 25–28.

112. Kunz, *Butter and Guns*, 114–15, tables 6-2 and 6-1; Schwartz, *Lyndon Johnson and Europe*, 64; U.S. Bureau of the Census, *Statistical Abstract of the United States, 1970* (Washington, DC: GPO, 1970), 764.

113. Fred L. Block, *The Origins of International Economic Disorder: A Study of United States International Monetary Policy from World War II to the Present* (Berkeley: University of California Press, 1977), 160, table 7.

114. Francis J. Gavin, *Gold, Dollars, and Power: The Politics of International Monetary Relations, 1958–1971* (Chapel Hill: University of North Carolina Press, 2004), 120–25; *FRUS, 1964–1968*, vol. 8, *International Monetary and Trade Policy* (Washington, DC: GPO, 1998), 71–72, 137.

115. *FRUS, 1964–1968*, vol. 12, *Western Europe* (Washington, DC: GPO, 2001), 91–92.

116. Ibid., 480–83; Under Secretary of the Treasury Frederick L. Deming to Secretary of the Treasury C. Douglas Dillon, March 9, 1965, Bator Papers, Subject File, UK, 1965, Box 22, LBJL.

117. *FRUS, 1964–1968*, 8: 171–77 (quotes 172, 173).

118. Ibid., 176.

119. *FRUS, 1964–1968*, 8:199.

120. Quoted in Richard N. Goodwin, *Remembering America: A Voice from the Sixties* (Boston: Little, Brown, 1988), 283.

121. *FRUS, 1964–1968*, 15:345–49, 352–54, 386–89 (quote 348).

122. Schwartz, *Lyndon Johnson and Europe*, 115–17.

123. *FRUS, 1964–1968*, 12:539–43 (quote 540).

124. *FRUS, 1964–1968*, 8:291.

125. Federal Reserve System, Division of International Finance, "Contingency Planning - Sterling," September 21, 1966, Bator Papers, Subject File, Contingency Planning - Sterling, Box 8, LBJL.

126. *FRUS, 1964–1968*, 8:299–30 (quote 301); Schwartz, *Lyndon Johnson and Europe*, 117–21.

127. Schwartz, *Lyndon Johnson and Europe*, 117–29; *FRUS, 1964–1968*, 13:471–77.

128. *FRUS, 1964–1968*, 13:471–77; *FRUS, 1964–1968*, 15:435.

129. Schwartz, *Lyndon Johnson and Europe*, 131–33.

130. *FRUS, 1964–1968*, 15:447.

131. *FRUS, 1964–1968*, 8:304–5; Calleo, *Imperious Economy*, 48–51.

132. Richard N. Gardner, "Economic Aspects of the Cold War, 1962–1975," in Leffler and Westad, *Cambridge History of the Cold War*, 2:59.

133. *FRUS, 1964–1968*, 8:352; Block, *Origins of International Economic Disorder*, 191–93; Calleo, *Imperious Economy*, 46–56.

134. *FRUS, 1964–1968*, 8:395.

135. "The Gold Crisis," NSF, National Security Council Histories, Gold Crisis, November 1967 - March 1968, Book I, Tabs 1–18, Box 53, LBJL; Gavin, *Gold, Dollars, and Power*, 165–71; Schwartz, *Lyndon Johnson and Europe*, 191–93.

136. Schwartz, *Lyndon Johnson and Europe*, 188–89.

137. The membership included the United States, Great Britain, West Germany, France, Italy, Belgium, the Netherlands, Sweden, Canada, and Japan.

138. *FRUS, 1964–1968*, 8:440, 447.

139. Ibid., 451–53.

140. Ibid., 456. On the decline of the postwar economic system and the rise of globalization, see Daniel Sargent, "Lyndon Johnson and the Challengers of Economic Globalization," in *Beyond the Cold War: Lyndon Johnson and the New Global Challenges of the 1960s*, ed. Francis J. Gavin and Mark Atwood Lawrence (New York: Oxford University Press, 2014), 17–43.

141. Gavin, *Gold, Dollars, and Power*, chapter 7.

142. *FRUS, 1964–1968*, 8:487, 507, 919–20.

143. Ibid., 471 (quotes 481, 482).

144. Robert M. Collins, "The Economic Crisis of 1968 and the Waning of the American Century," *American Historical Review* 101 (April 1996): 398.

145. *FRUS, 1964–1968*, 8:501.

146. CIA, Directorate of Intelligence, "French Actions in the Recent Gold Crisis," March 20, 1968, CIA, ERR, https://www.cia.gov/library/readingroom/docs/DOC _0000118650.pdf.

147. Calleo, *Imperious Economy*, 56–57, 235 n. 22.

148. *FRUS, 1964–1968*, 8:513; Fowler also quoted in Rostow to Johnson, March 14, 1968, NSF, National Security Council Histories, Gold Crisis, November 1967 - March 1968, Book I, Tabs 50–53, Box 53, LBJL.

149. *FRUS, 1964–1968*, 8:545.

150. Ibid., 559–70 (quote 562).

151. Ibid., 585–86, 600 (quote 578); Robert Solomon, *The International Monetary System: An Insider's View* (New York: Harper & Row, 1977), 155–61.

152. *FRUS, 1964–1968*, 8:602–10; Solomon, *International Monetary System*, 162–63.

153. David Milne, *America's Rasputin: Walt Rostow and the Vietnam War* (New York: Hill and Wang, 2008), 161–69.

154. *FRUS, 1964–1968*, 1:416–17; *FRUS, 1964–1968*, vol. 2, *Vietnam, January-June 1965* (Washington, DC: GPO, 1996), 409.

155. *FRUS, 1964–1968*, 2:721–24, 734–35 (quote 723); *FRUS, 1964–1968*, 3:205.

156. *PPP: Lyndon B. Johnson, 1965*, Book 1, *January 1, 1965 to June 30, 1965* (Washington, DC: GPO, 1966), 394–99; David Ekbladh, *The Great American Mission: Modernization and the Construction of an American World Order* (Princeton, NJ: Princeton University Press, 2009), 207–12.

157. James M. Carter, *Inventing Vietnam: The United States and State Building, 1954–1968* (New York: Cambridge University Press, 2008), 165–72; William J. Duiker, *Sacred War: Nationalism and Revolution in a Divided Vietnam* (New York: McGraw Hill, 1995), 173–75; *FRUS, 1964–1968*, 2:555–56, 562–63, 577–81 (quote 547).

158. Christopher T. Fisher, "The Illusion of Progress: CORDS and the Crisis of Modernization in South Vietnam, 1965–1968," *Pacific Historical Review* 75 (February 2006): 25–51.

159. *FRUS, 1964–1968*, vol. 4, *Vietnam, 1966* (Washington, DC: GPO, 1998), 227–28, 246–55 (quotes 218, 219).

160. Ibid., 419–20, 475–76, 609 n. 1, 672–77, 746–52 (quote 673); Daniel Ellsberg, *Papers on the War* (New York: Simon and Schuster, 1972), 156–70.

161. Carter, *Inventing Vietnam*, 210–12; Fisher, "Illusion of Progress," 37–40.

162. *FRUS, 1964–1968*, vol. 5, *Vietnam, 1967* (Washington, DC: GPO, 2002), 67–69, 584–87 (quotes 584, 585).

163. Ibid., 862.

164. Fisher, "Illusion of Progress," 43–45; *FRUS, 1964–1968*, 5:968; Ekbladh, *Great American Mission*, 217–18; Buzzanco, *Masters of War*, chapter 10; Milne, *America's Rasputin*, 213–15.

165. *FRUS, 1964–1968*, vol. 6, *Vietnam, January-August 1968* (Washington, DC: GPO, 2002), 875–82.

166. Bradley R. Simpson, *Economists with Guns: Authoritarian Development and U.S.-Indonesian Relations, 1960–1968* (Stanford, CA: Stanford University Press, 2008).

167. Ibid., 82–86; "Report of Civic Action Team to Indonesia," October 25, 1962, DDRS, CK3100495456.

168. Komer to McGeorge Bundy, July 7, 1965, NSF, Name File, Komer Memos, vol. 1 (2 of 3), Box 6 (1 of 2), LBJL; Simpson, *Economists with Guns*, 145–70 (quote 163).

169. Simpson, *Economists with Guns*, 171–206; *FRUS, 1964–1968*, 26:320, 323, 325, 329–33, 361–63 (quote 363).

170. Simpson, *Economists with Guns*, 191; *FRUS, 1964–1968*, 26:390–92, 419–21 (quote 419).

171. *FRUS, 1964–1968*, 26:449–57, 459–62, 465–74 (quote 477); NSF, NSC Meetings File, NSC Meetings, vol. 4: Tab 45, 8/4/66 - Indonesia, Box 2, LBJL.

172. *FRUS, 1964–1968*, 26:483.

173. NSF, NSC Meetings File, NSC Meetings, vol. 4: Tab 55, 8/9/67 - Indonesia, Box 2, LBJL (first quote); *FRUS, 1964–1968*, 26:537–38 (second quote 538 n. 6).

174. Simpson, *Economists with Guns*, 246–48; *FRUS, 1964–1968*, 26:557–59, 562–76 (quote 574).

175. Nick Cullather, *The Hungry World: America's Cold War Battle against Poverty in Asia* (Cambridge, MA: Harvard University Press, 2010), 206–15; *FRUS, 1964–1968*, 26:274, 483.

176. Cullather, *Hungry World*, 222–27; *FRUS, 1964–1968*, 26:579–81, 596–97, 764–65.

177. *FRUS, 1964–1968*, 26: 852–54, 882–84; Cullather, *Hungry World*, 228–30.

178. *FRUS, 1964–1968*, 26:1002–3, 1015–16, 1035–36 (quote 1015).

179. NIE 60/70-65, "Problems and Prospects in Sub-Saharan Africa," April 22, 1965, *FRUS, 1964–1968*, 24:297.

180. Ibid., 300–303, 306–7, 313–14 (quote 307).

181. Ibid., 308–15 (quote 311).

182. Ibid., 320–23, 330–49 (quote 340).

183. Ibid., 352–54, 362–63, 366–75, 404–6 (quote 404).

184. Levinson and de Onís, *Alliance That Lost Its Way*; Taffet, *Foreign Aid as Foreign Policy*; Rabe, *Most Dangerous Area in the World*, 148–72.

185. "U.S. Contributions to Alliance for Progress, March 13, 1961-January 31, 1964," Agency File, Alliance for Progress I, Box 4, LBJL.

186. Memorandum for McGeorge Bundy, November 3, 1964, Agency File, Alliance for Progress II, Box 5, LBJL; AID memorandum for McGeorge Bundy, October 29, 1965, ibid.

187. Levinson and de Onís, *Alliance That Lost Its Way*, 83.

188. Michael E. Latham, *The Right Kind of Revolution: Modernization, Development, and U.S. Foreign Policy from the Cold War to the Present* (Ithaca, NY: Cornell University Press, 2011), 131–33; Penny Lernoux, *Cry of the People: United States Involvement in the Rise of Fascism, Torture, and Murder and the Persecution of the Catholic Church in Latin America* (Garden City, NY: Doubleday, 1980), 285; CIA Intelligence Memorandum, "Guatemala: The Problem of Poverty," May 1968, CO File, Latin America, El Salvador-Guatemala, Guatemala Cables, vol. II, 1/66-11/68, Box 54, LBJL.

189. CIA Survey, April 1, 1964, pp. 121–22, CO File, Latin America, vol. I, Box 1, LBJL; Hughes to Rusk, October 23, 1967, CO File, Latin America, El Salvador-Guatemala, Guatemala Cables, vol. II, 1/66-11/68, Box 54, LBJL; Kennedy had named Hughes director of the Bureau of Intelligence and Research in April 1963.

190. Greg Grandin, *The Last Colonial Massacre: Latin America in the Cold War* (Chicago: University of Chicago Press, 2004), 95–100; Walter LaFeber, *Inevitable Revolutions: The United States in Central America*, 2nd ed. rev. and enlarged (New York: W. W. Norton, 1993), 166–73.

191. CIA, "Survey of Latin America," April 1, 1964, p. 1, CO File, Latin America, Vol. I, Box 1, LBJL.

192. *FRUS, 1964–1968*, 31:96–99 (quotes 97, 98).

193. William G. Bowdler memorandum for Walt W. Rostow, July 5, 1967, Intelligence File, Guerrilla Problem in Latin America, Box 2, LBJL; Military Assistance Program overview, [July 1967?], ibid.; Public Safety situation overview, [July 1967?], ibid; Kuzmarov, *Modernizing Repression*, 208–31.

194. Rostow to Johnson, June 24, 1967, Intelligence File, Guerrilla Problem in Latin America, Box 2, LBJL.

195. Kenneth D. Lehman, *Bolivia and the United States: A Limited Partnership* (Athens: University of Georgia Press, 1999), 138–46, 152–56.

196. Hughes to Rusk, May 24, 1965, CO File, Latin America, Bolivia, vol. VIII, Memos 12/64-9/65, Box 8, LBJL; CIA Intelligence Memorandum, "Situation in Bolivia," May 26, 1965, ibid.; State Department Report, "Bolivia," June 15, 1965, ibid.

197. *FRUS, 1964–1968*, 31:363–69.

198. Bowdler memorandum, June 29, 1967, CO File, Latin America, Bolivia, vol. IV, Memos 1/66-12/68, Box 8, LBJL.

199. *FRUS, 1964–1968*, 31:381–86.

200. CIA, "Survey of Latin America," April 1, 1964, p. 59, CO File, Latin America, vol. I, Box 1, LBJL.

201. James F. Rochlin, *Vanguard Revolutionaries in Latin America: Peru, Colombia, Mexico* (Boulder, CO: Lynne Rienner, 2003), 94–99, 102–3 (quote 95).

202. Dearborn to State Department, April 25, 1964, CO File, Latin America, Chile/Colombia, vol. I, Cables, Box 14, LBJL; Covey T. Oliver to State Department, October 20, 1964, ibid.

203. Benjamin H. Reed to Walt Rostow, September 15, 1966, ibid.; Gaud to Johnson, April 18, 1967, CO File, Latin America, Colombia/Costa Rica, vol. III, Memos, Box 15, ibid.

204. Hughes to Rusk, June 15, 1968, CO File, Latin America, Colombia/Costa Rica, vol. III, Memos, Box 15, LBJL; and "Colombia: One Year under President Lleras," August 18, 1967, p. 6, CIA, ERR, https://www.cia.gov/library/readingroom/docs/DOC_0000513768 Lleras Colombia.pdf.

205. CIA, "Survey of Latin America," April 1, 1964, pp. 191, 194, CO File, Latin America, vol. I, Box 1, LBJL.

206. Rochlin, *Vanguard Revolutionaries*, 29–33; Deborah Poole and Gerardo Rénique, *Peru: Time of Fear* (London: Latin American Bureau, 1992), 30–32; *FRUS, 1964–1968*, 31:74–77, 990.

207. *FRUS, 1964–1968*, 31:995, 1001–8; CIA, "Survey of Latin America," April 1, 1964, p. 193, CO File, Latin America, vol. I, Box 1, LBJL.

208. *FRUS, 1964–1968*, 31:1009–12, 1014.

209. Ibid., 1020.

210. Ibid., 1034–35, 1038–39, 1050–51, 1057–59.

211. Ibid., 1059 n. 3, 1068–69, 1077–78; Poole and Rénique, *Peru*, 31.

212. Gravel Edition, *Pentagon Papers*, 2: 336; Johnson, *Vantage Point*, 152.

213. *FRUS, 1964–1968*, 3:138.

214. Ibid., 110–13, 195 (quote 111); Duiker, *U.S. Containment Policy*, 311.

215. *FRUS, 1964–1968*, 3:230, 644–45, 749–51; Wilson, *Personal Record*, 79, 191–92, 247–48; Schwartz, *Lyndon Johnson and Europe*, 75, 79–80, 85–91.

216. *FRUS, 1964–1968*, 3:758.

217. Ilya V. Gaiduk, *The Soviet Union and the Vietnam War* (Chicago: Ivan R. Dee, 1996), 20–27, 35–56; *FRUS, 1964–1968*, vol. 14, *Soviet Union* (Washington, DC: GPO, 2001), 233–35, 243 n. 2 (quote), 244–49, 302.

218. *FRUS, 1964–1968*, 14:306–15 (quote 306).

219. Randall Bennett Woods, *Fulbright: A Biography* (New York: Cambridge University Press, 1995), 324–25 (quote 476). Columns suggestive of Lippmann's thinking about Vietnam are in the *Washington Post*, August 6, 1964; February 18, 1965; April 13, 1965; July 30, 1965; September 30, 1965; and December 21, 1965 (quote).

220. *PPP: Johnson, 1965*, Book I: 394–99 (quote 395).

221. Tom Wells, *The War Within: America's Battle over Vietnam* (Berkeley: University of California Press, 1994), 19–38; Carl Oglesby, *Ravens in the Storm: A Personal History of*

the 1960s Antiwar Movement (New York: Scribner, 2008), 93–97; David W. Levy, *The Debate over Vietnam*, 2nd ed. (Baltimore: Johns Hopkins University Press, 1995), 135.

222. Volker R. Berghahn, *America and the Intellectual Cold Wars in Europe: Shepard Stone between Philanthropy, Academy, and Diplomacy* (Princeton, NJ: Princeton University Press, 2001), 241–49; Martin Klimke, *The Other Alliance: Student Protest in West Germany and the United States in the Global Sixties* (Princeton, NJ: Princeton University Press, 2010), chapters 1–4; Interagency Youth Committee Meeting, August 31, 1966, Office Files of Harry McPherson, McPherson: Youth Committee (2 of 3), Box 18 [1 of 2], LBJL.

223. "Airlie House Conference on European Youth and Young Leaders," May 14–15, 1967 (quote 3), McPherson Files, McPherson: Youth Committee (3 of 3), Box 18 [1 of 2], LBJL; Klimke, *Other Alliance*, 221; Alessandro Brogi, *Confronting America: The Cold War between the United States and the Communists in France and Italy* (Chapel Hill: University of North Carolina Press, 2011), 207–9, 269.

224. On the global phenomenon that was 1968, see Carole Fink, Philipp Gassert, and Detlef Junker, eds., *1968: The World Transformed* (New York: Cambridge University Press, 1998); "*AHR* Forum: The International 1968, Part I," *American Historical Review* 114 (February 2009): 42–135; "*AHR* Forum: The International 1968, Part II," *American Historical Review* 114 (April 2009): 329–404.

225. Department of State circular telegram to U.S. diplomatic posts [summer 1968], Confidential File, WE/MC, WE 8 Youth Programs, Box 98, LBJL; Hughes to Rusk, September 12, 1968, ibid.; William Marotti, "Japan 1968: The Performance of Violence and the Theater of Protest," *American Historical Review* 114 (February 2009): 97–137.

226. CIA, "Restless Youth," September 1968, NSF, Files of Walt W. Rostow, Youth and Student Movements - CIA report, Box 13, LBJL; Cabinet Papers, Cabinet Meeting, September 18, 1968 [1 of 3], Box 15, ibid.

227. *PPP: Lyndon B. Johnson, 1964*, Book II, *July 1, 1964 to December 31, 1964* (Washington, DC: GPO, 1965), 927.

228. Levy, *Debate over Vietnam*, 131; Hans J. Morgenthau, *Truth and Power: Essays of a Decade, 1960–1970* (New York: Frederick A. Praeger, 1970), 170.

229. Levy, *Debate over Vietnam*, 136–46.

230. John Baylis, *Anglo-American Defence Relations 1939–1980: The Special Relationship* (New York: St. Martin's Press, 1981), 93–97.

231. Schwartz, *Lyndon Johnson and Europe*, 227–35. Our analyses of the effect of Vietnam on U.S.-European relations vary slightly in emphasis. "The war hurt the image of the United States in Europe . . . ," Schwartz writes, "[yet] political leaders still cooperated with U.S. policies they perceived to be in their interest and opposed those they did not" (235).

232. *FRUS, 1964–1968*, 12:722 (Martin quote); Schwartz, *Lyndon Johnson and Europe*, 229–30.

233. *FRUS, 1964–1968*, 12:147–49.

234. NSF, National Security Council Histories, Gold Crisis, November 1967-March 1968, "The Gold Crisis," Box 53, Book I, Tabs 1–18, LBJL; Wilson, *Personal Record*, 451–61.

235. NSF, National Security Council Histories, Gold Crisis, November 1967-March 1968, "The Gold Crisis," Box 53, Book I, Tabs 1–18, LBJL.

236. NSF, National Security Council Histories, Gold Crisis, November 1967-March 1968, Box 53, Book I, Tabs 50–53, LBJL.

7. ATTAINING PRIMACY

1. Nixon's chief interest in foreign policy was to "restore America's global primacy." See Robert G. Kaiser, "The Disaster of Richard Nixon," *New York Review of Books*, April 21, 2016, pp. 56, 58–60 (quote 58).

2. Bruce Kuklick, *Blind Oracles: Intellectuals and War from Kennan to Kissinger* (Princeton, NJ: Princeton University Press, 2006), 189.

3. Henry Kissinger, *White House Years* (Boston: Little, Brown, 1979), 229.

4. Anatoly Dobrynin, *In Confidence: Moscow's Ambassador to America's Six Cold War Presidents (1962–1986)* (New York: Crown, 1995), 194–95 (quote 195).

5. Henry Kissinger, *Years of Upheaval* (Boston: Little, Brown, 1982), 245.

6. U.S. Department of State, *Foreign Relations of the United States, 1969–1976*, vol. 1, *Foundations of Foreign Policy, 1969–1972 (FRUS, year,* volume) (Washington, DC: Government Printing Office [GPO], 2003), 120 n. 11.

7. See Barbara Keys, "Henry Kissinger: The Emotional Statesman," *Diplomatic History* 35 (September 2011): 587–609 for an insightful analysis of Kissinger, cognition, and emotion.

8. William O. Walker III, *National Security and Core Values in American History* (New York: Cambridge University Press, 2009), 167 ff.

9. Jeremi Suri, *Henry Kissinger and the American Century* (Cambridge, MA: Belknap Press of Harvard University Press, 2007), 204.

10. *FRUS, 1969–1976,* 1:24.

11. Margaret MacMillan, *Nixon and Mao: The Week That Changed the World* (New York: Random House, 2007).

12. *FRUS, 1969–1976,* vol. 30, *China* (Washington, DC: GPO, 1998), 638–39, 645, 656–57, 662–65.

13. William Bundy, *A Tangled Web: The Making of Foreign Policy in the Nixon Presidency* (New York: Hill and Wang, 1998), 100–110; Richard M. Nixon, "Asia after Vietnam," *Foreign Affairs* 46 (October 1967): 111–25 (quote 121).

14. David Milne, *Worldmaking: The Art and Science of American Diplomacy* (New York: Farrar, Straus and Giroux, 2015), 14; Milne writes that credibility was a "foreign-policy value that Kissinger revered above all others."

15. Kissinger, *White House Years,* 765.

16. Dobrynin, *In Confidence,* 235–38; *FRUS, 1961–1963,* vol. 19, *South Asia* (Washington, DC: GPO, 1996), 369–73.

17. Gary J. Bass, *The Blood Telegram: Nixon, Kissinger, and a Forgotten Genocide* (New York: Alfred A. Knopf, 2013). The "Blood telegram," sent to the State Department by Consul General Archer Blood on March 28, 1971, is found in *FRUS, 1969–1976,* vol. E-7, *Documents on South Asia, 1969–1972,* Document 125, https://history.state.gov/historical documents/frus1969-76ve07/d125.

18. CIA, President's Daily Brief, December 5, 1971, p. 2, Central Intelligence Agency, Electronic Reading Room (CIA, ERR), https://www.cia.gov/library/readingroom/docs /DOC_0005993012.pdf. Nixon likely paid less attention to the daily briefs than to Kissinger's cover memos.

19. *FRUS, 1969–1976,* vol. 11, *South Asia Crisis, 1971* (Washington, DC: GPO, 2005), 264–66, 323–29 (quote 499).

20. Ibid., 632–47, 779–83; Bundy, *Tangled Web,* 269–92.

21. Dobrynin, *In Confidence,* 242.

22. Bundy, *Tangled Web,* 322–27.

23. Walker, *National Security and Core Values,* 169–73.

24. Quoted in James Mann, *Rise of the Vulcans: The History of Bush's War Cabinet* (New York: Viking, 2004), 16; Robert Bothwell, "Thanks for the Fish: Nixon, Kissinger, and Canada," in *Nixon in the World: American Foreign Relations, 1969–1977,* ed. Fredrik Logevall and Andrew Preston (New York: Oxford University Press, 2008), 309–11.

25. *FRUS, 1969–1976,* 1:29.

26. Ibid., 140–41 (quote 176); William Burr and Jeffrey P. Kimball, *Nixon's Nuclear Specter: The Secret Alert of 1969, Madman Diplomacy, and the Vietnam War* (Lawrence: University Press of Kansas, 2015).

27. Douglas Little, *American Orientalism: The United States and the Middle East since 1945*, 3rd ed. (Chapel Hill: University of North Carolina Press, 2008), 105–6; *FRUS, 1969–1976*, vol. 24, *Middle East Region and Arabian Peninsula, 1969–1972; Jordan, September 1970* (Washington, DC: GPO, 2008), 875–78, 891, 914–15.

28. Nixon White House Tapes Online, Tape 866, Conversation 16, March 1973, Richard M. Nixon Presidential Library and Museum (RMNL), Yorba Linda, CA, http://www.nixonlibrary.gov/forresearchers/find/tapes/tape866/tape866.php.

29. *New York Times*, August 9, 1968.

30. Kissinger, *White House Years*, 81, 84.

31. *FRUS, 1969–1976*, 1:73.

32. The issue of consultation suffused relations with European allies during Nixon's presidency; Luke A. Nichter, *Richard Nixon and Europe: The Reshaping of the Postwar Atlantic World* (New York: Cambridge University Press, 2015).

33. Thomas A. Schwartz and Matthias Schulz, introduction to *The Strained Alliance: U.S.-European Relations from Nixon to Carter*, ed. Matthias Schulz and Thomas A. Schwartz (New York: Cambridge University Press, 2010), 9; Kissinger, *White House Years*, 381, 405–12.

34. *FRUS, 1969–1976*, vol. 40, *Germany and Berlin, 1969–1972* (Washington, DC: GPO, 2007), 34–35, 722.

35. Gottfried Niedhart, "U.S. Détente and West German *Ostpolitik*: Parallels and Frictions," in Schulz and Schwartz, *Strained Alliance*, 40.

36. Tony Judt, *Postwar: A History of Europe since 1945* (New York: Penguin Press, 2005), 497–502; Jussi Hannimäki, "Détente in Europe, 1962–1975," in *The Cambridge History of the Cold War*, 3 vols., vol. 2, *Crises and Détente*, ed. Melvyn P. Leffler and Odd Arne Westad (New York: Cambridge University Press, 2010), 198–218.

37. At the time of the USSR's invasion of Czechoslovakia in August 1968, the Warsaw Pact adopted a resolution, the Brezhnev Doctrine, authorizing the use of force in any Communist country where socialism was allegedly under attack; Judt, *Postwar*, 443–46.

38. Bernd Schaefer, "The Nixon Administration and West German *Ostpolitik*, 1969–1973," in Schulz and Schwartz, *Strained Alliance*, 58–62; Mary Elise Sarotte, "The Frailties of Grand Strategies: A Comparison of Détente and Ostpolitik," in Logevall and Preston, *Nixon in the World*, 146–63.

39. Lewis Sorley, *Arms Transfers under Nixon: A Policy Analysis* (Lexington: University Press of Kentucky, 1983), 5–21.

40. Little, *American Orientalism*, 189–91, 242–43; Kissinger, *White House Years*, 1258.

41. Sorely, *Arms Transfers under Nixon*, 194; Rachel Bronson, *Thicker Than Oil: America's Uneasy Partnership with Saudi Arabia* (New York: Oxford University Press, 2006), 117–28.

42. Fredrik Logevall and Andrew Preston, "Introduction: The Adventurous Journey of Nixon in the World," in Logevall and Preston, *Nixon in the World*, 3.

43. For trade figures, see Fred L. Block, *The Origins of International Economic Disorder: A Study of United States International Monetary Policy from World War II to the Present* (Berkeley: University of California Press, 1977), 145.

44. *FRUS, 1964–1968*, vol. 8, *International Monetary and Trade Policy* (Washington, DC: GPO, 1998), 414–15, 454–55, 461–65, 571–72; on patterns of investment, see Jeffrey A. Frieden, *Global Capitalism: Its Fall and Rise in the Twentieth Century* (New York: W. W. Norton, 2006), 292–96.

45. *FRUS, 1964–1968*, vol. 14, *Soviet Union* (Washington, DC: GPO, 2001), 322–23, 635–36 (quote 636); *FRUS, 1964–1968*, 8:181.

46. Francis J. Gavin, *Gold, Dollars, and Power: The Politics of International Monetary Relations, 1958–1971* (Chapel Hill: University of North Carolina Press, 2004), 184–85.

47. Campbell Craig and Fredrik Logevall, *America's Cold War: The Politics of Insecurity* (Cambridge, MA: Belknap Press of Harvard University Press, 2009), 252–64; Kuklick, *Blind Oracles*, 192–202.

48. On brinksmanship, see Francis J. Gavin, "Nuclear Nixon: Ironies, Puzzles, and the Triumph of Realpolitik," in Logevall and Preston, *Nixon in the World*, 136–38.

49. Joan Hoff, *Nixon Reconsidered* (New York: Basic Books, 1994), 138–44, 166–69.

50. Nixon quoted in *FRUS, 1969–1976*, 1:205, 206; *FRUS, 1969–1976*, vol. 3, *Foreign Economic Policy; International Monetary Policy, 1969–1972* (Washington, DC: GPO, 2001), 37–39, 42–43; Gavin, *Gold, Dollars, and Power*, 187 (Connally quote).

51. Allen J. Matusow, *Nixon's Economy: Booms, Busts, Dollars, and Votes* (Lawrence: University Press of Kansas, 1998), 55–83.

52. Thomas W. Zeiler, "Nixon Shocks Japan, Inc.," in Logevall and Preston, *Nixon in the World*, 289–93.

53. Robert Solomon, *The International Monetary System: An Insider's View* (New York: Harper & Row, 1977), 161–65, 173.

54. *FRUS, 1969–1976*, 3:85.

55. Gavin, *Gold, Dollars, and Power*, 192–93; Solomon, *International Monetary System*, 179; *FRUS, 1969–1976*, 3:433 (quote).

56. *FRUS, 1969–1976*, 3:433.

57. Ibid., 438, 440–45.

58. *FRUS, 1969–1976*, 1:323–24 (quote 323).

59. *Public Papers of the Presidents of the United States (PPP): Richard Nixon, 1971* (Washington, DC: GPO, 1972), 886–91 (quote 888).

60. *FRUS, 1969–1976*, 3:466–67; Matusow, *Nixon's Economy*, 149–53; Zeiler, "Nixon Shocks Japan, Inc.," 294–99.

61. *FRUS, 1969–1976*, vol. 4, *Foreign Assistance, International Development, Trade Policies, 1969–1972* (Washington, DC: GPO, 2002), 481.

62. Zeiler, "Nixon Shocks Japan, Inc.," 294–96; *FRUS, 1969–1976*, 4:638–39.

63. *FRUS, 1969–1976*, 3:468.

64. Ibid., 471–72, 479–84.

65. Solomon, *International Monetary System*, 188–90.

66. Ibid., 192–201; *FRUS, 1969–1976*, 3:561–66.

67. *FRUS, 1969–1976*, 3:599–601; Joanne S. Gowa, *Closing the Gold Window: Domestic Politics and the End of Bretton Woods* (Ithaca, NY: Cornell University Press, 1983); *PPP: Nixon, 1971*, 1195–96.

68. Kissinger, *White House Years*, 961–62 (quote 961).

69. C. Fred Bergsten, *Reforming the Dollar: An International Monetary Policy for the United States* (New York: Council on Foreign Relations, 1972), 16, 7.

70. Solomon, *International Monetary System*, 216–34; Block, *Origins of International Economic Disorder*, 198–99.

71. C. Fred Bergsten, *Toward a New International Economic Order: Selected Papers of C. Fred Bergsten, 1972–1974* (Lexington, MA: Lexington Books, 1975), 201; Saburo Okita, "Natural Resource Dependency and Japanese Foreign Policy," *Foreign Affairs* 52 (July 1974): 714–24.

72. Kissinger, *White House Years*, 1269–71.

73. Julian E. Zelizer, *Arsenal of Democracy: The Politics of National Security—from World War II to the War on Terrorism* (New York: Basic Books, 2010), 246–49; Dobrynin, *In Confidence*, 266–70 (quote 159).

74. William Burr, ed., *The Kissinger Transcripts: The Top-Secret Talks with Moscow and Beijing* (New York: New Press, 1998), 225.

75. *FRUS, 1964–1968*, vol. 30, China (Washington, DC: GPO, 1998), 645–50, 704–18, 729–30.

76. *FRUS, 1969–1976*, vol. 17, *China, 1969–1972* (Washington, DC: GPO, 2006), 39–41, 46–47, 297–99.

77. MacMillan, *Nixon and Mao*, 231–304; *FRUS, 1969–1976*, 17:1066, 1073; Burr, *The Kissinger Transcripts*, 93–94.

78. *FRUS, 1969–1976*, vol. 18, *China, 1973–1976* (Washington, DC: GPO, 2008), 447–51.

79. *FRUS, 1969–1976*, vol. 7, *Vietnam, July 1970- January 1972* (Washington, DC: GPO, 2010), 322.

80. Bundy, *Tangled Web*, 452–60.

81. *FRUS, 1969–1976*, 4:10–17, 128–30, 173, 302–3 (quote 303); David Ekbladh, *The Great American Mission: Modernization and the Construction of an American World Order* (Princeton, NJ: Princeton University Press, 2009), 222.

82. *FRUS, 1969–1976*, 4:318–30.

83. *PPP: Richard Nixon, 1970* (Washington, DC: GPO, 1971), 118–19 (quote), 745.

84. Kissinger, *White House Years*, 17–19. Kissinger subsequently conveys a less favorable view of Johnson and Rostow; ibid., 48–50, 230–31.

85. Michael E. Latham, *The Right Kind of Revolution: Modernization, Development, and U.S. Foreign Policy from the Cold War to the Present* (Ithaca, NY: Cornell University Press, 2011), 156–68; Ekbladh, *Great American Mission*, 220–25; *PPP: Richard Nixon, 1969* (Washington, DC: GPO, 1970), 412; see *FRUS, 1969–1976*, 4:224–26 for AID's reduced mission.

86. *FRUS, 1969–1976*, 4:14, 253–57; Robert Gilpin, *U.S. Power and the Multinational Corporation: The Political Economy of Foreign Direct Investment* (New York: Basic Books, 1975), 139.

87. *FRUS, 1969–1976*, 4:267–68; Paul E. Sigmund, *Multinationals in Latin America: The Politics of Nationalization* (Madison: University of Wisconsin Press, 1980), 314–16; Sol M. Linowitz, ed., *The Americas in a Changing World, including the Report of the Commission on United States-Latin American Relations* (New York: Quadrangle, New York Times Book Co., 1975), 54–55.

88. Sigmund, *Multinationals in Latin America*, 131–73; Nathaniel Davis, *The Last Two Years of Salvador Allende* (Ithaca, NY: Cornell University Press, 1985), 25.

89. Ekbladh, *Great American Mission*, 230–33; James A. Bill, *The Eagle and the Lion: The Tragedy of American-Iranian Relations* (New Haven, CT: Yale University Press, 1988), 120–27, 132–53 (quote 123).

90. Bill, *Eagle and the Lion*, 169–82 (quote 181); *FRUS, 1964–1968*, vol. 22, *Iran* (Washington, DC: GPO, 1999), 21–22, 154, 343–44, 445, 450, 514–15, 522–34, 543–45.

91. *FRUS, 1969–1976*, 4:64–65; *FRUS, 1969–1976*, vol. E-4, *Documents on Iran and Iraq, 1969–1972*, Documents 133, 158, http://history.state.gov/historicaldocuments/frus1969 -76ve04.

92. *FRUS, 1969–1976*, E-4: Document 84.

93. Bundy, *Tangled Web*, 327–28; *FRUS, 1969–1976*, E-4: Document 188.

94. *FRUS, 1969–1976*, E-4: Document 209.

95. Ibid., Document 217.

96. Roham Alvandi, "Nixon, Kissinger, and the Shah: The Origins of Iranian Primacy in the Persian Gulf," *Diplomatic History* 36 (April 2012): 337–72.

97. *FRUS, 1969–1976*, E-4: Document 97; Bundy, *Tangled Web*, 331.

98. *FRUS, 1969–1976*, vol. 20, *Southeast Asia, 1969–1972* (Washington, DC: GPO, 2006), 6–7, 19–20; Daniel Weimer, *Seeing Drugs: Modernization, Counterinsurgency, and*

U.S. Narcotics Control in the Third World, 1969–1976 (Kent, OH: Kent State University Press, 2010), 85–91.

99. *FRUS, 1969–1976*, 20:12–13, 32–35; Robert J. McMahon, *The Limits of Empire: The United States and Southeast Asia since World War II* (New York: Columbia University Press, 1999), 159.

100. Kissinger, *White House Years*, 223; *FRUS, 1969–1976*, 20:100–104, 151–54 (quote 100).

101. *FRUS, 1969–1976*, 20:216–19, 320–24 (quote 218).

102. Ibid., 243–44, 267–69, 355–56 (quote 356).

103. Weimer, *Seeing Drugs*, 94–101.

104. Timothy N. Castle, *At War in the Shadow of Vietnam: U.S. Military Aid to the Royal Lao Government, 1955–1975* (New York: Columbia University Press, 1993); Jane Hamilton-Merritt, *Tragic Mountains: The Hmong, the Americans, and the Secret Wars for Laos, 1942–1992* (Bloomington: Indiana University Press, 1993).

105. William O. Walker III, *Opium and Foreign Policy: The Anglo-American Search for Order in Asia, 1912–1954* (Chapel Hill: University of North Carolina Press, 1991), 189–213; Alfred W. McCoy, *The Politics of Heroin: CIA Complicity in the Global Drug Trade* (Brooklyn, NY: Lawrence Hill Books, 1991), 283–387; *FRUS, 1969–1976*, 20:285–87, 296–98, 372–74.

106. *FRUS, 1969–1976*, 20:299–300, 306–7, 356–57.

107. *FRUS, 1969–1976*, vol. E-12, *Documents on East and Southeast Asia, 1973–1976, Chapter 10: Thailand and Burma*, Documents 369, 372, 383, 386, 390 (quote, Document 371), http://history.state.gov/historicaldocuments/frus1969-76ve12.

108. George Herring, *America's Longest War: The United States and Vietnam, 1950–1975*, 4th ed. (Boston: McGraw Hill, 2002), 281–83; *PPP: Nixon, 1969*, 901–9; Henry A. Kissinger, "The Viet Nam Negotiations," *Foreign Affairs* 47 (January 1969): 211–34 (quote 218–19).

109. *PPP: Nixon, 1970*, 405–10 (quote 409).

110. David W. Levy, *The Debate over Vietnam*, 2nd ed. (Baltimore: Johns Hopkins University Press, 1995), 152, 157–67; Rick Perlstein, *Nixonland: The Rise of a President and the Fracturing of America* (New York: Scribner, 2008), 277–78, 429–39.

111. Ilya V. Gaiduk, *The Soviet Union and the Vietnam War* (Chicago: Ivan R. Dee, 1996), 194–212. On attempts to pressure the Soviet Union, see Memorandum of Conversation of the Ambassador of the USSR to the USA, A. F. Dobrynin with Kissinger, Aide to President Nixon, July 12, 1969, in *Cold War International History Project Bulletin*, Issue 3 (Fall 1993), 66; *FRUS, 1969–1976*, vol. 12, *Soviet Union, January 1969 - October 1970* (Washington, DC: GPO, 2006), 259–60.

112. *FRUS, 1969–1976*, 11:264–67, 323–25, 398, 850–52 (quote 851).

113. Perlstein, *Nixonland*, 722–46; J. Anthony Lukas, *Nightmare: The Underside of the Nixon Years* (Athens: Ohio University Press, 1999), 276–339.

114. Henry A. Kissinger, "The Year of Europe," *Department of State Bulletin*, May 14, 1973, pp. 593–98 (quote 593); Kissinger, *Years of Upheaval*, 128–62 (quote 131).

115. Daniel Möckli, "Asserting Europe's Distinct Identity: The EC Nine and Kissinger's Year of Europe," in Schulz and Schwartz, *Strained Alliance*, 195–96; *FRUS, 1969–1976*, vol. 31, *Foreign Economic Policy, 1973–1976* (Washington, DC: GPO, 2009), 119.

116. Edward Heath, *The Course of My Life: My Autobiography* (London: Hodder & Stoughton, 1998), 493; Kissinger, *Years of Upheaval*, 162–92 (quote 184).

117. Hubert Zimmermann, "Unraveling the Ties That Really Bind: The Dissolution of the Transatlantic Monetary Order and the European Monetary Cooperation, 1965–1973," in Schulz and Schwartz, *Strained Alliance*, 125–44; *FRUS, 1973–1976*, 31:178–80, 183–86; Bundy, *Tangled Web*, 418–19.

118. Zimmermann, "Unraveling the Ties That Really Bind," 205; Kissinger, *Years of Upheaval*, 191, 194; Brandt to Nixon, August 4, 1973, Cold War International History Project, e-Dossier No. 22: "Introduction to the Willy Brandt Document Collection," http://www.wilsoncenter.org/publication/e-dossier-no-22-introduction-to-the-willy-brandt-document-collection.

119. William O. Walker III, "The Johnson-Nixon-Castro Years: Superpower Containment of Cuba," in *Fifty Years of Revolution: Perspectives on Cuba, the United States, and the World*, ed. Soraya M. Castro Mariño and Ronald W. Pruessen (Gainesville: University Press of Florida, 2012), 213–16; *PPP: Nixon, 1969*, 893–901; Tanya Harmer, *Allende's Chile and the Inter-American Cold War* (Chapel Hill: University of North Carolina Press, 2011), 39–46 (quote 39).

120. Nixon-Rogers Conversation, October 5, 1971, in *The Nixon Tapes: Secret Recordings from the Nixon White House on Luis Echeverría [Alvarez] and Much Much More*, ed. Kate Doyle, August 18, 2003, National Security Archive, Electronic Briefing Book (NSA, EBB) No. 95, http://www.gwu.edu/~nsarchiv/NSAEBB/NSAEBB95/.

121. United States Congress, Senate, *Select Committee to Study Governmental Operations with Respect to Intelligence Activities*, "Covert Action in Chile, 1963–1973," 94 Cong., 1 Sess., December 18, 1975 (Washington, DC: GPO, 1975); Thomas L. Hughes interview, September 7, 1999, pp. 184–86, Library of Congress, Frontline Diplomacy: The Foreign Affairs Oral History Collection of the Association for Diplomatic Studies and Training, https://www.loc.gov/item/mfdipbib001565/.

122. Frank Chapin to Kissinger, March 23, 1970, December 9, 2010 Materials Release, Virtual Library, RMNL, http://www.nixonlibrary.gov/virtuallibrary/releases/dec10.php; Minutes of the March 25, 1970, Meeting of the 40 Committee, March 30, 1970, ibid.

123. TELCON: Helms/Kissinger, September 12, 1970, in *New Kissinger "TELCONS" Reveal Chile Plotting at Highest Levels of U.S. Government*, ed. Peter Kornbluh, NSA, EBB No. 255, http://www.gwu.edu/~nsarchiv/NSAEBB/NSAEBB255/19700912-1200-Helms1.pdf; TELCON: President/Kissinger, September 12, 1970, ibid., http://www.gwu.edu/~nsarchiv/NSAEBB/NSAEBB255/19700912-1200-Nixon2.pdf.

124. CIA, President's Daily Brief, November 13, 1970, p. 11, CIA, ERR, https://www.cia.gov/library/readingroom/docs/DOC_0005977796.pdf.

125. Memorandum of Conversation - NSC Meeting - Chile (NSSM 97), November 6, 1970, in *The Pinochet File: A Declassified Dossier on Atrocity and Accountability*, ed. Peter Kornbluh (New York: New Press, 2003), 116–20; Richard Nixon, *RN: The Memoirs of Richard Nixon* (New York: Grosset & Dunlap, 1978), 489–90.

126. Harmer, *Allende's Chile*, 98–109, 123–32.

127. *FRUS, 1969–1976*, vol. E-10, *Documents on American Republics, 1969–1972*, Memorandum of Meeting, December 8, 1971, Document 142, http://history.state.gov/historicaldocuments/frus1969-76ve10.

128. Memorandum by Kissinger for Nixon, December 9, 1971, Document 143, ibid.

129. Harmer, *Allende's Chile*, 212–28; Davis, *Last Two Years of Salvador Allende*, 331–32; Nixon, *RN*, 489.

130. Washington Special Action Group Meeting, September 13, 1973, Digital National Security Archive, #CL00975; TELCON: Kissinger/President, September 16, 1973, NSA, EBB No. 255, http://www.gwu.edu/~nsarchiv/NSAEBB/NSAEBB255/19730916KP5.pdf.

131. TELCON: President/Kissinger, July 4, 1973, NSA, EBB No. 255, http://www.gwu.edu/~nsarchiv/NSAEBB/NSAEBB255/19730704-1100-Nixon4.pdf.

132. Lukas, *Underside*, 389–441.

133. Salim Yaqub, "The Weight of Conquest: Henry Kissinger and the Arab-Israeli Conflict," in Logevall and Preston, *Nixon and the World*, 227–36; Little, *American Orientalism*, 106–7; Bundy, *Tangled Web*, 428–42.

134. Kissinger, *Years of Upheaval*, 565.

135. Yaqub, "Weight of Conquest," 232–33; Kissinger, *Years of Upheaval*, 210, 224–25, 481–82 (quote 482).

136. Victor Israelyan, *Inside the Kremlin during the Yom Kippur War* (University Park: Pennsylvania State University Press, 1995), 10–12, 27–28; Kissinger, *Years of Upheaval*, 580.

137. Vladislav M. Zubok, *A Failed Empire: The Soviet Union in the Cold War from Stalin to Gorbachev* (Chapel Hill: University of North Carolina Press, 2007), 240, suggests that conclusion; see also CIA, President's Daily Brief, October 27, p. 3, CIA, ERR, https://www.cia.gov/library/readingroom/docs/DOC_ 0005993968.pdf.

138. Israelyan, *Inside the Kremlin*, 126–27 (quotes 160, 214); for Brezhnev, see Dobrynin, *In Confidence*, 299; CIA, President's Daily Brief, October 27, 1973, p. 7, CIA, ERR, https://www.cia.gov/library/readingroom/docs/DOC_ 0005993968.pdf.

139. Kissinger, *Years of Upheaval*, 600; *FRUS, 1969–1976*, vol. 25, *Arab-Israeli Crisis and War, 1973* (Washington, DC: GPO, 2011), 421–22; Dobrynin, *In Confidence*, 301.

140. Bundy, *Tangled Web*, 441, 443; *FRUS, 1969–1976*, 25:763 n. 4 (quote); Kissinger's defense of his treatment of Europe is in *Years of Upheaval*, 707–22.

141. Little, *American Orientalism*, 69–71; Bundy, *Tangled Web*, 438.

142. Richard Helms to Kissinger, April 6 and 25, 1973, June 26, 2012, Materials Release, Virtual Library, RMNL, http://www.nixonlibrary.gov/virtuallibrary/releases/jun12.php; Edward Heath to Nixon, June 14, 1973, July 2, 2010, Materials Release, Virtual Library, RMNL, http://www.nixonlibrary.gov/virtuallibrary/releases/jul10.php.

143. Bundy, *Tangled Web*, 395–99; Kissinger, *Years of Upheaval*, 429, 510, 582, 593 (the text of this volume of his memoirs reaches 1214 pages); Nixon, *RN*, 889.

144. *FRUS, 1969–1976*, vol. 38, Part 1, *Foundations of Foreign Policy, 1973–1976* (Washington, DC: GPO, 2012), 234–49 (quote 235).

CONCLUSION

1. "A Letter from the Publisher, Aug. 19, 1974," *Time*, August 19, 1974; "The Resignation: Exit Nixon," ibid.; Hugh Sidey, "The Presidency: Trying to Ensure an Epitaph," ibid.

2. U.S. Department of State, *Foreign Relations of the United States, 1969–1976*, vol. 38 (in two parts), *Foundations of Foreign Policy, 1973–1976* (Washington, DC: Government Printing Office, 2012), pt. 1: 220.

3. Ibid., 222. Regarding Leonid Brezhnev's commitment to furthering a competitive détente, see Svetlana Savranskaya, ed., *Anatoly S. Chernyaev Diary, 1973*, National Security Archive, Electronic Briefing Book No. 430, May 25, 2013, especially for April 16, May 22, and June 24, 1973, http://www.gwu.edu/~nsarchiv/NSAEBB/NSAEBB430/.

4. George F. Kennan, *Around the Cragged Hill: A Personal and Political Philosophy* (New York: W. W. Norton, 1993), 182.

5. Walter F. LaFeber email to author, January 11, 2013.

6. Thomas L. Hughes, "Whose Century?," *Foreign Affairs* 50 (April 1972): 476–87 (quote 477); the idea of the American Century as a broadly defined cultural entity is at the heart of Donald W. White, *The American Century: The Rise and Decline of the United States as a World Power* (New Haven, CT: Yale University Press, 1996).

7. Hughes, "Whose Century?," 483.

8. Ibid., 484.

9. Andrew J. Bacevich, ed., *The Short American Century: A Postmortem* (Cambridge, MA: Harvard University Press, 2012); Alfred W. McCoy, *In the Shadows of the American Century: The Rise and Decline of US Global Power* (Chicago: Haymarket Books, 2017).

10. Walter LaFeber, "The Tension between Democracy and Capitalism in the American Century," *Diplomatic History* 23 (Spring 1999): 263–84 (quote 272); Emily S. Rosenberg, "Consuming the American Century," in Bacevich, *Short American Century*, 44.

11. Roberto Giorgio Rabel, introduction to *The American Century?: In Retrospect and Prospect*, ed. Roberto Giorgio Rabel (Westport, CT: Frederick A. Praeger, 2002), 12.

12. Ibid., 6, 5 (quotes).

13. Benedict Anderson, *Imagined Communities: Reflections on the Origins and Spread of Nationalism*, rev. ed. (London: Verso, 1991), 1–7 (quote 7); Rosenberg, "Consuming the American Century," identifies an imagined community in American consumer culture.

14. Randall B. Woods, *LBJ: Architect of American Ambition* (New York: Free Press, 2006), 384, makes a succinct case for Johnson's adroitness as a manager of U.S. foreign policy.

15. Fredrik Logevall, *Choosing War: The Lost Chance for Peace and the Escalation of War in Vietnam* (Berkeley: University of California Press, 1999).

16. Even in the confusion following Stalin's death in March 1953, leaders in Western Europe advocated a cautious response; Robert R. Bowie and Richard H. Immerman, *Waging Peace: How Eisenhower Shaped an Enduring Cold War Strategy* (New York: Oxford University Press, 1998), 113.

17. Thomas H. Carothers, *In the Name of Democracy: U.S. Policy toward Latin America in the Reagan Years* (Berkeley: University of California Press, 1991); Jeffrey A. Frieden, "From the American Century to Globalization," in Bacevich, *The Short American Century*, 154.

18. George H. W. Bush, August 18, 1988, The American Presidency Project, University of California, Santa Barbara, http://www.presidency.ucsb.edu/ws/?pid=25955.

19. McCoy, *In the Shadows of the American Century*, 170–90; John W. Dower, *The Violent American Century: War and Terror since World War II* (Chicago: Haymarket Books, 2017), 115–25.

20. http://www.newamericancentury.org/statementofprinciples.htm. The website is no longer active.

21. Hillary Clinton, "America's Pacific Century," *Foreign Policy* (November 2011): 56–63 (quote 57).

22. *Washington Post*, October 7, 2011; *USA Today*, May 23, 2012. Romney repeated his support for a new American Century in a speech on October 8, 2012, at the Virginia Military Institute, saying, "The 21st century can and must be an American century." See *New York Times*, October 9, 2012.

23. Clinton, "America's Pacific Century," 63. In an address to the Democratic National Convention on July 27, 2016, in support of Hillary Clinton, Vice President Joe Biden said near the end of his remarks, "The 21st century is going to be the American century." *Washington Post*, July 28, 2016.

24. For a thoughtful disquisition on hegemony, see Simon Reich and Richard Ned Lebow, *Good-Bye Hegemony!: Power and Influence in the Global System* (Princeton, NJ: Princeton University Press, 2014).

25. *International Herald Tribune*, March 7, 2013 (quote); *New York Times*, April 7, 2013.

26. The Constitution Project, *The Report of the Constitution Project's Task Force on Detainee Treatment* (Washington, DC: The Constitution Project, 2013), 3, http://www .constitutionproject.org.

27. Ibid., 1, 3.

28. In the midpoint of Obama's last year in the White House, his administration released a report claiming that civilian deaths resulting from drone strikes were no higher than 116 and perhaps as low as 64; *New York Times*, July 2, 2016.

29. Ibid., May 24, 2014, for the text of the speech.

30. On the eve of Donald J. Trump's inauguration as forty-fifth president of the United States, Matt Bai, national political columnist for Yahoo! News, wrote a column, "President Trump and the End of the American Century." About the demise of expansive glo-

balism, he concluded, "The price of maintaining global hegemony, both in lives and in credit, became harder to justify [over time]." See https://www.yahoo.com/news/president -trump-and-the-end-of-the-american-century-100054474.html.

31. Matthew Lee and Jonathan Lemire, "How Trump's Advisers Schooled Him on Globalism," AP News, September 18, 2017, https://apnews.com/4cef63caf6b34cb796bc4c 196d47c143/How-Trump's-advisers-schooled-him-on-globalism.

32. For the text of the speech, see http://www.politico.com/story/2017/08/21/trump -afghanistan-speech-text-241882.

33. The Rachel Maddow Show, MSNBC, July 18, 2017, www.msnbc.com/rachel -maddow/us-under-trump-shifts-toward-putin-worldview-1003059267865.

Index

CPSIA information can be obtained
at www.ICGtesting.com
Printed in the USA
LVHW111805310319
612460LV00005B/406/P